c⚲ntraband

words	tj behe
illustrations	phil elliott
inks	ian sharman
tones	cherie donovan
cover	mike bogadanovic & taka

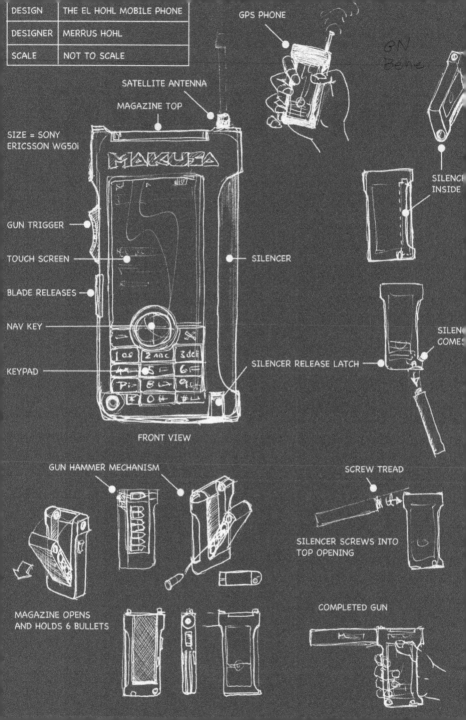

DESIGN	THE EL HOHL MOBILE PHONE
DESIGNER	MERRUS HOHL
SCALE	NOT TO SCALE

GPS PHONE

GN Behie

SATELLITE ANTENNA

MAGAZINE TOP

SIZE = SONY
ERICSSON WG50i

SILENCE
INSIDE

MAKUSA

GUN TRIGGER

TOUCH SCREEN

BLADE RELEASES

NAV KEY

SILENC
COMES

KEYPAD

SILENCER RELEASE LATCH

SILENCER

1 as 2 abc 3 def
4 5 6
Pi 8 9
* 0 #

FRONT VIEW

GUN HAMMER MECHANISM

SCREW TREAD

SILENCER SCREWS INTO
TOP OPENING

MAGAZINE OPENS
AND HOLDS 6 BULLETS

COMPLETED GUN

MAKUSA

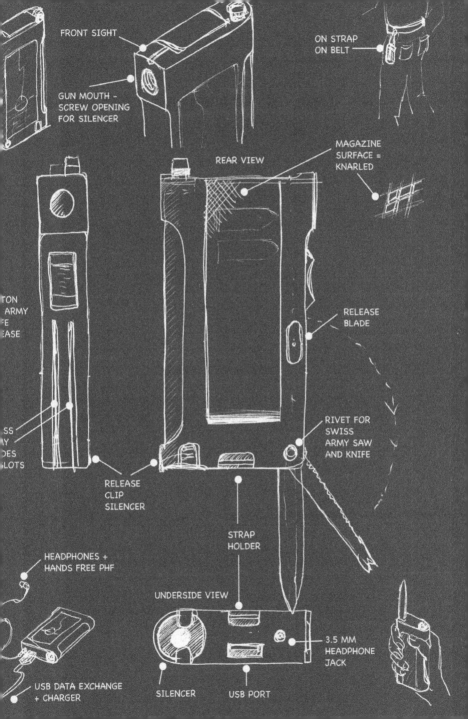

FRONT SIGHT

GUN MOUTH -
SCREW OPENING
FOR SILENCER

ON STRAP
ON BELT

REAR VIEW

MAGAZINE
SURFACE =
KNARLED

...TON
...ARMY
...FE
...EASE

RELEASE
BLADE

...SS
...Y
...DES
...LOTS

RIVET FOR
SWISS
ARMY SAW
AND KNIFE

RELEASE
CLIP
SILENCER

HEADPHONES +
HANDS FREE PHF

STRAP
HOLDER

UNDERSIDE VIEW

3.5 MM
HEADPHONE
JACK

USB DATA EXCHANGE
+ CHARGER

SILENCER

USB PORT

TJ and Phil would like to thank
Steph, Ian, Ian and Fiona for their
support in the creation of this book.

To contact the creators

TJ Behe - tjbehe@gmail.com
Phil Elliott - phil@elliott-design.com
Ian Sharman - ian@supremeknightstudios.com
Taka - atakads@gmail.com
Contraband website - www.contrabandgraphicnovel.com

For Markosia Enterprises Ltd

Harry Markos
Publisher & Managing Partner

Andy Briggs
Creative Consultant

GM Jordan
Special Projects Co-Ordinator

Meirion Jones
Marketing Director

Annika Eade
Media Manager

Ian Sharman
Editor In Chief

ISBN 978-1-913802-60-8
www.markosia.com

MY PHONE STILL GETS CLOGGED WITH SPAM.

TEXTS, PHOTOS, VIDEOS TONNES OF VIRAL STUFF.

THE MATES SENT ME ALL THE CLASSICS. THAT GREAT WHITE SHARK,
THE ONE SNAPPING AT THE SOLDIER HANGING FROM THE HELICOPTER.

THAT MULLET-HAIRED KID TIED TO A POLE OVER THE FOUR-
LANE HIGHWAY. AN ABSOLUTE CLASSIC.

...AND THAT SERBIAN GENERAL WHOSE TROOPS BLASTED BULLETS INTO
A THOUSAND VILLAGERS A COUPLE DECADES BACK,

I'M SURE THEY WOULD HAVE ALL BEEN TOP RANKED VIDEOS ON
CONTRABAND IF IT WAS AROUND BACK THEN,

EVERYONE'S ON THAT APP THESE DAYS. AND RIGHT NOW
THEY'RE ONLY TALKING ABOUT ONE THING. THOSE VIDEOS OF MY GIRLFRIEND,

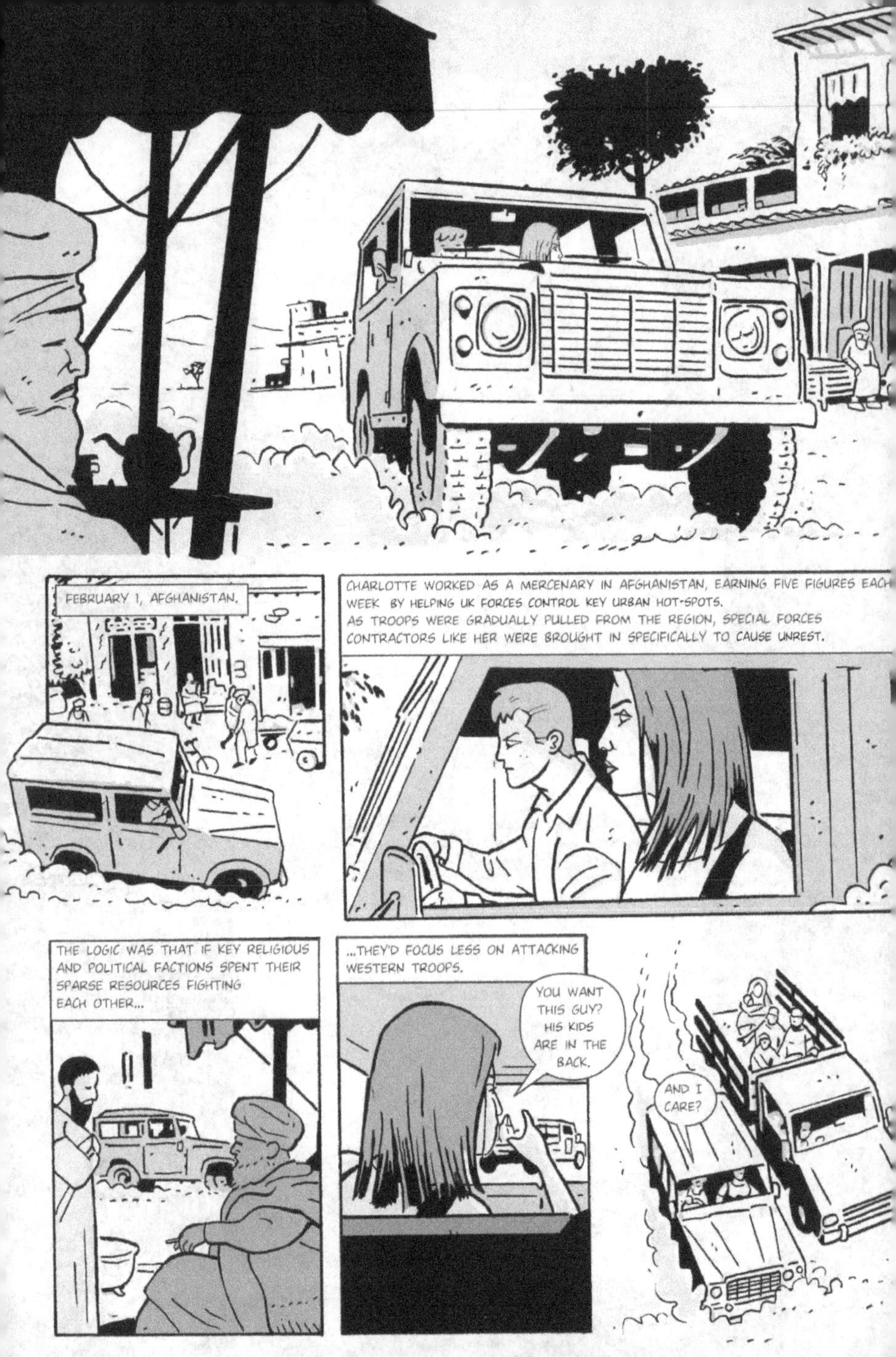
FEBRUARY 1, AFGHANISTAN.
CHARLOTTE WORKED AS A MERCENARY IN AFGHANISTAN, EARNING FIVE FIGURES EACH WEEK BY HELPING UK FORCES CONTROL KEY URBAN HOT-SPOTS.
AS TROOPS WERE GRADUALLY PULLED FROM THE REGION, SPECIAL FORCES CONTRACTORS LIKE HER WERE BROUGHT IN SPECIFICALLY TO CAUSE UNREST.
THE LOGIC WAS THAT IF KEY RELIGIOUS AND POLITICAL FACTIONS SPENT THEIR SPARSE RESOURCES FIGHTING EACH OTHER...
...THEY'D FOCUS LESS ON ATTACKING WESTERN TROOPS.
YOU WANT THIS GUY? HIS KIDS ARE IN THE BACK.
AND I CARE?

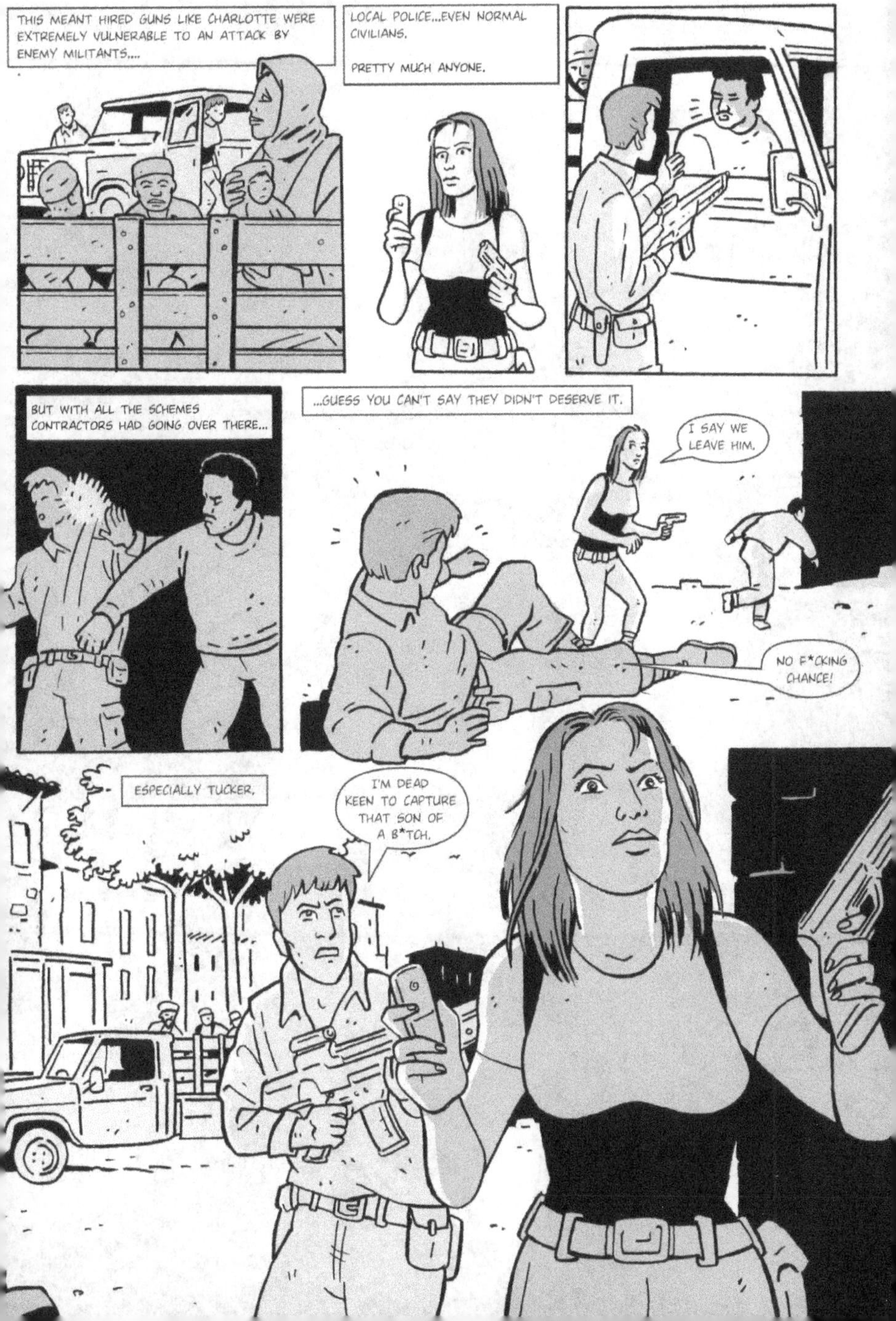
THIS MEANT HIRED GUNS LIKE CHARLOTTE WERE EXTREMELY VULNERABLE TO AN ATTACK BY ENEMY MILITANTS....
LOCAL POLICE...EVEN NORMAL CIVILIANS.
PRETTY MUCH ANYONE.
BUT WITH ALL THE SCHEMES CONTRACTORS HAD GOING OVER THERE...
...GUESS YOU CAN'T SAY THEY DIDN'T DESERVE IT.
I SAY WE LEAVE HIM.
NO F*CKING CHANCE!
ESPECIALLY TUCKER.
I'M DEAD KEEN TO CAPTURE THAT SON OF A B*TCH.

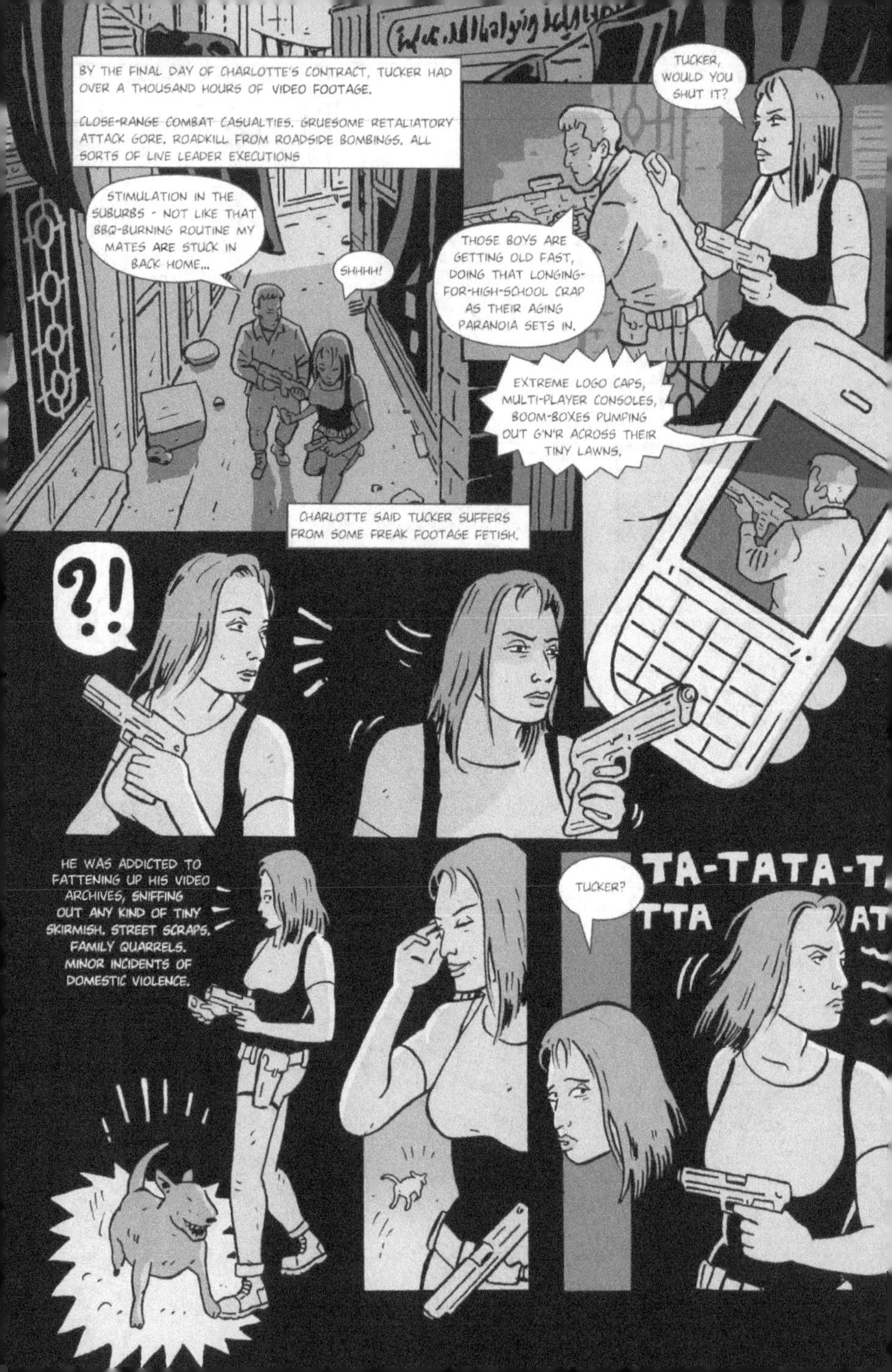
BY THE FINAL DAY OF CHARLOTTE'S CONTRACT, TUCKER HAD OVER A THOUSAND HOURS OF VIDEO FOOTAGE.
CLOSE-RANGE COMBAT CASUALTIES. GRUESOME RETALIATORY ATTACK GORE. ROADKILL FROM ROADSIDE BOMBINGS. ALL SORTS OF LIVE LEADER EXECUTIONS
STIMULATION IN THE SUBURBS - NOT LIKE THAT BBQ-BURNING ROUTINE MY MATES ARE STUCK IN BACK HOME...
SHHHH!
TUCKER, WOULD YOU SHUT IT?
THOSE BOYS ARE GETTING OLD FAST, DOING THAT LONGING-FOR-HIGH-SCHOOL CRAP AS THEIR AGING PARANOIA SETS IN.
EXTREME LOGO CAPS, MULTI-PLAYER CONSOLES, BOOM-BOXES PUMPING OUT G'N'R ACROSS THEIR TINY LAWNS.
CHARLOTTE SAID TUCKER SUFFERS FROM SOME FREAK FOOTAGE FETISH.
?!
HE WAS ADDICTED TO FATTENING UP HIS VIDEO ARCHIVES, SNIFFING OUT ANY KIND OF TINY SKIRMISH. STREET SCRAPS. FAMILY QUARRELS. MINOR INCIDENTS OF DOMESTIC VIOLENCE.
TUCKER?
TA-TATA-T
TTA
AT

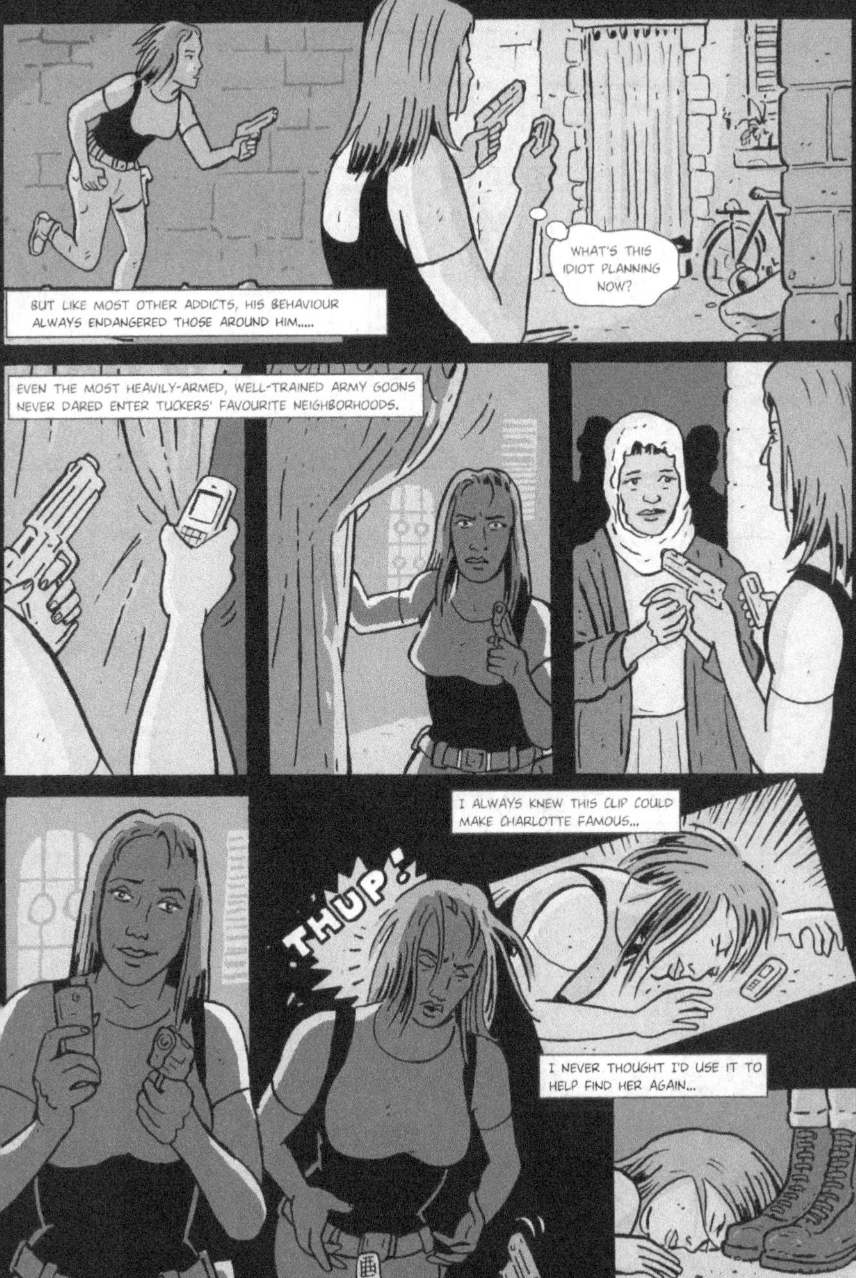
BUT LIKE MOST OTHER ADDICTS, HIS BEHAVIOUR ALWAYS ENDANGERED THOSE AROUND HIM.....
WHAT'S THIS IDIOT PLANNING NOW?
EVEN THE MOST HEAVILY-ARMED, WELL-TRAINED ARMY GOONS NEVER DARED ENTER TUCKERS' FAVOURITE NEIGHBORHOODS.
I ALWAYS KNEW THIS CLIP COULD MAKE CHARLOTTE FAMOUS...
THUP!
I NEVER THOUGHT I'D USE IT TO HELP FIND HER AGAIN...

two

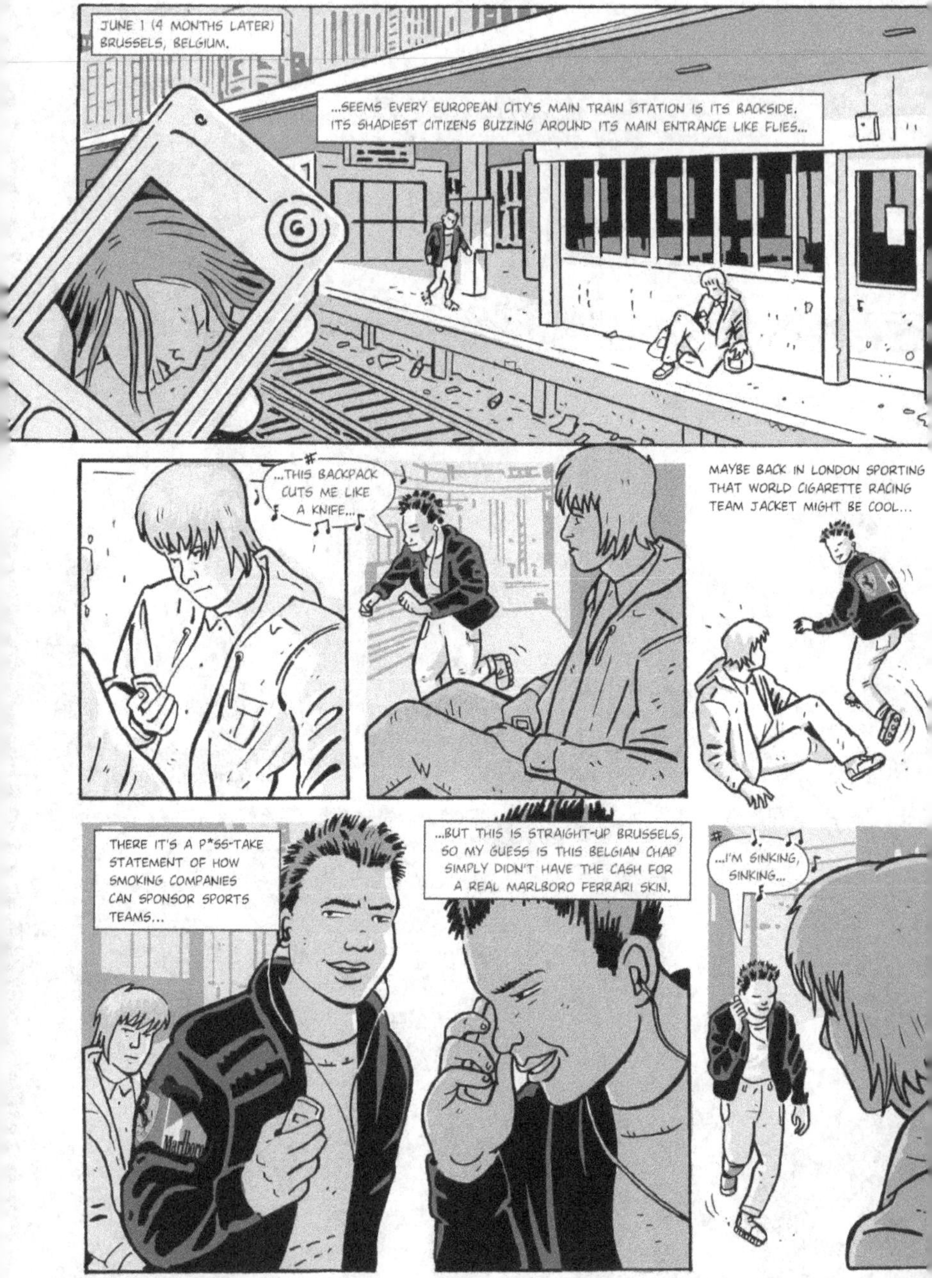
JUNE 1 (4 MONTHS LATER) BRUSSELS, BELGIUM.
...SEEMS EVERY EUROPEAN CITY'S MAIN TRAIN STATION IS ITS BACKSIDE. ITS SHADIEST CITIZENS BUZZING AROUND ITS MAIN ENTRANCE LIKE FLIES...
...THIS BACKPACK CUTS ME LIKE A KNIFE...
MAYBE BACK IN LONDON SPORTING THAT WORLD CIGARETTE RACING TEAM JACKET MIGHT BE COOL...
THERE IT'S A P*SS-TAKE STATEMENT OF HOW SMOKING COMPANIES CAN SPONSOR SPORTS TEAMS...
...BUT THIS IS STRAIGHT-UP BRUSSELS, SO MY GUESS IS THIS BELGIAN CHAP SIMPLY DIDN'T HAVE THE CASH FOR A REAL MARLBORO FERRARI SKIN.
...I'M SINKING, SINKING...

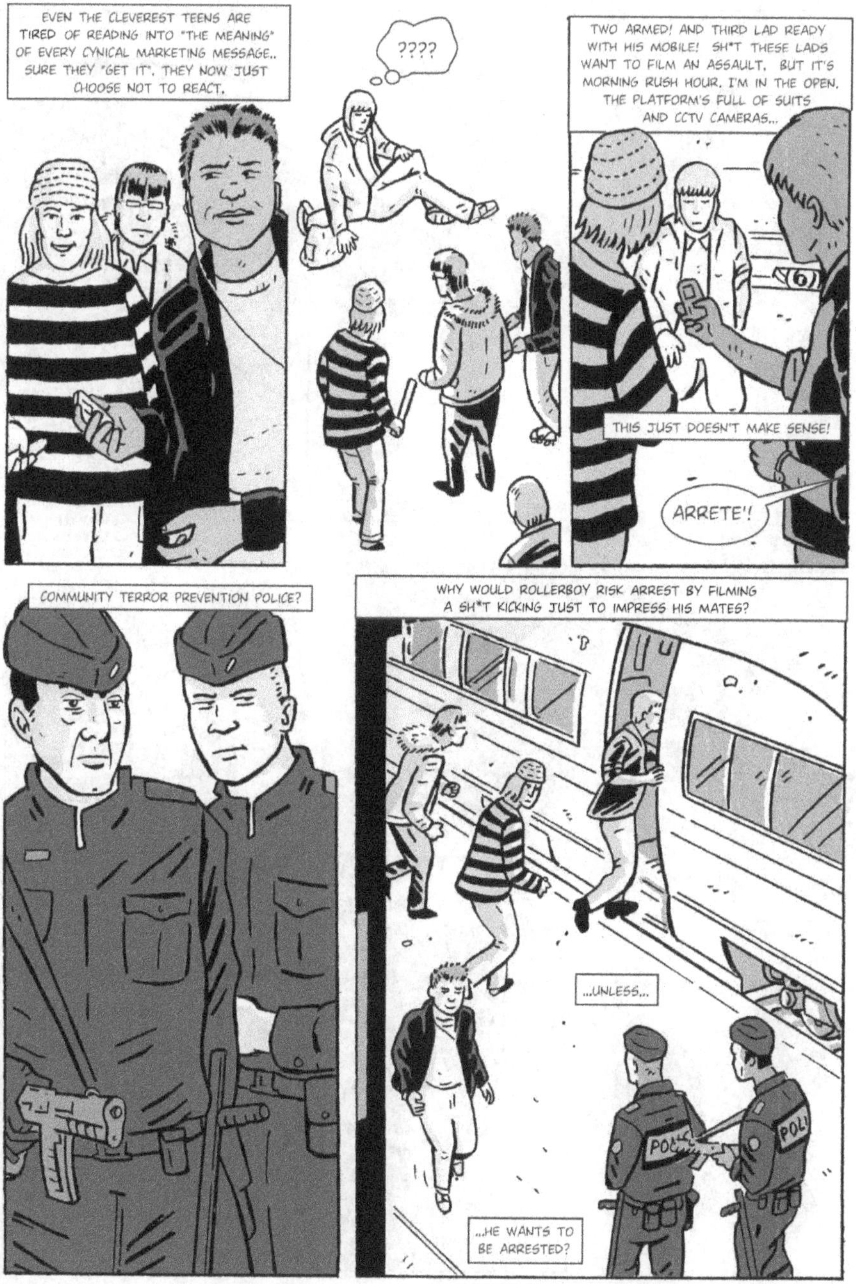
EVEN THE CLEVEREST TEENS ARE TIRED OF READING INTO "THE MEANING" OF EVERY CYNICAL MARKETING MESSAGE.. SURE THEY "GET IT". THEY NOW JUST CHOOSE NOT TO REACT.
????
TWO ARMED! AND THIRD LAD READY WITH HIS MOBILE! SH*T THESE LADS WANT TO FILM AN ASSAULT. BUT IT'S MORNING RUSH HOUR. I'M IN THE OPEN. THE PLATFORM'S FULL OF SUITS AND CCTV CAMERAS...
THIS JUST DOESN'T MAKE SENSE!
ARRETE'!
COMMUNITY TERROR PREVENTION POLICE?
WHY WOULD ROLLERBOY RISK ARREST BY FILMING A SH*T KICKING JUST TO IMPRESS HIS MATES?
...UNLESS...
...HE WANTS TO BE ARRESTED?

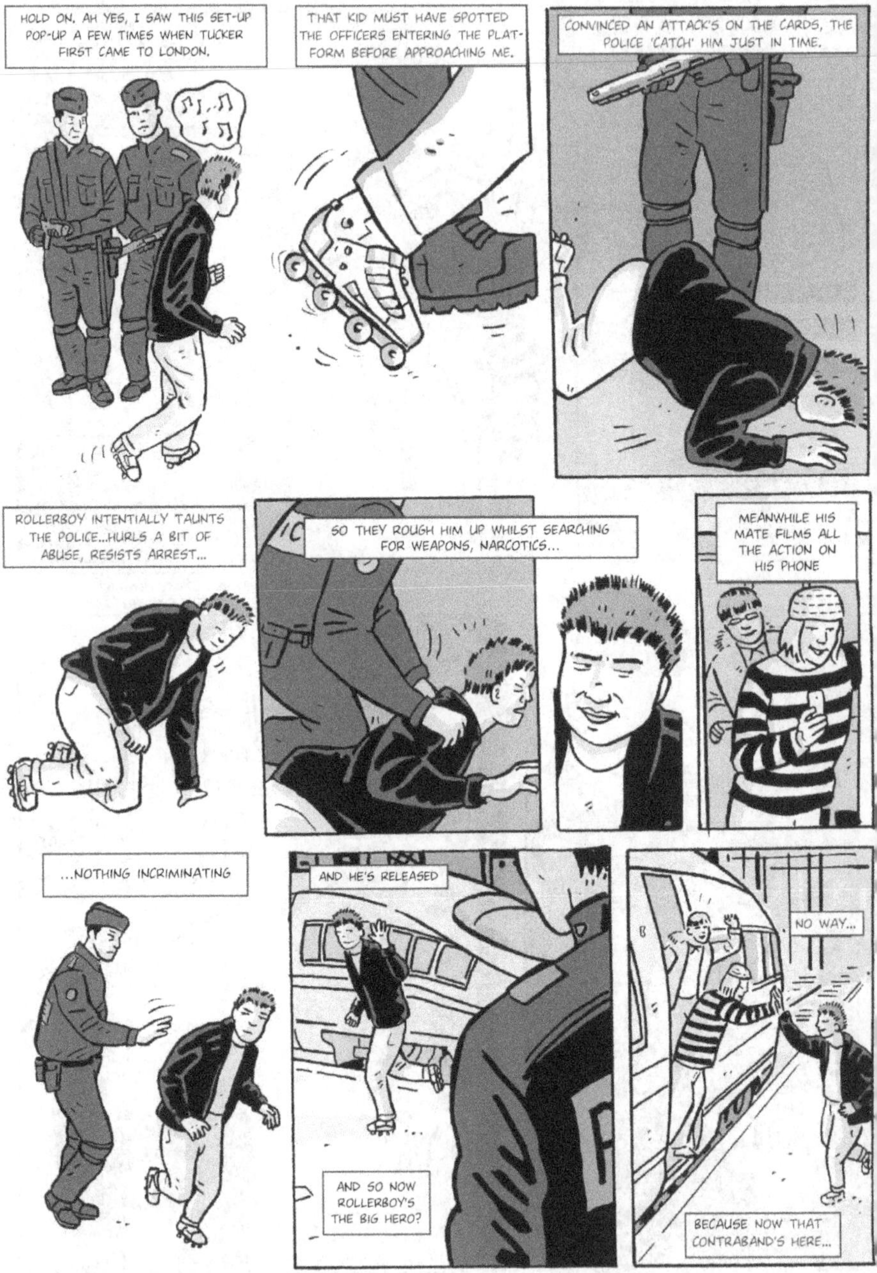
HOLD ON. AH YES, I SAW THIS SET-UP POP-UP A FEW TIMES WHEN TUCKER FIRST CAME TO LONDON.
THAT KID MUST HAVE SPOTTED THE OFFICERS ENTERING THE PLATFORM BEFORE APPROACHING ME.
CONVINCED AN ATTACK'S ON THE CARDS, THE POLICE 'CATCH' HIM JUST IN TIME.
ROLLERBOY INTENTIALLY TAUNTS THE POLICE...HURLS A BIT OF ABUSE, RESISTS ARREST...
SO THEY ROUGH HIM UP WHILST SEARCHING FOR WEAPONS, NARCOTICS...
MEANWHILE HIS MATE FILMS ALL THE ACTION ON HIS PHONE
...NOTHING INCRIMINATING
AND HE'S RELEASED
AND SO NOW ROLLERBOY'S THE BIG HERO?
NO WAY...
BECAUSE NOW THAT CONTRABAND'S HERE...

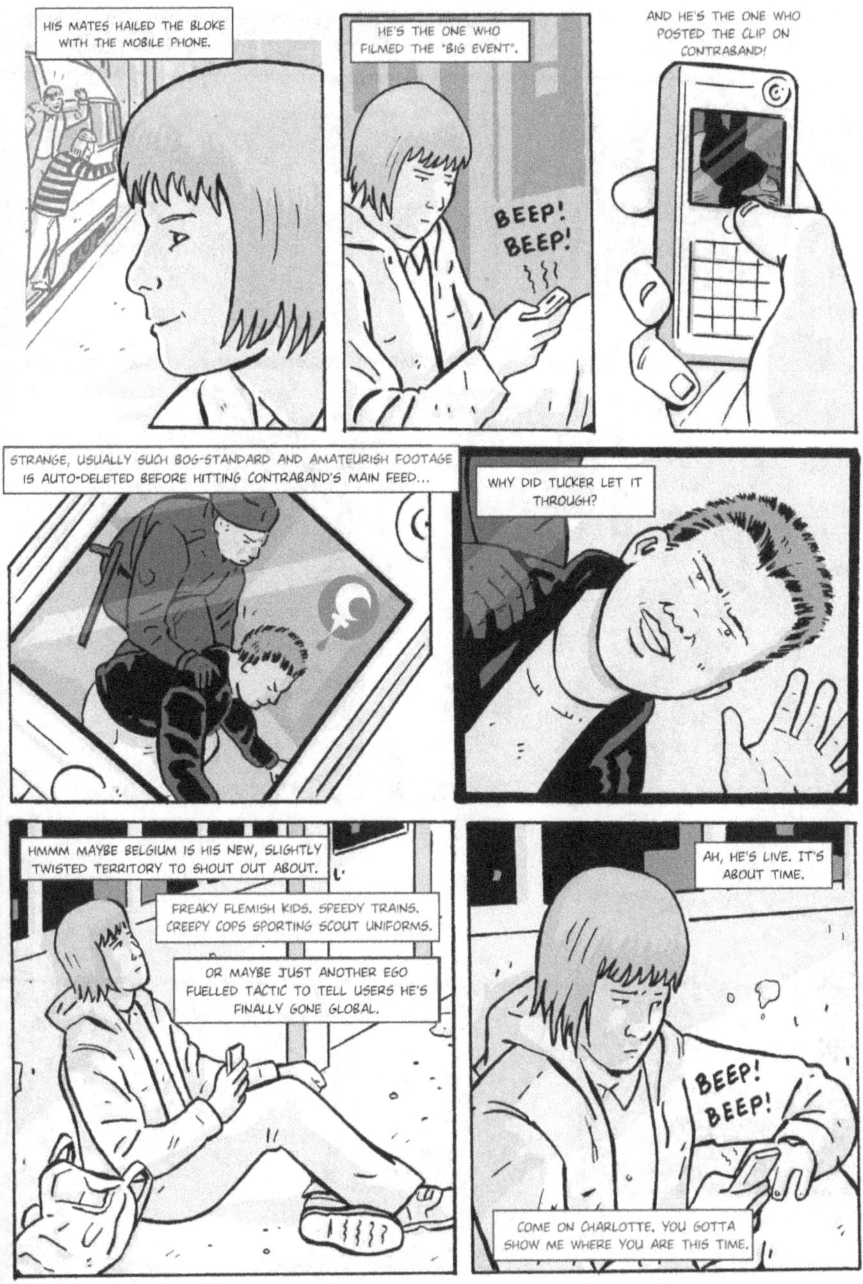
HIS MATES HAILED THE BLOKE WITH THE MOBILE PHONE.
HE'S THE ONE WHO FILMED THE "BIG EVENT".
BEEP! BEEP!
AND HE'S THE ONE WHO POSTED THE CLIP ON CONTRABAND!
STRANGE, USUALLY SUCH BOG-STANDARD AND AMATEURISH FOOTAGE IS AUTO-DELETED BEFORE HITTING CONTRABAND'S MAIN FEED...
WHY DID TUCKER LET IT THROUGH?
HMMM MAYBE BELGIUM IS HIS NEW, SLIGHTLY TWISTED TERRITORY TO SHOUT OUT ABOUT.
FREAKY FLEMISH KIDS. SPEEDY TRAINS. CREEPY COPS SPORTING SCOUT UNIFORMS.
OR MAYBE JUST ANOTHER EGO FUELLED TACTIC TO TELL USERS HE'S FINALLY GONE GLOBAL.
AH, HE'S LIVE. IT'S ABOUT TIME.
BEEP! BEEP!
COME ON CHARLOTTE. YOU GOTTA SHOW ME WHERE YOU ARE THIS TIME.

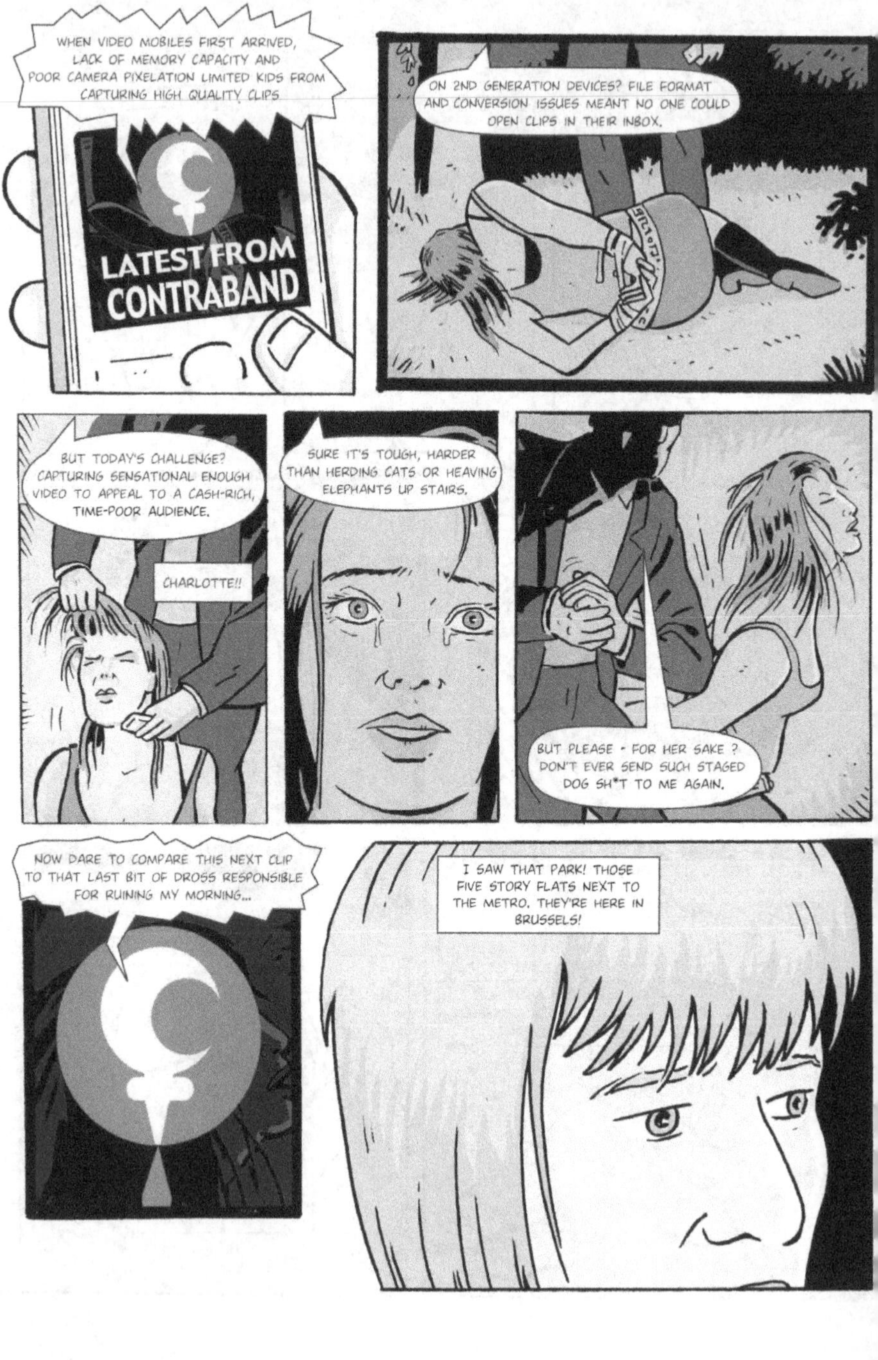
WHEN VIDEO MOBILES FIRST ARRIVED, LACK OF MEMORY CAPACITY AND POOR CAMERA PIXELATION LIMITED KIDS FROM CAPTURING HIGH QUALITY CLIPS
LATEST FROM CONTRABAND
ON 2ND GENERATION DEVICES? FILE FORMAT AND CONVERSION ISSUES MEANT NO ONE COULD OPEN CLIPS IN THEIR INBOX.
BUT TODAY'S CHALLENGE? CAPTURING SENSATIONAL ENOUGH VIDEO TO APPEAL TO A CASH-RICH, TIME-POOR AUDIENCE.
CHARLOTTE!!
SURE IT'S TOUGH, HARDER THAN HERDING CATS OR HEAVING ELEPHANTS UP STAIRS.
BUT PLEASE - FOR HER SAKE ? DON'T EVER SEND SUCH STAGED DOG SH*T TO ME AGAIN.
NOW DARE TO COMPARE THIS NEXT CLIP TO THAT LAST BIT OF DROSS RESPONSIBLE FOR RUINING MY MORNING...
I SAW THAT PARK! THOSE FIVE STORY FLATS NEXT TO THE METRO. THEY'RE HERE IN BRUSSELS!

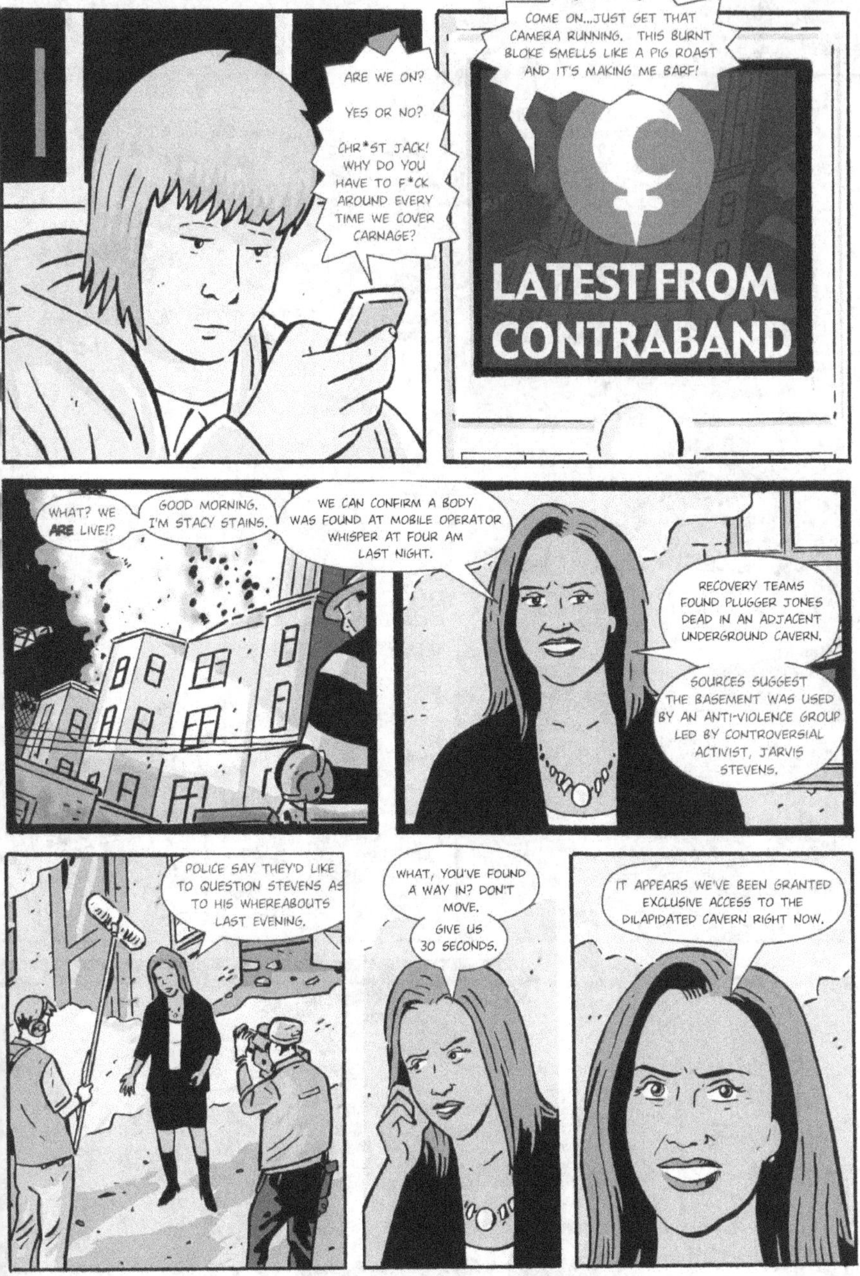
ARE WE ON?
YES OR NO?
CHR*ST JACK! WHY DO YOU HAVE TO F*CK AROUND EVERY TIME WE COVER CARNAGE?
COME ON...JUST GET THAT CAMERA RUNNING. THIS BURNT BLOKE SMELLS LIKE A PIG ROAST AND IT'S MAKING ME BARF!
LATEST FROM CONTRABAND
WHAT? WE ARE LIVE!?
GOOD MORNING. I'M STACY STAINS.
WE CAN CONFIRM A BODY WAS FOUND AT MOBILE OPERATOR WHISPER AT FOUR AM LAST NIGHT.
RECOVERY TEAMS FOUND PLUGGER JONES DEAD IN AN ADJACENT UNDERGROUND CAVERN.
SOURCES SUGGEST THE BASEMENT WAS USED BY AN ANTI-VIOLENCE GROUP LED BY CONTROVERSIAL ACTIVIST, JARVIS STEVENS.
POLICE SAY THEY'D LIKE TO QUESTION STEVENS AS TO HIS WHEREABOUTS LAST EVENING.
WHAT, YOU'VE FOUND A WAY IN? DON'T MOVE.
GIVE US 30 SECONDS.
IT APPEARS WE'VE BEEN GRANTED EXCLUSIVE ACCESS TO THE DILAPIDATED CAVERN RIGHT NOW.

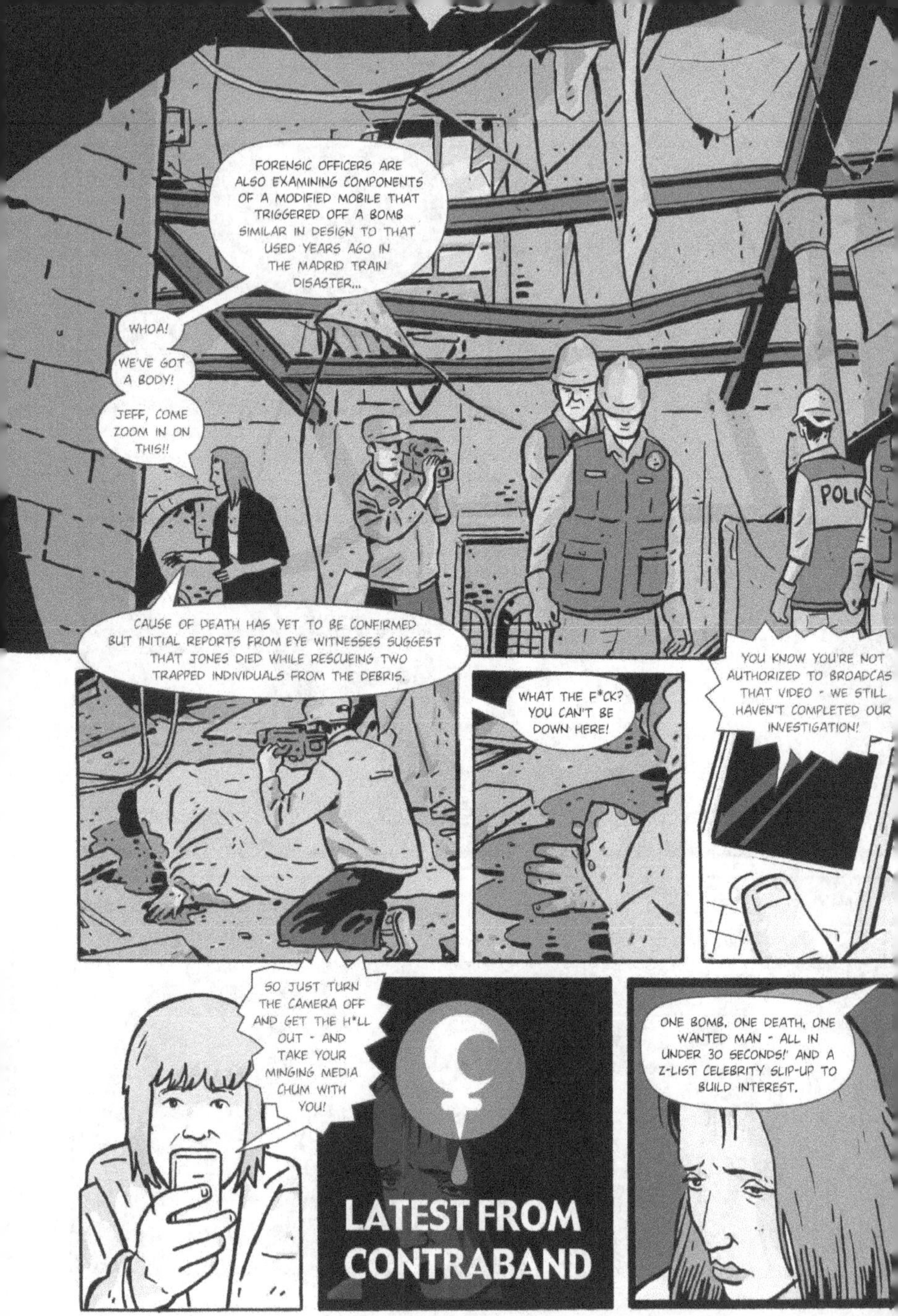
FORENSIC OFFICERS ARE ALSO EXAMINING COMPONENTS OF A MODIFIED MOBILE THAT TRIGGERED OFF A BOMB SIMILAR IN DESIGN TO THAT USED YEARS AGO IN THE MADRID TRAIN DISASTER...
WHOA!
WE'VE GOT A BODY!
JEFF, COME ZOOM IN ON THIS!!
CAUSE OF DEATH HAS YET TO BE CONFIRMED BUT INITIAL REPORTS FROM EYE WITNESSES SUGGEST THAT JONES DIED WHILE RESCUEING TWO TRAPPED INDIVIDUALS FROM THE DEBRIS.
WHAT THE F*CK? YOU CAN'T BE DOWN HERE!
YOU KNOW YOU'RE NOT AUTHORIZED TO BROADCAS THAT VIDEO - WE STILL HAVEN'T COMPLETED OUR INVESTIGATION!
SO JUST TURN THE CAMERA OFF AND GET THE H*LL OUT - AND TAKE YOUR MINGING MEDIA CHUM WITH YOU!
LATEST FROM CONTRABAND
ONE BOMB. ONE DEATH. ONE WANTED MAN - ALL IN UNDER 30 SECONDS!' AND A Z-LIST CELEBRITY SLIP-UP TO BUILD INTEREST.

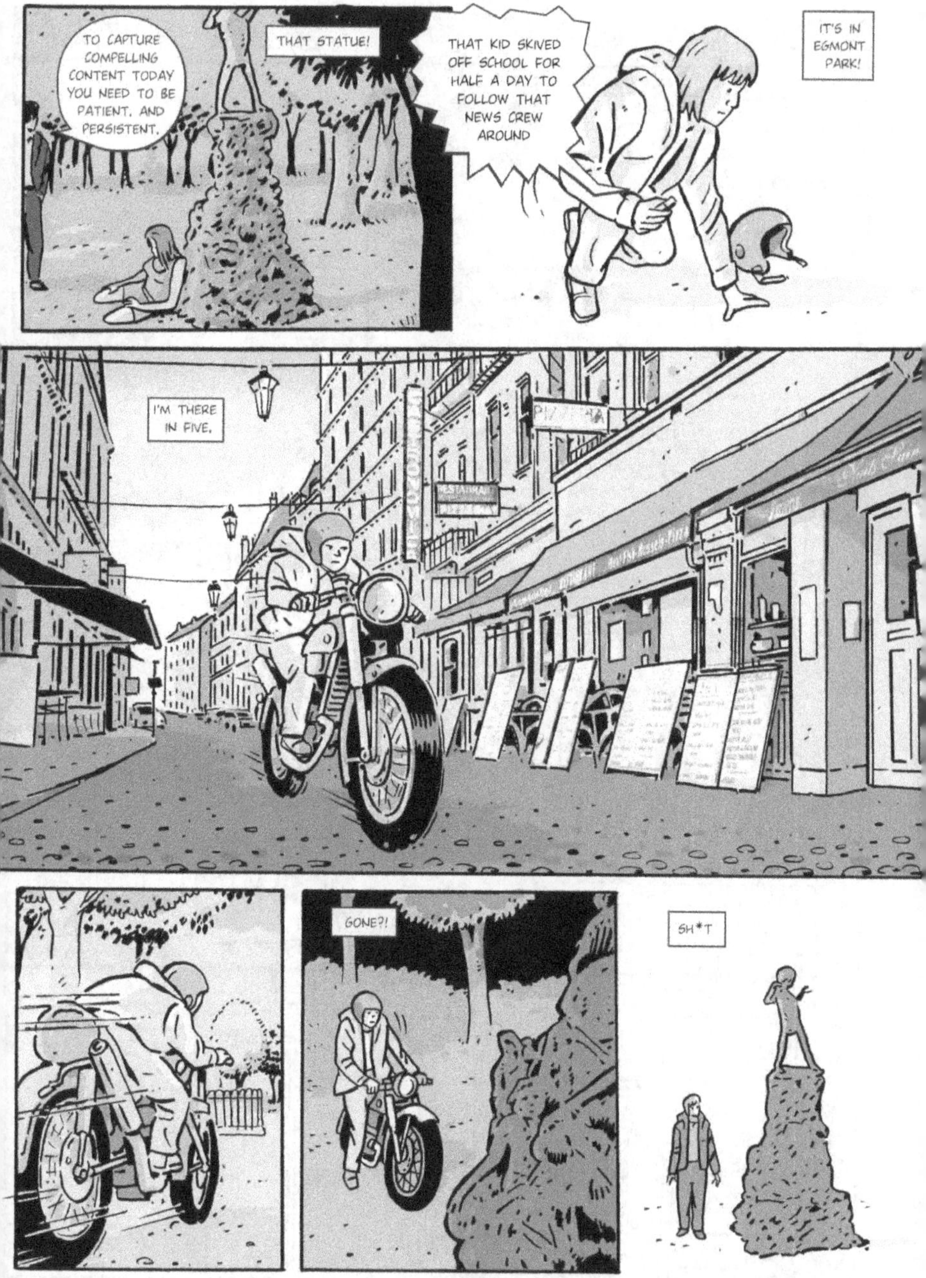
TO CAPTURE COMPELLING CONTENT TODAY YOU NEED TO BE PATIENT. AND PERSISTENT.
THAT STATUE!
THAT KID SKIVED OFF SCHOOL FOR HALF A DAY TO FOLLOW THAT NEWS CREW AROUND
IT'S IN EGMONT PARK!
I'M THERE IN FIVE.
PIZZERIA
RESTAURANT
GONE?!
SH*T

three

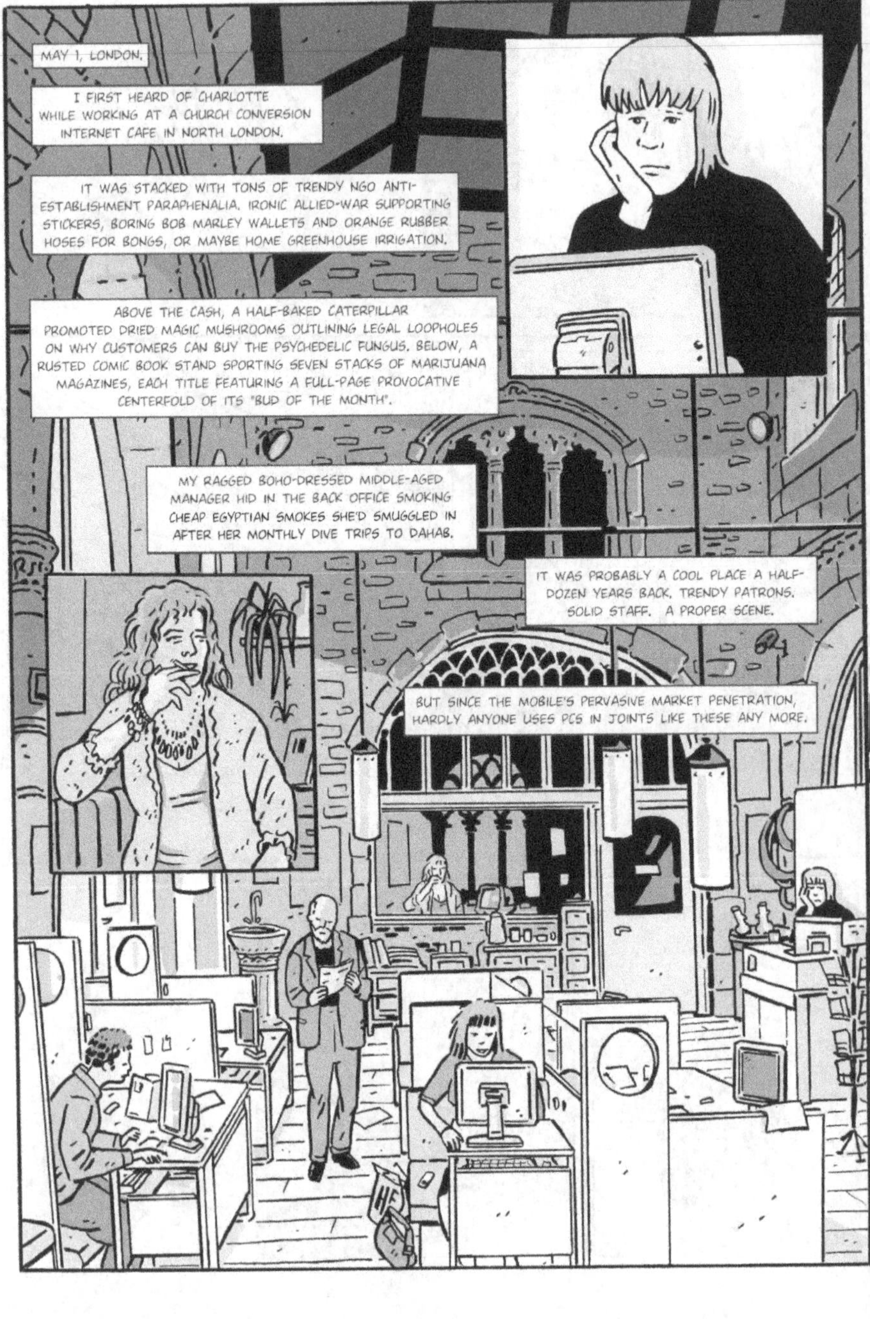
MAY 1, LONDON.
I FIRST HEARD OF CHARLOTTE WHILE WORKING AT A CHURCH CONVERSION INTERNET CAFE IN NORTH LONDON.
IT WAS STACKED WITH TONS OF TRENDY NGO ANTI-ESTABLISHMENT PARAPHENALIA. IRONIC ALLIED-WAR SUPPORTING STICKERS, BORING BOB MARLEY WALLETS AND ORANGE RUBBER HOSES FOR BONGS, OR MAYBE HOME GREENHOUSE IRRIGATION.
ABOVE THE CASH, A HALF-BAKED CATERPILLAR PROMOTED DRIED MAGIC MUSHROOMS OUTLINING LEGAL LOOPHOLES ON WHY CUSTOMERS CAN BUY THE PSYCHEDELIC FUNGUS. BELOW, A RUSTED COMIC BOOK STAND SPORTING SEVEN STACKS OF MARIJUANA MAGAZINES, EACH TITLE FEATURING A FULL-PAGE PROVOCATIVE CENTERFOLD OF ITS "BUD OF THE MONTH".
MY RAGGED BOHO-DRESSED MIDDLE-AGED MANAGER HID IN THE BACK OFFICE SMOKING CHEAP EGYPTIAN SMOKES SHE'D SMUGGLED IN AFTER HER MONTHLY DIVE TRIPS TO DAHAB.
IT WAS PROBABLY A COOL PLACE A HALF-DOZEN YEARS BACK. TRENDY PATRONS. SOLID STAFF. A PROPER SCENE.
BUT SINCE THE MOBILE'S PERVASIVE MARKET PENETRATION, HARDLY ANYONE USES PCS IN JOINTS LIKE THESE ANY MORE.

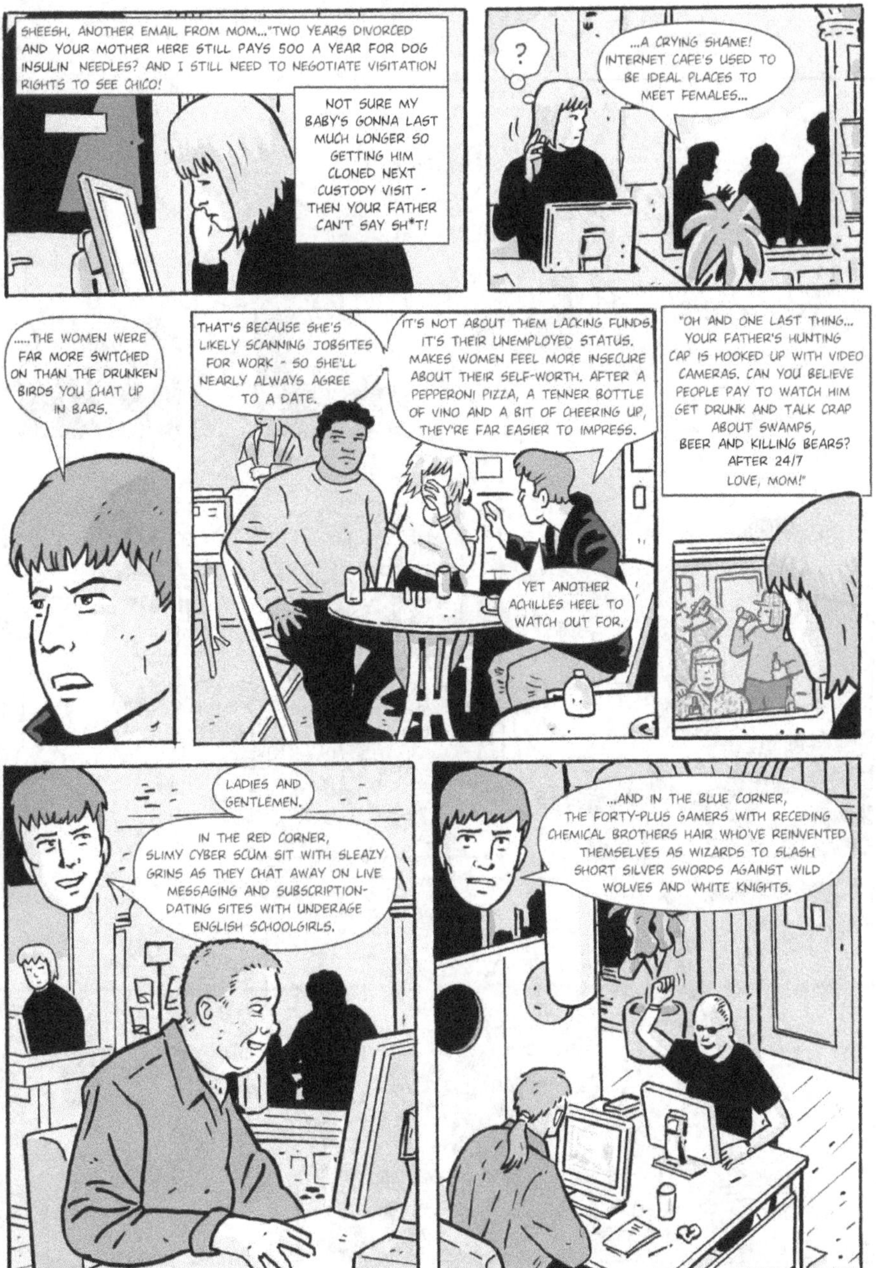
SHEESH, ANOTHER EMAIL FROM MOM..."TWO YEARS DIVORCED AND YOUR MOTHER HERE STILL PAYS 500 A YEAR FOR DOG INSULIN NEEDLES? AND I STILL NEED TO NEGOTIATE VISITATION RIGHTS TO SEE CHICO!
NOT SURE MY BABY'S GONNA LAST MUCH LONGER SO GETTING HIM CLONED NEXT CUSTODY VISIT - THEN YOUR FATHER CAN'T SAY SH*T!
?
...A CRYING SHAME! INTERNET CAFE'S USED TO BE IDEAL PLACES TO MEET FEMALES...
.....THE WOMEN WERE FAR MORE SWITCHED ON THAN THE DRUNKEN BIRDS YOU CHAT UP IN BARS.
THAT'S BECAUSE SHE'S LIKELY SCANNING JOBSITES FOR WORK - SO SHE'LL NEARLY ALWAYS AGREE TO A DATE.
IT'S NOT ABOUT THEM LACKING FUNDS. IT'S THEIR UNEMPLOYED STATUS. MAKES WOMEN FEEL MORE INSECURE ABOUT THEIR SELF-WORTH. AFTER A PEPPERONI PIZZA, A TENNER BOTTLE OF VINO AND A BIT OF CHEERING UP, THEY'RE FAR EASIER TO IMPRESS.
YET ANOTHER ACHILLES HEEL TO WATCH OUT FOR.
"OH AND ONE LAST THING... YOUR FATHER'S HUNTING CAP IS HOOKED UP WITH VIDEO CAMERAS. CAN YOU BELIEVE PEOPLE PAY TO WATCH HIM GET DRUNK AND TALK CRAP ABOUT SWAMPS, BEER AND KILLING BEARS? AFTER 24/7 LOVE, MOM!"
LADIES AND GENTLEMEN.
IN THE RED CORNER, SLIMY CYBER SCUM SIT WITH SLEAZY GRINS AS THEY CHAT AWAY ON LIVE MESSAGING AND SUBSCRIPTION-DATING SITES WITH UNDERAGE ENGLISH SCHOOLGIRLS.
...AND IN THE BLUE CORNER, THE FORTY-PLUS GAMERS WITH RECEDING CHEMICAL BROTHERS HAIR WHO'VE REINVENTED THEMSELVES AS WIZARDS TO SLASH SHORT SILVER SWORDS AGAINST WILD WOLVES AND WHITE KNIGHTS.

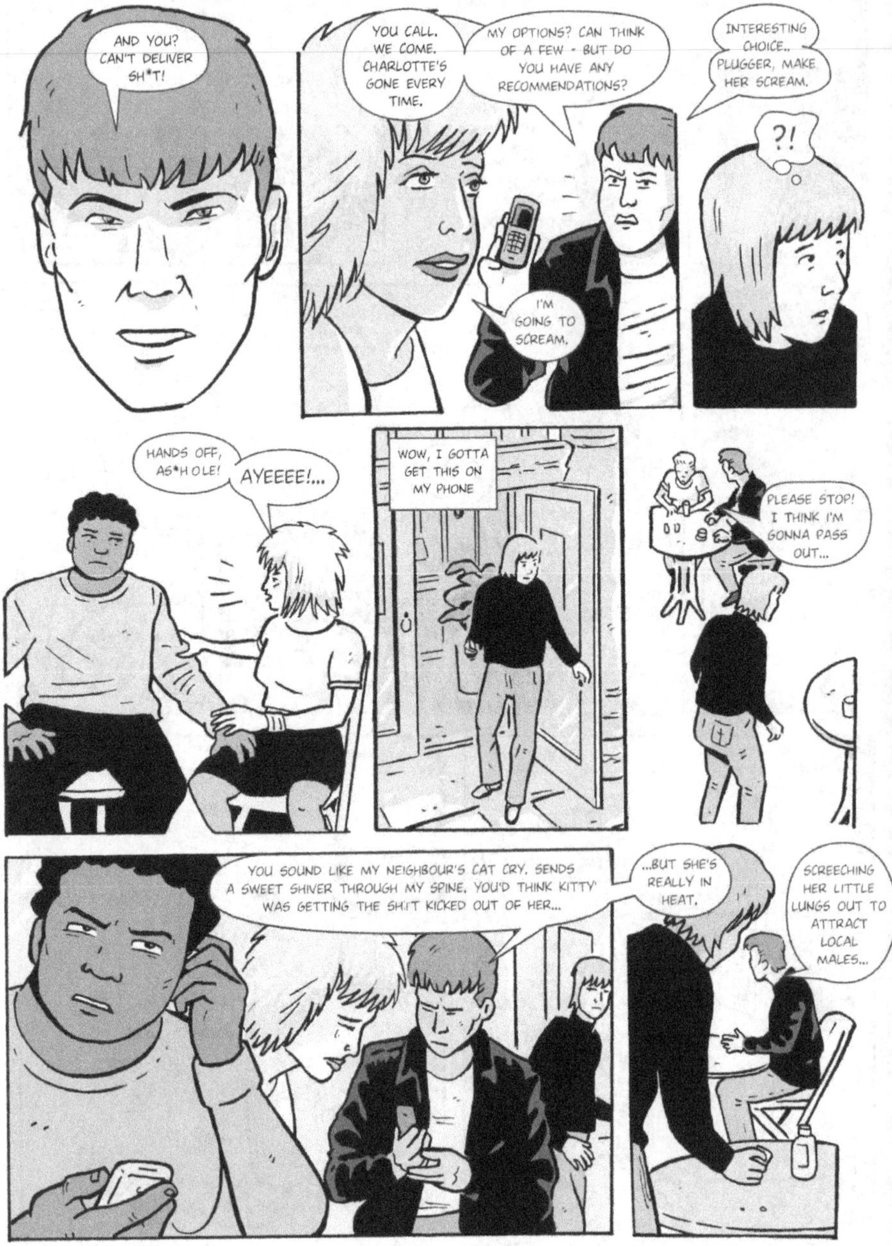
AND YOU? CAN'T DELIVER SH*T!
YOU CALL. WE COME. CHARLOTTE'S GONE EVERY TIME.
MY OPTIONS? CAN THINK OF A FEW - BUT DO YOU HAVE ANY RECOMMENDATIONS?
I'M GOING TO SCREAM.
INTERESTING CHOICE.. PLUGGER, MAKE HER SCREAM.
?!
HANDS OFF, AS*HOLE!
AYEEEE!...
WOW, I GOTTA GET THIS ON MY PHONE
PLEASE STOP! I THINK I'M GONNA PASS OUT...
YOU SOUND LIKE MY NEIGHBOUR'S CAT CRY. SENDS A SWEET SHIVER THROUGH MY SPINE. YOU'D THINK KITTY WAS GETTING THE SH!T KICKED OUT OF HER...
...BUT SHE'S REALLY IN HEAT.
SCREECHING HER LITTLE LUNGS OUT TO ATTRACT LOCAL MALES...

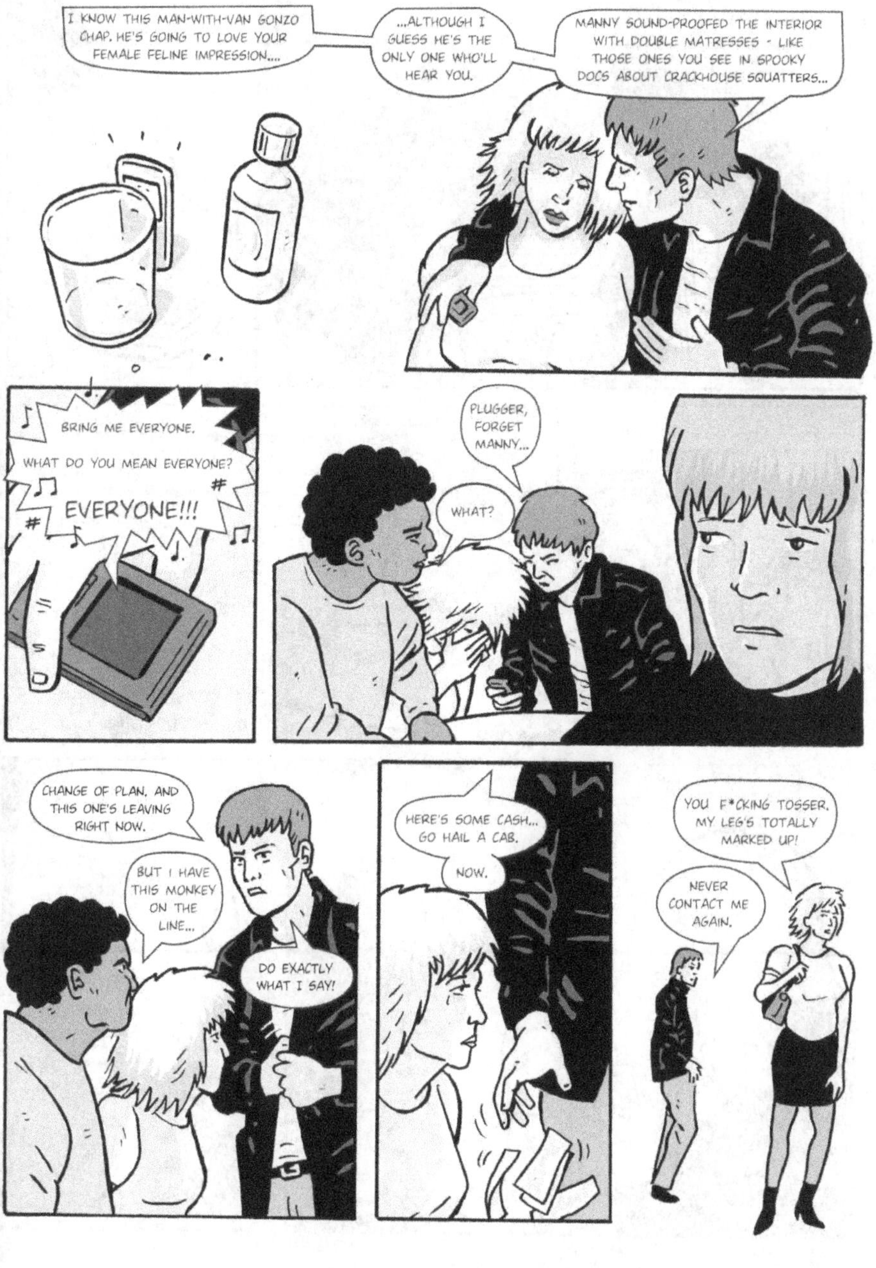
I KNOW THIS MAN-WITH-VAN GONZO CHAP. HE'S GOING TO LOVE YOUR FEMALE FELINE IMPRESSION....
...ALTHOUGH I GUESS HE'S THE ONLY ONE WHO'LL HEAR YOU.
MANNY SOUND-PROOFED THE INTERIOR WITH DOUBLE MATRESSES - LIKE THOSE ONES YOU SEE IN SPOOKY DOCS ABOUT CRACKHOUSE SQUATTERS...
BRING ME EVERYONE.
WHAT DO YOU MEAN EVERYONE?
EVERYONE!!!
PLUGGER, FORGET MANNY...
WHAT?
CHANGE OF PLAN. AND THIS ONE'S LEAVING RIGHT NOW.
BUT I HAVE THIS MONKEY ON THE LINE...
DO EXACTLY WHAT I SAY!
HERE'S SOME CASH... GO HAIL A CAB.
NOW.
YOU F*CKING TOSSER. MY LEG'S TOTALLY MARKED UP!
NEVER CONTACT ME AGAIN.

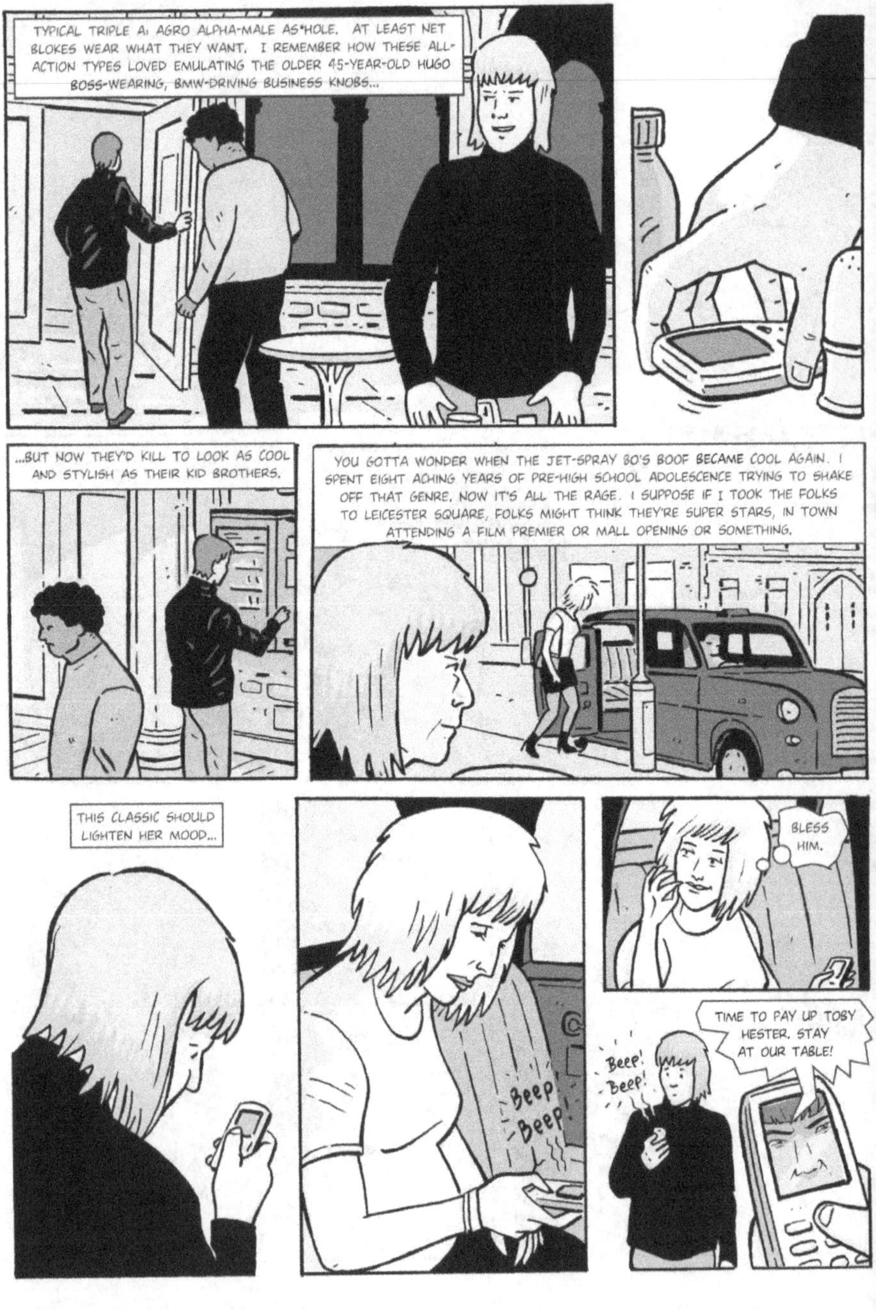
TYPICAL TRIPLE A: AGRO ALPHA-MALE AS*HOLE. AT LEAST NET BLOKES WEAR WHAT THEY WANT. I REMEMBER HOW THESE ALL-ACTION TYPES LOVED EMULATING THE OLDER 45-YEAR-OLD HUGO BOSS-WEARING, BMW-DRIVING BUSINESS KNOBS...
...BUT NOW THEY'D KILL TO LOOK AS COOL AND STYLISH AS THEIR KID BROTHERS.
YOU GOTTA WONDER WHEN THE JET-SPRAY 80'S BOOF BECAME COOL AGAIN. I SPENT EIGHT ACHING YEARS OF PRE-HIGH SCHOOL ADOLESCENCE TRYING TO SHAKE OFF THAT GENRE. NOW IT'S ALL THE RAGE. I SUPPOSE IF I TOOK THE FOLKS TO LEICESTER SQUARE, FOLKS MIGHT THINK THEY'RE SUPER STARS, IN TOWN ATTENDING A FILM PREMIER OR MALL OPENING OR SOMETHING.
THIS CLASSIC SHOULD LIGHTEN HER MOOD...
Beep Beep
BLESS HIM.
Beep! Beep!
TIME TO PAY UP TOBY HESTER. STAY AT OUR TABLE!

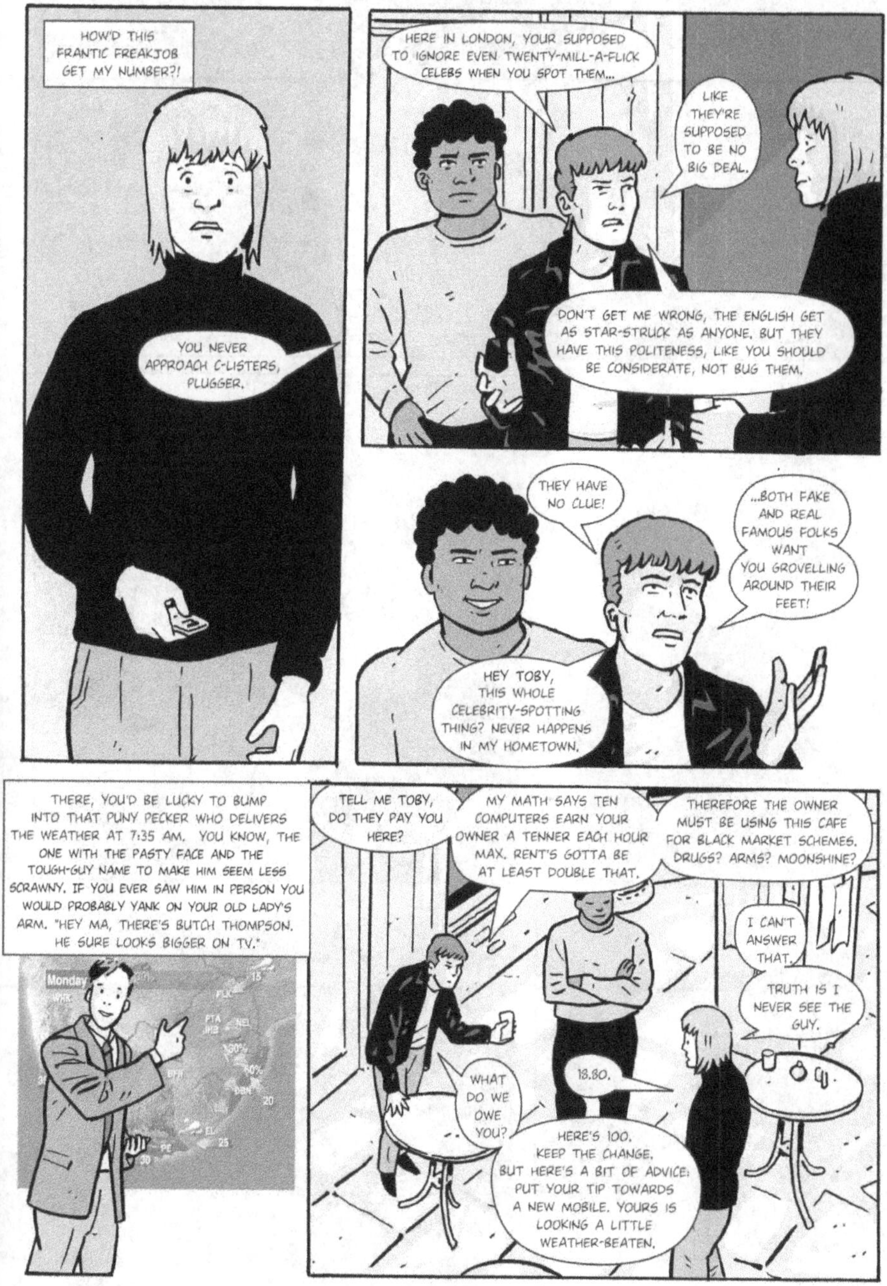
HOW'D THIS FRANTIC FREAKJOB GET MY NUMBER?!
YOU NEVER APPROACH C-LISTERS, PLUGGER.
HERE IN LONDON, YOUR SUPPOSED TO IGNORE EVEN TWENTY-MILL-A-FLICK CELEBS WHEN YOU SPOT THEM...
LIKE THEY'RE SUPPOSED TO BE NO BIG DEAL.
DON'T GET ME WRONG, THE ENGLISH GET AS STAR-STRUCK AS ANYONE. BUT THEY HAVE THIS POLITENESS, LIKE YOU SHOULD BE CONSIDERATE, NOT BUG THEM.
HEY TOBY, THIS WHOLE CELEBRITY-SPOTTING THING? NEVER HAPPENS IN MY HOMETOWN.
THEY HAVE NO CLUE!
...BOTH FAKE AND REAL FAMOUS FOLKS WANT YOU GROVELLING AROUND THEIR FEET!
THERE, YOU'D BE LUCKY TO BUMP INTO THAT PUNY PECKER WHO DELIVERS THE WEATHER AT 7:35 AM. YOU KNOW, THE ONE WITH THE PASTY FACE AND THE TOUGH-GUY NAME TO MAKE HIM SEEM LESS SCRAWNY. IF YOU EVER SAW HIM IN PERSON YOU WOULD PROBABLY YANK ON YOUR OLD LADY'S ARM. "HEY MA, THERE'S BUTCH THOMPSON. HE SURE LOOKS BIGGER ON TV."
Monday
TELL ME TOBY, DO THEY PAY YOU HERE?
MY MATH SAYS TEN COMPUTERS EARN YOUR OWNER A TENNER EACH HOUR MAX. RENT'S GOTTA BE AT LEAST DOUBLE THAT.
THEREFORE THE OWNER MUST BE USING THIS CAFE FOR BLACK MARKET SCHEMES. DRUGS? ARMS? MOONSHINE?
I CAN'T ANSWER THAT.
TRUTH IS I NEVER SEE THE GUY.
WHAT DO WE OWE YOU?
18.80.
HERE'S 100. KEEP THE CHANGE. BUT HERE'S A BIT OF ADVICE: PUT YOUR TIP TOWARDS A NEW MOBILE. YOURS IS LOOKING A LITTLE WEATHER-BEATEN.

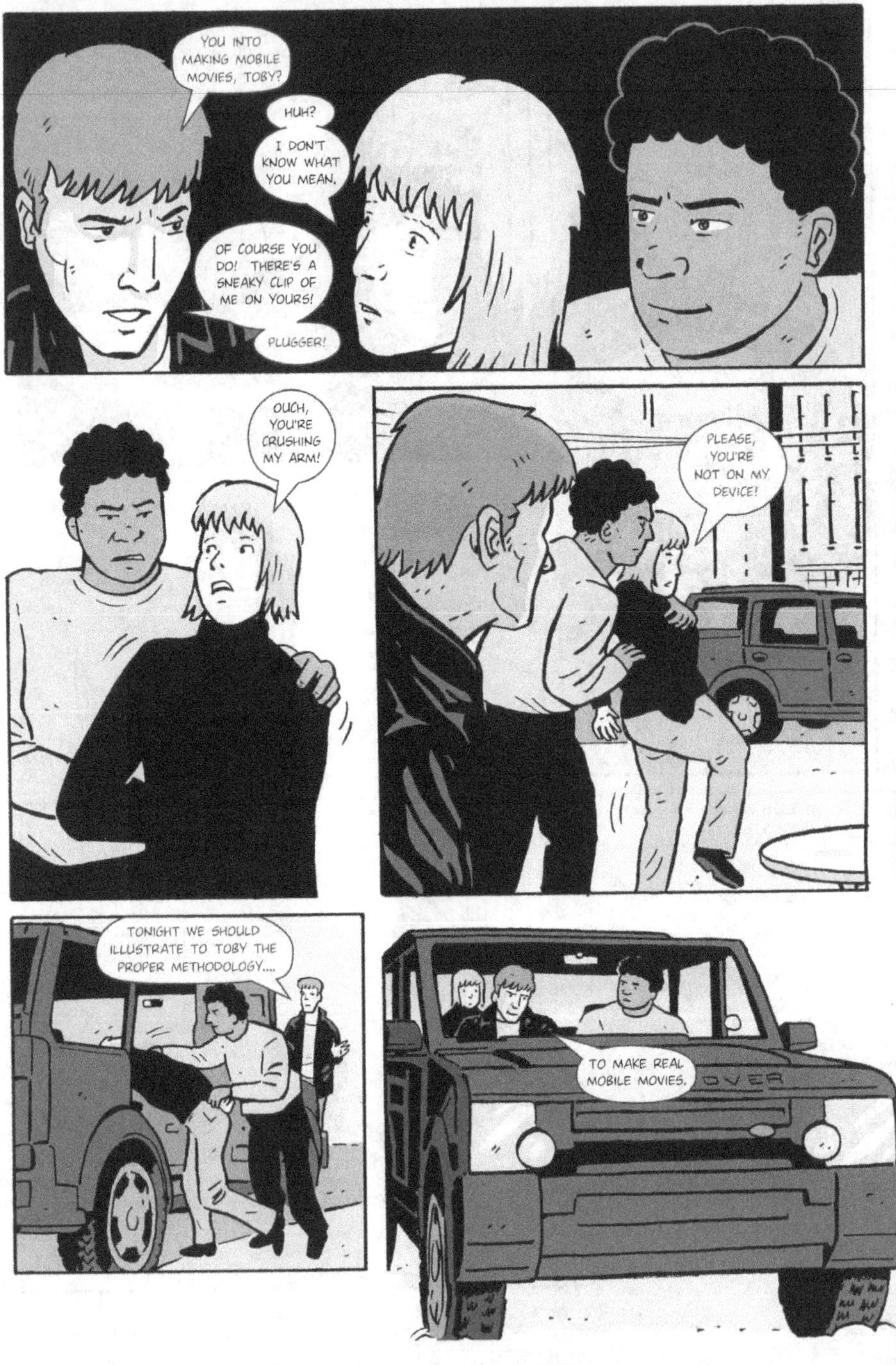
YOU INTO MAKING MOBILE MOVIES, TOBY?
HUH?
I DON'T KNOW WHAT YOU MEAN.
OF COURSE YOU DO! THERE'S A SNEAKY CLIP OF ME ON YOURS!
PLUGGER!
OUCH, YOU'RE CRUSHING MY ARM!
PLEASE, YOU'RE NOT ON MY DEVICE!
TONIGHT WE SHOULD ILLUSTRATE TO TOBY THE PROPER METHODOLOGY....
TO MAKE REAL MOBILE MOVIES.
OVER

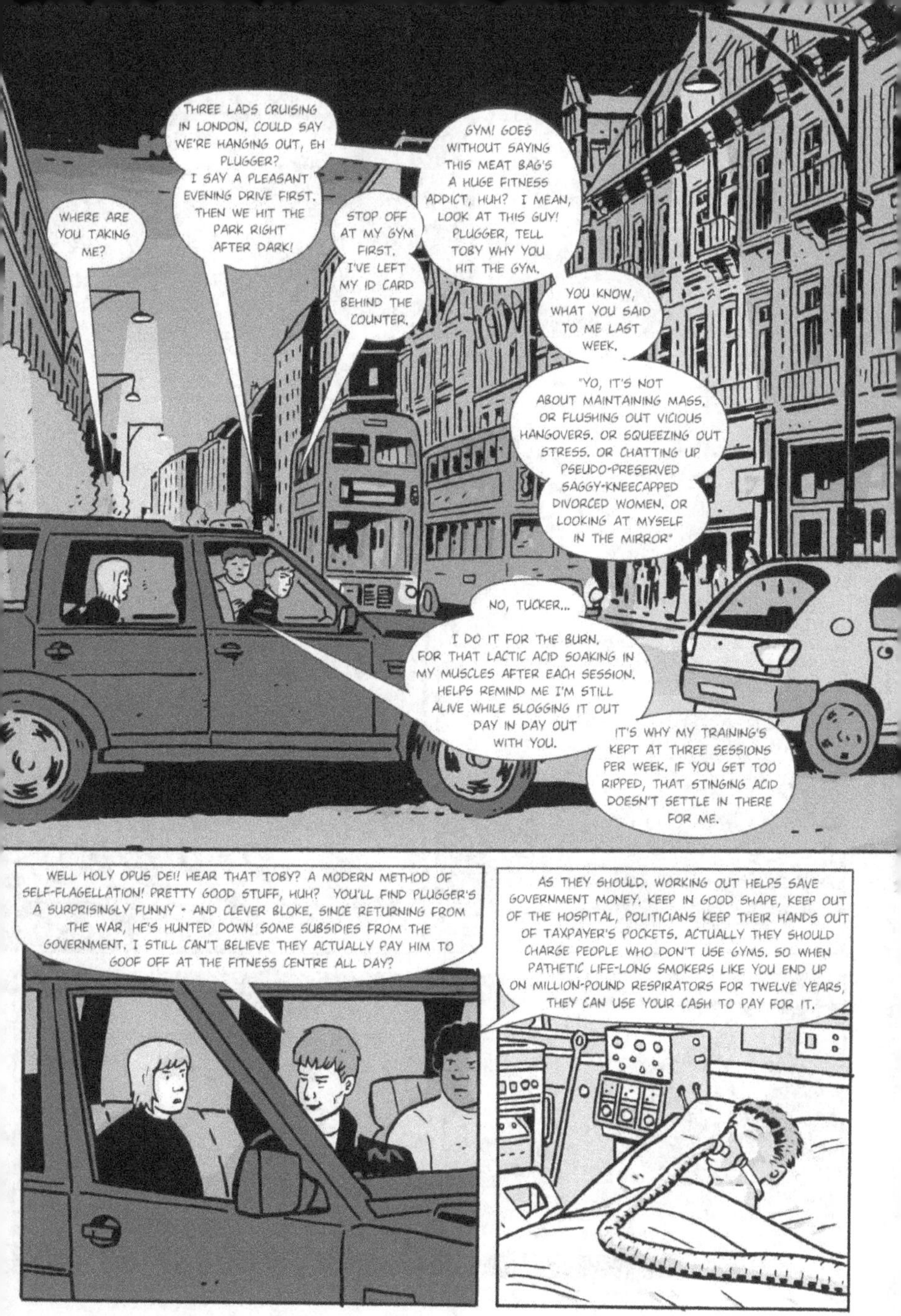
WHERE ARE YOU TAKING ME?
THREE LADS CRUISING IN LONDON. COULD SAY WE'RE HANGING OUT, EH PLUGGER? I SAY A PLEASANT EVENING DRIVE FIRST. THEN WE HIT THE PARK RIGHT AFTER DARK!
STOP OFF AT MY GYM FIRST. I'VE LEFT MY ID CARD BEHIND THE COUNTER.
GYM! GOES WITHOUT SAYING THIS MEAT BAG'S A HUGE FITNESS ADDICT, HUH? I MEAN, LOOK AT THIS GUY! PLUGGER, TELL TOBY WHY YOU HIT THE GYM.
YOU KNOW, WHAT YOU SAID TO ME LAST WEEK.
"YO, IT'S NOT ABOUT MAINTAINING MASS. OR FLUSHING OUT VICIOUS HANGOVERS. OR SQUEEZING OUT STRESS. OR CHATTING UP PSEUDO-PRESERVED SAGGY-KNEECAPPED DIVORCED WOMEN. OR LOOKING AT MYSELF IN THE MIRROR"
NO, TUCKER...
I DO IT FOR THE BURN. FOR THAT LACTIC ACID SOAKING IN MY MUSCLES AFTER EACH SESSION. HELPS REMIND ME I'M STILL ALIVE WHILE SLOGGING IT OUT DAY IN DAY OUT WITH YOU.
IT'S WHY MY TRAINING'S KEPT AT THREE SESSIONS PER WEEK. IF YOU GET TOO RIPPED, THAT STINGING ACID DOESN'T SETTLE IN THERE FOR ME.
WELL HOLY OPUS DEI! HEAR THAT TOBY? A MODERN METHOD OF SELF-FLAGELLATION! PRETTY GOOD STUFF, HUH? YOU'LL FIND PLUGGER'S A SURPRISINGLY FUNNY - AND CLEVER BLOKE. SINCE RETURNING FROM THE WAR, HE'S HUNTED DOWN SOME SUBSIDIES FROM THE GOVERNMENT. I STILL CAN'T BELIEVE THEY ACTUALLY PAY HIM TO GOOF OFF AT THE FITNESS CENTRE ALL DAY?
AS THEY SHOULD. WORKING OUT HELPS SAVE GOVERNMENT MONEY. KEEP IN GOOD SHAPE, KEEP OUT OF THE HOSPITAL, POLITICIANS KEEP THEIR HANDS OUT OF TAXPAYER'S POCKETS. ACTUALLY THEY SHOULD CHARGE PEOPLE WHO DON'T USE GYMS. SO WHEN PATHETIC LIFE-LONG SMOKERS LIKE YOU END UP ON MILLION-POUND RESPIRATORS FOR TWELVE YEARS, THEY CAN USE YOUR CASH TO PAY FOR IT.

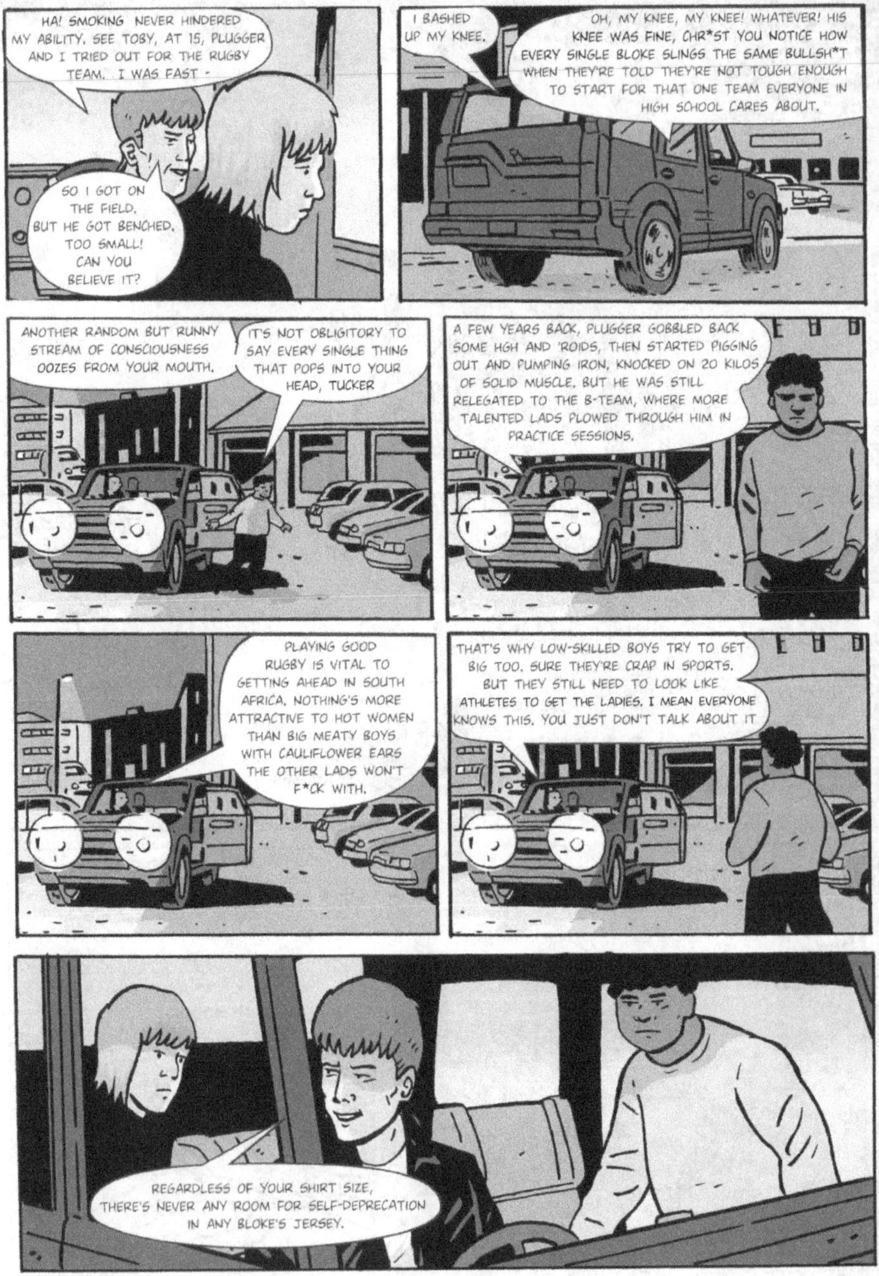
HA! SMOKING NEVER HINDERED MY ABILITY. SEE TOBY, AT 15, PLUGGER AND I TRIED OUT FOR THE RUGBY TEAM. I WAS FAST -
SO I GOT ON THE FIELD. BUT HE GOT BENCHED. TOO SMALL! CAN YOU BELIEVE IT?
I BASHED UP MY KNEE.
OH, MY KNEE, MY KNEE! WHATEVER! HIS KNEE WAS FINE, CHR*ST YOU NOTICE HOW EVERY SINGLE BLOKE SLINGS THE SAME BULLSH*T WHEN THEY'RE TOLD THEY'RE NOT TOUGH ENOUGH TO START FOR THAT ONE TEAM EVERYONE IN HIGH SCHOOL CARES ABOUT.
ANOTHER RANDOM BUT RUNNY STREAM OF CONSCIOUSNESS OOZES FROM YOUR MOUTH.
IT'S NOT OBLIGITORY TO SAY EVERY SINGLE THING THAT POPS INTO YOUR HEAD, TUCKER
A FEW YEARS BACK, PLUGGER GOBBLED BACK SOME HGH AND 'ROIDS, THEN STARTED PIGGING OUT AND PUMPING IRON, KNOCKED ON 20 KILOS OF SOLID MUSCLE. BUT HE WAS STILL RELEGATED TO THE B-TEAM, WHERE MORE TALENTED LADS PLOWED THROUGH HIM IN PRACTICE SESSIONS.
PLAYING GOOD RUGBY IS VITAL TO GETTING AHEAD IN SOUTH AFRICA. NOTHING'S MORE ATTRACTIVE TO HOT WOMEN THAN BIG MEATY BOYS WITH CAULIFLOWER EARS THE OTHER LADS WON'T F*CK WITH.
THAT'S WHY LOW-SKILLED BOYS TRY TO GET BIG TOO. SURE THEY'RE CRAP IN SPORTS. BUT THEY STILL NEED TO LOOK LIKE ATHLETES TO GET THE LADIES. I MEAN EVERYONE KNOWS THIS. YOU JUST DON'T TALK ABOUT IT
REGARDLESS OF YOUR SHIRT SIZE, THERE'S NEVER ANY ROOM FOR SELF-DEPRECATION IN ANY BLOKE'S JERSEY.

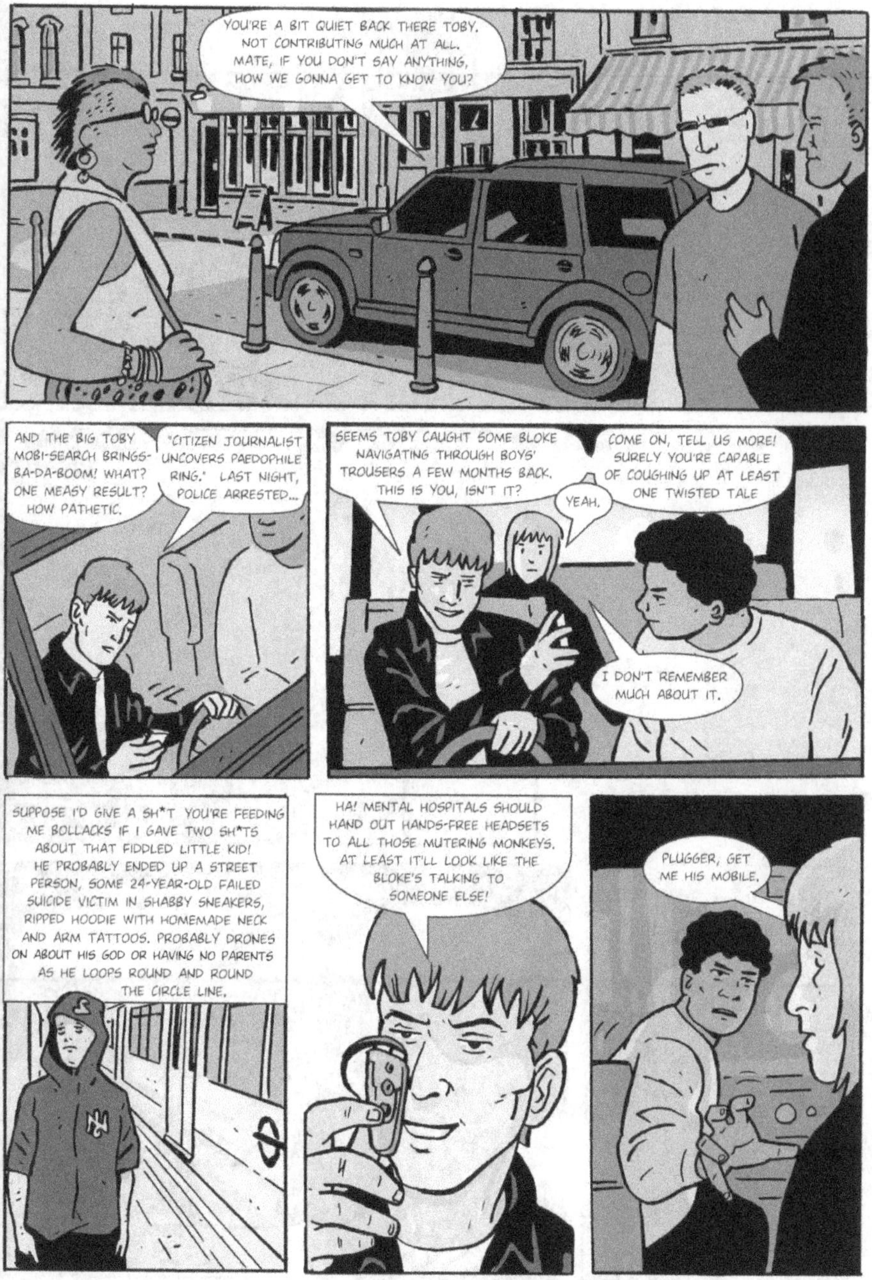
YOU'RE A BIT QUIET BACK THERE TOBY. NOT CONTRIBUTING MUCH AT ALL. MATE, IF YOU DON'T SAY ANYTHING, HOW WE GONNA GET TO KNOW YOU?
AND THE BIG TOBY MOBI-SEARCH BRINGS-BA-DA-BOOM! WHAT? ONE MEASY RESULT? HOW PATHETIC.
"CITIZEN JOURNALIST UNCOVERS PAEDOPHILE RING." LAST NIGHT, POLICE ARRESTED...
SEEMS TOBY CAUGHT SOME BLOKE NAVIGATING THROUGH BOYS' TROUSERS A FEW MONTHS BACK. THIS IS YOU, ISN'T IT?
YEAH.
COME ON, TELL US MORE! SURELY YOU'RE CAPABLE OF COUGHING UP AT LEAST ONE TWISTED TALE
I DON'T REMEMBER MUCH ABOUT IT.
SUPPOSE I'D GIVE A SH*T YOU'RE FEEDING ME BOLLACKS IF I GAVE TWO SH*TS ABOUT THAT FIDDLED LITTLE KID! HE PROBABLY ENDED UP A STREET PERSON, SOME 24-YEAR-OLD FAILED SUICIDE VICTIM IN SHABBY SNEAKERS, RIPPED HOODIE WITH HOMEMADE NECK AND ARM TATTOOS. PROBABLY DRONES ON ABOUT HIS GOD OR HAVING NO PARENTS AS HE LOOPS ROUND AND ROUND THE CIRCLE LINE.
HA! MENTAL HOSPITALS SHOULD HAND OUT HANDS-FREE HEADSETS TO ALL THOSE MUTERING MONKEYS. AT LEAST IT'LL LOOK LIKE THE BLOKE'S TALKING TO SOMEONE ELSE!
PLUGGER, GET ME HIS MOBILE.

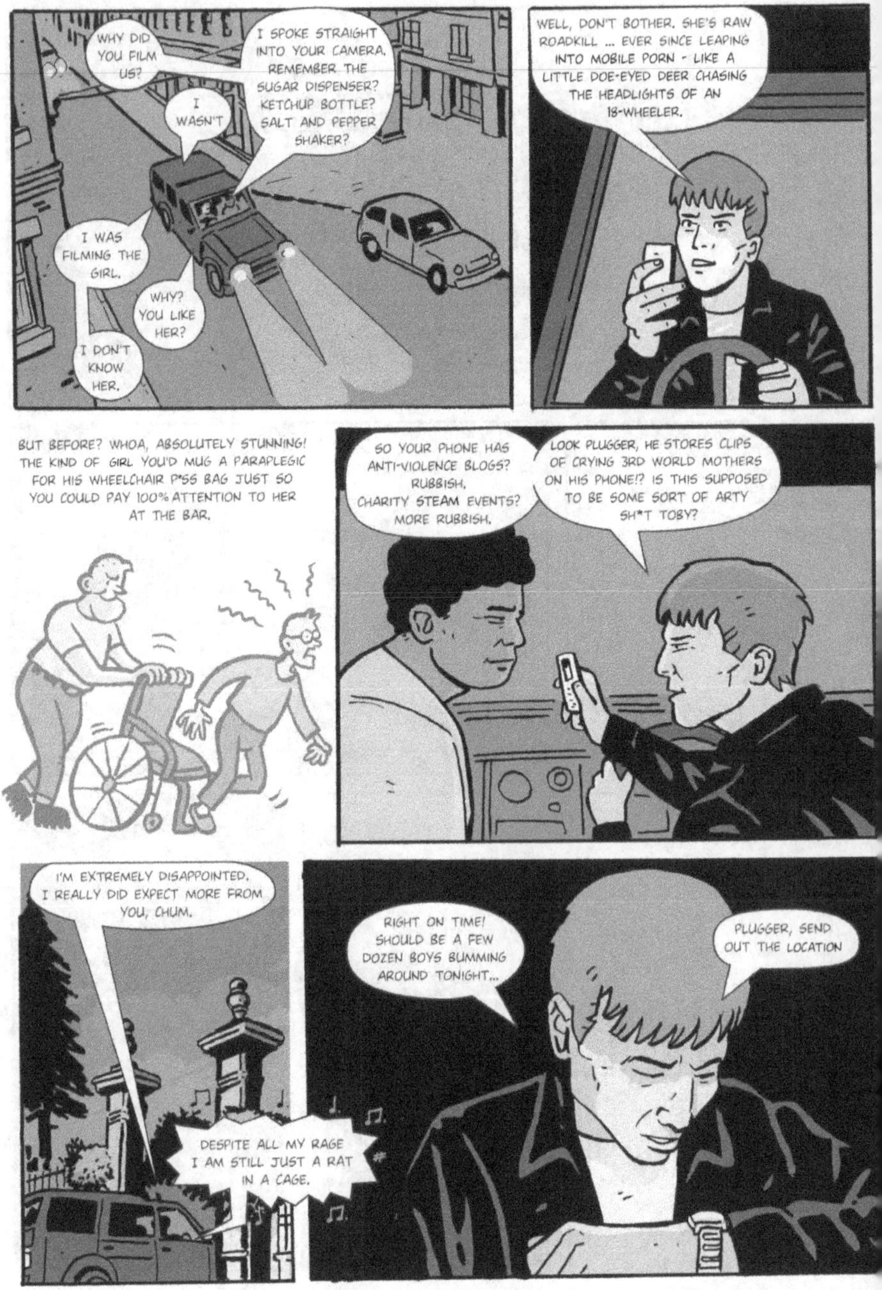
WHY DID YOU FILM US?
I WASN'T
I SPOKE STRAIGHT INTO YOUR CAMERA. REMEMBER THE SUGAR DISPENSER? KETCHUP BOTTLE? SALT AND PEPPER SHAKER?
I WAS FILMING THE GIRL.
WHY? YOU LIKE HER?
I DON'T KNOW HER.
WELL, DON'T BOTHER. SHE'S RAW ROADKILL ... EVER SINCE LEAPING INTO MOBILE PORN - LIKE A LITTLE DOE-EYED DEER CHASING THE HEADLIGHTS OF AN 18-WHEELER.
BUT BEFORE? WHOA, ABSOLUTELY STUNNING! THE KIND OF GIRL YOU'D MUG A PARAPLEGIC FOR HIS WHEELCHAIR P*SS BAG JUST SO YOU COULD PAY 100% ATTENTION TO HER AT THE BAR.
SO YOUR PHONE HAS ANTI-VIOLENCE BLOGS? RUBBISH. CHARITY STEAM EVENTS? MORE RUBBISH.
LOOK PLUGGER, HE STORES CLIPS OF CRYING 3RD WORLD MOTHERS ON HIS PHONE!? IS THIS SUPPOSED TO BE SOME SORT OF ARTY SH*T TOBY?
I'M EXTREMELY DISAPPOINTED. I REALLY DID EXPECT MORE FROM YOU, CHUM.
DESPITE ALL MY RAGE I AM STILL JUST A RAT IN A CAGE.
RIGHT ON TIME! SHOULD BE A FEW DOZEN BOYS BUMMING AROUND TONIGHT...
PLUGGER, SEND OUT THE LOCATION

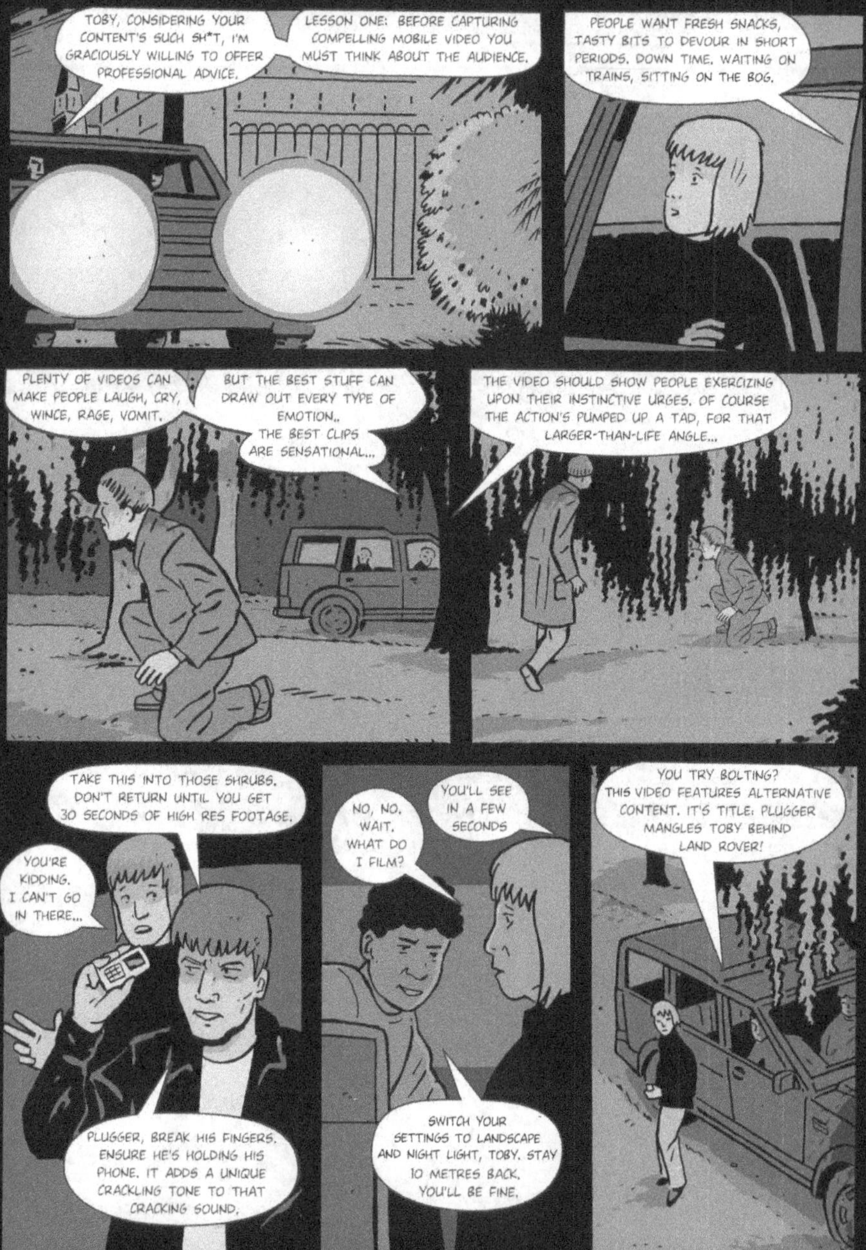
TOBY, CONSIDERING YOUR CONTENT'S SUCH SH*T, I'M GRACIOUSLY WILLING TO OFFER PROFESSIONAL ADVICE.
LESSON ONE: BEFORE CAPTURING COMPELLING MOBILE VIDEO YOU MUST THINK ABOUT THE AUDIENCE.
PEOPLE WANT FRESH SNACKS, TASTY BITS TO DEVOUR IN SHORT PERIODS. DOWN TIME. WAITING ON TRAINS, SITTING ON THE BOG.
PLENTY OF VIDEOS CAN MAKE PEOPLE LAUGH, CRY, WINCE, RAGE, VOMIT.
BUT THE BEST STUFF CAN DRAW OUT EVERY TYPE OF EMOTION.. THE BEST CLIPS ARE SENSATIONAL...
THE VIDEO SHOULD SHOW PEOPLE EXERCIZING UPON THEIR INSTINCTIVE URGES. OF COURSE THE ACTION'S PUMPED UP A TAD, FOR THAT LARGER-THAN-LIFE ANGLE...
TAKE THIS INTO THOSE SHRUBS. DON'T RETURN UNTIL YOU GET 30 SECONDS OF HIGH RES FOOTAGE.
YOU'RE KIDDING. I CAN'T GO IN THERE...
PLUGGER, BREAK HIS FINGERS. ENSURE HE'S HOLDING HIS PHONE. IT ADDS A UNIQUE CRACKLING TONE TO THAT CRACKING SOUND.
NO, NO. WAIT. WHAT DO I FILM?
YOU'LL SEE IN A FEW SECONDS
SWITCH YOUR SETTINGS TO LANDSCAPE AND NIGHT LIGHT, TOBY. STAY 10 METRES BACK. YOU'LL BE FINE.
YOU TRY BOLTING? THIS VIDEO FEATURES ALTERNATIVE CONTENT. IT'S TITLE: PLUGGER MANGLES TOBY BEHIND LAND ROVER!

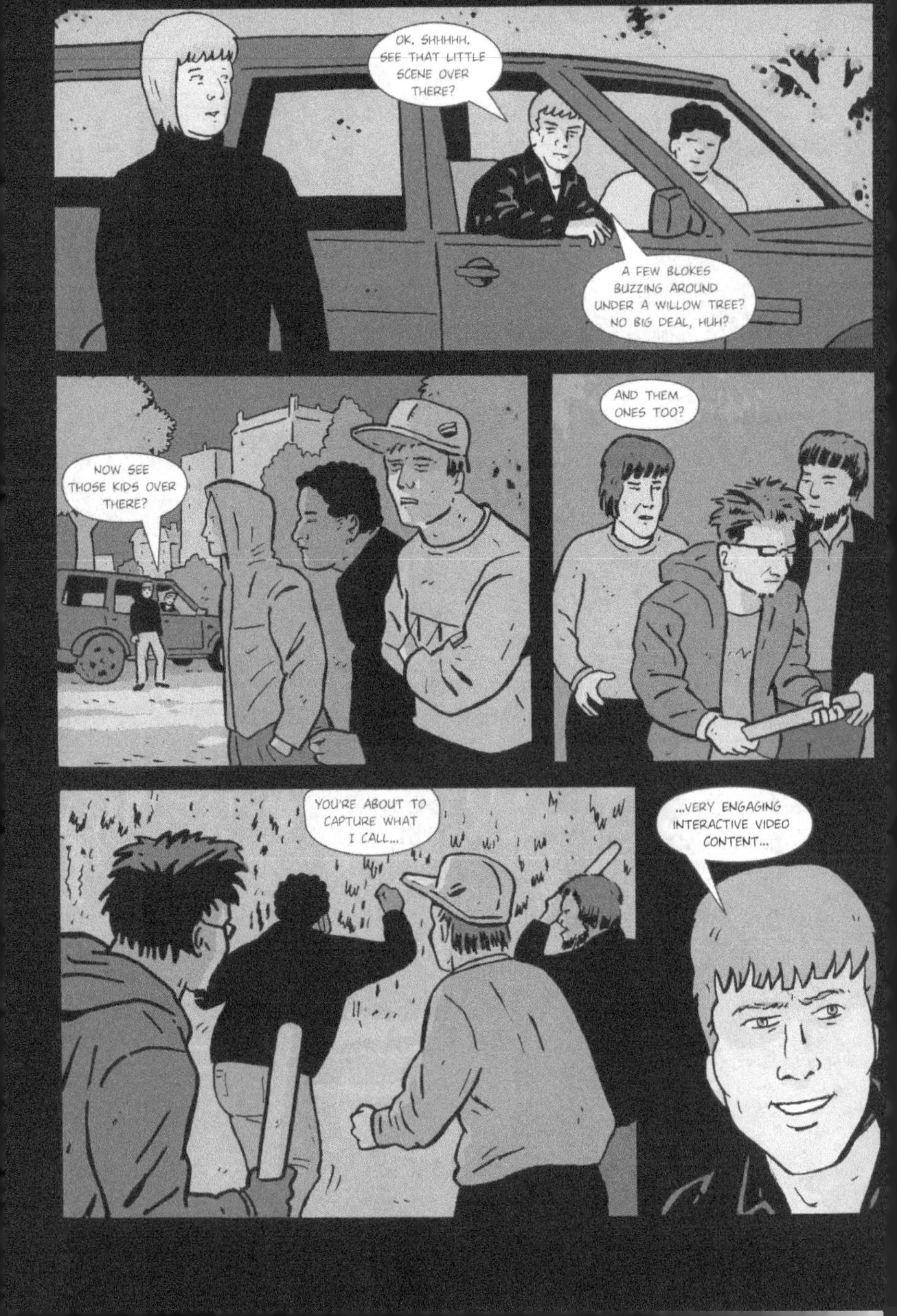
OK. SHHHHH. SEE THAT LITTLE SCENE OVER THERE?
A FEW BLOKES BUZZING AROUND UNDER A WILLOW TREE? NO BIG DEAL, HUH?
NOW SEE THOSE KIDS OVER THERE?
AND THEM ONES TOO?
YOU'RE ABOUT TO CAPTURE WHAT I CALL...
...VERY ENGAGING INTERACTIVE VIDEO CONTENT...

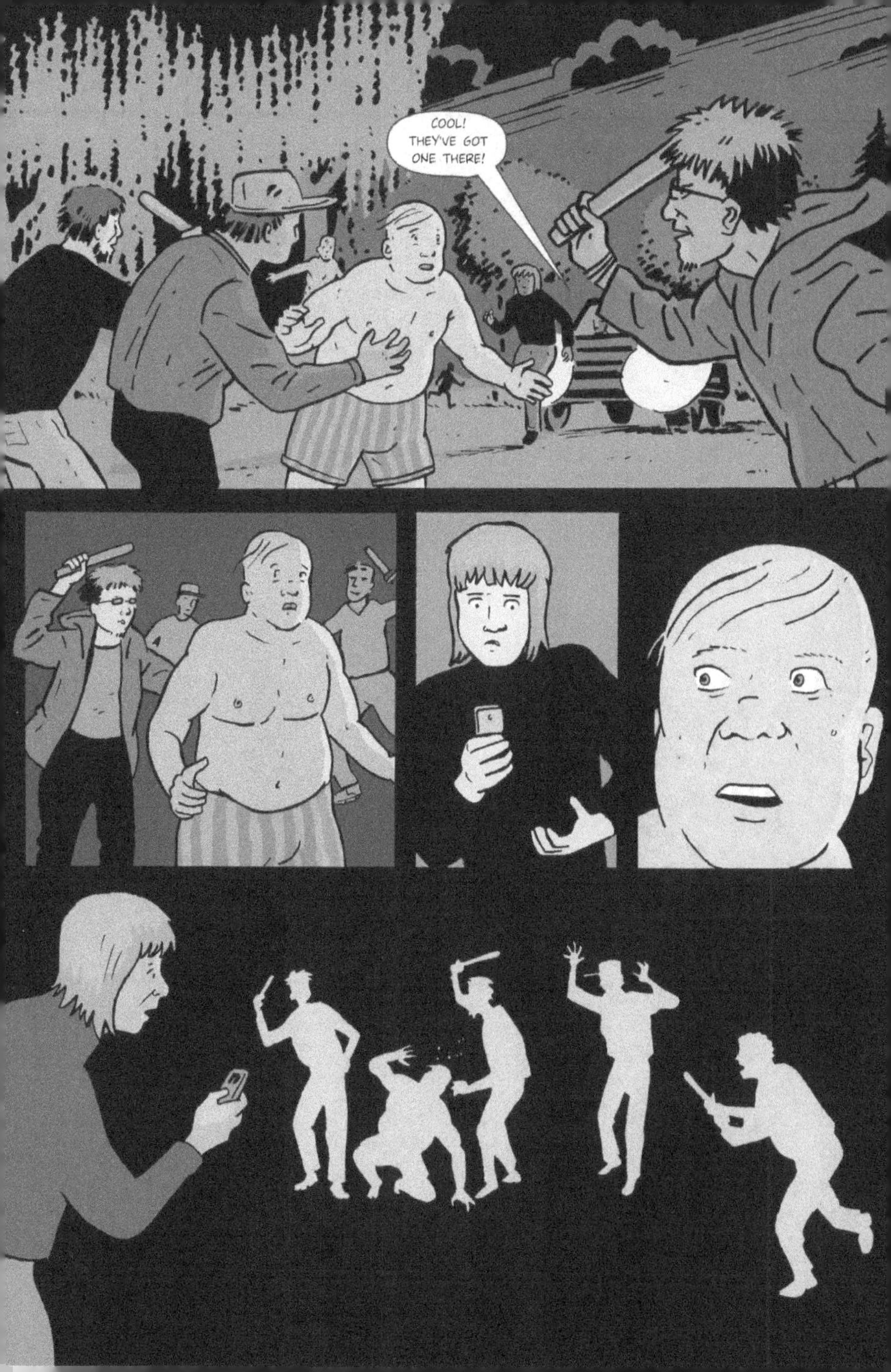
COOL! THEY'VE GOT ONE THERE!

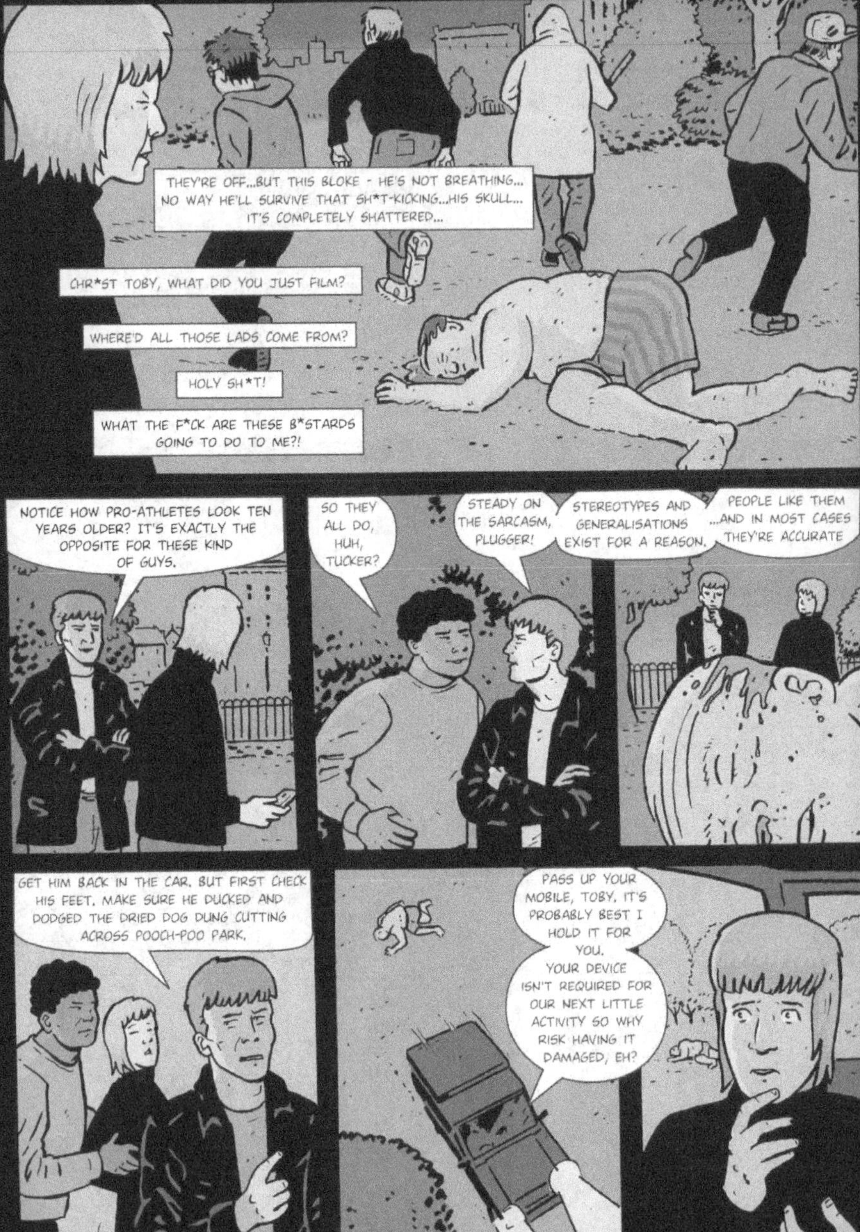
THEY'RE OFF...BUT THIS BLOKE - HE'S NOT BREATHING... NO WAY HE'LL SURVIVE THAT SH*T-KICKING...HIS SKULL... IT'S COMPLETELY SHATTERED...
CHR*ST TOBY, WHAT DID YOU JUST FILM?
WHERE'D ALL THOSE LADS COME FROM?
HOLY SH*T!
WHAT THE F*CK ARE THESE B*STARDS GOING TO DO TO ME?!
NOTICE HOW PRO-ATHLETES LOOK TEN YEARS OLDER? IT'S EXACTLY THE OPPOSITE FOR THESE KIND OF GUYS.
SO THEY ALL DO, HUH, TUCKER?
STEADY ON THE SARCASM, PLUGGER!
STEREOTYPES AND GENERALISATIONS EXIST FOR A REASON.
PEOPLE LIKE THEM ...AND IN MOST CASES THEY'RE ACCURATE
GET HIM BACK IN THE CAR. BUT FIRST CHECK HIS FEET. MAKE SURE HE DUCKED AND DODGED THE DRIED DOG DUNG CUTTING ACROSS POOCH-POO PARK.
PASS UP YOUR MOBILE, TOBY. IT'S PROBABLY BEST I HOLD IT FOR YOU. YOUR DEVICE ISN'T REQUIRED FOR OUR NEXT LITTLE ACTIVITY SO WHY RISK HAVING IT DAMAGED, EH?

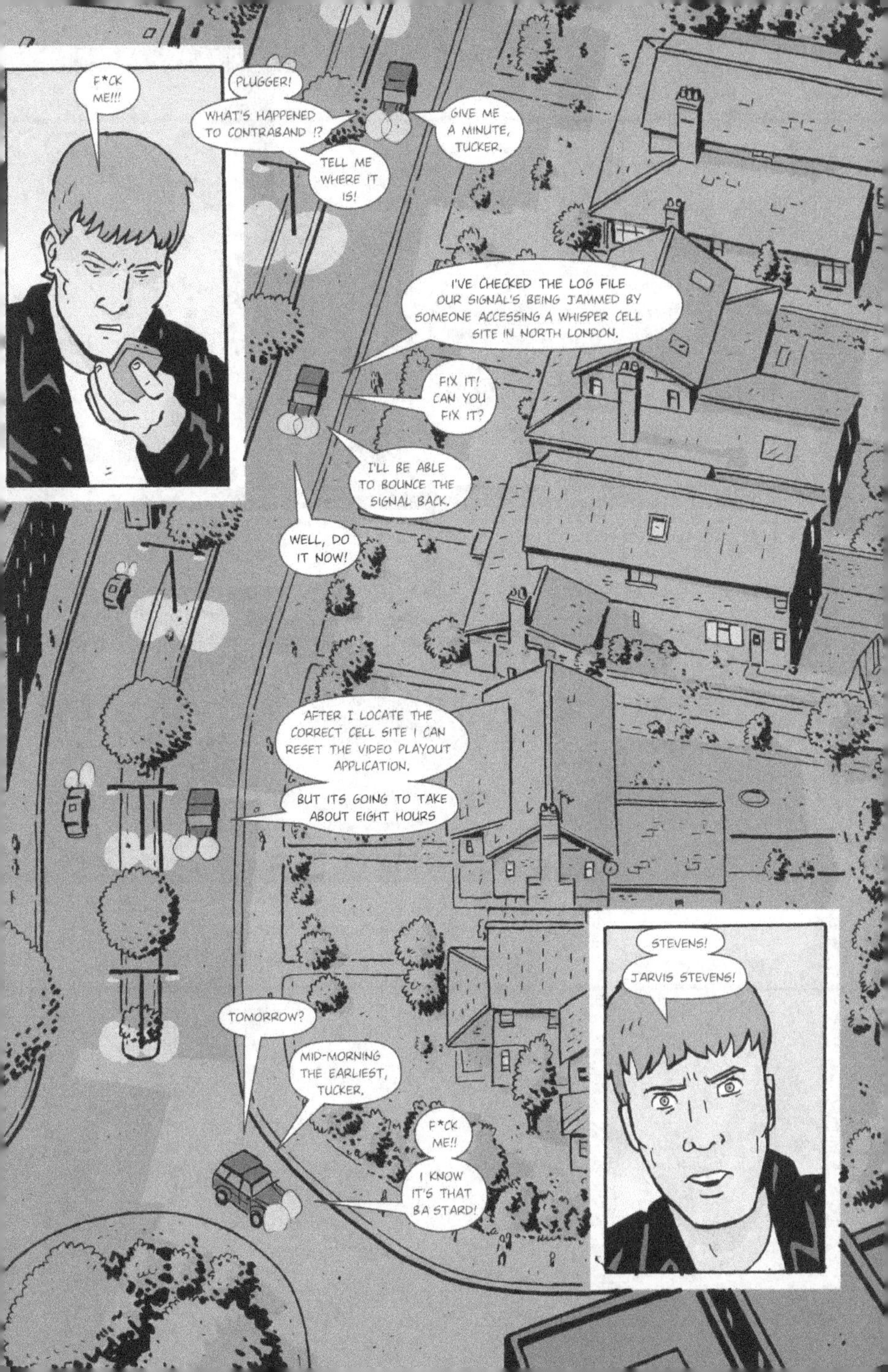
F*CK ME!!!
PLUGGER!
WHAT'S HAPPENED TO CONTRABAND !?
GIVE ME A MINUTE, TUCKER.
TELL ME WHERE IT IS!
I'VE CHECKED THE LOG FILE OUR SIGNAL'S BEING JAMMED BY SOMEONE ACCESSING A WHISPER CELL SITE IN NORTH LONDON.
FIX IT! CAN YOU FIX IT?
I'LL BE ABLE TO BOUNCE THE SIGNAL BACK.
WELL, DO IT NOW!
AFTER I LOCATE THE CORRECT CELL SITE I CAN RESET THE VIDEO PLAYOUT APPLICATION.
BUT ITS GOING TO TAKE ABOUT EIGHT HOURS
TOMORROW?
MID-MORNING THE EARLIEST, TUCKER.
F*CK ME!!
I KNOW IT'S THAT BA STARD!
STEVENS!
JARVIS STEVENS!

LATER...

SO PLUGGER TELL TOBY WHAT INSPIRED YOU TO BUILD MY NEW PHONE

CROATIAN POLICE OFFICERS MADE A HUGE DRUG BUST A FEW YEARS BACK. BROKE INTO A SEASIDE VILLA. SHOT A FEW HEAVY-HITTING DEALERS. AND THEY CONFISCATED 4KG OF HEROIN, 1.5M CASH, DOZENS OF FAKE PASSPORTS - AND ONE HOMEMADE MOBILE DEVICE ABLE TO SHOOT .22 MM CALIBER BULLETS.

SOMEBODY ACTUALLY MADE A PHONE GUN! I MEAN, HOW INCREDIBLE IS THAT?

FROM MOBILE NEWS FOOTAGE AND A FEW DESIGNS I PINCHED FROM WHISPER I DEVELOPED AN ADVANCED VERSION FOR TUCKER.

AND I MUST SAY THE RESULTS WERE ASTONISHING.

THE EL HOHL AMBUSH HAS ALL THE STANDARD FEATURES. VOICE, TEXT, WIFI, CAMERA, PLAYER, HANDS-FREE, ROAMING, STEEL CASING, WATER PROOFING, SHOCK RESISTANCE, BACK-UP POWER...

WHOA, STOP!

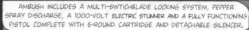

CUT THE PHONE SHOP SALES SH...T AND TELL HIM ABOUT THE GOOD STUFF, THE VALUE ADDING CAPABILITIES.

AMBUSH INCLUDES A MULTI-SWTICHBLADE LOCKING SYSTEM, PEPPER SPRAY DISCHARGE, A 1000-VOLT ELECTRIC STUNNER AND A FULLY FUNCTIONING PISTOL COMPLETE WITH 6-ROUND CARTRIDGE AND DETACHABLE SILENCER.

THAT'S THE BIT OF FUNCTIONALITY I'M KEEN TO DEMONSTRATE

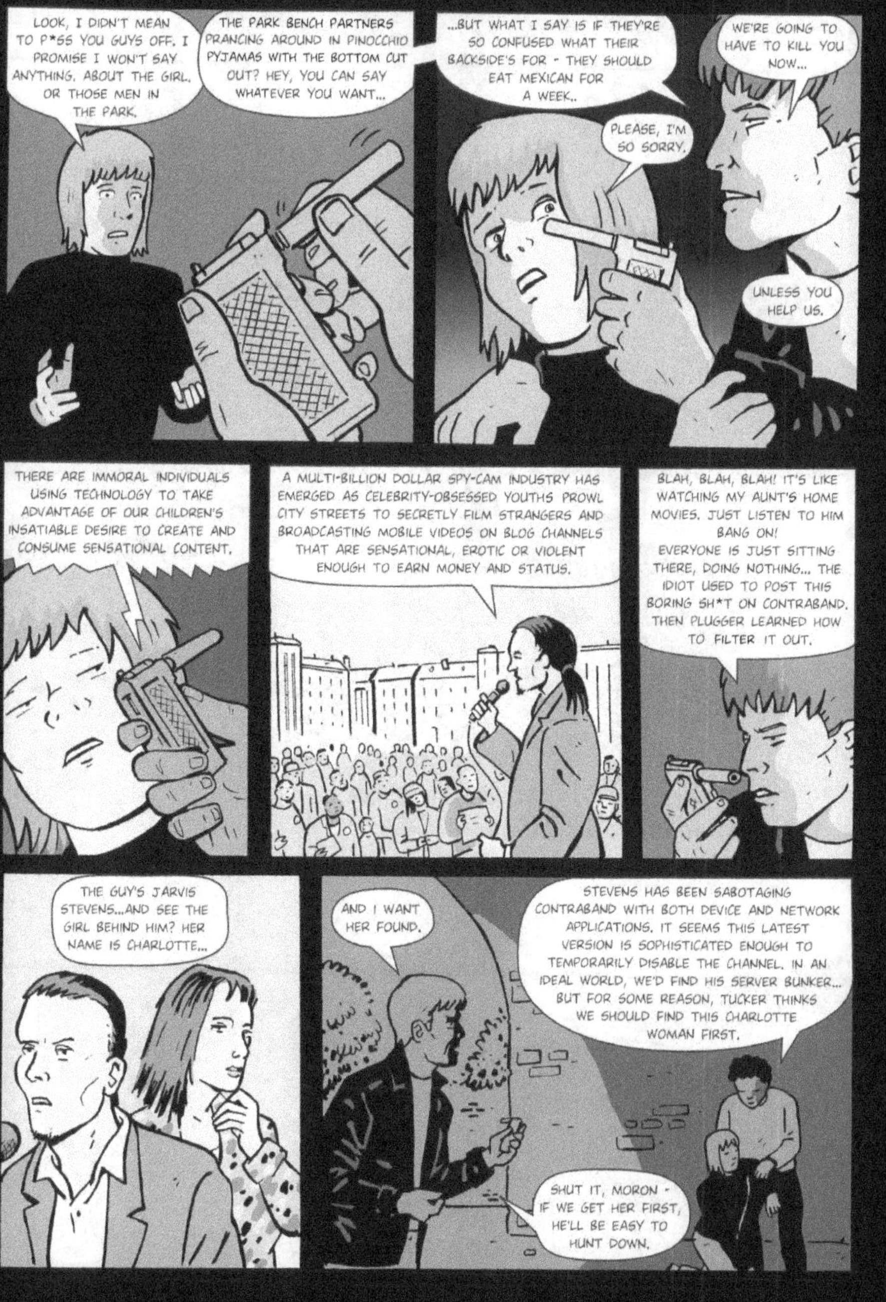
LOOK, I DIDN'T MEAN TO P*SS YOU GUYS OFF. I PROMISE I WON'T SAY ANYTHING. ABOUT THE GIRL. OR THOSE MEN IN THE PARK.
THE PARK BENCH PARTNERS PRANCING AROUND IN PINOCCHIO PYJAMAS WITH THE BOTTOM CUT OUT? HEY, YOU CAN SAY WHATEVER YOU WANT...
...BUT WHAT I SAY IS IF THEY'RE SO CONFUSED WHAT THEIR BACKSIDE'S FOR - THEY SHOULD EAT MEXICAN FOR A WEEK..
WE'RE GOING TO HAVE TO KILL YOU NOW...
PLEASE, I'M SO SORRY.
UNLESS YOU HELP US.
THERE ARE IMMORAL INDIVIDUALS USING TECHNOLOGY TO TAKE ADVANTAGE OF OUR CHILDREN'S INSATIABLE DESIRE TO CREATE AND CONSUME SENSATIONAL CONTENT.
A MULTI-BILLION DOLLAR SPY-CAM INDUSTRY HAS EMERGED AS CELEBRITY-OBSESSED YOUTHS PROWL CITY STREETS TO SECRETLY FILM STRANGERS AND BROADCASTING MOBILE VIDEOS ON BLOG CHANNELS THAT ARE SENSATIONAL, EROTIC OR VIOLENT ENOUGH TO EARN MONEY AND STATUS.
BLAH, BLAH, BLAH! IT'S LIKE WATCHING MY AUNT'S HOME MOVIES. JUST LISTEN TO HIM BANG ON! EVERYONE IS JUST SITTING THERE, DOING NOTHING... THE IDIOT USED TO POST THIS BORING SH*T ON CONTRABAND. THEN PLUGGER LEARNED HOW TO FILTER IT OUT.
THE GUY'S JARVIS STEVENS...AND SEE THE GIRL BEHIND HIM? HER NAME IS CHARLOTTE...
AND I WANT HER FOUND.
STEVENS HAS BEEN SABOTAGING CONTRABAND WITH BOTH DEVICE AND NETWORK APPLICATIONS. IT SEEMS THIS LATEST VERSION IS SOPHISTICATED ENOUGH TO TEMPORARILY DISABLE THE CHANNEL. IN AN IDEAL WORLD, WE'D FIND HIS SERVER BUNKER... BUT FOR SOME REASON, TUCKER THINKS WE SHOULD FIND THIS CHARLOTTE WOMAN FIRST.
SHUT IT, MORON - IF WE GET HER FIRST, HE'LL BE EASY TO HUNT DOWN.

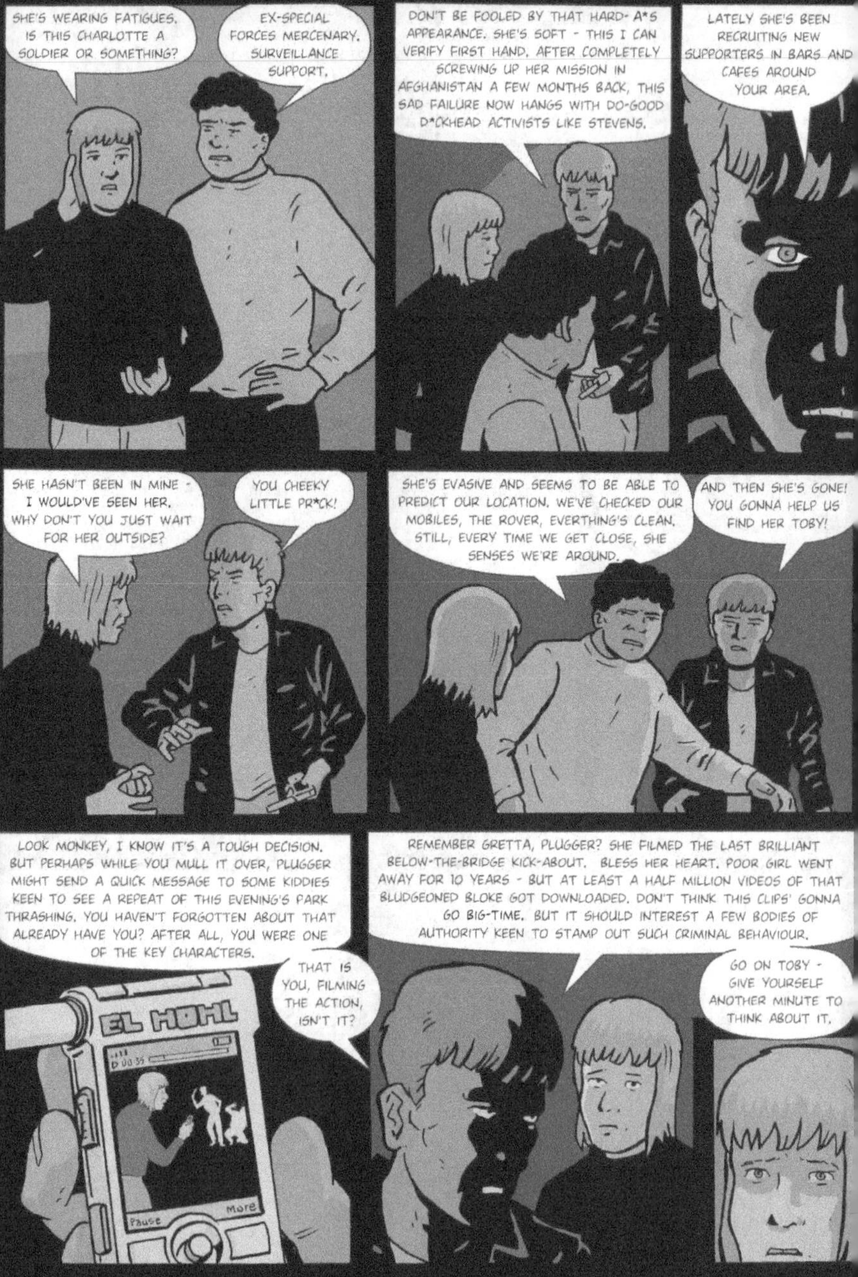
SHE'S WEARING FATIGUES. IS THIS CHARLOTTE A SOLDIER OR SOMETHING?
EX-SPECIAL FORCES MERCENARY. SURVEILLANCE SUPPORT.
DON'T BE FOOLED BY THAT HARD- A*S APPEARANCE. SHE'S SOFT - THIS I CAN VERIFY FIRST HAND. AFTER COMPLETELY SCREWING UP HER MISSION IN AFGHANISTAN A FEW MONTHS BACK, THIS SAD FAILURE NOW HANGS WITH DO-GOOD D*CKHEAD ACTIVISTS LIKE STEVENS.
LATELY SHE'S BEEN RECRUITING NEW SUPPORTERS IN BARS AND CAFES AROUND YOUR AREA.
SHE HASN'T BEEN IN MINE - I WOULD'VE SEEN HER. WHY DON'T YOU JUST WAIT FOR HER OUTSIDE?
YOU CHEEKY LITTLE PR*CK!
SHE'S EVASIVE AND SEEMS TO BE ABLE TO PREDICT OUR LOCATION. WE'VE CHECKED OUR MOBILES, THE ROVER, EVERTHING'S CLEAN. STILL, EVERY TIME WE GET CLOSE, SHE SENSES WE'RE AROUND.
AND THEN SHE'S GONE! YOU GONNA HELP US FIND HER TOBY!
LOOK MONKEY, I KNOW IT'S A TOUGH DECISION. BUT PERHAPS WHILE YOU MULL IT OVER, PLUGGER MIGHT SEND A QUICK MESSAGE TO SOME KIDDIES KEEN TO SEE A REPEAT OF THIS EVENING'S PARK THRASHING. YOU HAVEN'T FORGOTTEN ABOUT THAT ALREADY HAVE YOU? AFTER ALL, YOU WERE ONE OF THE KEY CHARACTERS.
THAT IS YOU, FILMING THE ACTION, ISN'T IT?
EL MOHL
Pause
More
REMEMBER GRETTA, PLUGGER? SHE FILMED THE LAST BRILLIANT BELOW-THE-BRIDGE KICK-ABOUT. BLESS HER HEART. POOR GIRL WENT AWAY FOR 10 YEARS - BUT AT LEAST A HALF MILLION VIDEOS OF THAT BLUDGEONED BLOKE GOT DOWNLOADED. DON'T THINK THIS CLIPS' GONNA GO BIG-TIME. BUT IT SHOULD INTEREST A FEW BODIES OF AUTHORITY KEEN TO STAMP OUT SUCH CRIMINAL BEHAVIOUR.
GO ON TOBY - GIVE YOURSELF ANOTHER MINUTE TO THINK ABOUT IT.

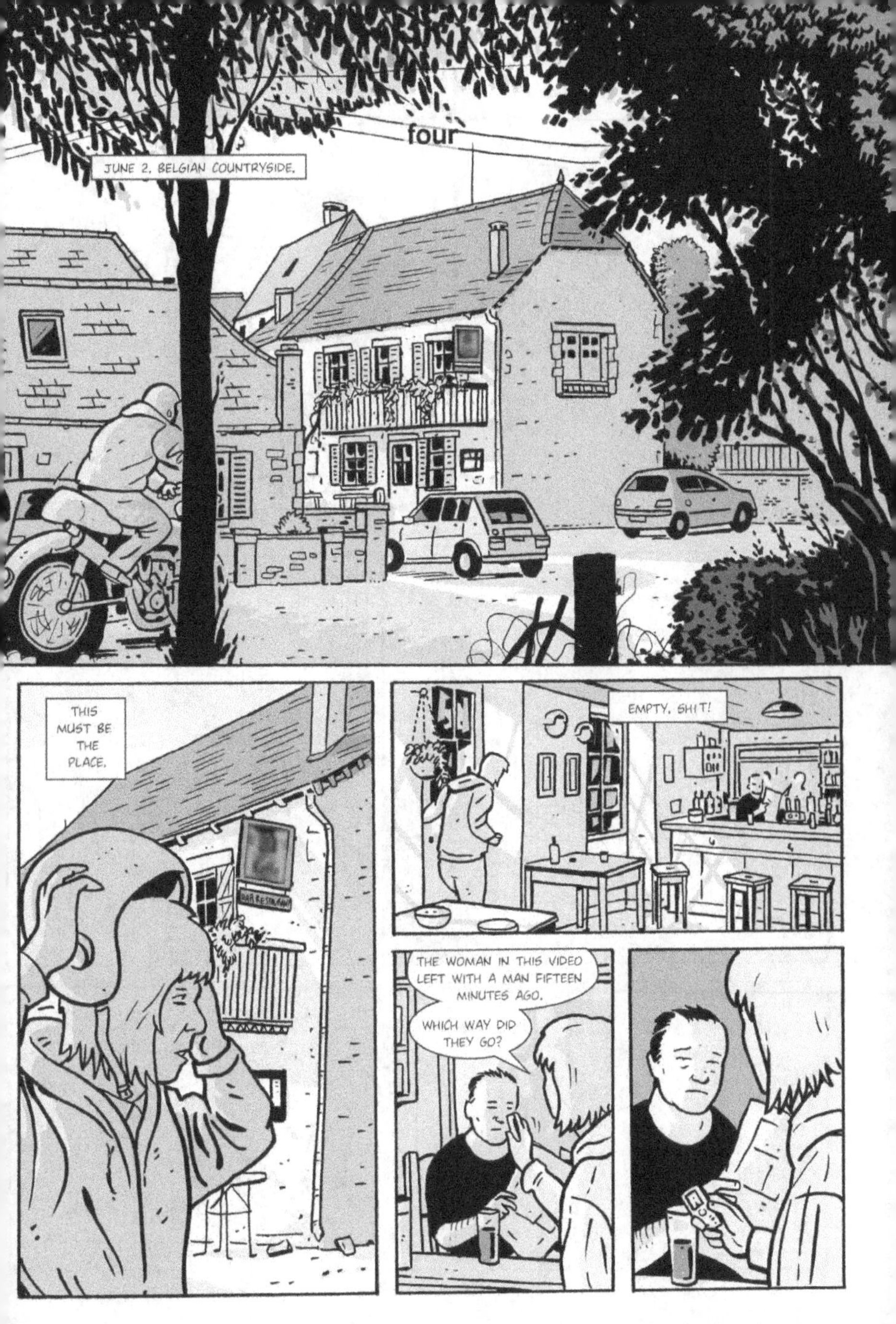
four
JUNE 2, BELGIAN COUNTRYSIDE.
THIS MUST BE THE PLACE.
EMPTY. SHIT!
THE WOMAN IN THIS VIDEO LEFT WITH A MAN FIFTEEN MINUTES AGO.
WHICH WAY DID THEY GO?

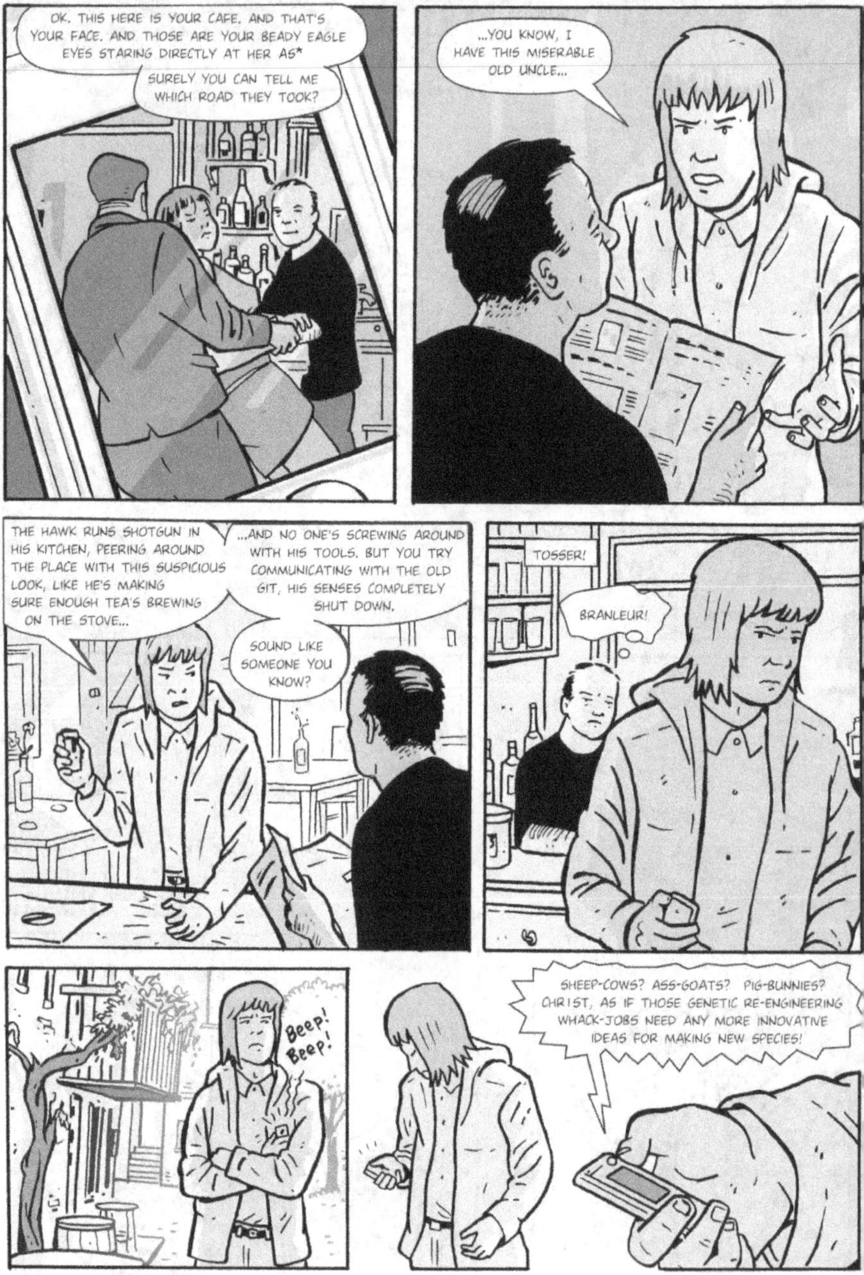
OK. THIS HERE IS YOUR CAFE. AND THAT'S YOUR FACE. AND THOSE ARE YOUR BEADY EAGLE EYES STARING DIRECTLY AT HER AS*
SURELY YOU CAN TELL ME WHICH ROAD THEY TOOK?
...YOU KNOW, I HAVE THIS MISERABLE OLD UNCLE...
THE HAWK RUNS SHOTGUN IN HIS KITCHEN, PEERING AROUND THE PLACE WITH THIS SUSPICIOUS LOOK, LIKE HE'S MAKING SURE ENOUGH TEA'S BREWING ON THE STOVE...
...AND NO ONE'S SCREWING AROUND WITH HIS TOOLS. BUT YOU TRY COMMUNICATING WITH THE OLD GIT, HIS SENSES COMPLETELY SHUT DOWN.
SOUND LIKE SOMEONE YOU KNOW?
TOSSER!
BRANLEUR!
Beep! Beep!
SHEEP-COWS? ASS-GOATS? PIG-BUNNIES? CHRIST, AS IF THOSE GENETIC RE-ENGINEERING WHACK-JOBS NEED ANY MORE INNOVATIVE IDEAS FOR MAKING NEW SPECIES!

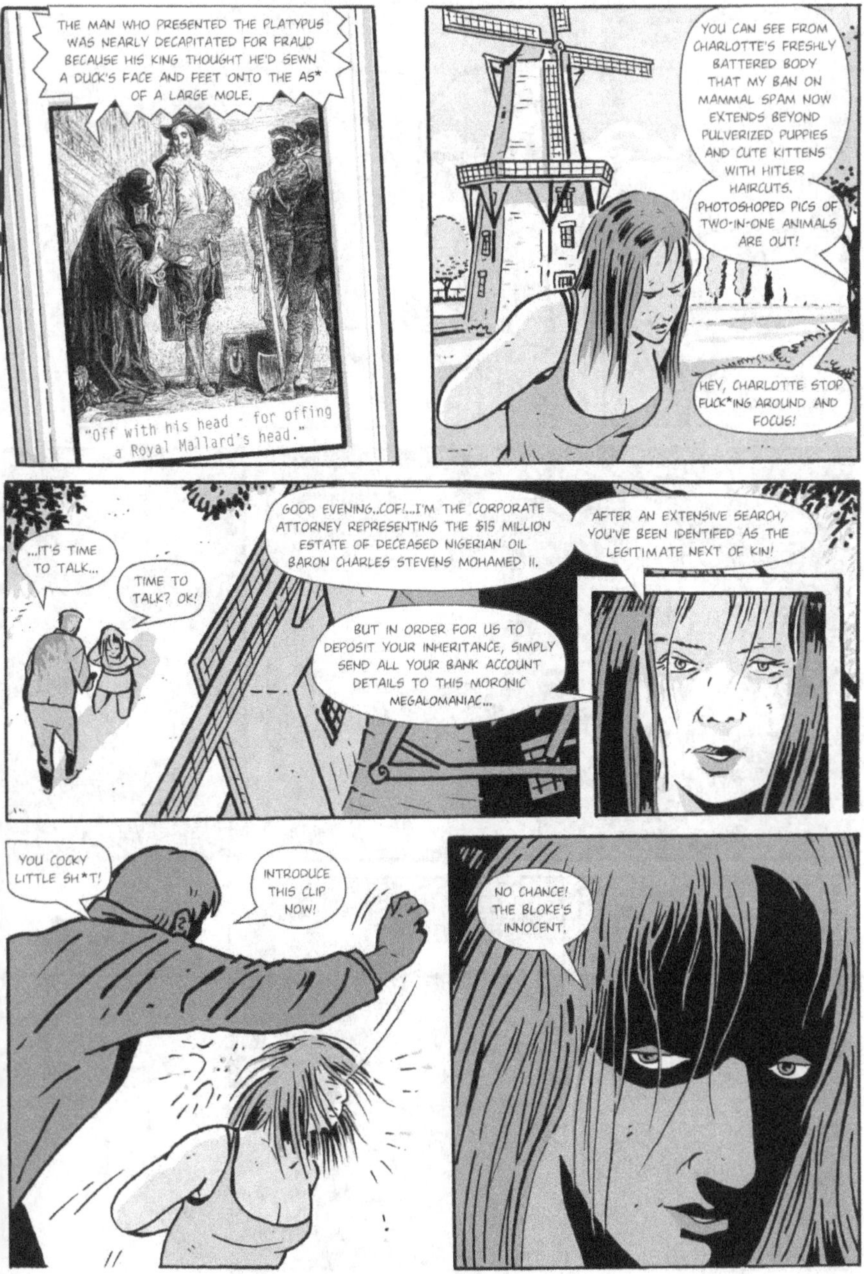
THE MAN WHO PRESENTED THE PLATYPUS WAS NEARLY DECAPITATED FOR FRAUD BECAUSE HIS KING THOUGHT HE'D SEWN A DUCK'S FACE AND FEET ONTO THE AS* OF A LARGE MOLE.
"Off with his head - for offing a Royal Mallard's head."
YOU CAN SEE FROM CHARLOTTE'S FRESHLY BATTERED BODY THAT MY BAN ON MAMMAL SPAM NOW EXTENDS BEYOND PULVERIZED PUPPIES AND CUTE KITTENS WITH HITLER HAIRCUTS. PHOTOSHOPED PICS OF TWO-IN-ONE ANIMALS ARE OUT!
HEY, CHARLOTTE STOP FUCK*ING AROUND AND FOCUS!
...IT'S TIME TO TALK...
TIME TO TALK? OK!
GOOD EVENING..COF!...I'M THE CORPORATE ATTORNEY REPRESENTING THE $15 MILLION ESTATE OF DECEASED NIGERIAN OIL BARON CHARLES STEVENS MOHAMED II.
AFTER AN EXTENSIVE SEARCH, YOU'VE BEEN IDENTIFED AS THE LEGITIMATE NEXT OF KIN!
BUT IN ORDER FOR US TO DEPOSIT YOUR INHERITANCE, SIMPLY SEND ALL YOUR BANK ACCOUNT DETAILS TO THIS MORONIC MEGALOMANIAC...
YOU COCKY LITTLE SH*T!
INTRODUCE THIS CLIP NOW!
NO CHANCE! THE BLOKE'S INNOCENT.

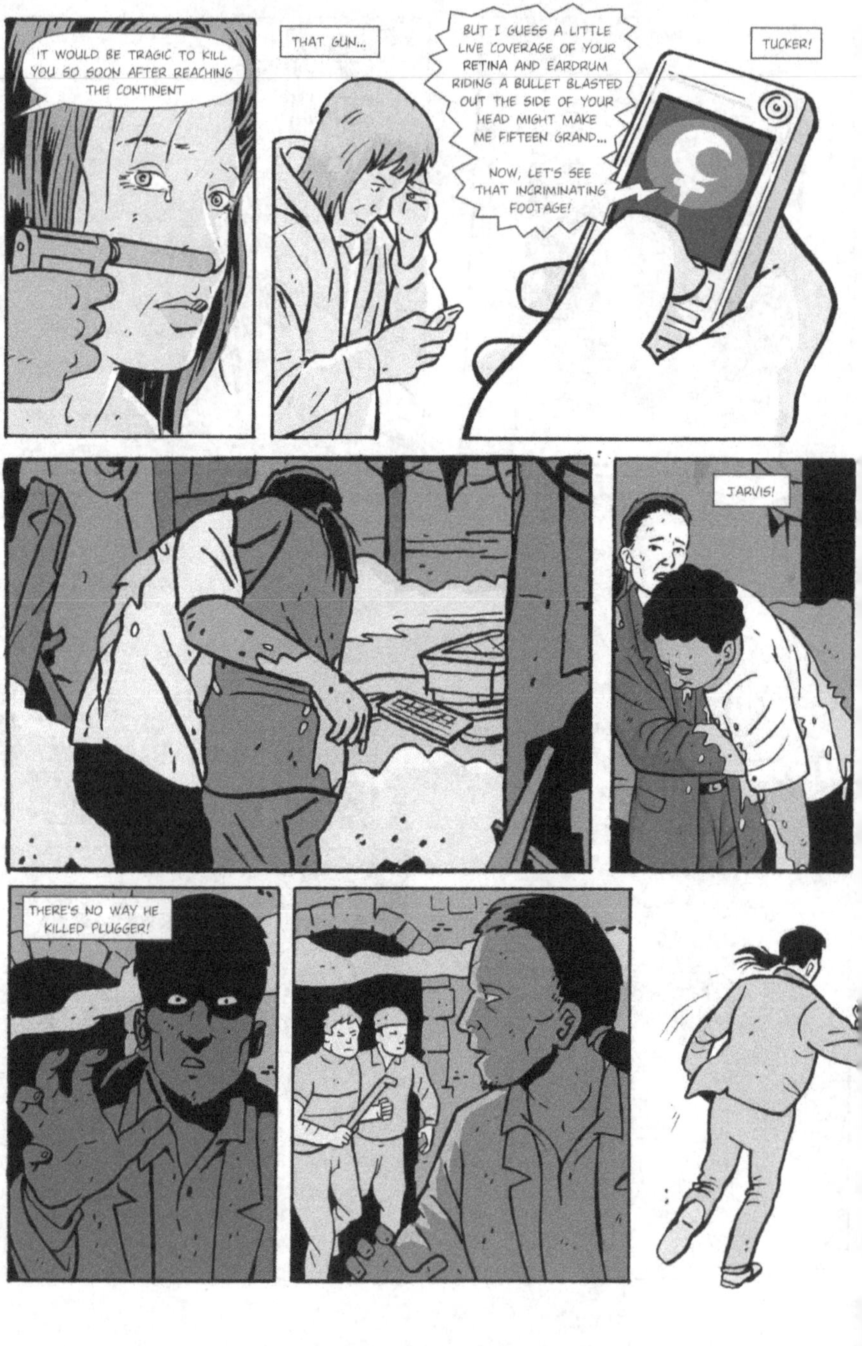
IT WOULD BE TRAGIC TO KILL YOU SO SOON AFTER REACHING THE CONTINENT
THAT GUN...
BUT I GUESS A LITTLE LIVE COVERAGE OF YOUR RETINA AND EARDRUM RIDING A BULLET BLASTED OUT THE SIDE OF YOUR HEAD MIGHT MAKE ME FIFTEEN GRAND...
NOW, LET'S SEE THAT INCRIMINATING FOOTAGE!
TUCKER!
JARVIS!
THERE'S NO WAY HE KILLED PLUGGER!

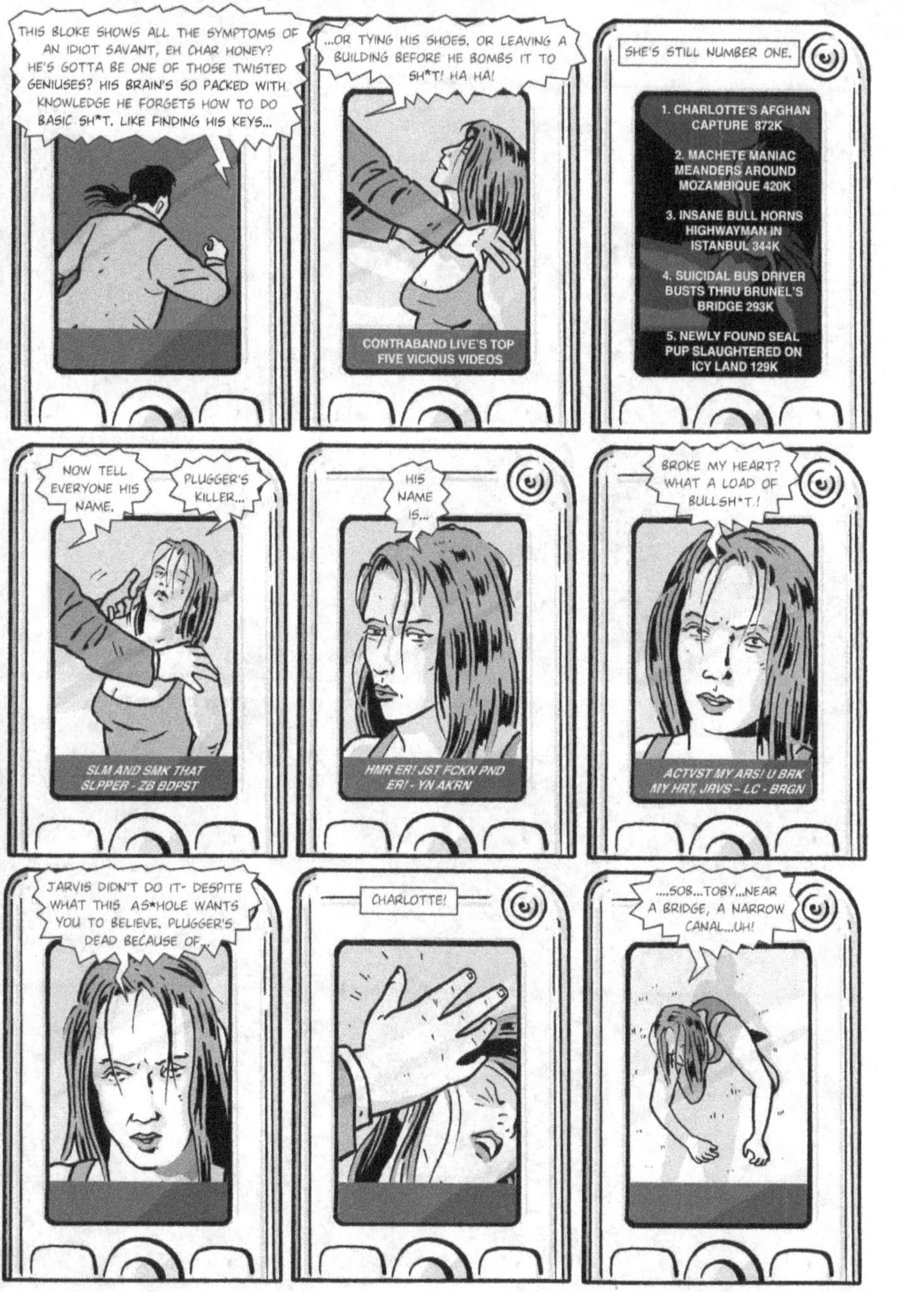
THIS BLOKE SHOWS ALL THE SYMPTOMS OF AN IDIOT SAVANT, EH CHAR HONEY? HE'S GOTTA BE ONE OF THOSE TWISTED GENIUSES? HIS BRAIN'S SO PACKED WITH KNOWLEDGE HE FORGETS HOW TO DO BASIC SH*T. LIKE FINDING HIS KEYS...
...OR TYING HIS SHOES. OR LEAVING A BUILDING BEFORE HE BOMBS IT TO SH*T! HA HA!
CONTRABAND LIVE'S TOP FIVE VICIOUS VIDEOS
SHE'S STILL NUMBER ONE.
1. CHARLOTTE'S AFGHAN CAPTURE 872K
2. MACHETE MANIAC MEANDERS AROUND MOZAMBIQUE 420K
3. INSANE BULL HORNS HIGHWAYMAN IN ISTANBUL 344K
4. SUICIDAL BUS DRIVER BUSTS THRU BRUNEL'S BRIDGE 293K
5. NEWLY FOUND SEAL PUP SLAUGHTERED ON ICY LAND 129K
NOW TELL EVERYONE HIS NAME.
PLUGGER'S KILLER...
SLM AND SMK THAT SLPPER - ZB BDPST
HIS NAME IS...
HMR ER! JST FCKN PND ER! - YN AKRN
BROKE MY HEART? WHAT A LOAD OF BULLSH*T!
ACTVST MY ARS! U BRK MY HRT, JRVS – LC - BRGN
JARVIS DIDN'T DO IT- DESPITE WHAT THIS AS*HOLE WANTS YOU TO BELIEVE. PLUGGER'S DEAD BECAUSE OF...
CHARLOTTE!
...SOB...TOBY...NEAR A BRIDGE, A NARROW CANAL...UH!

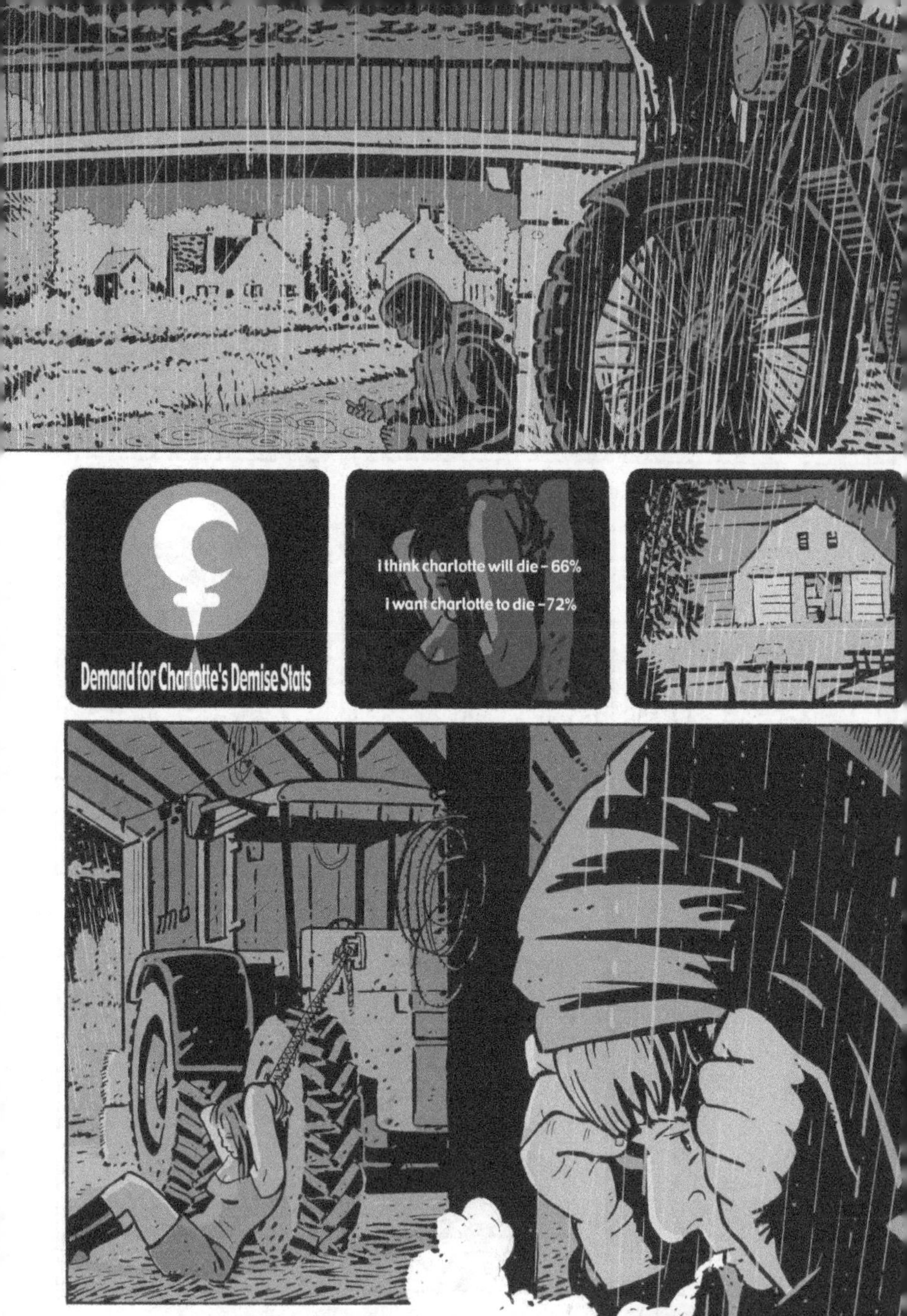
Demand for Charlotte's Demise Stats
i think charlotte will die - 66%
i want charlotte to die - 72%

five

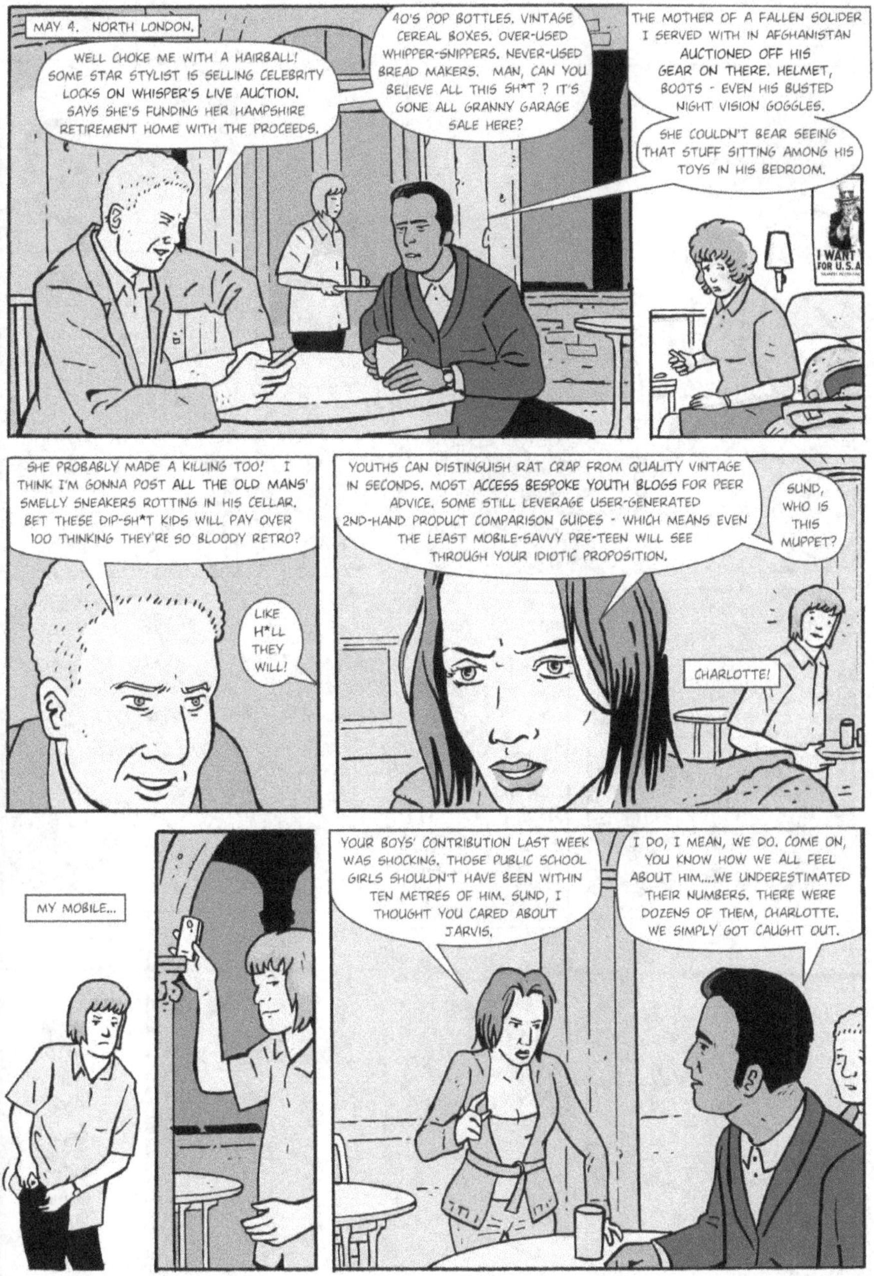
MAY 4. NORTH LONDON.
WELL CHOKE ME WITH A HAIRBALL! SOME STAR STYLIST IS SELLING CELEBRITY LOCKS ON WHISPER'S LIVE AUCTION. SAYS SHE'S FUNDING HER HAMPSHIRE RETIREMENT HOME WITH THE PROCEEDS.
40'S POP BOTTLES. VINTAGE CEREAL BOXES. OVER-USED WHIPPER-SNIPPERS. NEVER-USED BREAD MAKERS. MAN, CAN YOU BELIEVE ALL THIS SH*T ? IT'S GONE ALL GRANNY GARAGE SALE HERE?
THE MOTHER OF A FALLEN SOLIDER I SERVED WITH IN AFGHANISTAN AUCTIONED OFF HIS GEAR ON THERE. HELMET, BOOTS - EVEN HIS BUSTED NIGHT VISION GOGGLES.
SHE COULDN'T BEAR SEEING THAT STUFF SITTING AMONG HIS TOYS IN HIS BEDROOM.
I WANT
FOR U.S.A
SHE PROBABLY MADE A KILLING TOO! I THINK I'M GONNA POST ALL THE OLD MANS' SMELLY SNEAKERS ROTTING IN HIS CELLAR. BET THESE DIP-SH*T KIDS WILL PAY OVER 100 THINKING THEY'RE SO BLOODY RETRO?
LIKE H*LL THEY WILL!
YOUTHS CAN DISTINGUISH RAT CRAP FROM QUALITY VINTAGE IN SECONDS. MOST ACCESS BESPOKE YOUTH BLOGS FOR PEER ADVICE. SOME STILL LEVERAGE USER-GENERATED 2ND-HAND PRODUCT COMPARISON GUIDES - WHICH MEANS EVEN THE LEAST MOBILE-SAVVY PRE-TEEN WILL SEE THROUGH YOUR IDIOTIC PROPOSITION.
SUND, WHO IS THIS MUPPET?
CHARLOTTE!
MY MOBILE...
YOUR BOYS' CONTRIBUTION LAST WEEK WAS SHOCKING. THOSE PUBLIC SCHOOL GIRLS SHOULDN'T HAVE BEEN WITHIN TEN METRES OF HIM. SUND, I THOUGHT YOU CARED ABOUT JARVIS.
I DO, I MEAN, WE DO. COME ON, YOU KNOW HOW WE ALL FEEL ABOUT HIM....WE UNDERESTIMATED THEIR NUMBERS. THERE WERE DOZENS OF THEM, CHARLOTTE. WE SIMPLY GOT CAUGHT OUT.

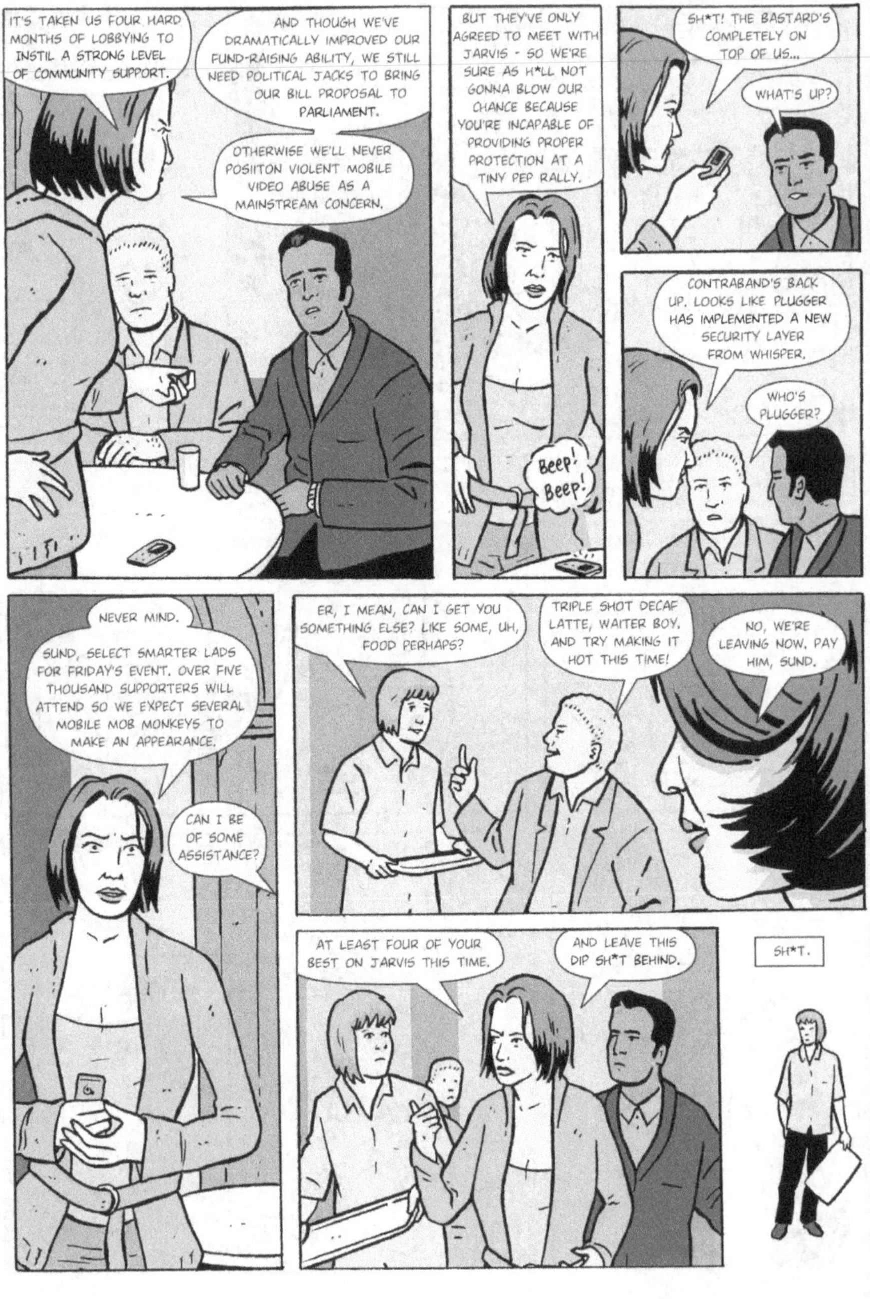
IT'S TAKEN US FOUR HARD MONTHS OF LOBBYING TO INSTIL A STRONG LEVEL OF COMMUNITY SUPPORT.
AND THOUGH WE'VE DRAMATICALLY IMPROVED OUR FUND-RAISING ABILITY, WE STILL NEED POLITICAL JACKS TO BRING OUR BILL PROPOSAL TO PARLIAMENT.
OTHERWISE WE'LL NEVER POSIITON VIOLENT MOBILE VIDEO ABUSE AS A MAINSTREAM CONCERN.
BUT THEY'VE ONLY AGREED TO MEET WITH JARVIS - SO WE'RE SURE AS H*LL NOT GONNA BLOW OUR CHANCE BECAUSE YOU'RE INCAPABLE OF PROVIDING PROPER PROTECTION AT A TINY PEP RALLY.
Beep! Beep!
SH*T! THE BASTARD'S COMPLETELY ON TOP OF US...
WHAT'S UP?
CONTRABAND'S BACK UP. LOOKS LIKE PLUGGER HAS IMPLEMENTED A NEW SECURITY LAYER FROM WHISPER.
WHO'S PLUGGER?
NEVER MIND.
SUND, SELECT SMARTER LADS FOR FRIDAY'S EVENT. OVER FIVE THOUSAND SUPPORTERS WILL ATTEND SO WE EXPECT SEVERAL MOBILE MOB MONKEYS TO MAKE AN APPEARANCE.
CAN I BE OF SOME ASSISTANCE?
ER, I MEAN, CAN I GET YOU SOMETHING ELSE? LIKE SOME, UH, FOOD PERHAPS?
TRIPLE SHOT DECAF LATTE, WAITER BOY, AND TRY MAKING IT HOT THIS TIME!
NO, WE'RE LEAVING NOW. PAY HIM, SUND.
AT LEAST FOUR OF YOUR BEST ON JARVIS THIS TIME.
AND LEAVE THIS DIP SH*T BEHIND.
SH*T.

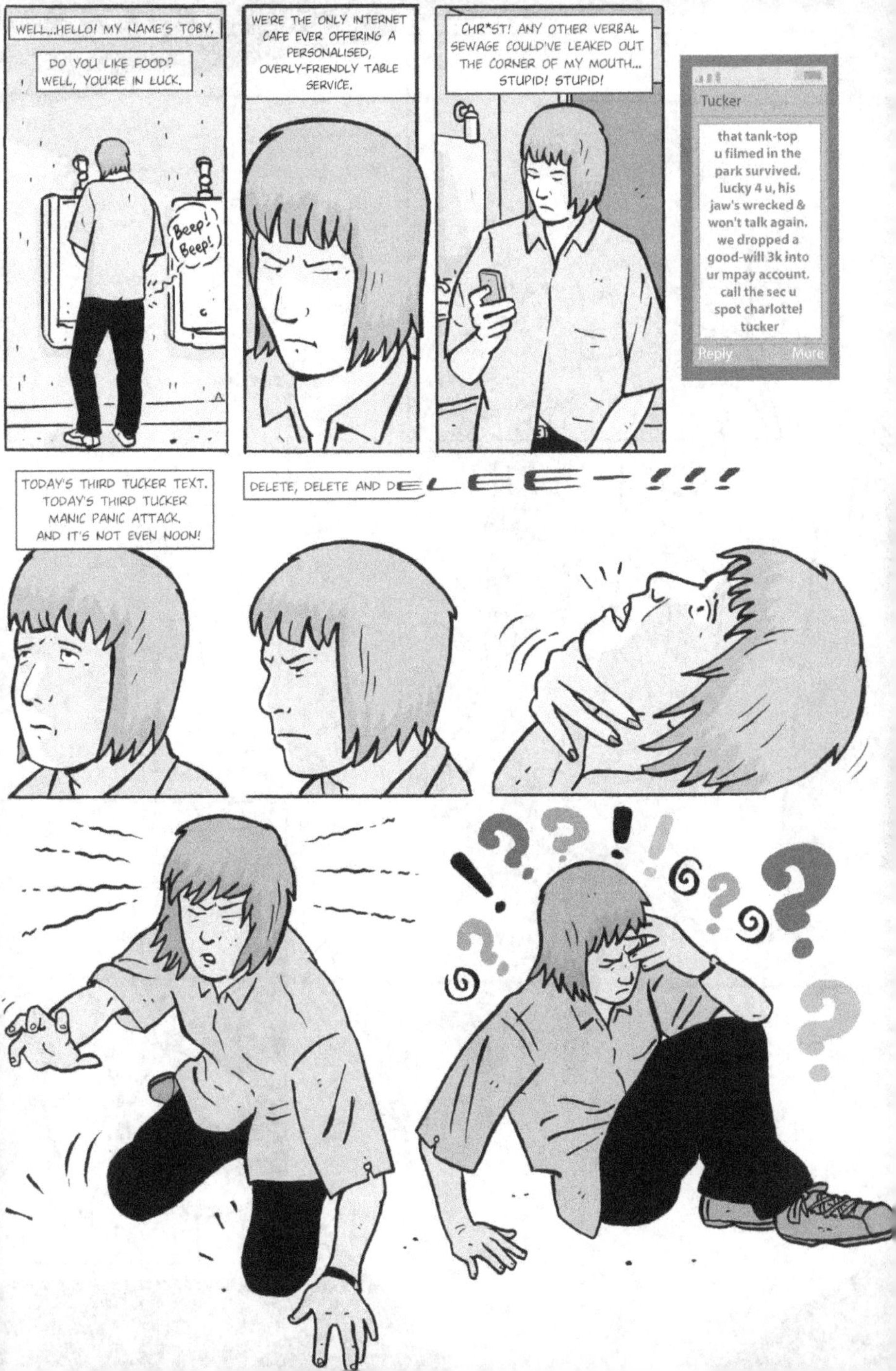
WELL...HELLO! MY NAME'S TOBY.
DO YOU LIKE FOOD? WELL, YOU'RE IN LUCK.
Beep! Beep!
WE'RE THE ONLY INTERNET CAFE EVER OFFERING A PERSONALISED, OVERLY-FRIENDLY TABLE SERVICE.
CHR*ST! ANY OTHER VERBAL SEWAGE COULD'VE LEAKED OUT THE CORNER OF MY MOUTH... STUPID! STUPID!
Tucker
that tank-top u filmed in the park survived. lucky 4 u, his jaw's wrecked & won't talk again. we dropped a good-will 3k into ur mpay account. call the sec u spot charlotte! tucker
Reply
More
TODAY'S THIRD TUCKER TEXT. TODAY'S THIRD TUCKER MANIC PANIC ATTACK. AND IT'S NOT EVEN NOON!
DELETE, DELETE AND DELEE—!!!

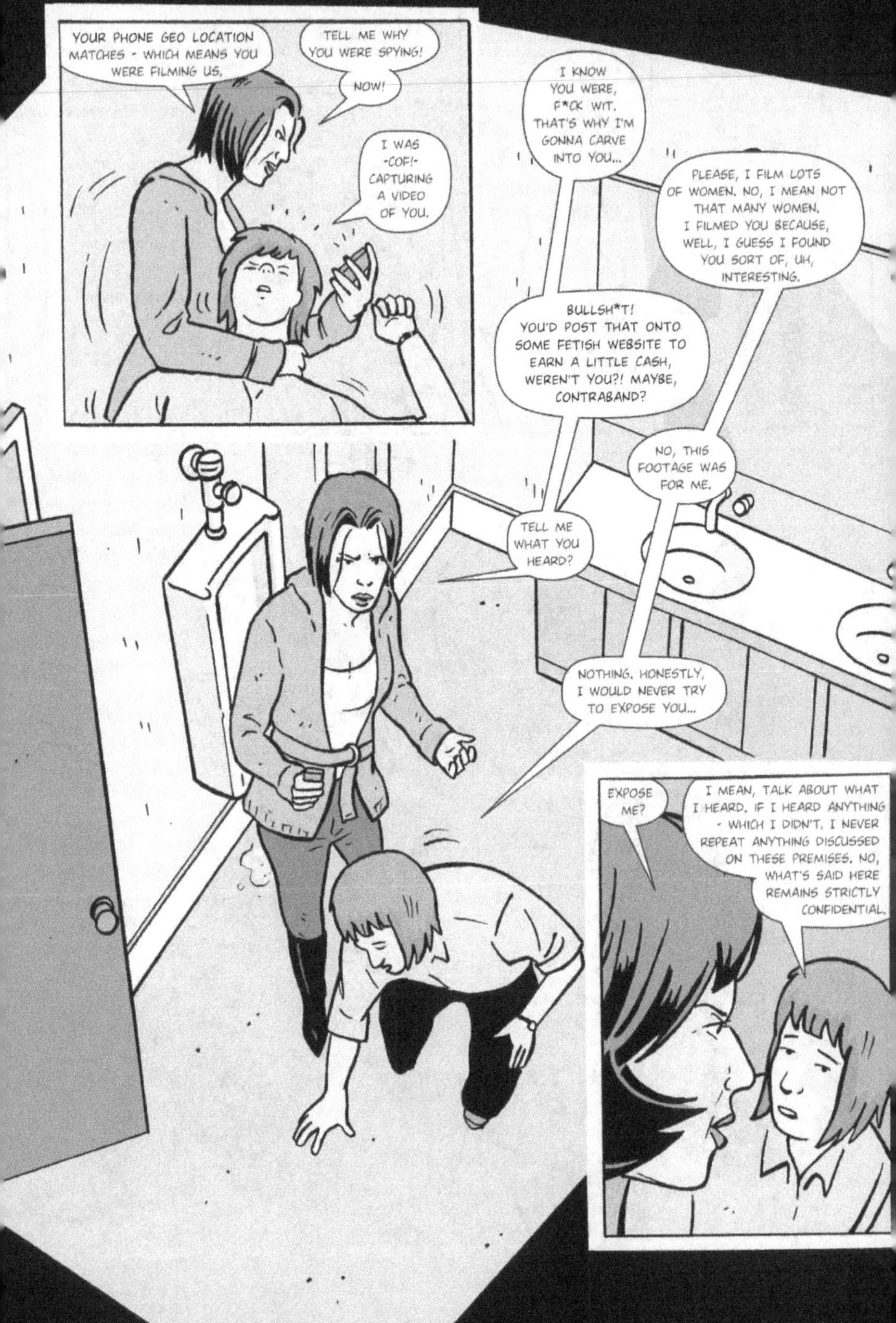
YOUR PHONE GEO LOCATION MATCHES - WHICH MEANS YOU WERE FILMING US.
TELL ME WHY YOU WERE SPYING!
NOW!
I WAS -COF!- CAPTURING A VIDEO OF YOU.
I KNOW YOU WERE, F*CK WIT. THAT'S WHY I'M GONNA CARVE INTO YOU...
PLEASE, I FILM LOTS OF WOMEN. NO, I MEAN NOT THAT MANY WOMEN. I FILMED YOU BECAUSE, WELL, I GUESS I FOUND YOU SORT OF, UH, INTERESTING.
BULLSH*T! YOU'D POST THAT ONTO SOME FETISH WEBSITE TO EARN A LITTLE CASH, WEREN'T YOU?! MAYBE, CONTRABAND?
NO, THIS FOOTAGE WAS FOR ME.
TELL ME WHAT YOU HEARD?
NOTHING. HONESTLY, I WOULD NEVER TRY TO EXPOSE YOU...
EXPOSE ME?
I MEAN, TALK ABOUT WHAT I HEARD. IF I HEARD ANYTHING - WHICH I DIDN'T. I NEVER REPEAT ANYTHING DISCUSSED ON THESE PREMISES. NO, WHAT'S SAID HERE REMAINS STRICTLY CONFIDENTIAL.

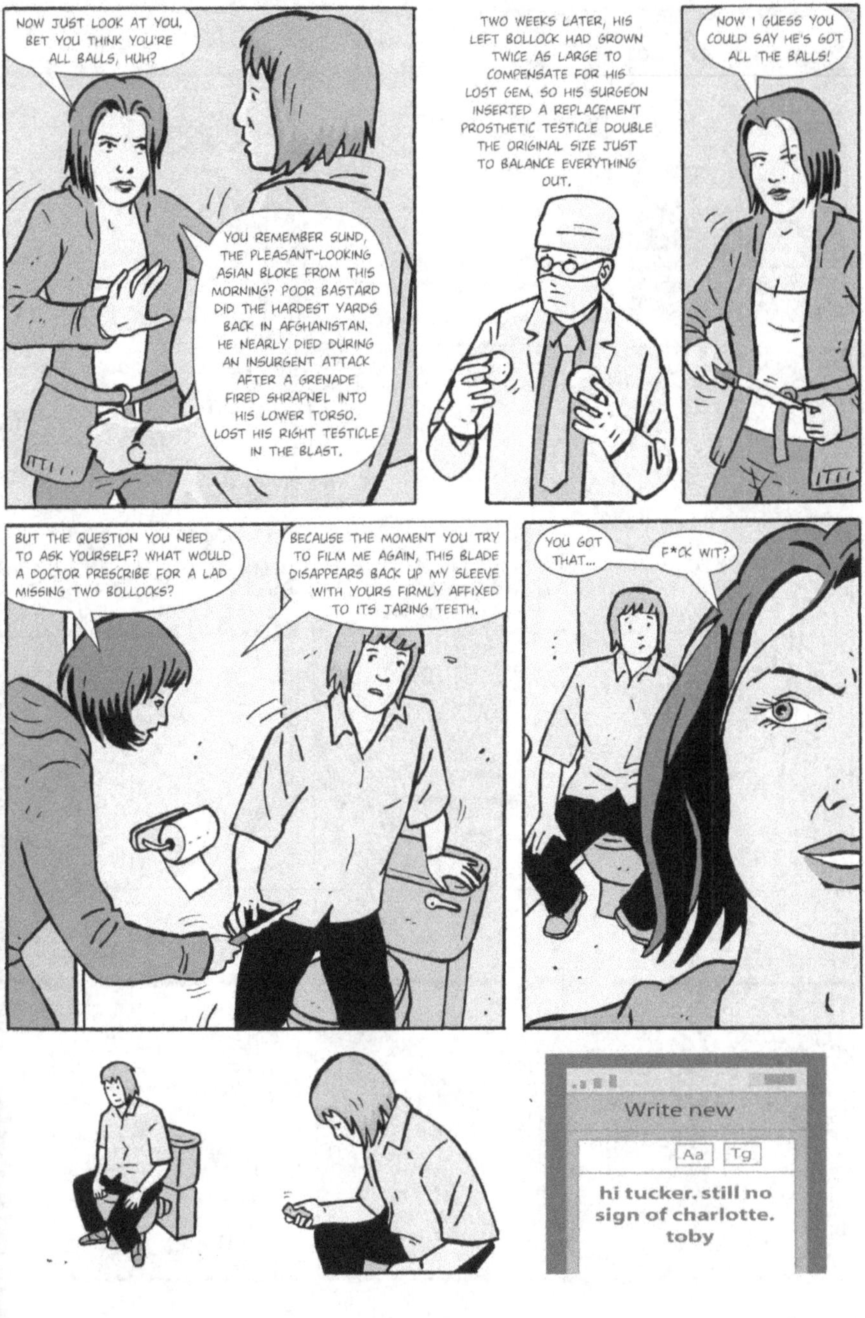
NOW JUST LOOK AT YOU. BET YOU THINK YOU'RE ALL BALLS, HUH?
YOU REMEMBER SUND, THE PLEASANT-LOOKING ASIAN BLOKE FROM THIS MORNING? POOR BASTARD DID THE HARDEST YARDS BACK IN AFGHANISTAN. HE NEARLY DIED DURING AN INSURGENT ATTACK AFTER A GRENADE FIRED SHRAPNEL INTO HIS LOWER TORSO. LOST HIS RIGHT TESTICLE IN THE BLAST.
TWO WEEKS LATER, HIS LEFT BOLLOCK HAD GROWN TWICE AS LARGE TO COMPENSATE FOR HIS LOST GEM, SO HIS SURGEON INSERTED A REPLACEMENT PROSTHETIC TESTICLE DOUBLE THE ORIGINAL SIZE JUST TO BALANCE EVERYTHING OUT.
NOW I GUESS YOU COULD SAY HE'S GOT ALL THE BALLS!
BUT THE QUESTION YOU NEED TO ASK YOURSELF? WHAT WOULD A DOCTOR PRESCRIBE FOR A LAD MISSING TWO BOLLOCKS?
BECAUSE THE MOMENT YOU TRY TO FILM ME AGAIN, THIS BLADE DISAPPEARS BACK UP MY SLEEVE WITH YOURS FIRMLY AFFIXED TO ITS JARING TEETH.
YOU GOT THAT...
F*CK WIT?
Write new
Aa
Tg
hi tucker. still no sign of charlotte. toby

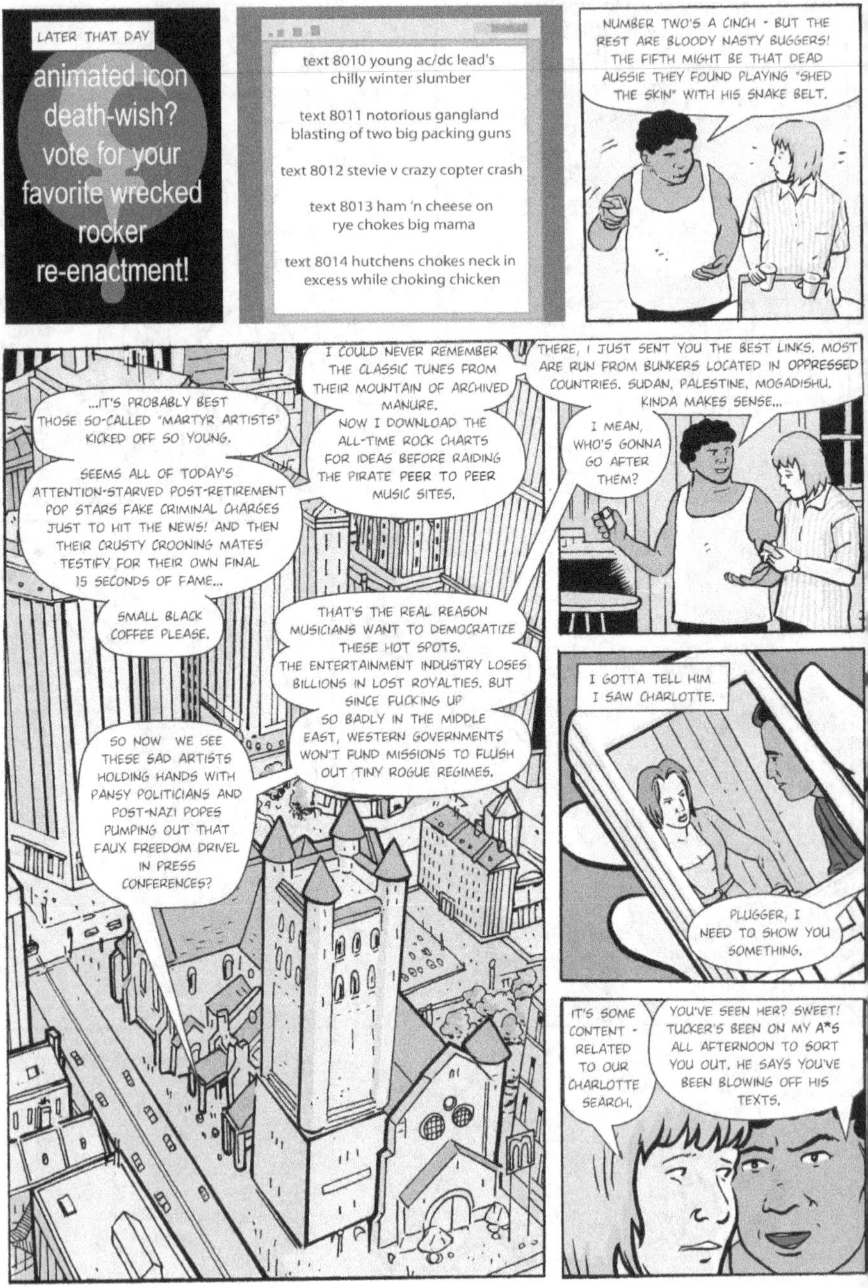
LATER THAT DAY
animated icon death-wish? vote for your favorite wrecked rocker re-enactment!
text 8010 young ac/dc lead's chilly winter slumber
text 8011 notorious gangland blasting of two big packing guns
text 8012 stevie v crazy copter crash
text 8013 ham 'n cheese on rye chokes big mama
text 8014 hutchens chokes neck in excess while choking chicken
NUMBER TWO'S A CINCH - BUT THE REST ARE BLOODY NASTY BUGGERS! THE FIFTH MIGHT BE THAT DEAD AUSSIE THEY FOUND PLAYING "SHED THE SKIN" WITH HIS SNAKE BELT.
...IT'S PROBABLY BEST THOSE SO-CALLED "MARTYR ARTISTS" KICKED OFF SO YOUNG.
SEEMS ALL OF TODAY'S ATTENTION-STARVED POST-RETIREMENT POP STARS FAKE CRIMINAL CHARGES JUST TO HIT THE NEWS! AND THEN THEIR CRUSTY CROONING MATES TESTIFY FOR THEIR OWN FINAL 15 SECONDS OF FAME...
SMALL BLACK COFFEE PLEASE.
I COULD NEVER REMEMBER THE CLASSIC TUNES FROM THEIR MOUNTAIN OF ARCHIVED MANURE. NOW I DOWNLOAD THE ALL-TIME ROCK CHARTS FOR IDEAS BEFORE RAIDING THE PIRATE PEER TO PEER MUSIC SITES.
SO NOW WE SEE THESE SAD ARTISTS HOLDING HANDS WITH PANSY POLITICIANS AND POST-NAZI POPES PUMPING OUT THAT FAUX FREEDOM DRIVEL IN PRESS CONFERENCES?
THAT'S THE REAL REASON MUSICIANS WANT TO DEMOCRATIZE THESE HOT SPOTS. THE ENTERTAINMENT INDUSTRY LOSES BILLIONS IN LOST ROYALTIES. BUT SINCE FUCKING UP SO BADLY IN THE MIDDLE EAST, WESTERN GOVERNMENTS WON'T FUND MISSIONS TO FLUSH OUT TINY ROGUE REGIMES.
THERE, I JUST SENT YOU THE BEST LINKS. MOST ARE RUN FROM BUNKERS LOCATED IN OPPRESSED COUNTRIES. SUDAN, PALESTINE, MOGADISHU. KINDA MAKES SENSE...
I MEAN, WHO'S GONNA GO AFTER THEM?
I GOTTA TELL HIM I SAW CHARLOTTE.
PLUGGER, I NEED TO SHOW YOU SOMETHING.
IT'S SOME CONTENT - RELATED TO OUR CHARLOTTE SEARCH.
YOU'VE SEEN HER? SWEET! TUCKER'S BEEN ON MY A*S ALL AFTERNOON TO SORT YOU OUT. HE SAYS YOU'VE BEEN BLOWING OFF HIS TEXTS.

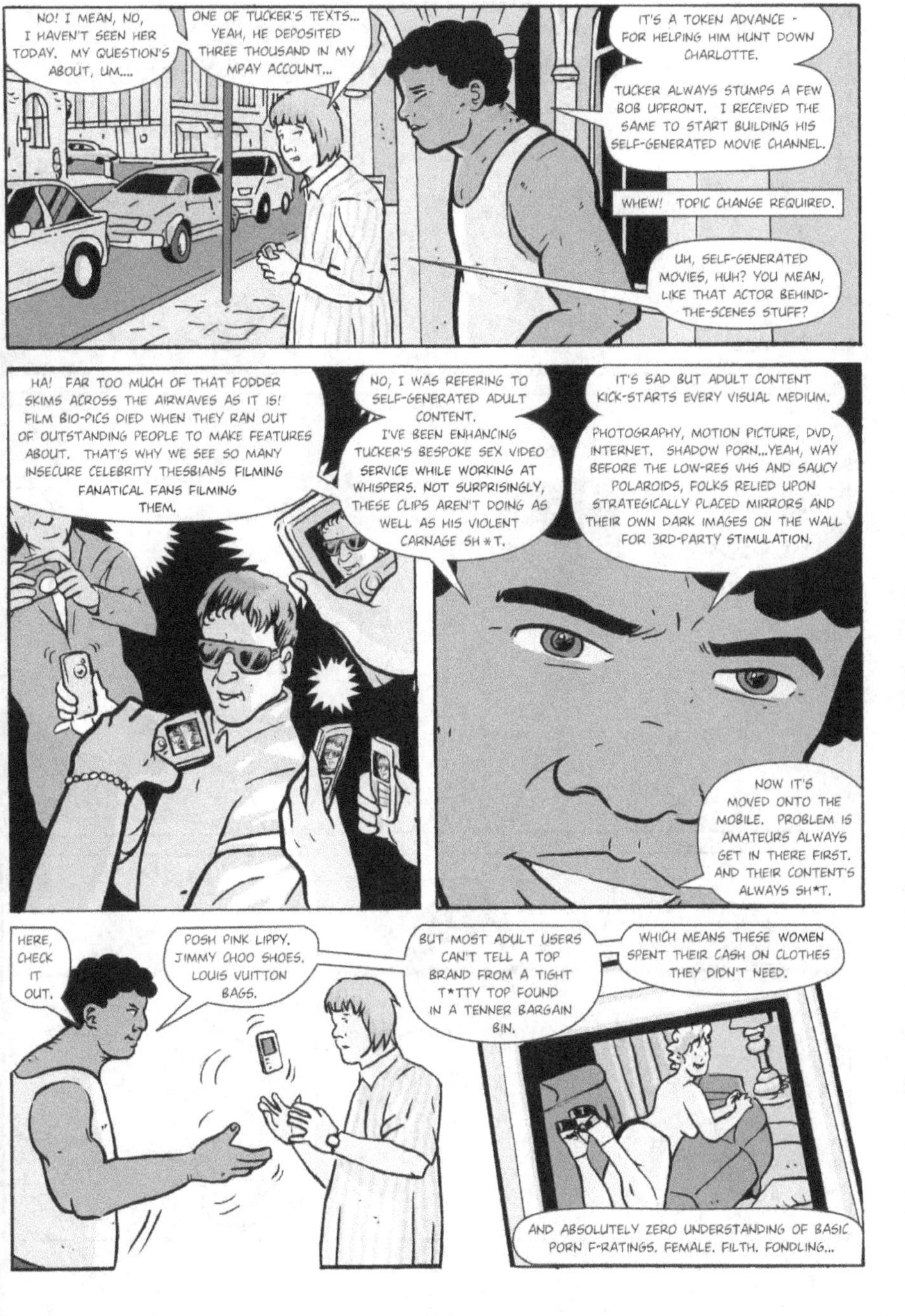
NO! I MEAN, NO, I HAVEN'T SEEN HER TODAY. MY QUESTION'S ABOUT, UM....
ONE OF TUCKER'S TEXTS... YEAH, HE DEPOSITED THREE THOUSAND IN MY MPAY ACCOUNT...
IT'S A TOKEN ADVANCE - FOR HELPING HIM HUNT DOWN CHARLOTTE.
TUCKER ALWAYS STUMPS A FEW BOB UPFRONT. I RECEIVED THE SAME TO START BUILDING HIS SELF-GENERATED MOVIE CHANNEL.
WHEW! TOPIC CHANGE REQUIRED.
UH, SELF-GENERATED MOVIES, HUH? YOU MEAN, LIKE THAT ACTOR BEHIND-THE-SCENES STUFF?
HA! FAR TOO MUCH OF THAT FODDER SKIMS ACROSS THE AIRWAVES AS IT IS! FILM BIO-PICS DIED WHEN THEY RAN OUT OF OUTSTANDING PEOPLE TO MAKE FEATURES ABOUT. THAT'S WHY WE SEE SO MANY INSECURE CELEBRITY THESBIANS FILMING FANATICAL FANS FILMING THEM.
NO, I WAS REFERING TO SELF-GENERATED ADULT CONTENT.
I'VE BEEN ENHANCING TUCKER'S BESPOKE SEX VIDEO SERVICE WHILE WORKING AT WHISPERS. NOT SURPRISINGLY, THESE CLIPS AREN'T DOING AS WELL AS HIS VIOLENT CARNAGE SH*T.
IT'S SAD BUT ADULT CONTENT KICK-STARTS EVERY VISUAL MEDIUM.
PHOTOGRAPHY, MOTION PICTURE, DVD, INTERNET. SHADOW PORN...YEAH, WAY BEFORE THE LOW-RES VHS AND SAUCY POLAROIDS, FOLKS RELIED UPON STRATEGICALLY PLACED MIRRORS AND THEIR OWN DARK IMAGES ON THE WALL FOR 3RD-PARTY STIMULATION.
NOW IT'S MOVED ONTO THE MOBILE. PROBLEM IS AMATEURS ALWAYS GET IN THERE FIRST. AND THEIR CONTENT'S ALWAYS SH*T.
HERE, CHECK IT OUT.
POSH PINK LIPPY. JIMMY CHOO SHOES. LOUIS VUITTON BAGS.
BUT MOST ADULT USERS CAN'T TELL A TOP BRAND FROM A TIGHT T*TTY TOP FOUND IN A TENNER BARGAIN BIN.
WHICH MEANS THESE WOMEN SPENT THEIR CASH ON CLOTHES THEY DIDN'T NEED.
AND ABSOLUTELY ZERO UNDERSTANDING OF BASIC PORN F-RATINGS. FEMALE. FILTH. FONDLING...

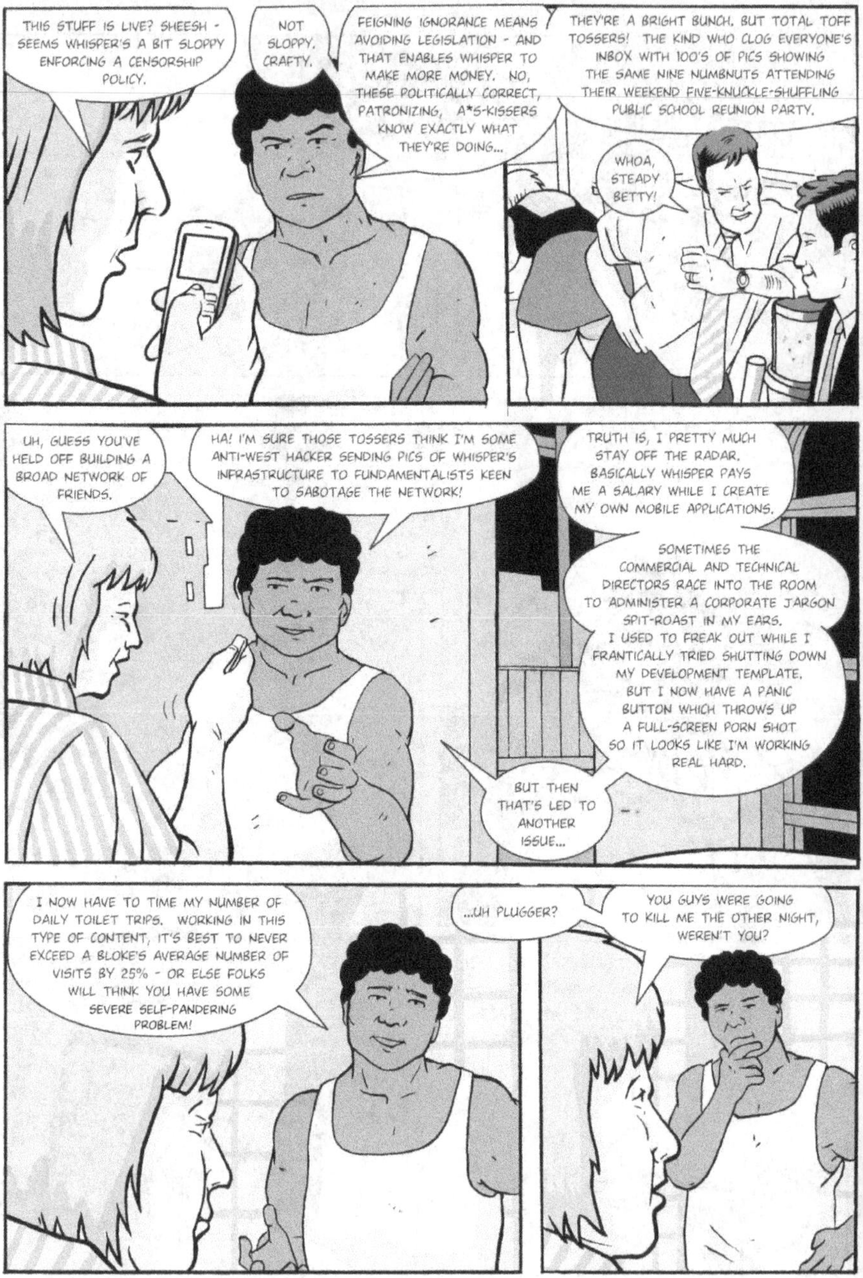
THIS STUFF IS LIVE? SHEESH - SEEMS WHISPER'S A BIT SLOPPY ENFORCING A CENSORSHIP POLICY.
NOT SLOPPY. CRAFTY.
FEIGNING IGNORANCE MEANS AVOIDING LEGISLATION - AND THAT ENABLES WHISPER TO MAKE MORE MONEY. NO, THESE POLITICALLY CORRECT, PATRONIZING, A*S-KISSERS KNOW EXACTLY WHAT THEY'RE DOING...
THEY'RE A BRIGHT BUNCH, BUT TOTAL TOFF TOSSERS! THE KIND WHO CLOG EVERYONE'S INBOX WITH 100'S OF PICS SHOWING THE SAME NINE NUMBNUTS ATTENDING THEIR WEEKEND FIVE-KNUCKLE-SHUFFLING PUBLIC SCHOOL REUNION PARTY.
WHOA, STEADY BETTY!
UH, GUESS YOU'VE HELD OFF BUILDING A BROAD NETWORK OF FRIENDS.
HA! I'M SURE THOSE TOSSERS THINK I'M SOME ANTI-WEST HACKER SENDING PICS OF WHISPER'S INFRASTRUCTURE TO FUNDAMENTALISTS KEEN TO SABOTAGE THE NETWORK!
TRUTH IS, I PRETTY MUCH STAY OFF THE RADAR. BASICALLY WHISPER PAYS ME A SALARY WHILE I CREATE MY OWN MOBILE APPLICATIONS.
SOMETIMES THE COMMERCIAL AND TECHNICAL DIRECTORS RACE INTO THE ROOM TO ADMINISTER A CORPORATE JARGON SPIT-ROAST IN MY EARS. I USED TO FREAK OUT WHILE I FRANTICALLY TRIED SHUTTING DOWN MY DEVELOPMENT TEMPLATE. BUT I NOW HAVE A PANIC BUTTON WHICH THROWS UP A FULL-SCREEN PORN SHOT SO IT LOOKS LIKE I'M WORKING REAL HARD.
BUT THEN THAT'S LED TO ANOTHER ISSUE...
I NOW HAVE TO TIME MY NUMBER OF DAILY TOILET TRIPS. WORKING IN THIS TYPE OF CONTENT, IT'S BEST TO NEVER EXCEED A BLOKE'S AVERAGE NUMBER OF VISITS BY 25% - OR ELSE FOLKS WILL THINK YOU HAVE SOME SEVERE SELF-PANDERING PROBLEM!
...UH PLUGGER?
YOU GUYS WERE GOING TO KILL ME THE OTHER NIGHT, WEREN'T YOU?

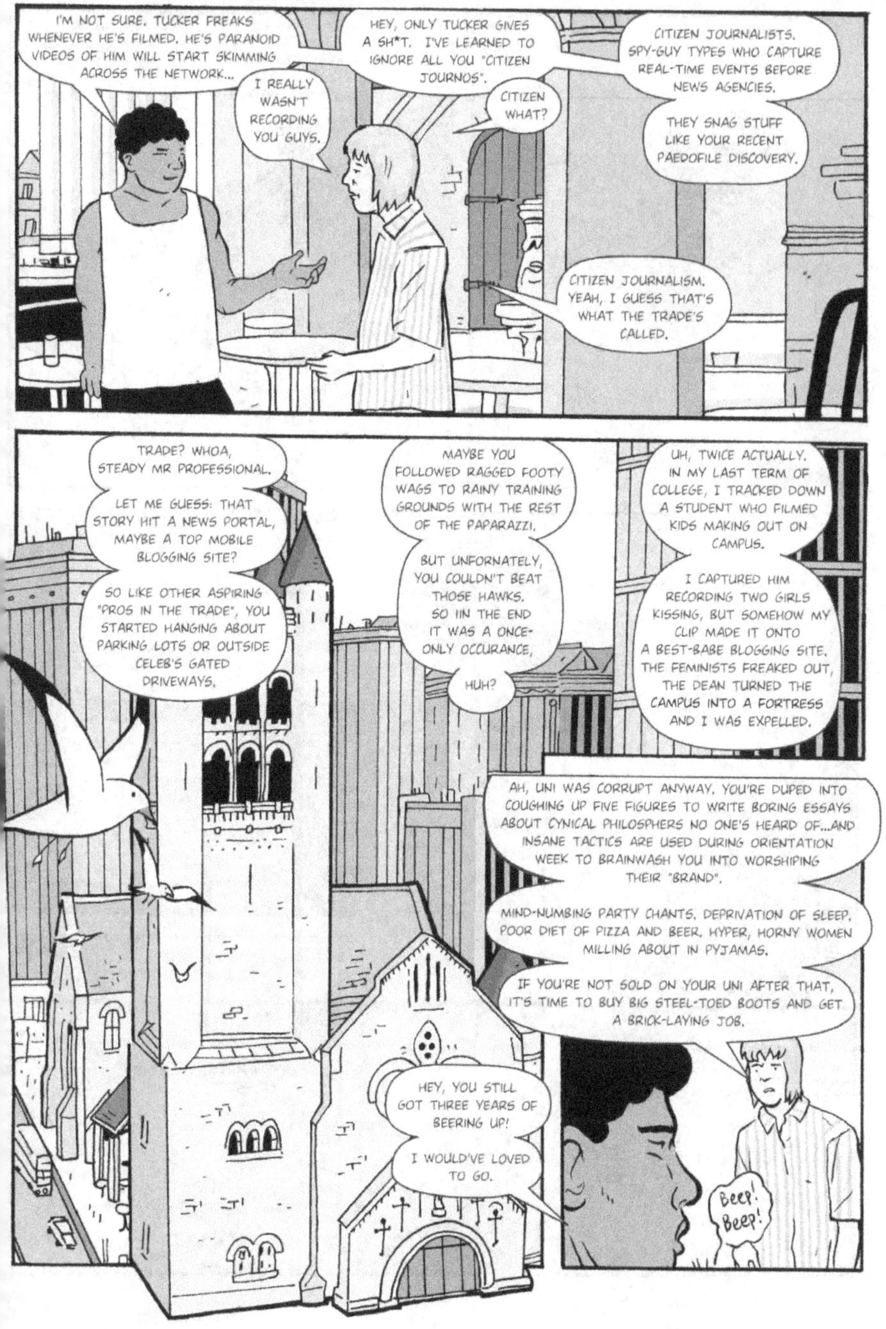
I'M NOT SURE. TUCKER FREAKS WHENEVER HE'S FILMED. HE'S PARANOID VIDEOS OF HIM WILL START SKIMMING ACROSS THE NETWORK...
I REALLY WASN'T RECORDING YOU GUYS.
HEY, ONLY TUCKER GIVES A SH*T. I'VE LEARNED TO IGNORE ALL YOU "CITIZEN JOURNOS".
CITIZEN WHAT?
CITIZEN JOURNALISTS. SPY-GUY TYPES WHO CAPTURE REAL-TIME EVENTS BEFORE NEWS AGENCIES.
THEY SNAG STUFF LIKE YOUR RECENT PAEDOFILE DISCOVERY.
CITIZEN JOURNALISM. YEAH, I GUESS THAT'S WHAT THE TRADE'S CALLED.
TRADE? WHOA, STEADY MR PROFESSIONAL.
LET ME GUESS: THAT STORY HIT A NEWS PORTAL, MAYBE A TOP MOBILE BLOGGING SITE?
SO LIKE OTHER ASPIRING "PROS IN THE TRADE", YOU STARTED HANGING ABOUT PARKING LOTS OR OUTSIDE CELEB'S GATED DRIVEWAYS.
MAYBE YOU FOLLOWED RAGGED FOOTY WAGS TO RAINY TRAINING GROUNDS WITH THE REST OF THE PAPARAZZI.
BUT UNFORNATELY, YOU COULDN'T BEAT THOSE HAWKS. SO IIN THE END IT WAS A ONCE-ONLY OCCURANCE,
HUH?
UH, TWICE ACTUALLY. IN MY LAST TERM OF COLLEGE, I TRACKED DOWN A STUDENT WHO FILMED KIDS MAKING OUT ON CAMPUS.
I CAPTURED HIM RECORDING TWO GIRLS KISSING, BUT SOMEHOW MY CLIP MADE IT ONTO A BEST-BABE BLOGGING SITE. THE FEMINISTS FREAKED OUT, THE DEAN TURNED THE CAMPUS INTO A FORTRESS AND I WAS EXPELLED.
AH, UNI WAS CORRUPT ANYWAY. YOU'RE DUPED INTO COUGHING UP FIVE FIGURES TO WRITE BORING ESSAYS ABOUT CYNICAL PHILOSPHERS NO ONE'S HEARD OF...AND INSANE TACTICS ARE USED DURING ORIENTATION WEEK TO BRAINWASH YOU INTO WORSHIPING THEIR "BRAND".
MIND-NUMBING PARTY CHANTS. DEPRIVATION OF SLEEP. POOR DIET OF PIZZA AND BEER. HYPER, HORNY WOMEN MILLING ABOUT IN PYJAMAS.
IF YOU'RE NOT SOLD ON YOUR UNI AFTER THAT, IT'S TIME TO BUY BIG STEEL-TOED BOOTS AND GET A BRICK-LAYING JOB.
HEY, YOU STILL GOT THREE YEARS OF BEERING UP!
I WOULD'VE LOVED TO GO.
Beep! Beep!

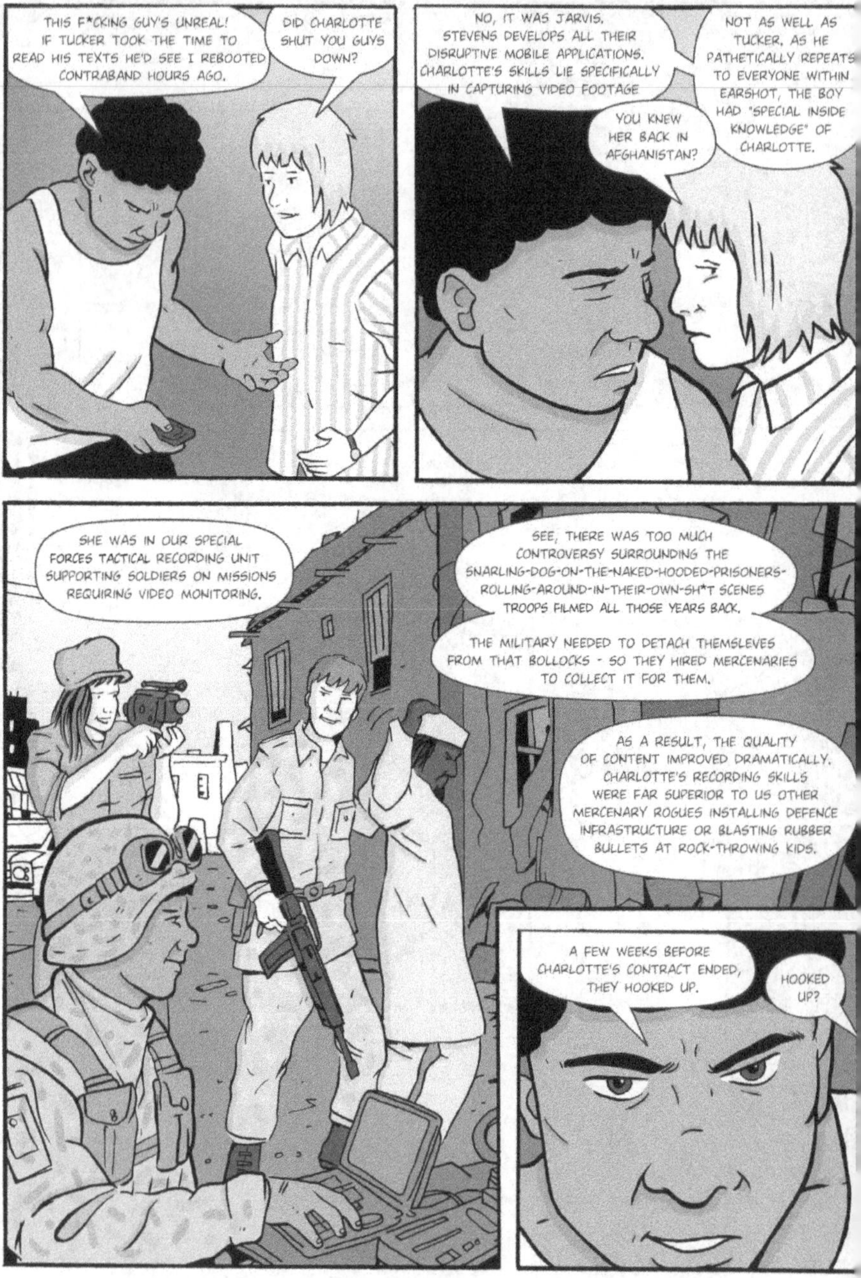
THIS F*CKING GUY'S UNREAL! IF TUCKER TOOK THE TIME TO READ HIS TEXTS HE'D SEE I REBOOTED CONTRABAND HOURS AGO.
DID CHARLOTTE SHUT YOU GUYS DOWN?
NO, IT WAS JARVIS. STEVENS DEVELOPS ALL THEIR DISRUPTIVE MOBILE APPLICATIONS. CHARLOTTE'S SKILLS LIE SPECIFICALLY IN CAPTURING VIDEO FOOTAGE
NOT AS WELL AS TUCKER, AS HE PATHETICALLY REPEATS TO EVERYONE WITHIN EARSHOT, THE BOY HAD "SPECIAL INSIDE KNOWLEDGE" OF CHARLOTTE.
YOU KNEW HER BACK IN AFGHANISTAN?
SHE WAS IN OUR SPECIAL FORCES TACTICAL RECORDING UNIT SUPPORTING SOLDIERS ON MISSIONS REQUIRING VIDEO MONITORING.
SEE, THERE WAS TOO MUCH CONTROVERSY SURROUNDING THE SNARLING-DOG-ON-THE-NAKED-HOODED-PRISONERS-ROLLING-AROUND-IN-THEIR-OWN-SH*T SCENES TROOPS FILMED ALL THOSE YEARS BACK.
THE MILITARY NEEDED TO DETACH THEMSLEVES FROM THAT BOLLOCKS - SO THEY HIRED MERCENARIES TO COLLECT IT FOR THEM.
AS A RESULT, THE QUALITY OF CONTENT IMPROVED DRAMATICALLY. CHARLOTTE'S RECORDING SKILLS WERE FAR SUPERIOR TO US OTHER MERCENARY ROGUES INSTALLING DEFENCE INFRASTRUCTURE OR BLASTING RUBBER BULLETS AT ROCK-THROWING KIDS.
A FEW WEEKS BEFORE CHARLOTTE'S CONTRACT ENDED, THEY HOOKED UP.
HOOKED UP?

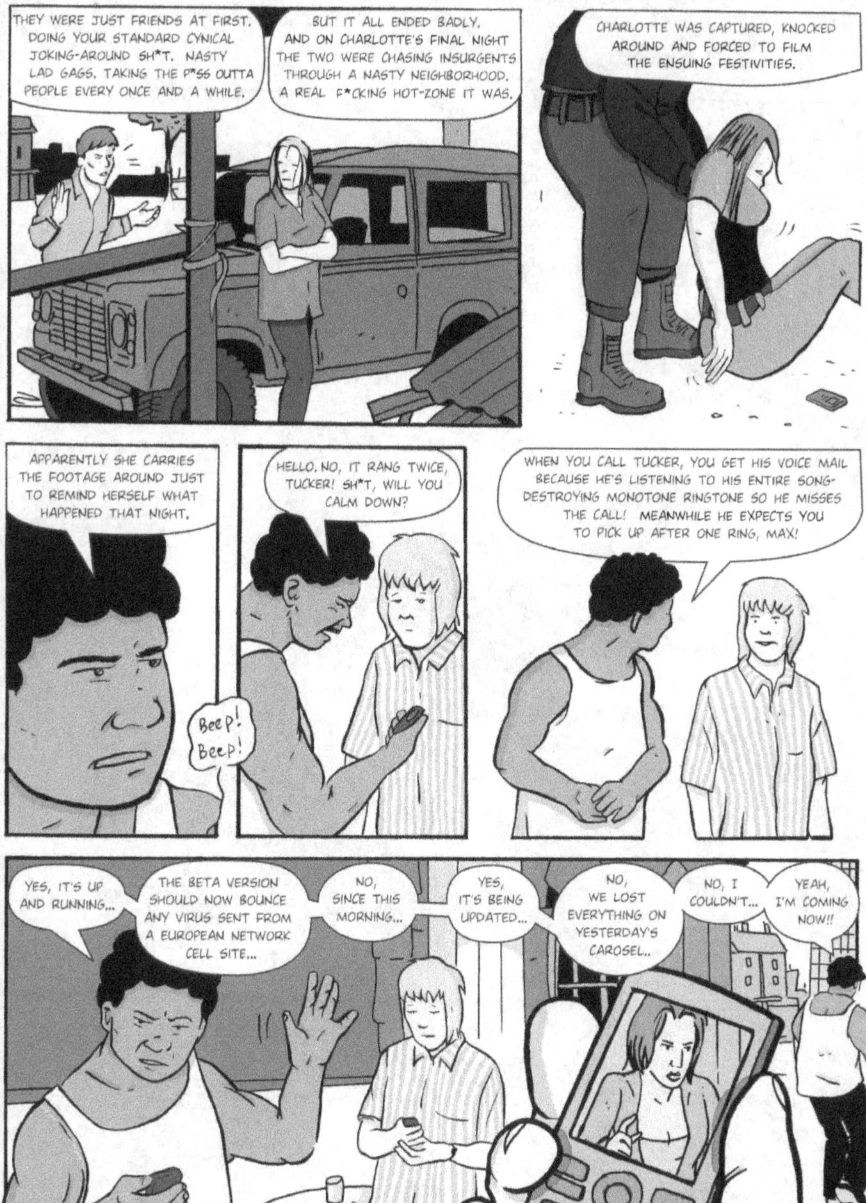

THEY WERE JUST FRIENDS AT FIRST. DOING YOUR STANDARD CYNICAL JOKING-AROUND SH*T. NASTY LAD GAGS. TAKING THE P*SS OUTTA PEOPLE EVERY ONCE AND A WHILE.
BUT IT ALL ENDED BADLY. AND ON CHARLOTTE'S FINAL NIGHT THE TWO WERE CHASING INSURGENTS THROUGH A NASTY NEIGHBORHOOD. A REAL F*CKING HOT-ZONE IT WAS.
CHARLOTTE WAS CAPTURED, KNOCKED AROUND AND FORCED TO FILM THE ENSUING FESTIVITIES.
APPARENTLY SHE CARRIES THE FOOTAGE AROUND JUST TO REMIND HERSELF WHAT HAPPENED THAT NIGHT.
Beep! Beep!
HELLO. NO, IT RANG TWICE, TUCKER! SH*T, WILL YOU CALM DOWN?
WHEN YOU CALL TUCKER, YOU GET HIS VOICE MAIL BECAUSE HE'S LISTENING TO HIS ENTIRE SONG-DESTROYING MONOTONE RINGTONE SO HE MISSES THE CALL! MEANWHILE HE EXPECTS YOU TO PICK UP AFTER ONE RING, MAX!
YES, IT'S UP AND RUNNING...
THE BETA VERSION SHOULD NOW BOUNCE ANY VIRUS SENT FROM A EUROPEAN NETWORK CELL SITE...
NO, SINCE THIS MORNING...
YES, IT'S BEING UPDATED...
NO, WE LOST EVERYTHING ON YESTERDAY'S CAROSEL..
NO, I COULDN'T...
YEAH, I'M COMING NOW!!

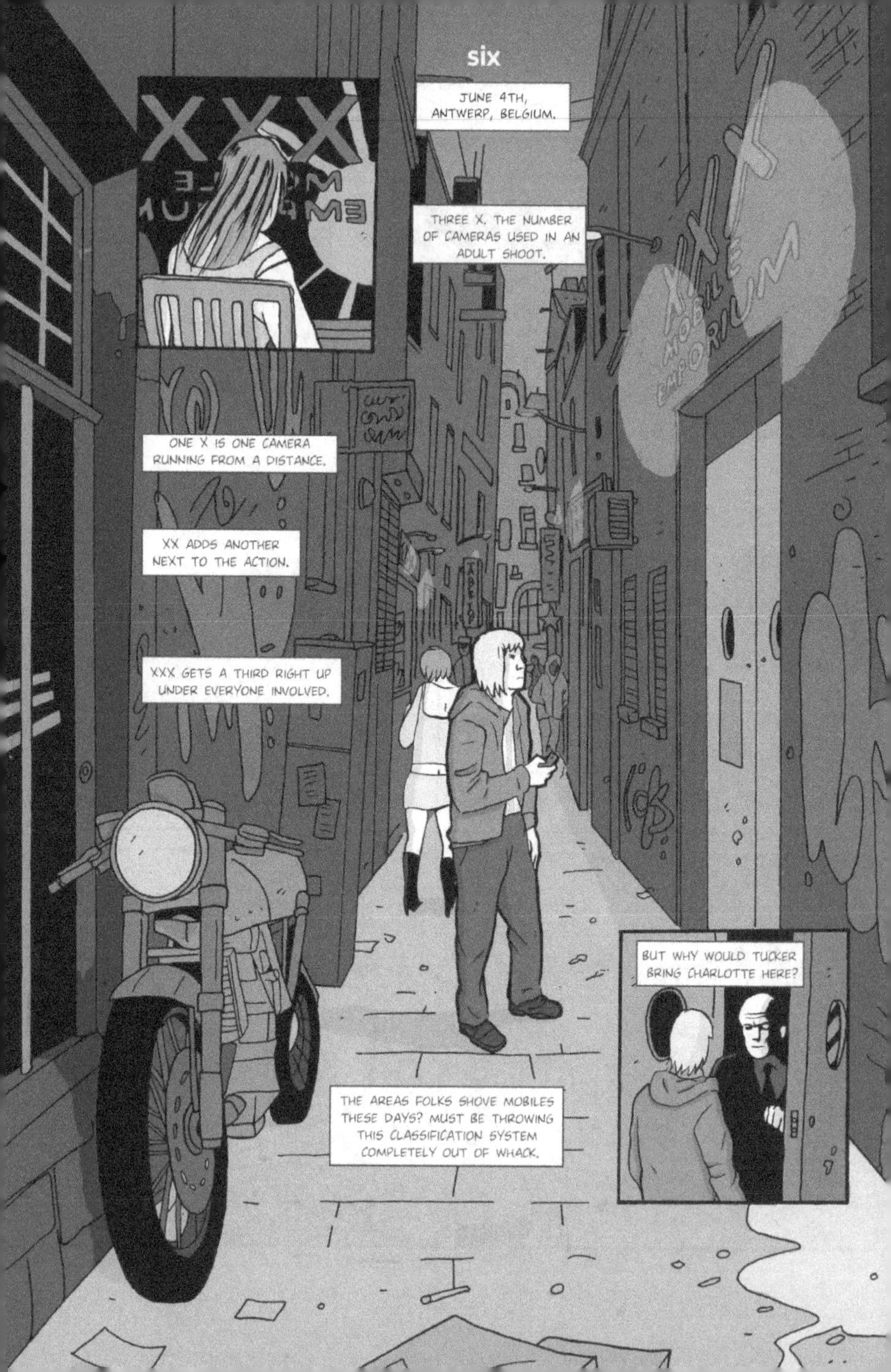
six
JUNE 4TH, ANTWERP, BELGIUM.
THREE X. THE NUMBER OF CAMERAS USED IN AN ADULT SHOOT.
XXX MOBILE EMPORIUM
ONE X IS ONE CAMERA RUNNING FROM A DISTANCE.
XX ADDS ANOTHER NEXT TO THE ACTION.
XXX GETS A THIRD RIGHT UP UNDER EVERYONE INVOLVED.
BUT WHY WOULD TUCKER BRING CHARLOTTE HERE?
THE AREAS FOLKS SHOVE MOBILES THESE DAYS? MUST BE THROWING THIS CLASSIFICATION SYSTEM COMPLETELY OUT OF WHACK.

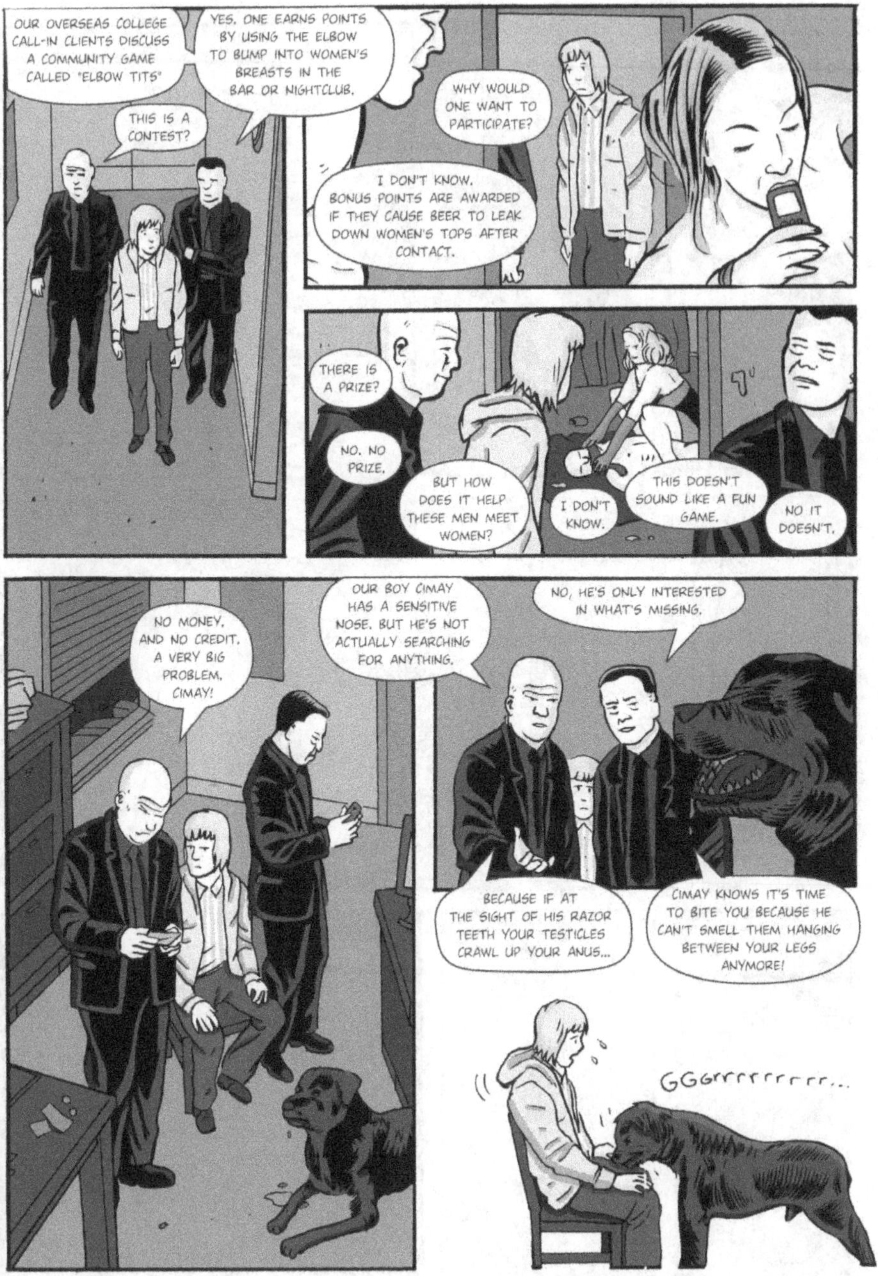
OUR OVERSEAS COLLEGE CALL-IN CLIENTS DISCUSS A COMMUNITY GAME CALLED "ELBOW TITS"
YES. ONE EARNS POINTS BY USING THE ELBOW TO BUMP INTO WOMEN'S BREASTS IN THE BAR OR NIGHTCLUB.
THIS IS A CONTEST?
WHY WOULD ONE WANT TO PARTICIPATE?
I DON'T KNOW. BONUS POINTS ARE AWARDED IF THEY CAUSE BEER TO LEAK DOWN WOMEN'S TOPS AFTER CONTACT.
THERE IS A PRIZE?
NO. NO PRIZE.
BUT HOW DOES IT HELP THESE MEN MEET WOMEN?
I DON'T KNOW.
THIS DOESN'T SOUND LIKE A FUN GAME.
NO IT DOESN'T.
NO MONEY, AND NO CREDIT. A VERY BIG PROBLEM, CIMAY!
OUR BOY CIMAY HAS A SENSITIVE NOSE. BUT HE'S NOT ACTUALLY SEARCHING FOR ANYTHING.
NO, HE'S ONLY INTERESTED IN WHAT'S MISSING.
BECAUSE IF AT THE SIGHT OF HIS RAZOR TEETH YOUR TESTICLES CRAWL UP YOUR ANUS...
CIMAY KNOWS IT'S TIME TO BITE YOU BECAUSE HE CAN'T SMELL THEM HANGING BETWEEN YOUR LEGS ANYMORE!
GGrrrrrrrrr...

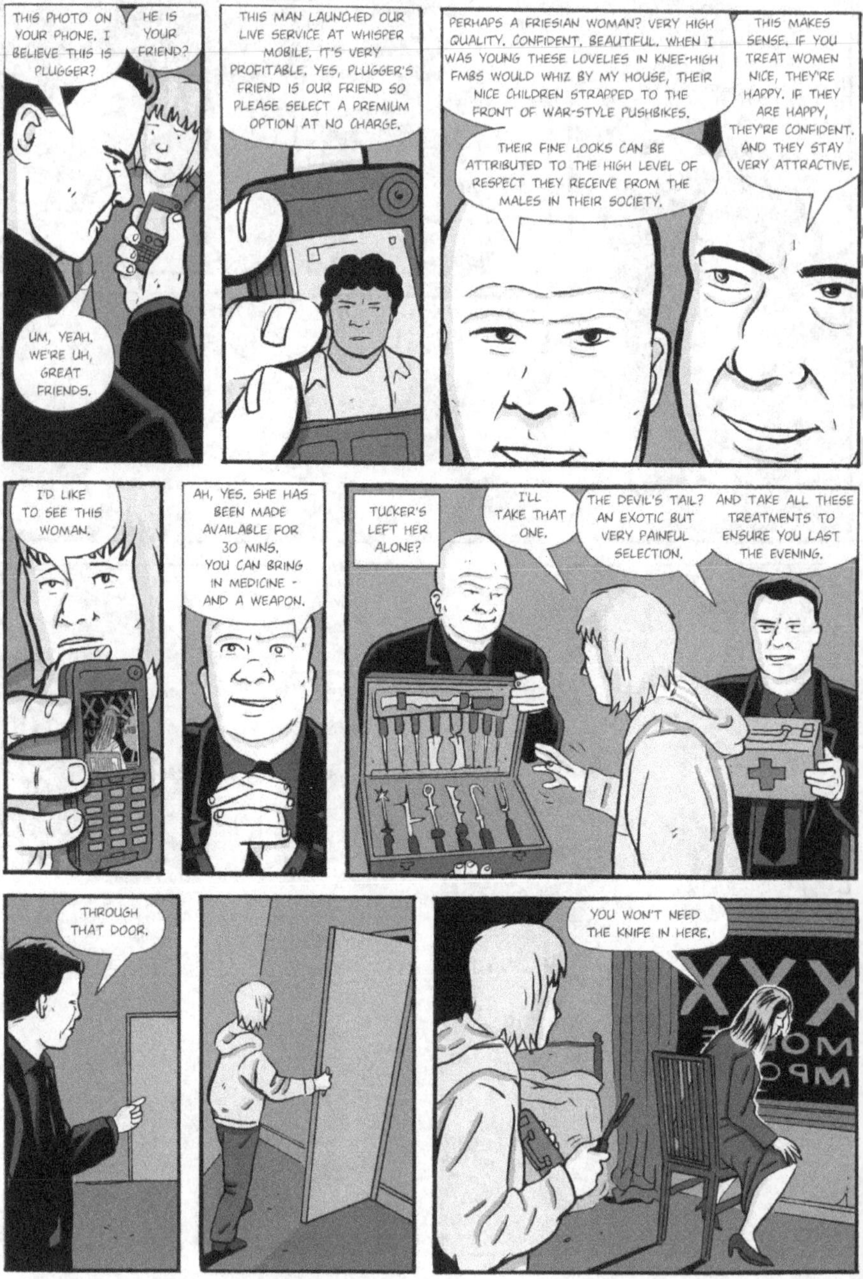
THIS PHOTO ON YOUR PHONE. I BELIEVE THIS IS PLUGGER?
HE IS YOUR FRIEND?
UM, YEAH. WE'RE UH, GREAT FRIENDS.
THIS MAN LAUNCHED OUR LIVE SERVICE AT WHISPER MOBILE. IT'S VERY PROFITABLE. YES, PLUGGER'S FRIEND IS OUR FRIEND SO PLEASE SELECT A PREMIUM OPTION AT NO CHARGE.
PERHAPS A FRIESIAN WOMAN? VERY HIGH QUALITY. CONFIDENT. BEAUTIFUL. WHEN I WAS YOUNG THESE LOVELIES IN KNEE-HIGH FMBS WOULD WHIZ BY MY HOUSE, THEIR NICE CHILDREN STRAPPED TO THE FRONT OF WAR-STYLE PUSHBIKES.
THEIR FINE LOOKS CAN BE ATTRIBUTED TO THE HIGH LEVEL OF RESPECT THEY RECEIVE FROM THE MALES IN THEIR SOCIETY.
THIS MAKES SENSE. IF YOU TREAT WOMEN NICE, THEY'RE HAPPY. IF THEY ARE HAPPY, THEY'RE CONFIDENT. AND THEY STAY VERY ATTRACTIVE.
I'D LIKE TO SEE THIS WOMAN.
AH, YES. SHE HAS BEEN MADE AVAILABLE FOR 30 MINS. YOU CAN BRING IN MEDICINE - AND A WEAPON.
TUCKER'S LEFT HER ALONE?
I'LL TAKE THAT ONE.
THE DEVIL'S TAIL? AN EXOTIC BUT VERY PAINFUL SELECTION.
AND TAKE ALL THESE TREATMENTS TO ENSURE YOU LAST THE EVENING.
THROUGH THAT DOOR.
YOU WON'T NEED THE KNIFE IN HERE.

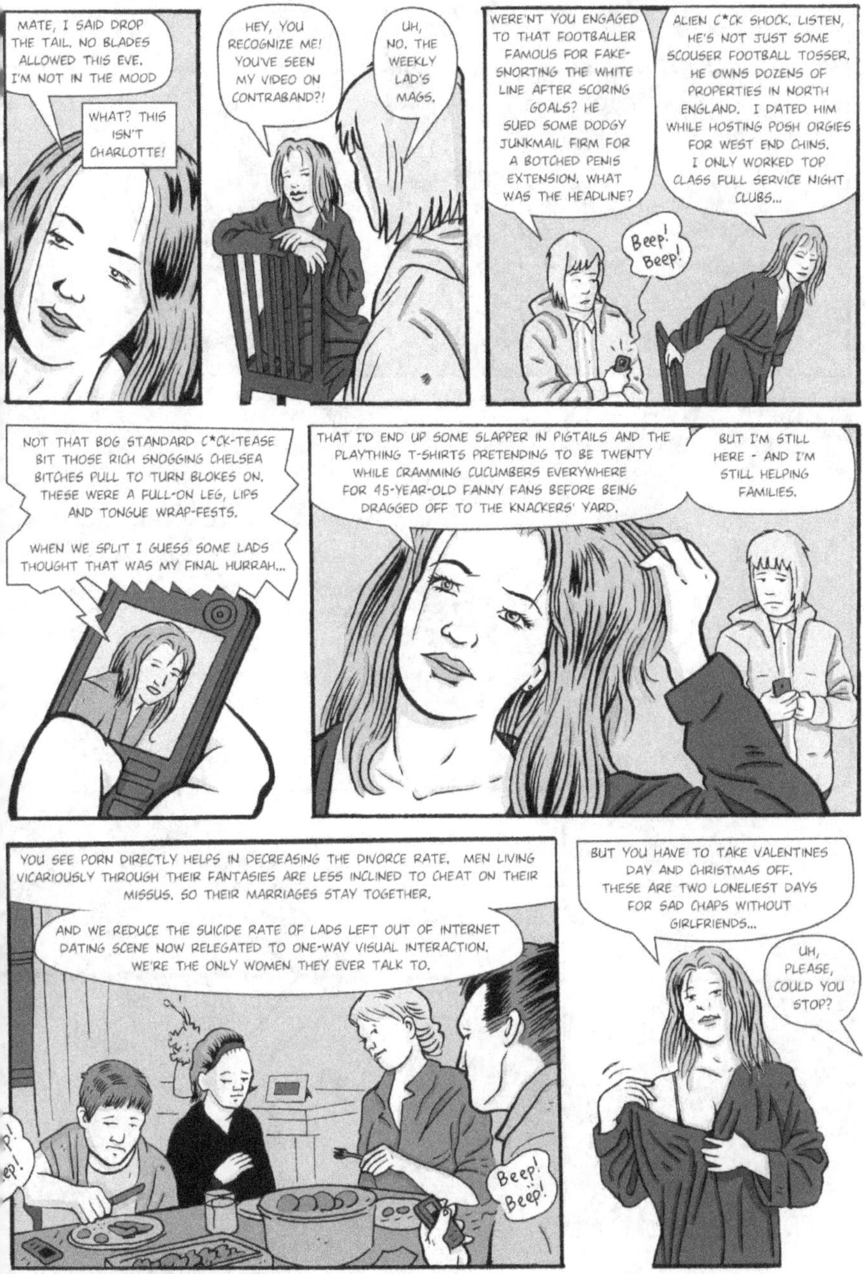
MATE, I SAID DROP THE TAIL. NO BLADES ALLOWED THIS EVE. I'M NOT IN THE MOOD
WHAT? THIS ISN'T CHARLOTTE!
HEY, YOU RECOGNIZE ME! YOU'VE SEEN MY VIDEO ON CONTRABAND?!
UH, NO. THE WEEKLY LAD'S MAGS.
WERE'NT YOU ENGAGED TO THAT FOOTBALLER FAMOUS FOR FAKE-SNORTING THE WHITE LINE AFTER SCORING GOALS? HE SUED SOME DODGY JUNKMAIL FIRM FOR A BOTCHED PENIS EXTENSION. WHAT WAS THE HEADLINE?
ALIEN C*CK SHOCK. LISTEN, HE'S NOT JUST SOME SCOUSER FOOTBALL TOSSER, HE OWNS DOZENS OF PROPERTIES IN NORTH ENGLAND. I DATED HIM WHILE HOSTING POSH ORGIES FOR WEST END CHINS. I ONLY WORKED TOP CLASS FULL SERVICE NIGHT CLUBS...
Beep! Beep!
NOT THAT BOG STANDARD C*CK-TEASE BIT THOSE RICH SNOGGING CHELSEA BITCHES PULL TO TURN BLOKES ON. THESE WERE A FULL-ON LEG, LIPS AND TONGUE WRAP-FESTS.
WHEN WE SPLIT I GUESS SOME LADS THOUGHT THAT WAS MY FINAL HURRAH...
THAT I'D END UP SOME SLAPPER IN PIGTAILS AND THE PLAYTHING T-SHIRTS PRETENDING TO BE TWENTY WHILE CRAMMING CUCUMBERS EVERYWHERE FOR 45-YEAR-OLD FANNY FANS BEFORE BEING DRAGGED OFF TO THE KNACKERS' YARD.
BUT I'M STILL HERE - AND I'M STILL HELPING FAMILIES.
YOU SEE PORN DIRECTLY HELPS IN DECREASING THE DIVORCE RATE. MEN LIVING VICARIOUSLY THROUGH THEIR FANTASIES ARE LESS INCLINED TO CHEAT ON THEIR MISSUS. SO THEIR MARRIAGES STAY TOGETHER.
AND WE REDUCE THE SUICIDE RATE OF LADS LEFT OUT OF INTERNET DATING SCENE NOW RELEGATED TO ONE-WAY VISUAL INTERACTION. WE'RE THE ONLY WOMEN THEY EVER TALK TO.
Beep! Beep!
BUT YOU HAVE TO TAKE VALENTINES DAY AND CHRISTMAS OFF. THESE ARE TWO LONELIEST DAYS FOR SAD CHAPS WITHOUT GIRLFRIENDS...
UH, PLEASE, COULD YOU STOP?

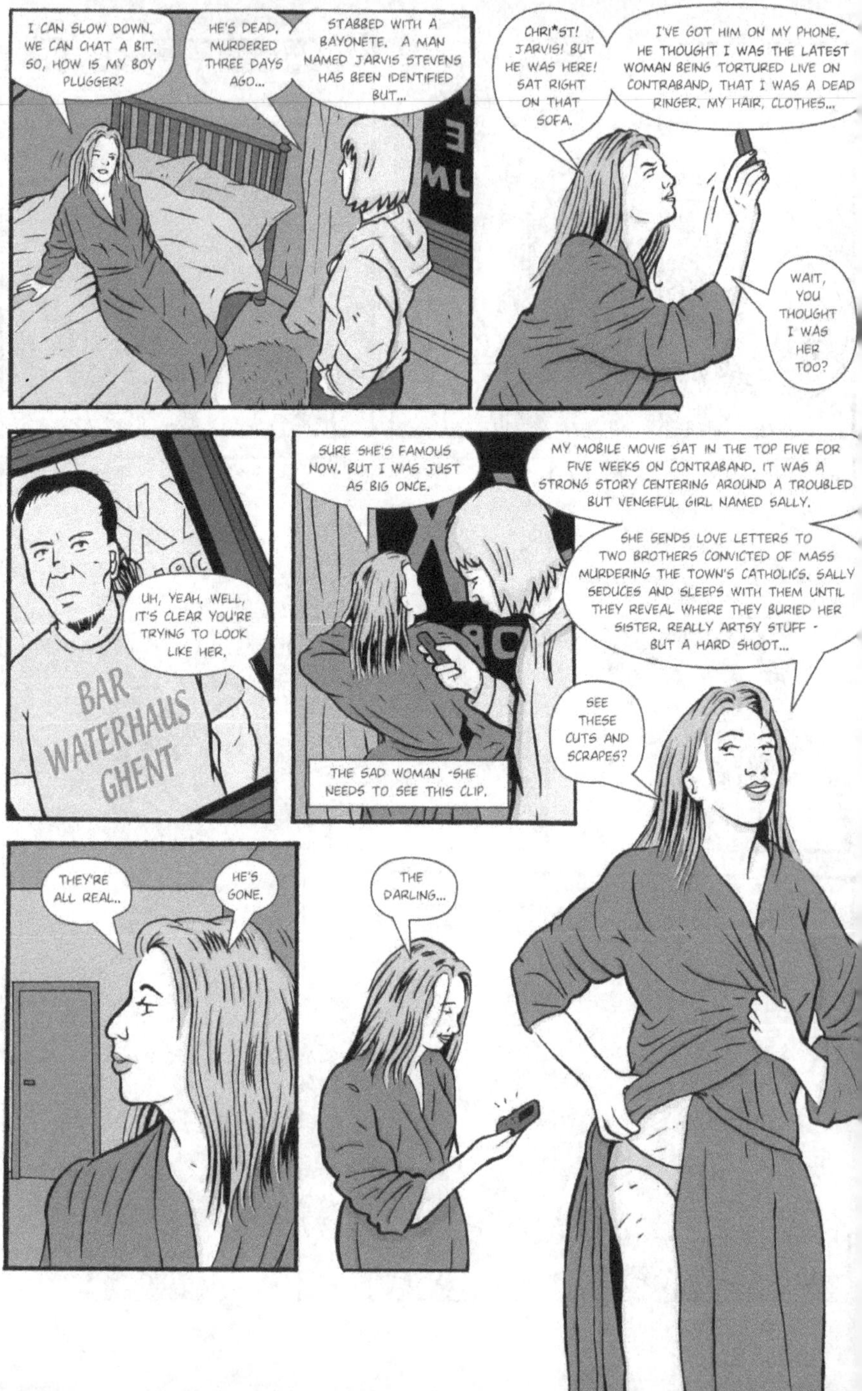
I CAN SLOW DOWN. WE CAN CHAT A BIT. SO, HOW IS MY BOY PLUGGER?
HE'S DEAD. MURDERED THREE DAYS AGO...
STABBED WITH A BAYONETE. A MAN NAMED JARVIS STEVENS HAS BEEN IDENTIFIED BUT...
CHRI*ST! JARVIS! BUT HE WAS HERE! SAT RIGHT ON THAT SOFA.
I'VE GOT HIM ON MY PHONE. HE THOUGHT I WAS THE LATEST WOMAN BEING TORTURED LIVE ON CONTRABAND, THAT I WAS A DEAD RINGER. MY HAIR, CLOTHES...
WAIT, YOU THOUGHT I WAS HER TOO?
BAR WATERHAUS GHENT
UH, YEAH. WELL, IT'S CLEAR YOU'RE TRYING TO LOOK LIKE HER.
SURE SHE'S FAMOUS NOW. BUT I WAS JUST AS BIG ONCE.
THE SAD WOMAN -SHE NEEDS TO SEE THIS CLIP.
MY MOBILE MOVIE SAT IN THE TOP FIVE FOR FIVE WEEKS ON CONTRABAND. IT WAS A STRONG STORY CENTERING AROUND A TROUBLED BUT VENGEFUL GIRL NAMED SALLY.
SHE SENDS LOVE LETTERS TO TWO BROTHERS CONVICTED OF MASS MURDERING THE TOWN'S CATHOLICS. SALLY SEDUCES AND SLEEPS WITH THEM UNTIL THEY REVEAL WHERE THEY BURIED HER SISTER. REALLY ARTSY STUFF - BUT A HARD SHOOT...
SEE THESE CUTS AND SCRAPES?
THEY'RE ALL REAL..
HE'S GONE.
THE DARLING...

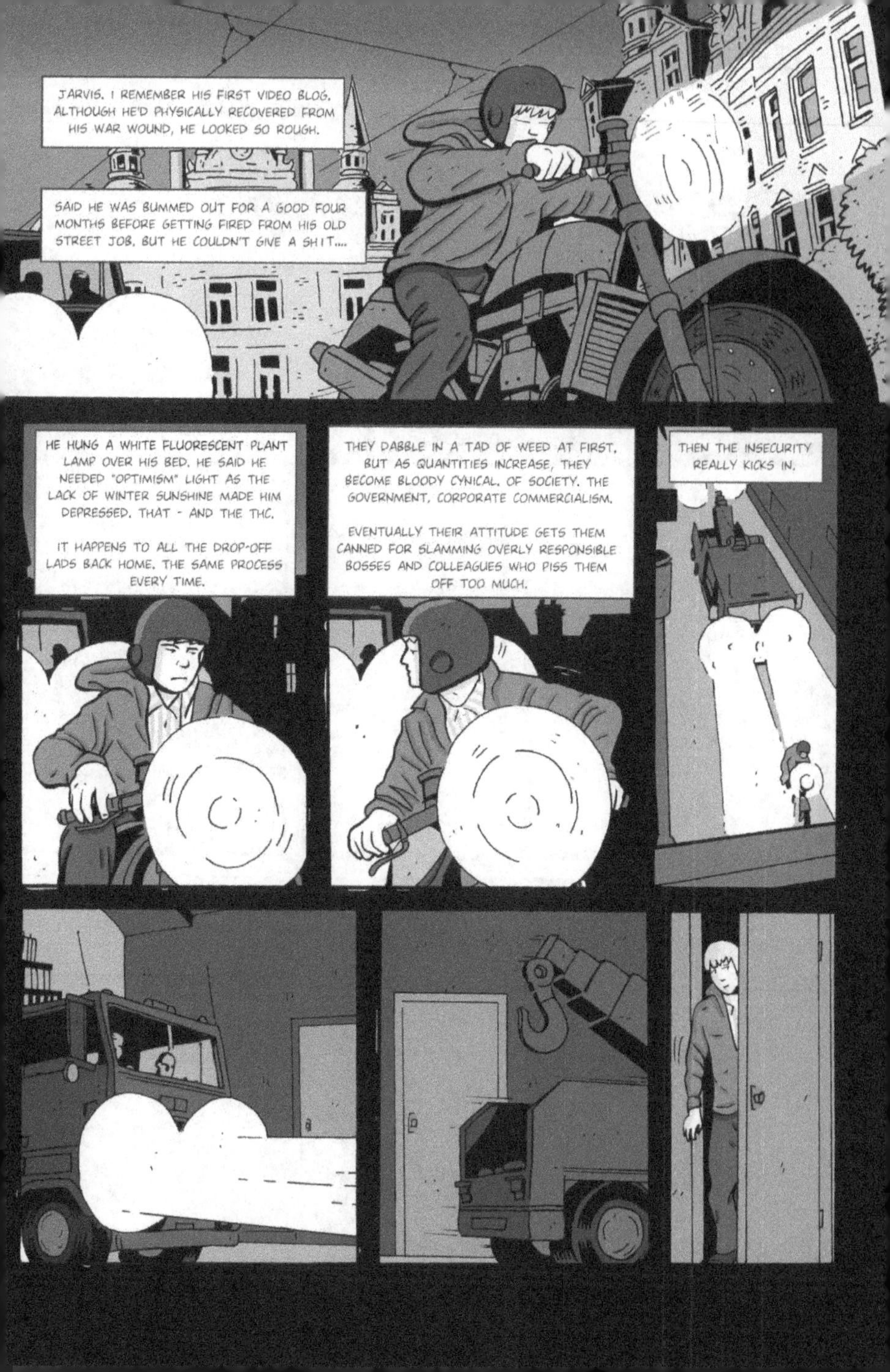
JARVIS. I REMEMBER HIS FIRST VIDEO BLOG. ALTHOUGH HE'D PHYSICALLY RECOVERED FROM HIS WAR WOUND, HE LOOKED SO ROUGH.
SAID HE WAS BUMMED OUT FOR A GOOD FOUR MONTHS BEFORE GETTING FIRED FROM HIS OLD STREET JOB. BUT HE COULDN'T GIVE A SHIT....
HE HUNG A WHITE FLUORESCENT PLANT LAMP OVER HIS BED. HE SAID HE NEEDED "OPTIMISM" LIGHT AS THE LACK OF WINTER SUNSHINE MADE HIM DEPRESSED. THAT - AND THE THC.
IT HAPPENS TO ALL THE DROP-OFF LADS BACK HOME. THE SAME PROCESS EVERY TIME.
THEY DABBLE IN A TAD OF WEED AT FIRST, BUT AS QUANTITIES INCREASE, THEY BECOME BLOODY CYNICAL. OF SOCIETY. THE GOVERNMENT. CORPORATE COMMERCIALISM.
EVENTUALLY THEIR ATTITUDE GETS THEM CANNED FOR SLAMMING OVERLY RESPONSIBLE BOSSES AND COLLEAGUES WHO PISS THEM OFF TOO MUCH.
THEN THE INSECURITY REALLY KICKS IN.

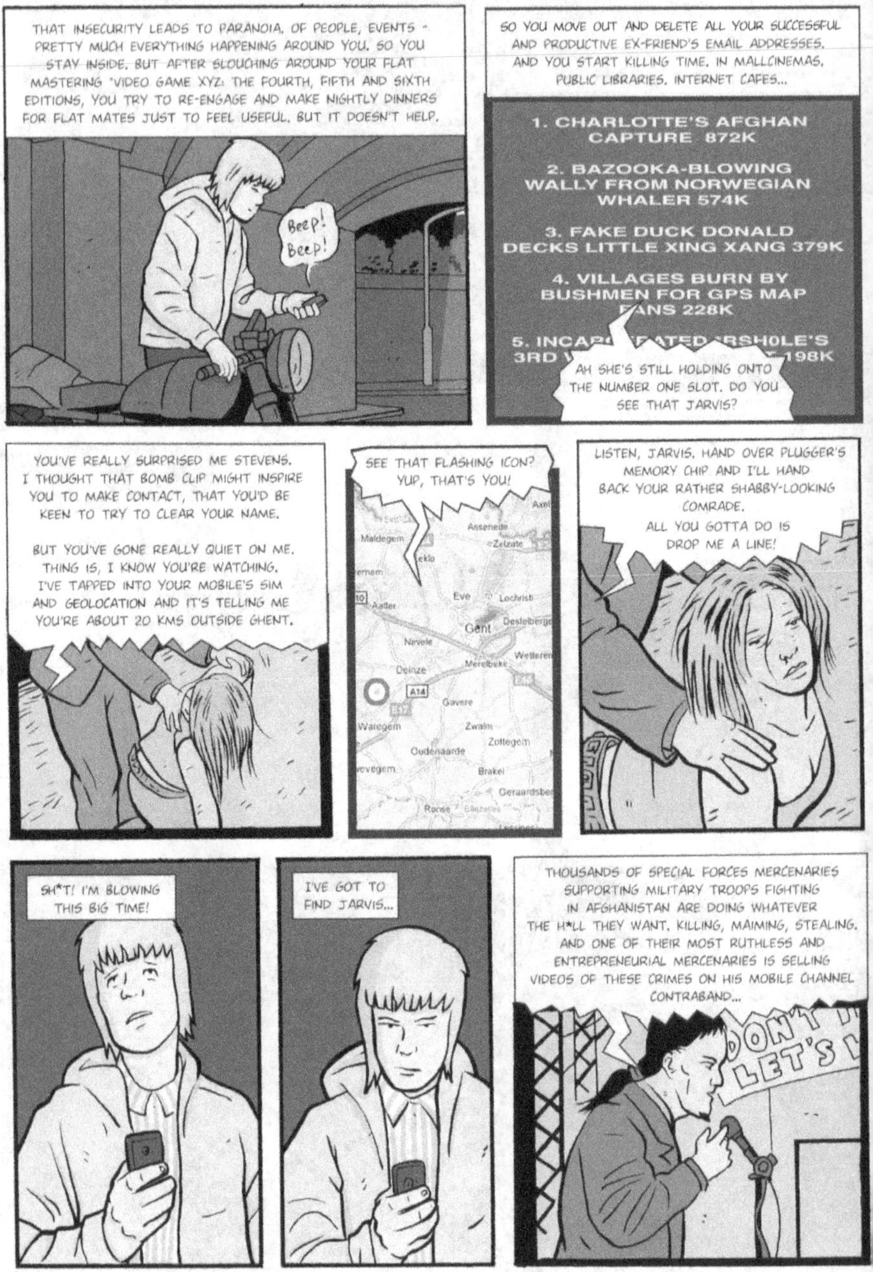
THAT INSECURITY LEADS TO PARANOIA. OF PEOPLE, EVENTS - PRETTY MUCH EVERYTHING HAPPENING AROUND YOU. SO YOU STAY INSIDE. BUT AFTER SLOUCHING AROUND YOUR FLAT MASTERING 'VIDEO GAME XYZ: THE FOURTH, FIFTH AND SIXTH EDITIONS, YOU TRY TO RE-ENGAGE AND MAKE NIGHTLY DINNERS FOR FLAT MATES JUST TO FEEL USEFUL. BUT IT DOESN'T HELP.
Beep! Beep!
SO YOU MOVE OUT AND DELETE ALL YOUR SUCCESSFUL AND PRODUCTIVE EX-FRIEND'S EMAIL ADDRESSES. AND YOU START KILLING TIME. IN MALLCINEMAS. PUBLIC LIBRARIES. INTERNET CAFES...
1. CHARLOTTE'S AFGHAN CAPTURE 872K
2. BAZOOKA-BLOWING WALLY FROM NORWEGIAN WHALER 574K
3. FAKE DUCK DONALD DECKS LITTLE XING XANG 379K
4. VILLAGES BURN BY BUSHMEN FOR GPS MAP FANS 228K
5. INCAR
3RD
198K
AH SHE'S STILL HOLDING ONTO THE NUMBER ONE SLOT. DO YOU SEE THAT JARVIS?
YOU'VE REALLY SURPRISED ME STEVENS. I THOUGHT THAT BOMB CLIP MIGHT INSPIRE YOU TO MAKE CONTACT, THAT YOU'D BE KEEN TO TRY TO CLEAR YOUR NAME.
BUT YOU'VE GONE REALLY QUIET ON ME. THING IS, I KNOW YOU'RE WATCHING. I'VE TAPPED INTO YOUR MOBILE'S SIM AND GEOLOCATION AND IT'S TELLING ME YOU'RE ABOUT 20 KMS OUTSIDE GHENT.
SEE THAT FLASHING ICON? YUP, THAT'S YOU!
Assenede
Maldegem
Zelzate
Eve
Lochristi
Aalter
Gent
Nevele
Merelbeke
Deinze
A14
Gavere
Waregem
Zwalm
Zottegem
Oudenaarde
Brakel
Ronse
LISTEN, JARVIS. HAND OVER PLUGGER'S MEMORY CHIP AND I'LL HAND BACK YOUR RATHER SHABBY-LOOKING COMRADE.
ALL YOU GOTTA DO IS DROP ME A LINE!
SH*T! I'M BLOWING THIS BIG TIME!
I'VE GOT TO FIND JARVIS...
THOUSANDS OF SPECIAL FORCES MERCENARIES SUPPORTING MILITARY TROOPS FIGHTING IN AFGHANISTAN ARE DOING WHATEVER THE H*LL THEY WANT. KILLING, MAIMING, STEALING. AND ONE OF THEIR MOST RUTHLESS AND ENTREPRENEURIAL MERCENARIES IS SELLING VIDEOS OF THESE CRIMES ON HIS MOBILE CHANNEL CONTRABAND...

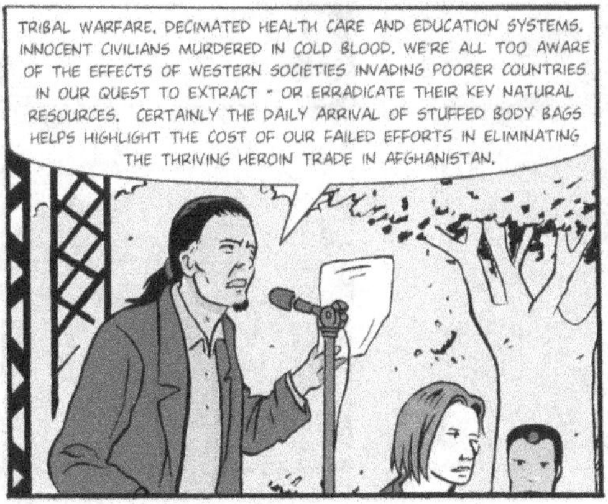
TRIBAL WARFARE. DECIMATED HEALTH CARE AND EDUCATION SYSTEMS. INNOCENT CIVILIANS MURDERED IN COLD BLOOD. WE'RE ALL TOO AWARE OF THE EFFECTS OF WESTERN SOCIETIES INVADING POORER COUNTRIES IN OUR QUEST TO EXTRACT - OR ERRADICATE THEIR KEY NATURAL RESOURCES. CERTAINLY THE DAILY ARRIVAL OF STUFFED BODY BAGS HELPS HIGHLIGHT THE COST OF OUR FAILED EFFORTS IN ELIMINATING THE THRIVING HEROIN TRADE IN AFGHANISTAN.

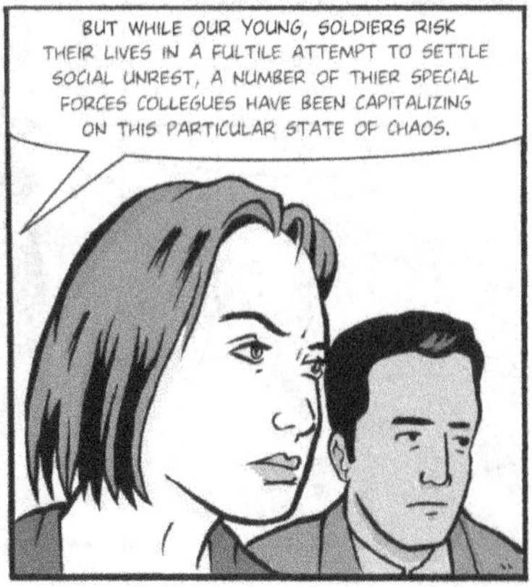
BUT WHILE OUR YOUNG, SOLDIERS RISK THEIR LIVES IN A FULTILE ATTEMPT TO SETTLE SOCIAL UNREST, A NUMBER OF THIER SPECIAL FORCES COLLEGUES HAVE BEEN CAPITALIZING ON THIS PARTICULAR STATE OF CHAOS.

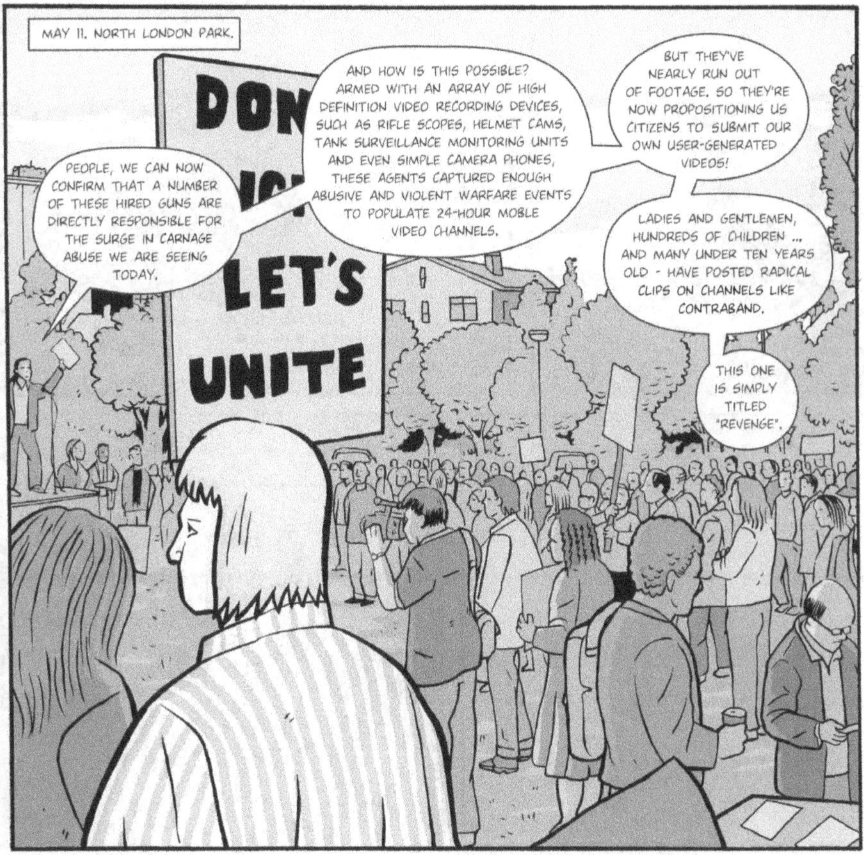
MAY 11. NORTH LONDON PARK.
PEOPLE, WE CAN NOW CONFIRM THAT A NUMBER OF THESE HIRED GUNS ARE DIRECTLY RESPONSIBLE FOR THE SURGE IN CARNAGE ABUSE WE ARE SEEING TODAY.
AND HOW IS THIS POSSIBLE? ARMED WITH AN ARRAY OF HIGH DEFINITION VIDEO RECORDING DEVICES, SUCH AS RIFLE SCOPES, HELMET CAMS, TANK SURVEILLANCE MONITORING UNITS AND EVEN SIMPLE CAMERA PHONES, THESE AGENTS CAPTURED ENOUGH ABUSIVE AND VIOLENT WARFARE EVENTS TO POPULATE 24-HOUR MOBLE VIDEO CHANNELS.
BUT THEY'VE NEARLY RUN OUT OF FOOTAGE. SO THEY'RE NOW PROPOSITIONING US CITIZENS TO SUBMIT OUR OWN USER-GENERATED VIDEOS!
LADIES AND GENTLEMEN, HUNDREDS OF CHILDREN ... AND MANY UNDER TEN YEARS OLD - HAVE POSTED RADICAL CLIPS ON CHANNELS LIKE CONTRABAND.
THIS ONE IS SIMPLY TITLED "REVENGE".
DON
LET'S
UNITE

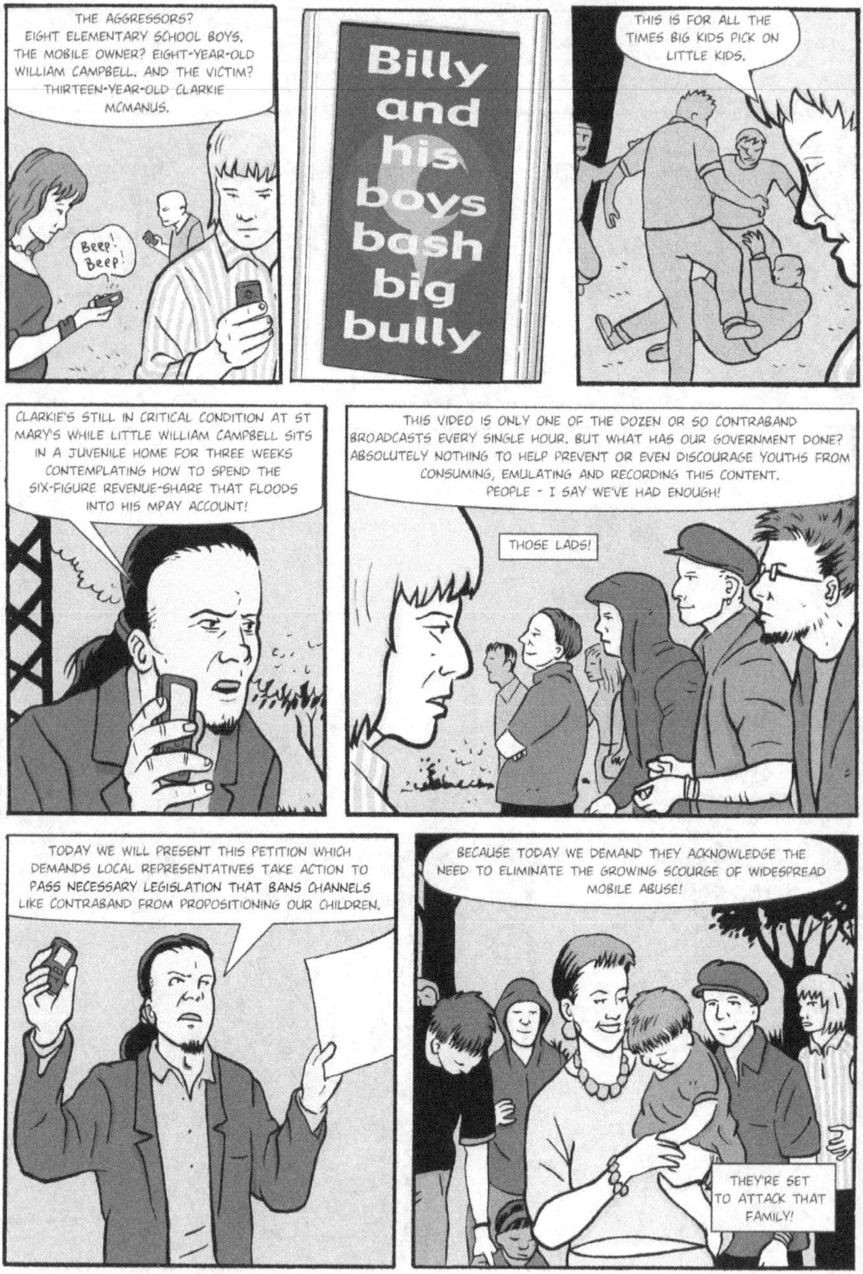
THE AGGRESSORS? EIGHT ELEMENTARY SCHOOL BOYS. THE MOBILE OWNER? EIGHT-YEAR-OLD WILLIAM CAMPBELL. AND THE VICTIM? THIRTEEN-YEAR-OLD CLARKIE MCMANUS.
Beep! Beep!
Billy and his boys bash big bully
THIS IS FOR ALL THE TIMES BIG KIDS PICK ON LITTLE KIDS.
CLARKIE'S STILL IN CRITICAL CONDITION AT ST MARY'S WHILE LITTLE WILLIAM CAMPBELL SITS IN A JUVENILE HOME FOR THREE WEEKS CONTEMPLATING HOW TO SPEND THE SIX-FIGURE REVENUE-SHARE THAT FLOODS INTO HIS MPAY ACCOUNT!
THIS VIDEO IS ONLY ONE OF THE DOZEN OR SO CONTRABAND BROADCASTS EVERY SINGLE HOUR. BUT WHAT HAS OUR GOVERNMENT DONE? ABSOLUTELY NOTHING TO HELP PREVENT OR EVEN DISCOURAGE YOUTHS FROM CONSUMING, EMULATING AND RECORDING THIS CONTENT. PEOPLE - I SAY WE'VE HAD ENOUGH!
THOSE LADS!
TODAY WE WILL PRESENT THIS PETITION WHICH DEMANDS LOCAL REPRESENTATIVES TAKE ACTION TO PASS NECESSARY LEGISLATION THAT BANS CHANNELS LIKE CONTRABAND FROM PROPOSITIONING OUR CHILDREN.
BECAUSE TODAY WE DEMAND THEY ACKNOWLEDGE THE NEED TO ELIMINATE THE GROWING SCOURGE OF WIDESPREAD MOBILE ABUSE!
THEY'RE SET TO ATTACK THAT FAMILY!

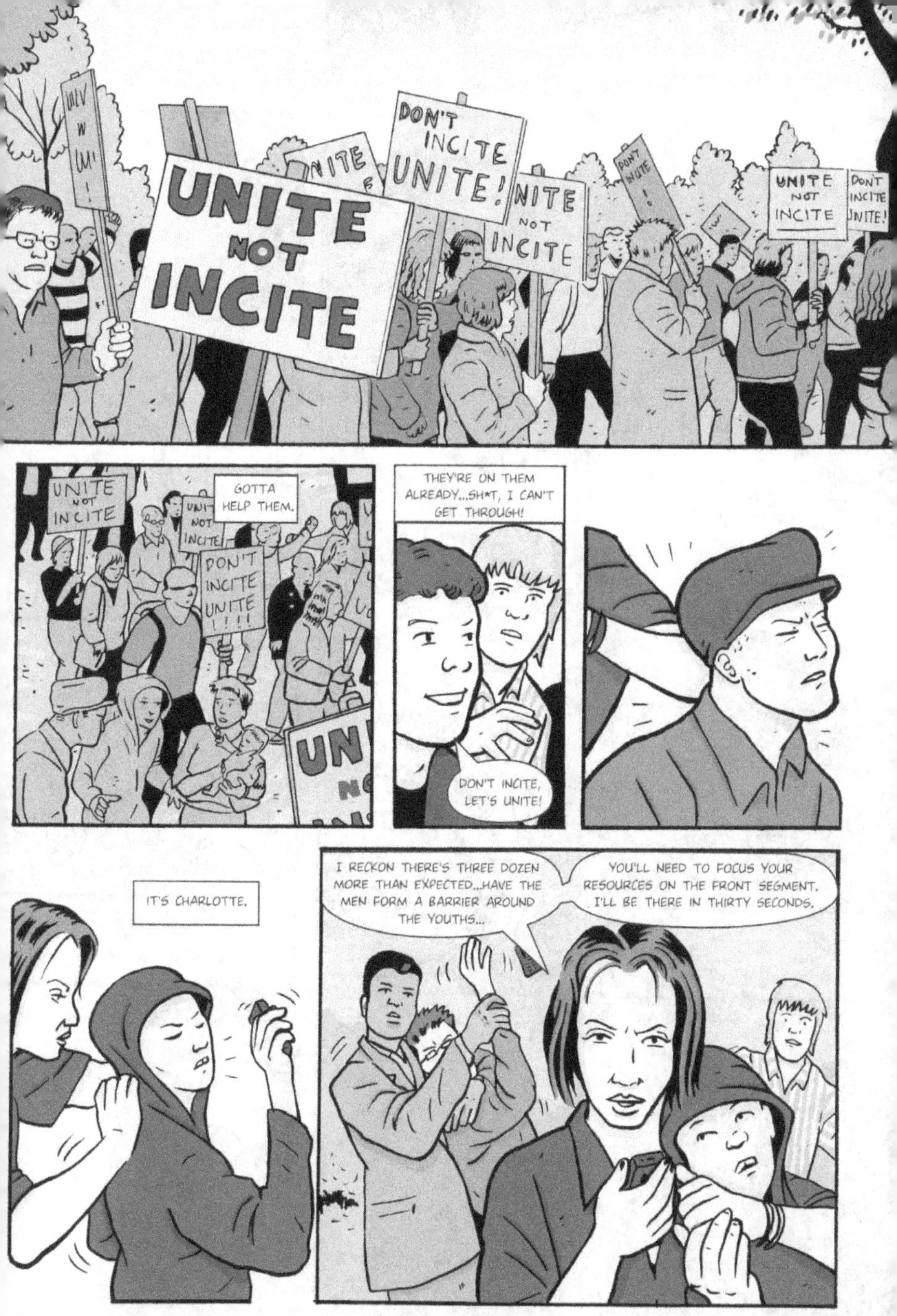
UNITE NOT INCITE
DON'T INCITE UNITE!
UNITE NOT INCITE
UNITE NOT INCITE
DON'T INCITE UNITE!
UNITE NOT INCITE
GOTTA HELP THEM.
DON'T INCITE UNITE !!!!
THEY'RE ON THEM ALREADY...SH*T, I CAN'T GET THROUGH!
DON'T INCITE, LET'S UNITE!
IT'S CHARLOTTE.
I RECKON THERE'S THREE DOZEN MORE THAN EXPECTED...HAVE THE MEN FORM A BARRIER AROUND THE YOUTHS...
YOU'LL NEED TO FOCUS YOUR RESOURCES ON THE FRONT SEGMENT. I'LL BE THERE IN THIRTY SECONDS.

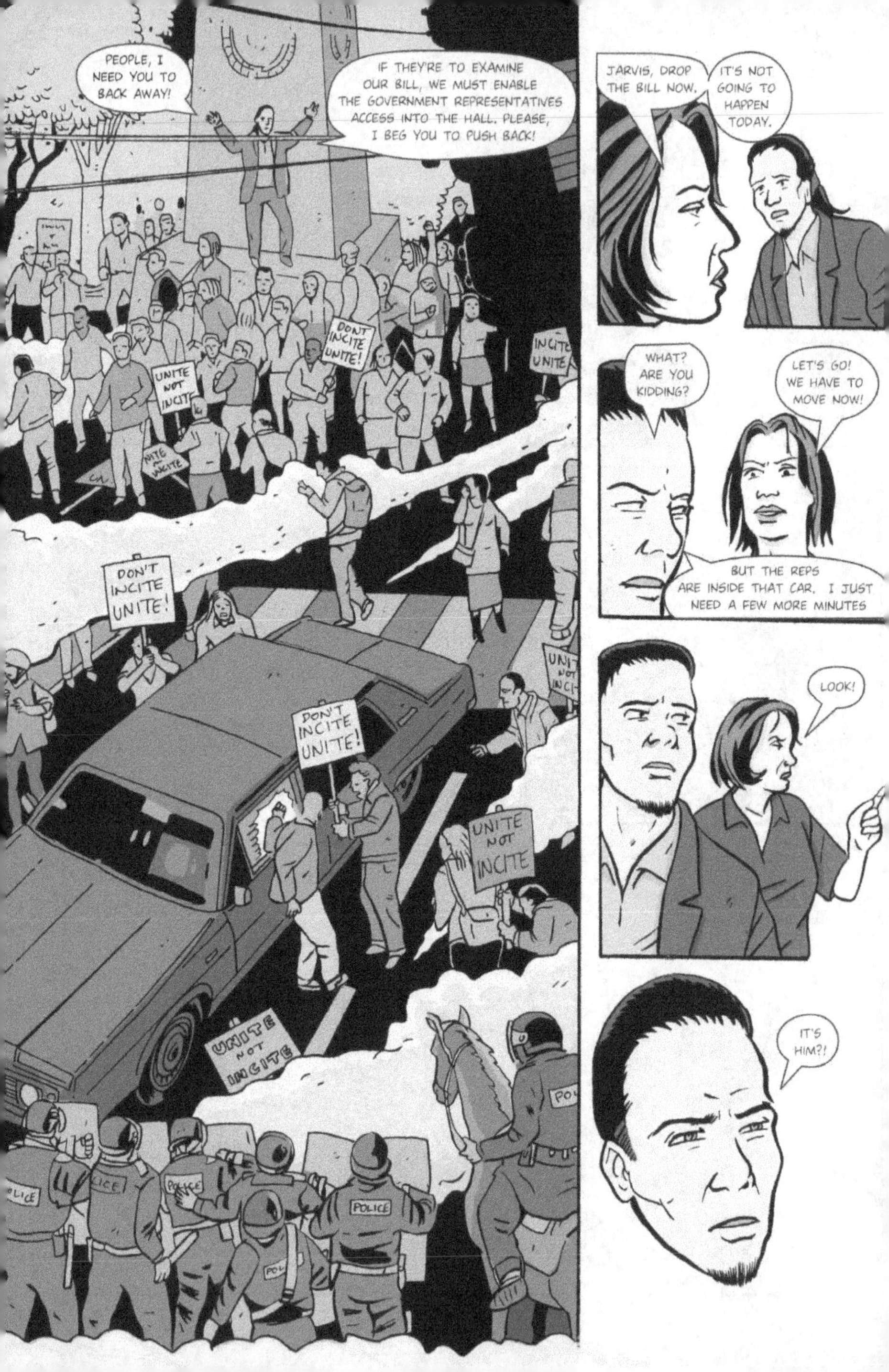
PEOPLE, I NEED YOU TO BACK AWAY!
IF THEY'RE TO EXAMINE OUR BILL, WE MUST ENABLE THE GOVERNMENT REPRESENTATIVES ACCESS INTO THE HALL. PLEASE, I BEG YOU TO PUSH BACK!
DON'T INCITE UNITE!
UNITE NOT INCITE
INCITE UNITE
DON'T INCITE UNITE!
DON'T INCITE UNITE!
UNITE NOT INCITE
UNITE NOT INCITE
POLICE
JARVIS, DROP THE BILL NOW.
IT'S NOT GOING TO HAPPEN TODAY.
WHAT? ARE YOU KIDDING?
LET'S GO! WE HAVE TO MOVE NOW!
BUT THE REPS ARE INSIDE THAT CAR. I JUST NEED A FEW MORE MINUTES
LOOK!
IT'S HIM?!

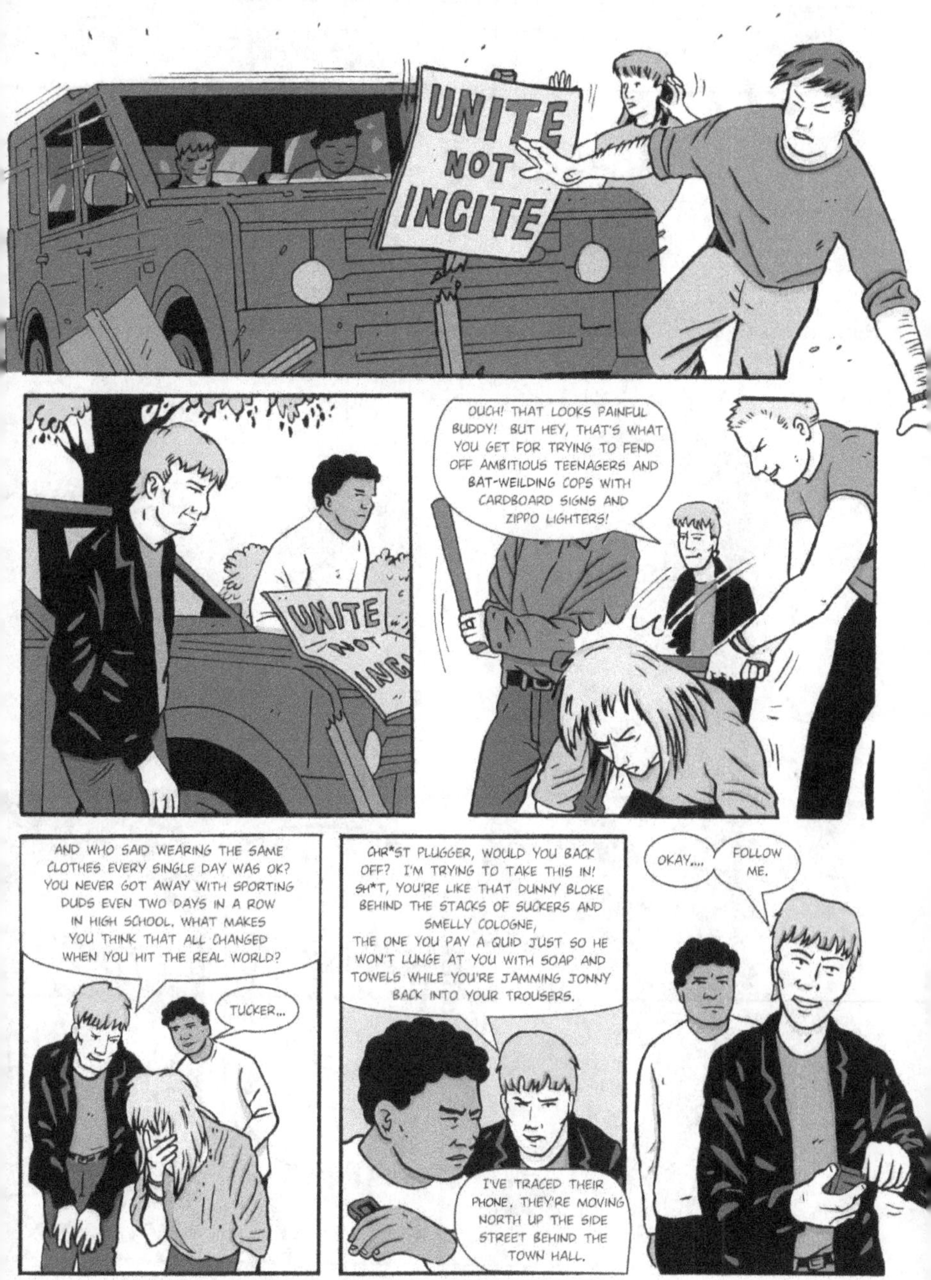
UNITE NOT INCITE
UNITE NOT INC
OUCH! THAT LOOKS PAINFUL BUDDY! BUT HEY, THAT'S WHAT YOU GET FOR TRYING TO FEND OFF AMBITIOUS TEENAGERS AND BAT-WEILDING COPS WITH CARDBOARD SIGNS AND ZIPPO LIGHTERS!
AND WHO SAID WEARING THE SAME CLOTHES EVERY SINGLE DAY WAS OK? YOU NEVER GOT AWAY WITH SPORTING DUDS EVEN TWO DAYS IN A ROW IN HIGH SCHOOL. WHAT MAKES YOU THINK THAT ALL CHANGED WHEN YOU HIT THE REAL WORLD?
TUCKER...
CHR*ST PLUGGER, WOULD YOU BACK OFF? I'M TRYING TO TAKE THIS IN! SH*T, YOU'RE LIKE THAT DUNNY BLOKE BEHIND THE STACKS OF SUCKERS AND SMELLY COLOGNE, THE ONE YOU PAY A QUID JUST SO HE WON'T LUNGE AT YOU WITH SOAP AND TOWELS WHILE YOU'RE JAMMING JONNY BACK INTO YOUR TROUSERS.
I'VE TRACED THEIR PHONE. THEY'RE MOVING NORTH UP THE SIDE STREET BEHIND THE TOWN HALL.
OKAY....
FOLLOW ME.

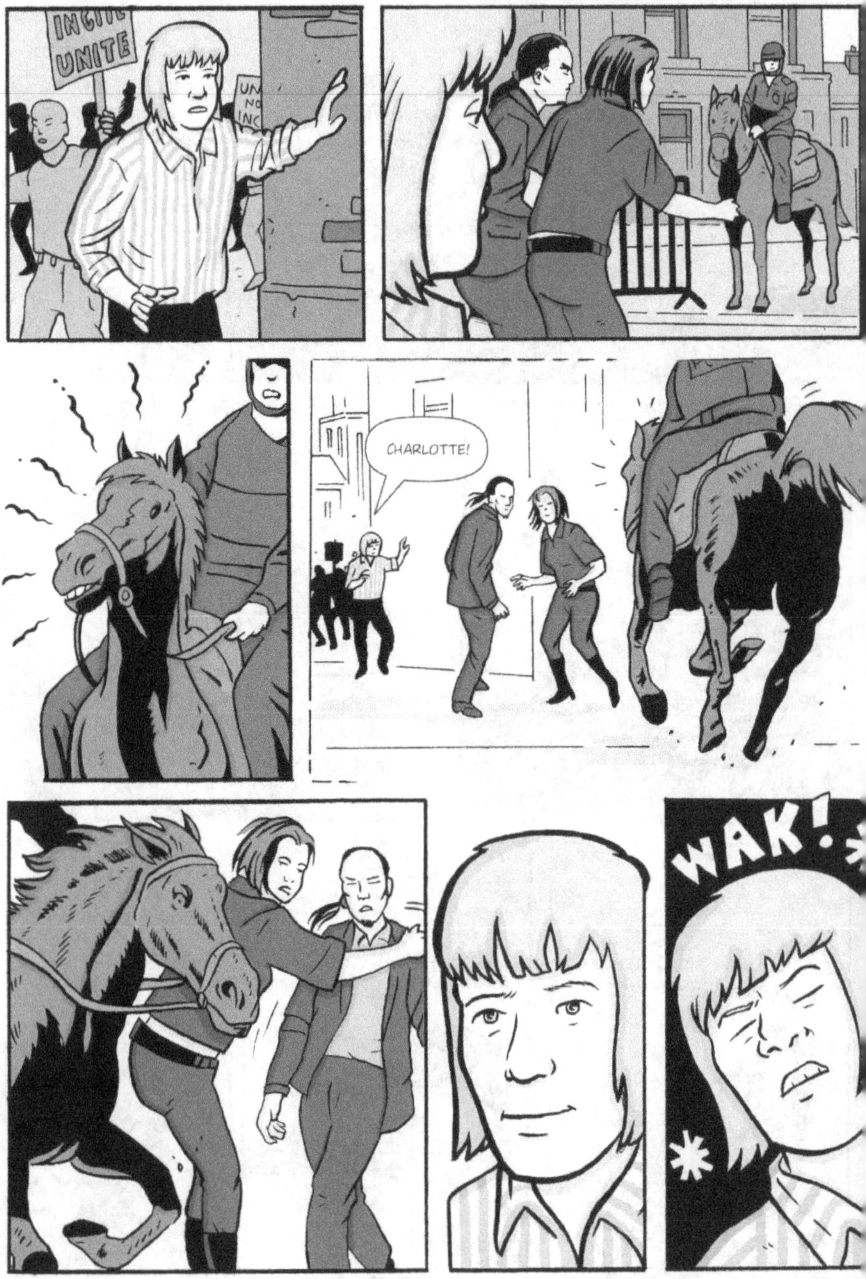
INCITE
UNITE
CHARLOTTE!
WAK!

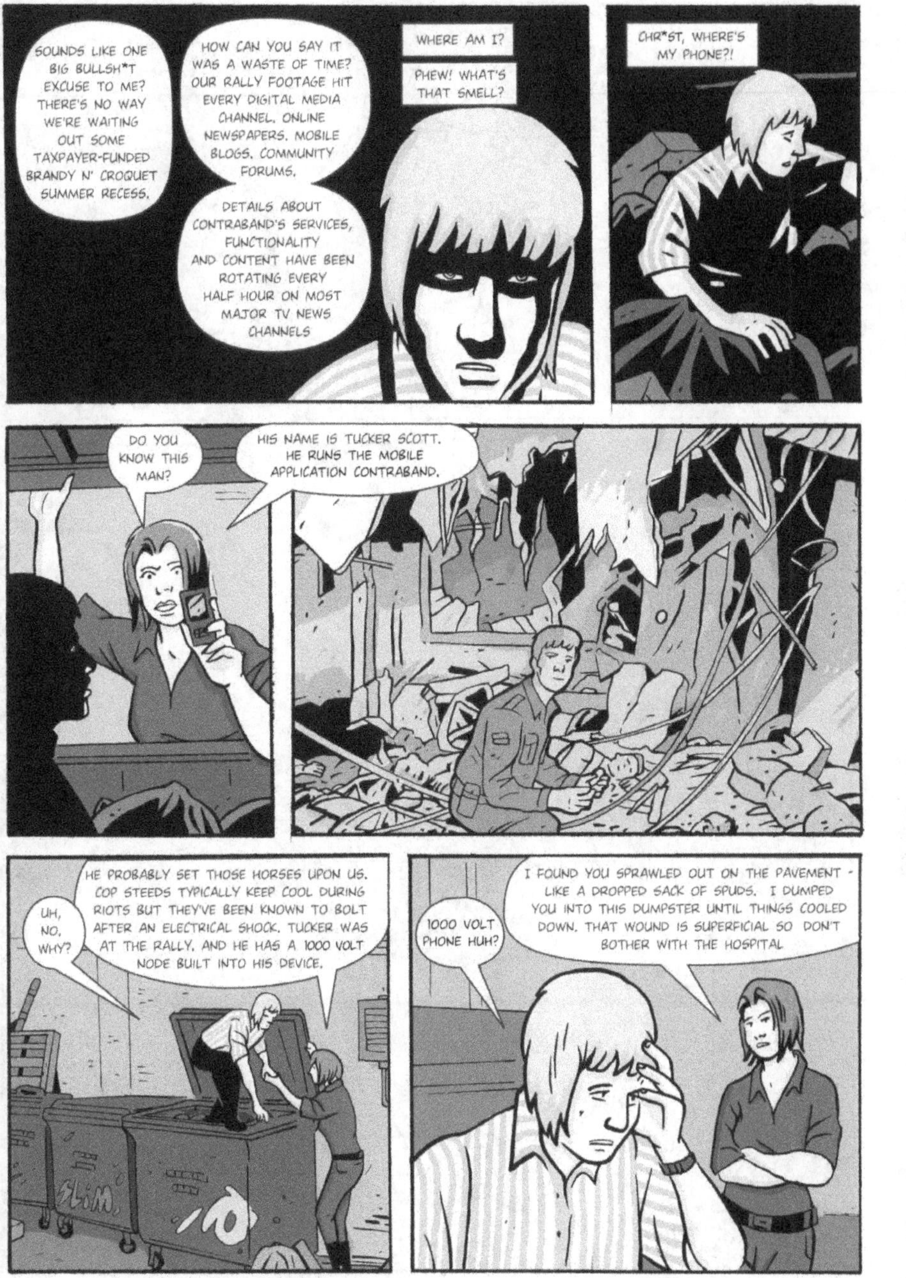
SOUNDS LIKE ONE BIG BULLSH*T EXCUSE TO ME? THERE'S NO WAY WE'RE WAITING OUT SOME TAXPAYER-FUNDED BRANDY N' CROQUET SUMMER RECESS.
HOW CAN YOU SAY IT WAS A WASTE OF TIME? OUR RALLY FOOTAGE HIT EVERY DIGITAL MEDIA CHANNEL. ONLINE NEWSPAPERS. MOBILE BLOGS. COMMUNITY FORUMS.
DETAILS ABOUT CONTRABAND'S SERVICES, FUNCTIONALITY AND CONTENT HAVE BEEN ROTATING EVERY HALF HOUR ON MOST MAJOR TV NEWS CHANNELS
WHERE AM I?
PHEW! WHAT'S THAT SMELL?
CHR*ST, WHERE'S MY PHONE?!
DO YOU KNOW THIS MAN?
HIS NAME IS TUCKER SCOTT. HE RUNS THE MOBILE APPLICATION CONTRABAND.
UH, NO, WHY?
HE PROBABLY SET THOSE HORSES UPON US. COP STEEDS TYPICALLY KEEP COOL DURING RIOTS BUT THEY'VE BEEN KNOWN TO BOLT AFTER AN ELECTRICAL SHOCK. TUCKER WAS AT THE RALLY. AND HE HAS A 1000 VOLT NODE BUILT INTO HIS DEVICE.
1000 VOLT PHONE HUH?
I FOUND YOU SPRAWLED OUT ON THE PAVEMENT - LIKE A DROPPED SACK OF SPUDS. I DUMPED YOU INTO THIS DUMPSTER UNTIL THINGS COOLED DOWN. THAT WOUND IS SUPERFICIAL SO DON'T BOTHER WITH THE HOSPITAL

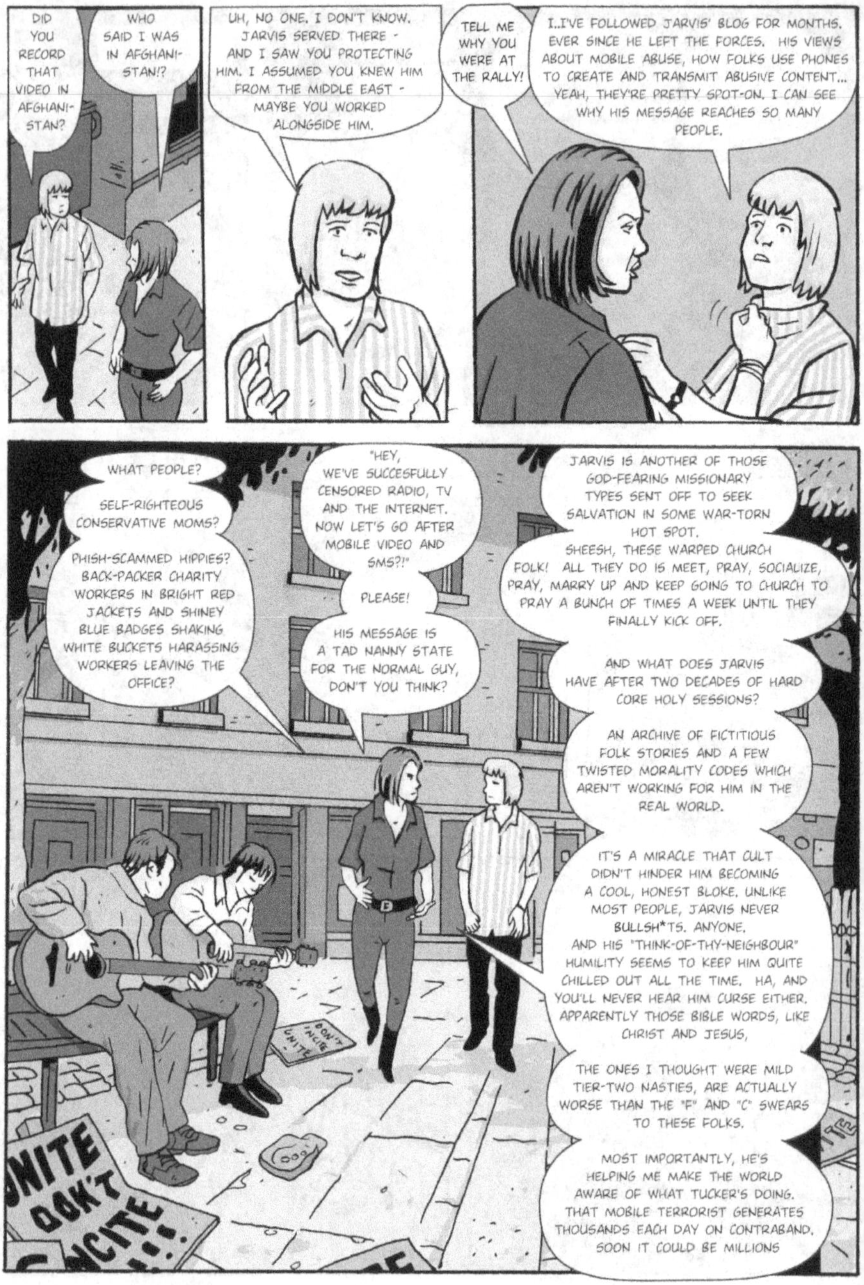
DID YOU RECORD THAT VIDEO IN AFGHANISTAN?
WHO SAID I WAS IN AFGHANISTAN!?
UH, NO ONE. I DON'T KNOW. JARVIS SERVED THERE - AND I SAW YOU PROTECTING HIM. I ASSUMED YOU KNEW HIM FROM THE MIDDLE EAST - MAYBE YOU WORKED ALONGSIDE HIM.
TELL ME WHY YOU WERE AT THE RALLY!
I..I'VE FOLLOWED JARVIS' BLOG FOR MONTHS. EVER SINCE HE LEFT THE FORCES. HIS VIEWS ABOUT MOBILE ABUSE, HOW FOLKS USE PHONES TO CREATE AND TRANSMIT ABUSIVE CONTENT... YEAH, THEY'RE PRETTY SPOT-ON. I CAN SEE WHY HIS MESSAGE REACHES SO MANY PEOPLE.
WHAT PEOPLE?
SELF-RIGHTEOUS CONSERVATIVE MOMS?
PHISH-SCAMMED HIPPIES? BACK-PACKER CHARITY WORKERS IN BRIGHT RED JACKETS AND SHINEY BLUE BADGES SHAKING WHITE BUCKETS HARASSING WORKERS LEAVING THE OFFICE?
"HEY, WE'VE SUCCESFULLY CENSORED RADIO, TV AND THE INTERNET. NOW LET'S GO AFTER MOBILE VIDEO AND SMS?!"
PLEASE!
HIS MESSAGE IS A TAD NANNY STATE FOR THE NORMAL GUY, DON'T YOU THINK?
JARVIS IS ANOTHER OF THOSE GOD-FEARING MISSIONARY TYPES SENT OFF TO SEEK SALVATION IN SOME WAR-TORN HOT SPOT. SHEESH, THESE WARPED CHURCH FOLK! ALL THEY DO IS MEET, PRAY, SOCIALIZE, PRAY, MARRY UP AND KEEP GOING TO CHURCH TO PRAY A BUNCH OF TIMES A WEEK UNTIL THEY FINALLY KICK OFF.
AND WHAT DOES JARVIS HAVE AFTER TWO DECADES OF HARD CORE HOLY SESSIONS?
AN ARCHIVE OF FICTITIOUS FOLK STORIES AND A FEW TWISTED MORALITY CODES WHICH AREN'T WORKING FOR HIM IN THE REAL WORLD.
IT'S A MIRACLE THAT CULT DIDN'T HINDER HIM BECOMING A COOL, HONEST BLOKE. UNLIKE MOST PEOPLE, JARVIS NEVER BULLSH*TS. ANYONE. AND HIS "THINK-OF-THY-NEIGHBOUR" HUMILITY SEEMS TO KEEP HIM QUITE CHILLED OUT ALL THE TIME. HA, AND YOU'LL NEVER HEAR HIM CURSE EITHER. APPARENTLY THOSE BIBLE WORDS, LIKE CHRIST AND JESUS,
THE ONES I THOUGHT WERE MILD TIER-TWO NASTIES, ARE ACTUALLY WORSE THAN THE "F" AND "C" SWEARS TO THESE FOLKS.
MOST IMPORTANTLY, HE'S HELPING ME MAKE THE WORLD AWARE OF WHAT TUCKER'S DOING. THAT MOBILE TERRORIST GENERATES THOUSANDS EACH DAY ON CONTRABAND. SOON IT COULD BE MILLIONS
DON'T INCITE UNITE
UNITE DON'T INCITE!!

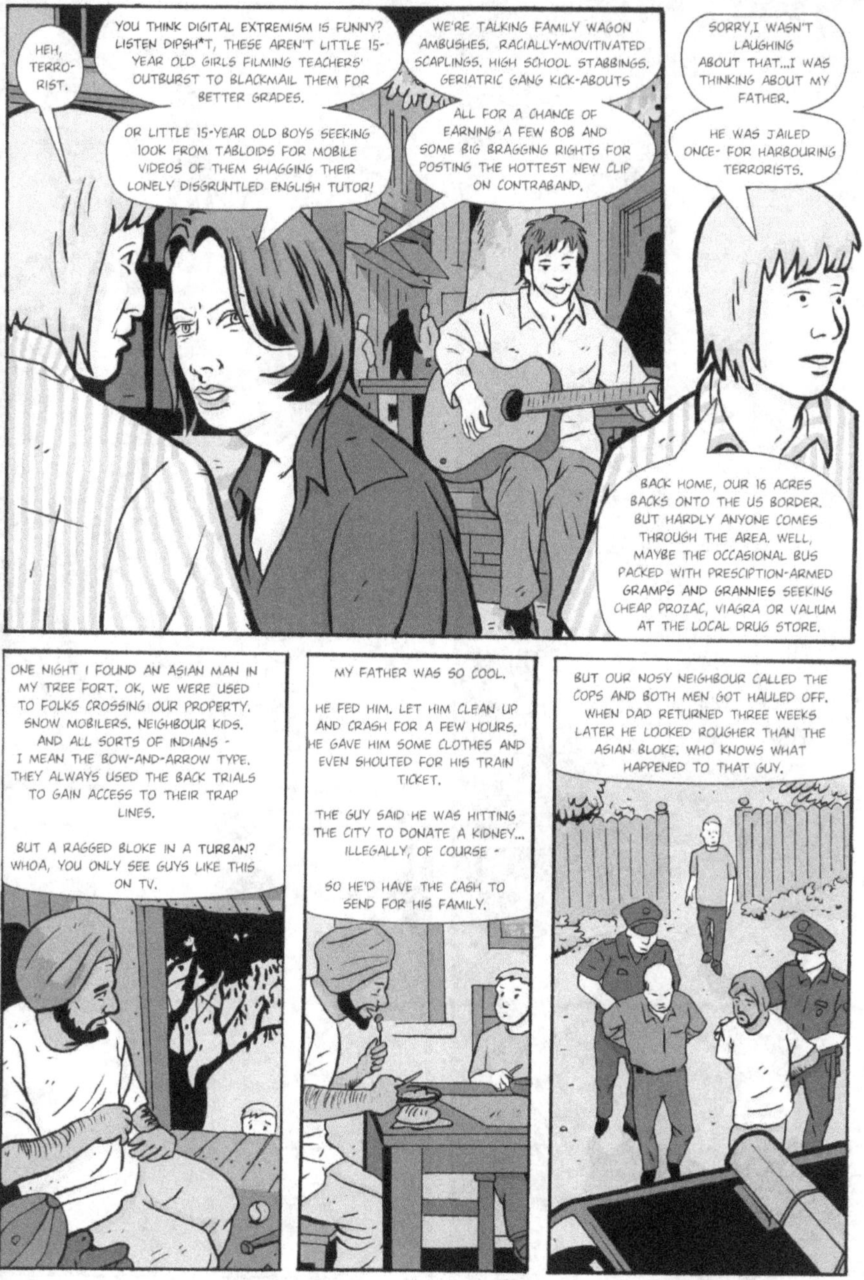
HEH, TERRO-RIST.
YOU THINK DIGITAL EXTREMISM IS FUNNY? LISTEN DIPSH*T, THESE AREN'T LITTLE 15-YEAR OLD GIRLS FILMING TEACHERS' OUTBURST TO BLACKMAIL THEM FOR BETTER GRADES.
OR LITTLE 15-YEAR OLD BOYS SEEKING 100K FROM TABLOIDS FOR MOBILE VIDEOS OF THEM SHAGGING THEIR LONELY DISGRUNTLED ENGLISH TUTOR!
WE'RE TALKING FAMILY WAGON AMBUSHES. RACIALLY-MOVITIVATED SCAPLINGS. HIGH SCHOOL STABBINGS. GERIATRIC GANG KICK-ABOUTS
ALL FOR A CHANCE OF EARNING A FEW BOB AND SOME BIG BRAGGING RIGHTS FOR POSTING THE HOTTEST NEW CLIP ON CONTRABAND.
SORRY, I WASN'T LAUGHING ABOUT THAT...I WAS THINKING ABOUT MY FATHER.
HE WAS JAILED ONCE- FOR HARBOURING TERRORISTS.
BACK HOME, OUR 16 ACRES BACKS ONTO THE US BORDER. BUT HARDLY ANYONE COMES THROUGH THE AREA. WELL, MAYBE THE OCCASIONAL BUS PACKED WITH PRESCIPTION-ARMED GRAMPS AND GRANNIES SEEKING CHEAP PROZAC, VIAGRA OR VALIUM AT THE LOCAL DRUG STORE.
ONE NIGHT I FOUND AN ASIAN MAN IN MY TREE FORT. OK, WE WERE USED TO FOLKS CROSSING OUR PROPERTY. SNOW MOBILERS. NEIGHBOUR KIDS. AND ALL SORTS OF INDIANS - I MEAN THE BOW-AND-ARROW TYPE. THEY ALWAYS USED THE BACK TRIALS TO GAIN ACCESS TO THEIR TRAP LINES.
BUT A RAGGED BLOKE IN A TURBAN? WHOA, YOU ONLY SEE GUYS LIKE THIS ON TV.
MY FATHER WAS SO COOL.
HE FED HIM. LET HIM CLEAN UP AND CRASH FOR A FEW HOURS. HE GAVE HIM SOME CLOTHES AND EVEN SHOUTED FOR HIS TRAIN TICKET.
THE GUY SAID HE WAS HITTING THE CITY TO DONATE A KIDNEY... ILLEGALLY, OF COURSE -
SO HE'D HAVE THE CASH TO SEND FOR HIS FAMILY.
BUT OUR NOSY NEIGHBOUR CALLED THE COPS AND BOTH MEN GOT HAULED OFF. WHEN DAD RETURNED THREE WEEKS LATER HE LOOKED ROUGHER THAN THE ASIAN BLOKE. WHO KNOWS WHAT HAPPENED TO THAT GUY.

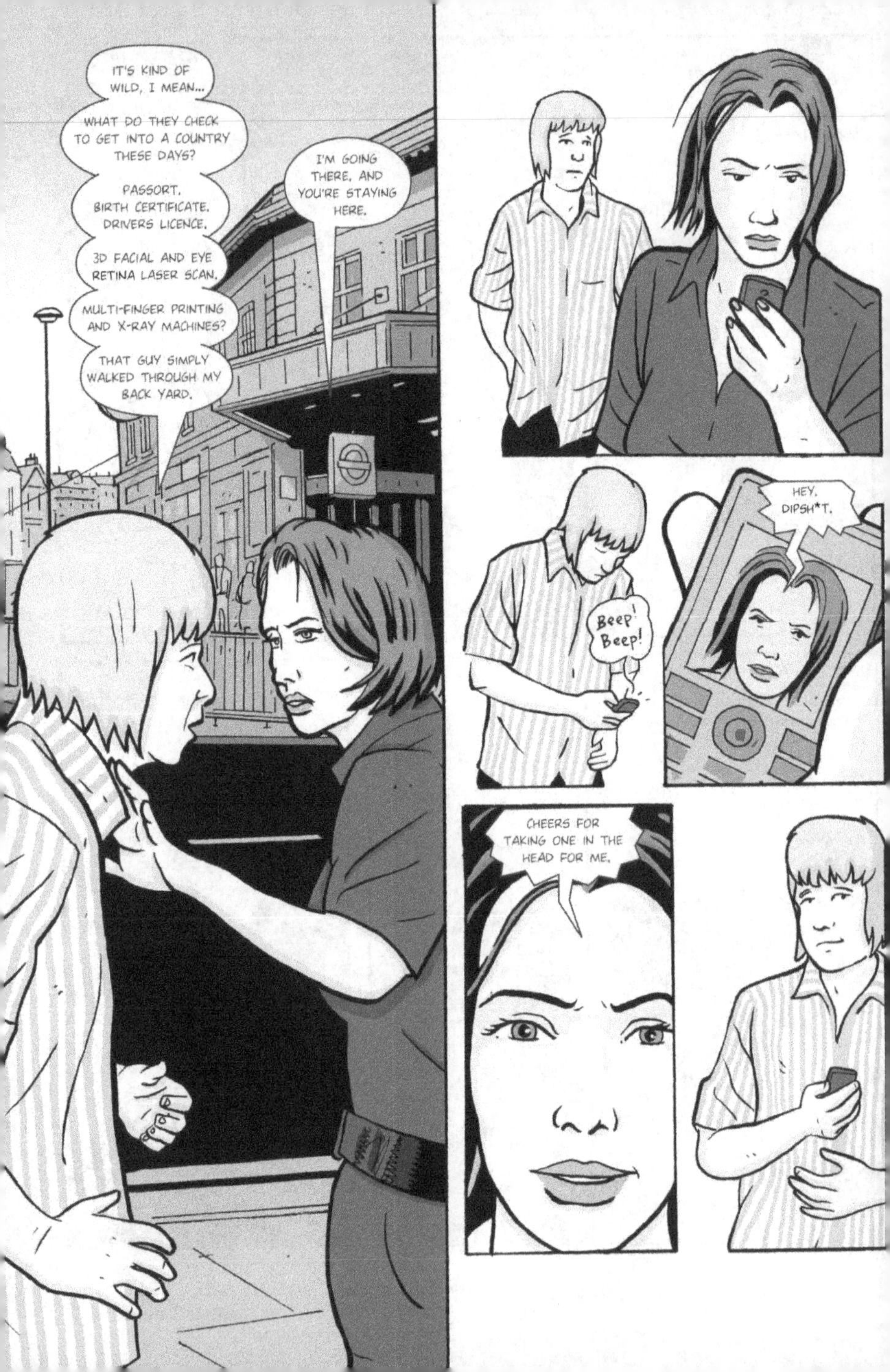
IT'S KIND OF WILD, I MEAN...
WHAT DO THEY CHECK TO GET INTO A COUNTRY THESE DAYS?
PASSORT. BIRTH CERTIFICATE. DRIVERS LICENCE.
3D FACIAL AND EYE RETINA LASER SCAN.
MULTI-FINGER PRINTING AND X-RAY MACHINES?
THAT GUY SIMPLY WALKED THROUGH MY BACK YARD.
I'M GOING THERE, AND YOU'RE STAYING HERE.
HEY, DIPSH*T.
Beep! Beep!
CHEERS FOR TAKING ONE IN THE HEAD FOR ME.

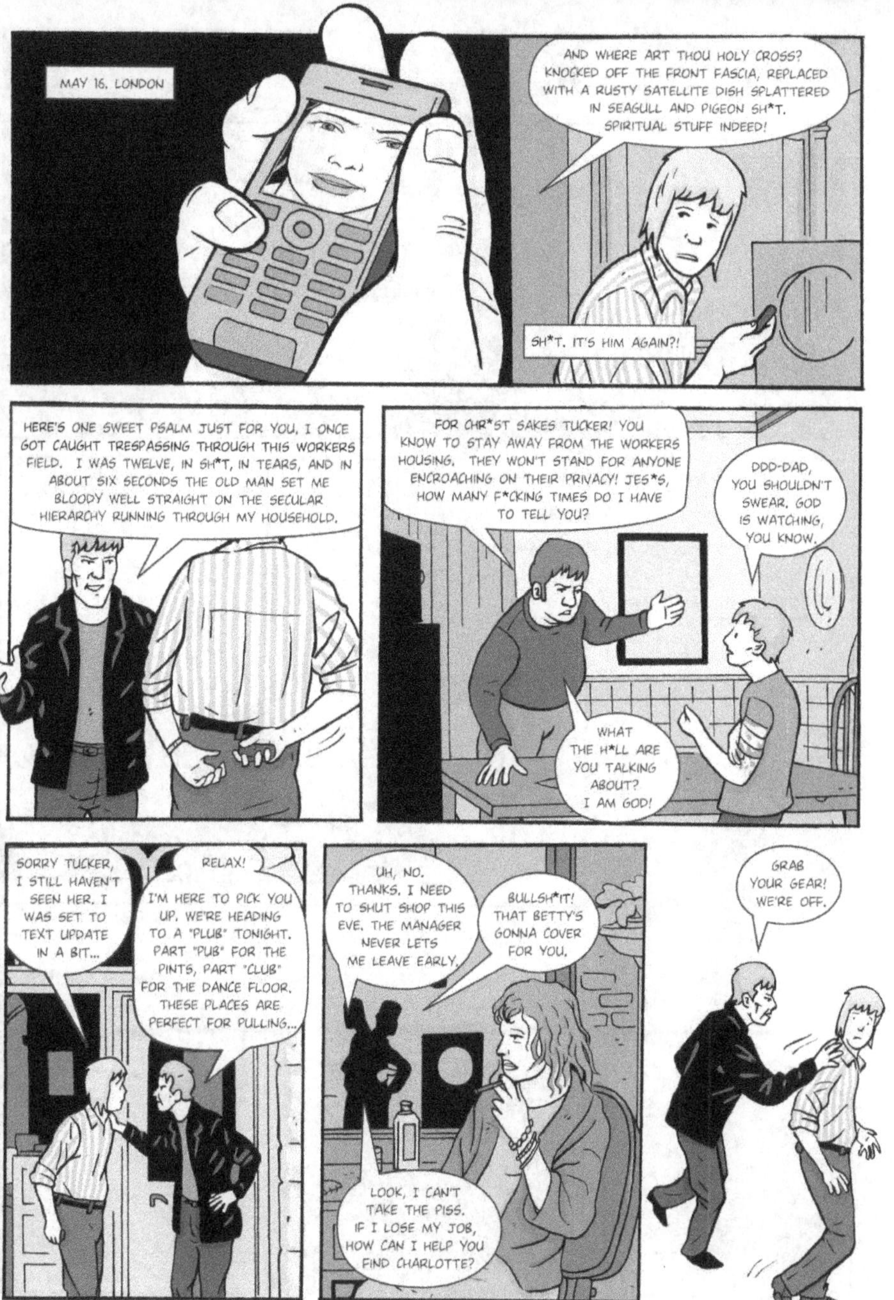
MAY 16, LONDON
AND WHERE ART THOU HOLY CROSS? KNOCKED OFF THE FRONT FASCIA, REPLACED WITH A RUSTY SATELLITE DISH SPLATTERED IN SEAGULL AND PIGEON SH*T. SPIRITUAL STUFF INDEED!
SH*T. IT'S HIM AGAIN?!
HERE'S ONE SWEET PSALM JUST FOR YOU. I ONCE GOT CAUGHT TRESPASSING THROUGH THIS WORKERS FIELD. I WAS TWELVE, IN SH*T, IN TEARS, AND IN ABOUT SIX SECONDS THE OLD MAN SET ME BLOODY WELL STRAIGHT ON THE SECULAR HIERARCHY RUNNING THROUGH MY HOUSEHOLD.
FOR CHR*ST SAKES TUCKER! YOU KNOW TO STAY AWAY FROM THE WORKERS HOUSING. THEY WON'T STAND FOR ANYONE ENCROACHING ON THEIR PRIVACY! JES*S, HOW MANY F*CKING TIMES DO I HAVE TO TELL YOU?
DDD-DAD, YOU SHOULDN'T SWEAR. GOD IS WATCHING, YOU KNOW.
WHAT THE H*LL ARE YOU TALKING ABOUT? I AM GOD!
SORRY TUCKER, I STILL HAVEN'T SEEN HER. I WAS SET TO TEXT UPDATE IN A BIT...
RELAX!
I'M HERE TO PICK YOU UP. WE'RE HEADING TO A "PLUB" TONIGHT. PART "PUB" FOR THE PINTS, PART "CLUB" FOR THE DANCE FLOOR. THESE PLACES ARE PERFECT FOR PULLING...
UH, NO. THANKS. I NEED TO SHUT SHOP THIS EVE. THE MANAGER NEVER LETS ME LEAVE EARLY.
BULLSH*IT! THAT BETTY'S GONNA COVER FOR YOU.
LOOK, I CAN'T TAKE THE PISS. IF I LOSE MY JOB, HOW CAN I HELP YOU FIND CHARLOTTE?
GRAB YOUR GEAR! WE'RE OFF.

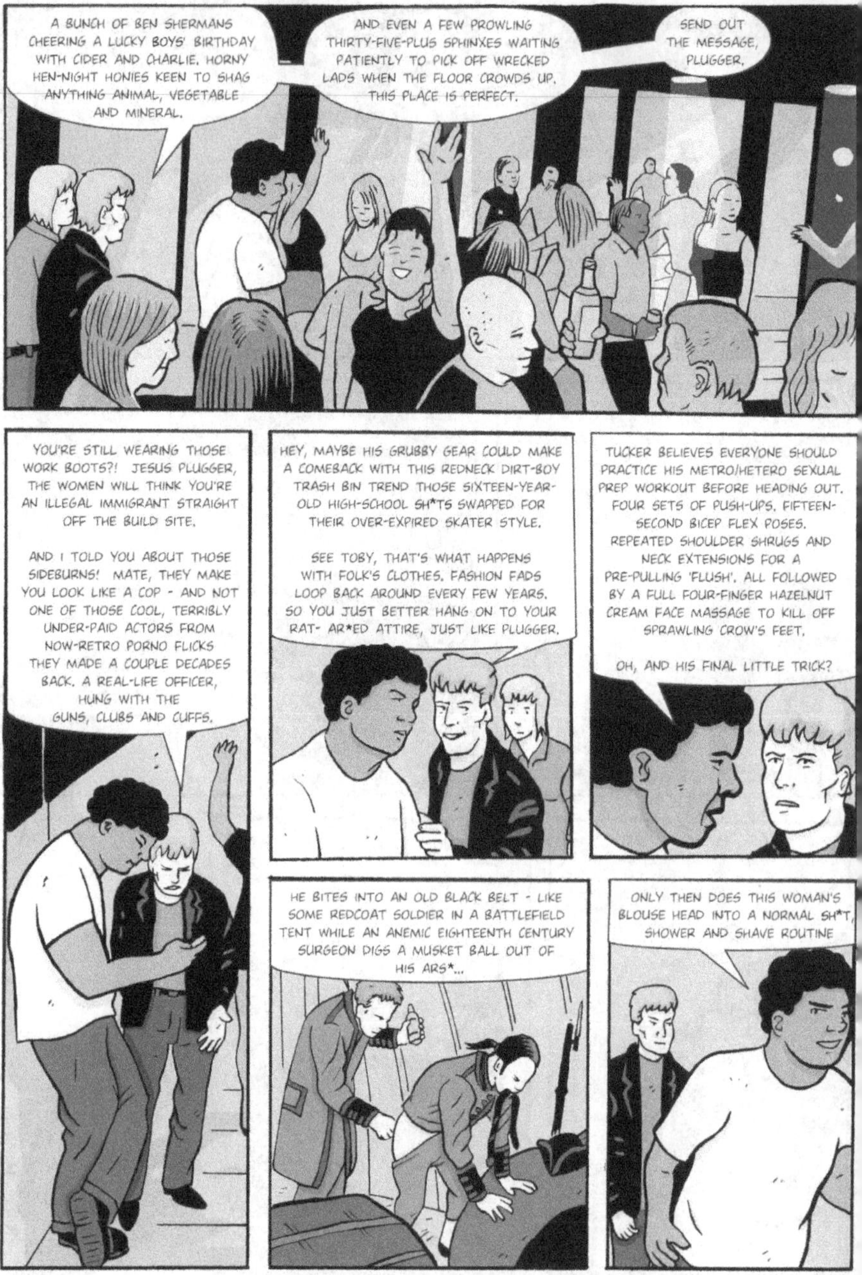
A BUNCH OF BEN SHERMANS CHEERING A LUCKY BOYS' BIRTHDAY WITH CIDER AND CHARLIE. HORNY HEN-NIGHT HONIES KEEN TO SHAG ANYTHING ANIMAL, VEGETABLE AND MINERAL.
AND EVEN A FEW PROWLING THIRTY-FIVE-PLUS SPHINXES WAITING PATIENTLY TO PICK OFF WRECKED LADS WHEN THE FLOOR CROWDS UP. THIS PLACE IS PERFECT.
SEND OUT THE MESSAGE, PLUGGER.
YOU'RE STILL WEARING THOSE WORK BOOTS?! JESUS PLUGGER, THE WOMEN WILL THINK YOU'RE AN ILLEGAL IMMIGRANT STRAIGHT OFF THE BUILD SITE.
AND I TOLD YOU ABOUT THOSE SIDEBURNS! MATE, THEY MAKE YOU LOOK LIKE A COP - AND NOT ONE OF THOSE COOL, TERRIBLY UNDER-PAID ACTORS FROM NOW-RETRO PORNO FLICKS THEY MADE A COUPLE DECADES BACK. A REAL-LIFE OFFICER, HUNG WITH THE GUNS, CLUBS AND CUFFS.
HEY, MAYBE HIS GRUBBY GEAR COULD MAKE A COMEBACK WITH THIS REDNECK DIRT-BOY TRASH BIN TREND THOSE SIXTEEN-YEAR-OLD HIGH-SCHOOL SH*TS SWAPPED FOR THEIR OVER-EXPIRED SKATER STYLE.
SEE TOBY, THAT'S WHAT HAPPENS WITH FOLK'S CLOTHES. FASHION FADS LOOP BACK AROUND EVERY FEW YEARS. SO YOU JUST BETTER HANG ON TO YOUR RAT- AR*ED ATTIRE, JUST LIKE PLUGGER.
TUCKER BELIEVES EVERYONE SHOULD PRACTICE HIS METRO/HETERO SEXUAL PREP WORKOUT BEFORE HEADING OUT. FOUR SETS OF PUSH-UPS. FIFTEEN-SECOND BICEP FLEX POSES. REPEATED SHOULDER SHRUGS AND NECK EXTENSIONS FOR A PRE-PULLING 'FLUSH'. ALL FOLLOWED BY A FULL FOUR-FINGER HAZELNUT CREAM FACE MASSAGE TO KILL OFF SPRAWLING CROW'S FEET.
OH, AND HIS FINAL LITTLE TRICK?
HE BITES INTO AN OLD BLACK BELT - LIKE SOME REDCOAT SOLDIER IN A BATTLEFIELD TENT WHILE AN ANEMIC EIGHTEENTH CENTURY SURGEON DIGS A MUSKET BALL OUT OF HIS ARS*...
ONLY THEN DOES THIS WOMAN'S BLOUSE HEAD INTO A NORMAL SH*T, SHOWER AND SHAVE ROUTINE

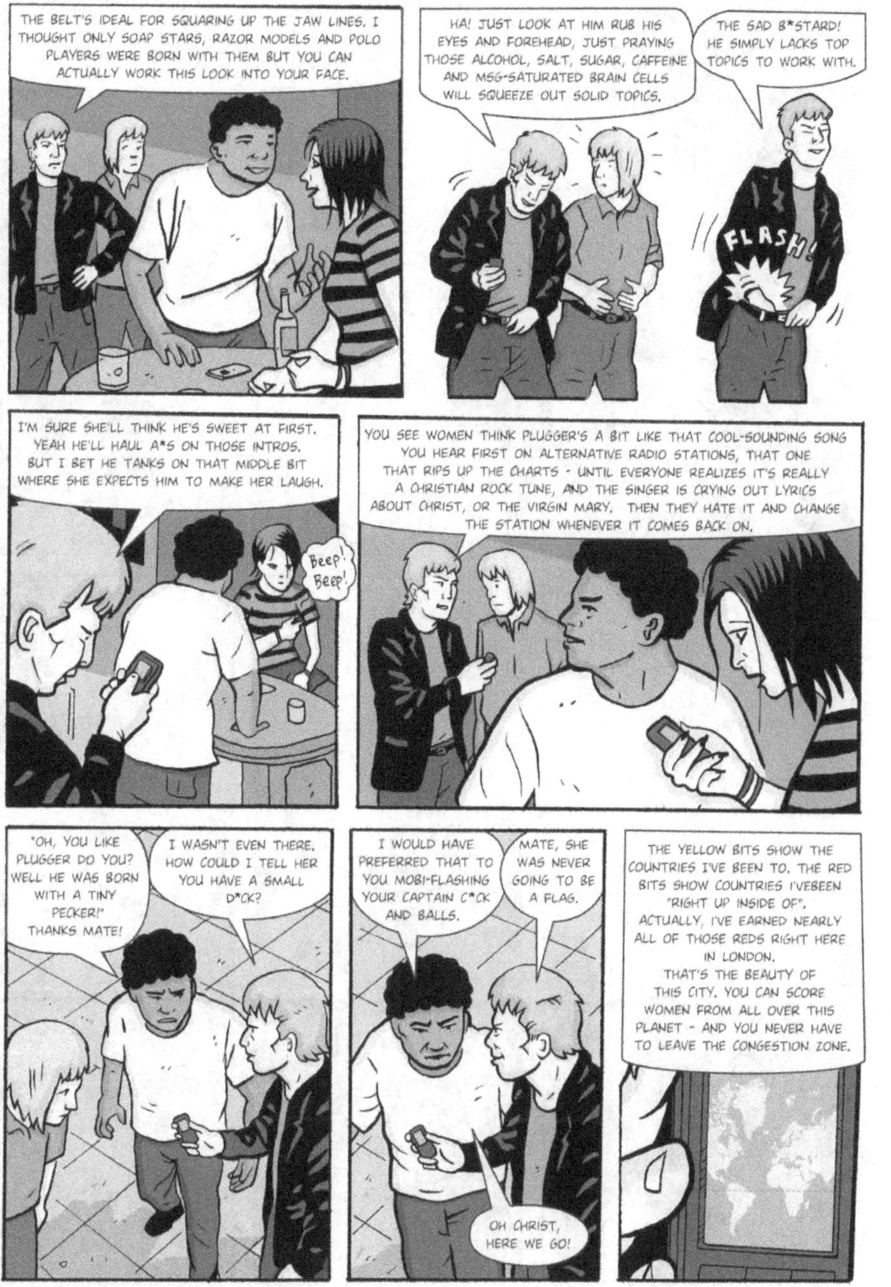
THE BELT'S IDEAL FOR SQUARING UP THE JAW LINES. I THOUGHT ONLY SOAP STARS, RAZOR MODELS AND POLO PLAYERS WERE BORN WITH THEM BUT YOU CAN ACTUALLY WORK THIS LOOK INTO YOUR FACE.
HA! JUST LOOK AT HIM RUB HIS EYES AND FOREHEAD, JUST PRAYING THOSE ALCOHOL, SALT, SUGAR, CAFFEINE AND MSG-SATURATED BRAIN CELLS WILL SQUEEZE OUT SOLID TOPICS.
THE SAD B*STARD! HE SIMPLY LACKS TOP TOPICS TO WORK WITH.
FLASH!
I'M SURE SHE'LL THINK HE'S SWEET AT FIRST. YEAH HE'LL HAUL A*S ON THOSE INTROS. BUT I BET HE TANKS ON THAT MIDDLE BIT WHERE SHE EXPECTS HIM TO MAKE HER LAUGH.
Beep! Beep!
YOU SEE WOMEN THINK PLUGGER'S A BIT LIKE THAT COOL-SOUNDING SONG YOU HEAR FIRST ON ALTERNATIVE RADIO STATIONS, THAT ONE THAT RIPS UP THE CHARTS - UNTIL EVERYONE REALIZES IT'S REALLY A CHRISTIAN ROCK TUNE, AND THE SINGER IS CRYING OUT LYRICS ABOUT CHRIST, OR THE VIRGIN MARY. THEN THEY HATE IT AND CHANGE THE STATION WHENEVER IT COMES BACK ON.
"OH, YOU LIKE PLUGGER DO YOU? WELL HE WAS BORN WITH A TINY PECKER!" THANKS MATE!
I WASN'T EVEN THERE. HOW COULD I TELL HER YOU HAVE A SMALL D*CK?
I WOULD HAVE PREFERRED THAT TO YOU MOBI-FLASHING YOUR CAPTAIN C*CK AND BALLS.
MATE, SHE WAS NEVER GOING TO BE A FLAG.
OH CHRIST, HERE WE GO!
THE YELLOW BITS SHOW THE COUNTRIES I'VE BEEN TO. THE RED BITS SHOW COUNTRIES I'VEBEEN "RIGHT UP INSIDE OF". ACTUALLY, I'VE EARNED NEARLY ALL OF THOSE REDS RIGHT HERE IN LONDON. THAT'S THE BEAUTY OF THIS CITY. YOU CAN SCORE WOMEN FROM ALL OVER THIS PLANET - AND YOU NEVER HAVE TO LEAVE THE CONGESTION ZONE.

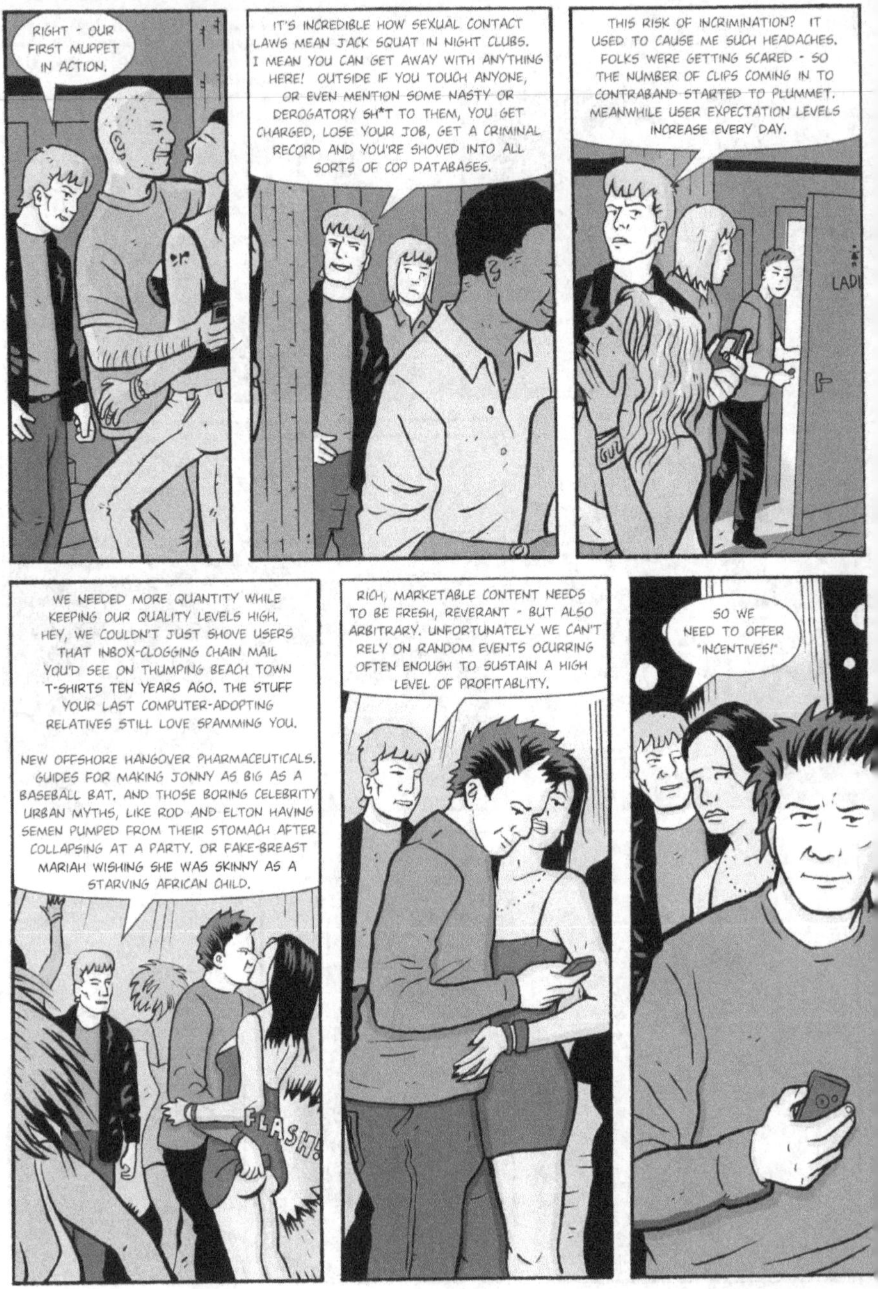
RIGHT - OUR FIRST MUPPET IN ACTION.
IT'S INCREDIBLE HOW SEXUAL CONTACT LAWS MEAN JACK SQUAT IN NIGHT CLUBS. I MEAN YOU CAN GET AWAY WITH ANYTHING HERE! OUTSIDE IF YOU TOUCH ANYONE, OR EVEN MENTION SOME NASTY OR DEROGATORY SH*T TO THEM, YOU GET CHARGED, LOSE YOUR JOB, GET A CRIMINAL RECORD AND YOU'RE SHOVED INTO ALL SORTS OF COP DATABASES.
THIS RISK OF INCRIMINATION? IT USED TO CAUSE ME SUCH HEADACHES. FOLKS WERE GETTING SCARED - SO THE NUMBER OF CLIPS COMING IN TO CONTRABAND STARTED TO PLUMMET. MEANWHILE USER EXPECTATION LEVELS INCREASE EVERY DAY.
LADI
WE NEEDED MORE QUANTITY WHILE KEEPING OUR QUALITY LEVELS HIGH. HEY, WE COULDN'T JUST SHOVE USERS THAT INBOX-CLOGGING CHAIN MAIL YOU'D SEE ON THUMPING BEACH TOWN T-SHIRTS TEN YEARS AGO. THE STUFF YOUR LAST COMPUTER-ADOPTING RELATIVES STILL LOVE SPAMMING YOU.
NEW OFFSHORE HANGOVER PHARMACEUTICALS. GUIDES FOR MAKING JONNY AS BIG AS A BASEBALL BAT. AND THOSE BORING CELEBRITY URBAN MYTHS, LIKE ROD AND ELTON HAVING SEMEN PUMPED FROM THEIR STOMACH AFTER COLLAPSING AT A PARTY. OR FAKE-BREAST MARIAH WISHING SHE WAS SKINNY AS A STARVING AFRICAN CHILD.
FLASH!
RICH, MARKETABLE CONTENT NEEDS TO BE FRESH, REVERANT - BUT ALSO ARBITRARY. UNFORTUNATELY WE CAN'T RELY ON RANDOM EVENTS OCURRING OFTEN ENOUGH TO SUSTAIN A HIGH LEVEL OF PROFITABLITY.
SO WE NEED TO OFFER "INCENTIVES!"

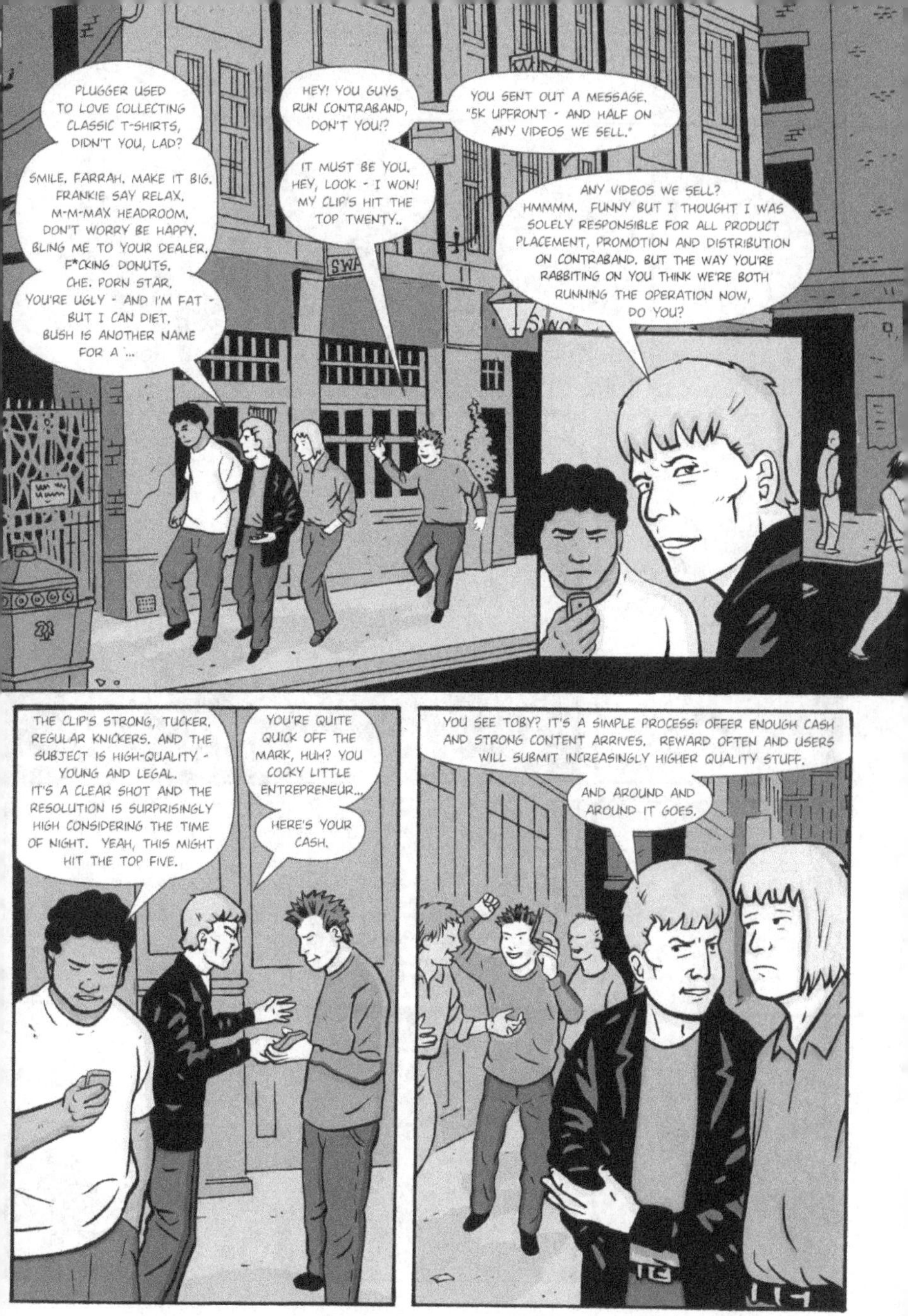
PLUGGER USED TO LOVE COLLECTING CLASSIC T-SHIRTS, DIDN'T YOU, LAD?
SMILE. FARRAH. MAKE IT BIG. FRANKIE SAY RELAX. M-M-MAX HEADROOM. DON'T WORRY BE HAPPY. BLING ME TO YOUR DEALER. F*CKING DONUTS. CHE. PORN STAR. YOU'RE UGLY - AND I'M FAT - BUT I CAN DIET. BUSH IS ANOTHER NAME FOR A ...
HEY! YOU GUYS RUN CONTRABAND, DON'T YOU!?
IT MUST BE YOU. HEY, LOOK - I WON! MY CLIP'S HIT THE TOP TWENTY..
YOU SENT OUT A MESSAGE. "5K UPFRONT - AND HALF ON ANY VIDEOS WE SELL."
ANY VIDEOS WE SELL? HMMMM. FUNNY BUT I THOUGHT I WAS SOLELY RESPONSIBLE FOR ALL PRODUCT PLACEMENT, PROMOTION AND DISTRIBUTION ON CONTRABAND. BUT THE WAY YOU'RE RABBITING ON YOU THINK WE'RE BOTH RUNNING THE OPERATION NOW, DO YOU?
THE CLIP'S STRONG, TUCKER. REGULAR KNICKERS. AND THE SUBJECT IS HIGH-QUALITY - YOUNG AND LEGAL. IT'S A CLEAR SHOT AND THE RESOLUTION IS SURPRISINGLY HIGH CONSIDERING THE TIME OF NIGHT. YEAH, THIS MIGHT HIT THE TOP FIVE.
YOU'RE QUITE QUICK OFF THE MARK, HUH? YOU COCKY LITTLE ENTREPRENEUR...
HERE'S YOUR CASH.
YOU SEE TOBY? IT'S A SIMPLE PROCESS: OFFER ENOUGH CASH AND STRONG CONTENT ARRIVES. REWARD OFTEN AND USERS WILL SUBMIT INCREASINGLY HIGHER QUALITY STUFF.
AND AROUND AND AROUND IT GOES.

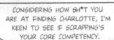

SO FELLA, YOU KEEN TO TREBLE YOUR WINNINGS?

SH*T YEAH! BUT THE PLACE IS DEAD. NOT SURE I'LL EXTRACT MUCH MORE VIDEO OUTTA HERE....

NO, YOUR UPSKIRTING SKILLS ARE NO LONGER REQUIRED. THIS NEW PROPOSITION IS VERY SIMPLE INDEED.

IF YOU CAN DROP TOBY, WE'LL DROP YOU AN EXTRA TEN GRAND INTO YOUR MPAY ACCOUNT.

?!

CONSIDERING HOW SH*T YOU ARE AT FINDING CHARLOTTE, I'M KEEN TO SEE IF SCRAPPING'S YOUR CORE COMPETENCY.

I'LL APOLOGIZE NOW BECAUSE WHEN I KNOCK YOU FOR SIX, I'LL FEEL MODERATELY BAD. BUT MATE, I'VE BEEN IN FIGHTS FOR NOTHING, LET ALONE 10 GRAND. OFFER ACCEPTED!

PLEASE, TUCKER! THIS ISN'T ON.

RELAX, YOU'RE GONNA COME OUT ON TOP. TELL ME, WHEN'S THE LAST TIME YOU WON A FIGHT?

BY THE WAY THERE'S ONE RULE: THERE'S ONE WEAPON, AND TOBY GETS IT.

WHAT? THAT'S BOLLOCKS! SCREW THIS SH*T!

COME ON TUCKER, HE'S BAILING...

WRONG! HE ACCEPTED THE OFFER. A VERBAL CONTRACT IS BINDING SO HE MUST EXECUTE ON HIS REQUIREMENTS BASED ON THE AGREED TERMS.

HERE, TAKE YOUR MONEY BACK!

BE CALM, FRIEND. HERE'S WHAT'S GONNA HAPPEN: TOBY'LL BOUNCE THIS BAT OFF YOUR SKULL A FEW TIMES. SURE, IT'LL PROBABLY HURT - AND YOU MIGHT FEEL STUPID FOR A FEW WEEKS - BUT DON'T WORRY, NEW BRAIN CELLS DO RE-GENERATE TO REPLACE THOSE KILLED OFF. THAT'S WHAT THIS TIDY NURSE SARAH TOLD ME BACK IN AFGHANISTAN. YOU KNOW, THIS SINGLE FACT CHANGED MY PHILOSOPHY ABOUT BOOZING FOREVER. SEE, MY FOLKS SCARED ME INTO BELIEVING THE OPPOSITE WAS TRUE.

SWING THE F*CKING BAT NOW - OR I HAND IT TO HIM!

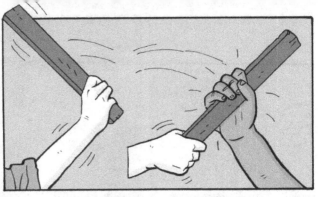

WOULD YOU LOOK AT PLUGGER. GLARING. STARING. JUDGING. HIS LEFT EYEBROW HALFWAY UP HIS HAIRLINE.

HEY, HE KIND OF LOOKS LIKE THAT WRESTLER WHO PUMPED OUT COMPUTER-GENERATED FLICKS ABOUT PHANTOMS OR MUMMIES A DECADE BACK.

SURE THOSE MOVIES LOOKED REAL BACK THEN BUT WITH THE ADVENT OF VISUAL TECHNOLOGY, THEY'RE ALL PRETTY PHONY-LOOKING NOW, EH?

YOU KNOW MY COUSIN LOVED STEROID BOY SO MUCH HE CHANGED HIS MOBILE MAIL TO "THEGRANITEHEAD", BUT HE THEN HAD TO ADD "_2239" ON THE END. NOW THERE'S ONE POPULAR GUY!

SOMETIMES IT'S GOOD TO UNDERSTAND HOW OTHERS PERCEIVE YOU. MY ADVICE? READ THE OUTGOING TEXTS IN YOUR OUTBOX AND YOU'LL REALIZE JUST HOW MUCH OF PR*CK YOU CAN BE TO PEOPLE.

SHUT UP! JUST SHUT THE F*CK UP!

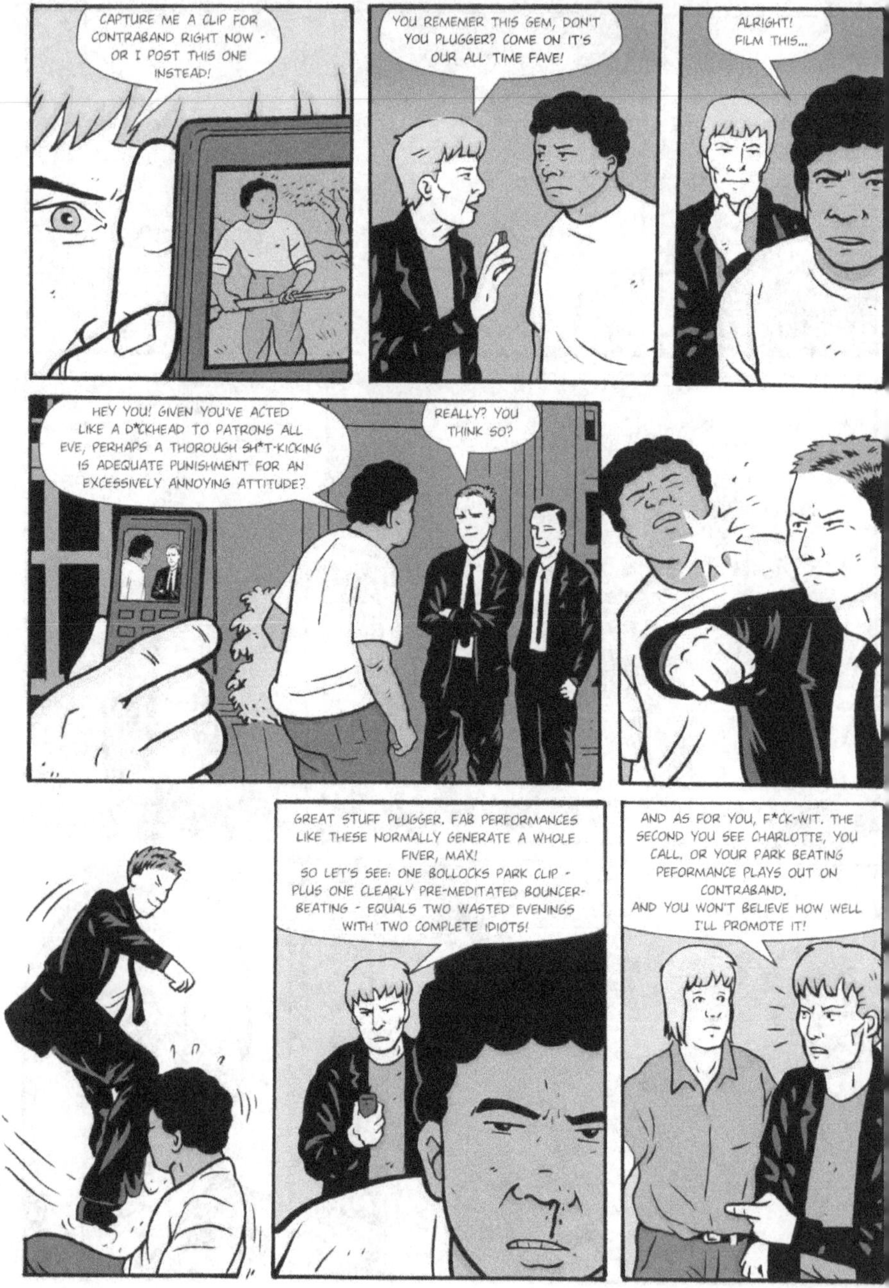
CAPTURE ME A CLIP FOR CONTRABAND RIGHT NOW - OR I POST THIS ONE INSTEAD!
YOU REMEMER THIS GEM, DON'T YOU PLUGGER? COME ON IT'S OUR ALL TIME FAVE!
ALRIGHT! FILM THIS...
HEY YOU! GIVEN YOU'VE ACTED LIKE A D*CKHEAD TO PATRONS ALL EVE, PERHAPS A THOROUGH SH*T-KICKING IS ADEQUATE PUNISHMENT FOR AN EXCESSIVELY ANNOYING ATTITUDE?
REALLY? YOU THINK SO?
GREAT STUFF PLUGGER. FAB PERFORMANCES LIKE THESE NORMALLY GENERATE A WHOLE FIVER, MAX!
SO LET'S SEE: ONE BOLLOCKS PARK CLIP - PLUS ONE CLEARLY PRE-MEDITATED BOUNCER-BEATING - EQUALS TWO WASTED EVENINGS WITH TWO COMPLETE IDIOTS!
AND AS FOR YOU, F*CK-WIT. THE SECOND YOU SEE CHARLOTTE, YOU CALL. OR YOUR PARK BEATING PEFORMANCE PLAYS OUT ON CONTRABAND.
AND YOU WON'T BELIEVE HOW WELL I'LL PROMOTE IT!

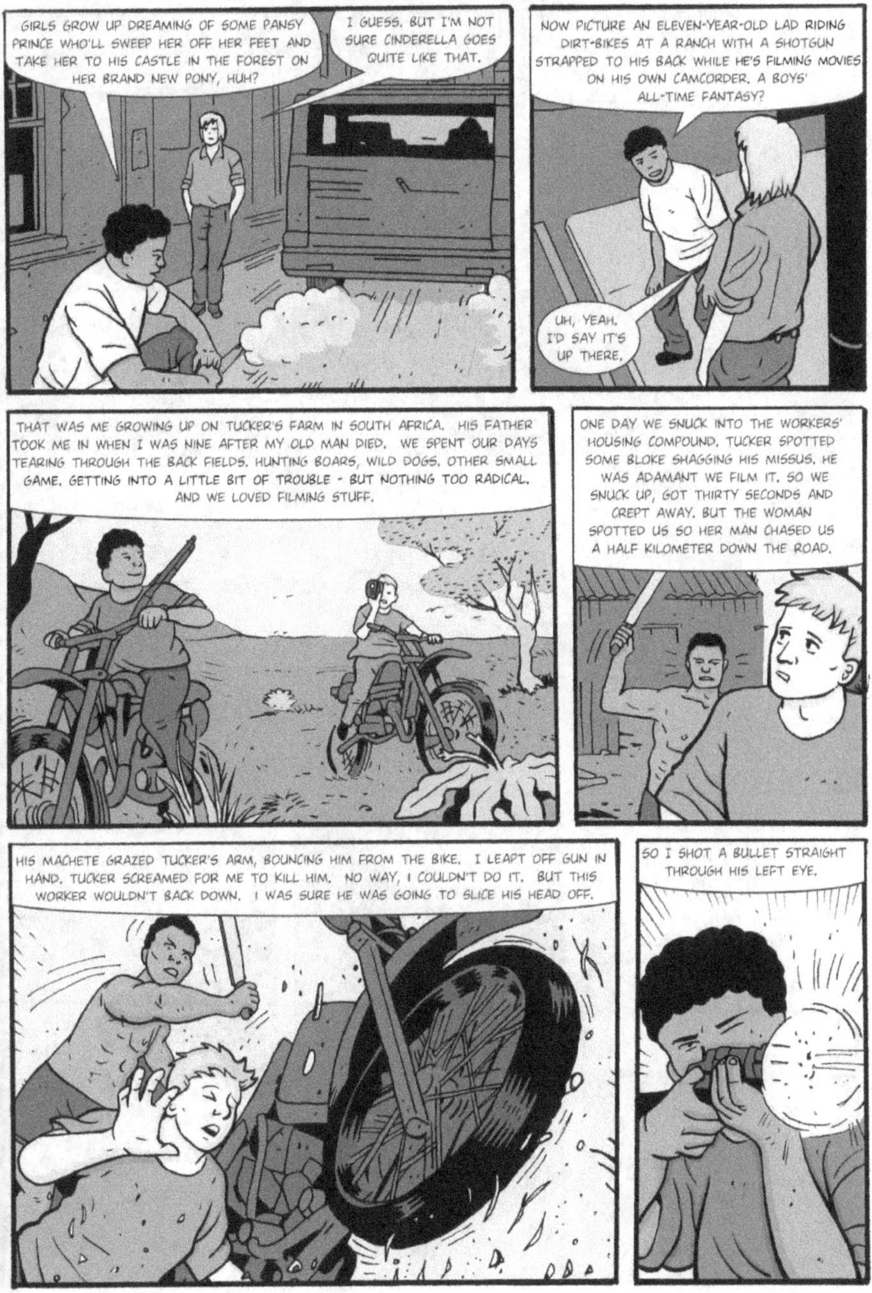
GIRLS GROW UP DREAMING OF SOME PANSY PRINCE WHO'LL SWEEP HER OFF HER FEET AND TAKE HER TO HIS CASTLE IN THE FOREST ON HER BRAND NEW PONY, HUH?
I GUESS. BUT I'M NOT SURE CINDERELLA GOES QUITE LIKE THAT.
NOW PICTURE AN ELEVEN-YEAR-OLD LAD RIDING DIRT-BIKES AT A RANCH WITH A SHOTGUN STRAPPED TO HIS BACK WHILE HE'S FILMING MOVIES ON HIS OWN CAMCORDER. A BOYS' ALL-TIME FANTASY?
UH, YEAH. I'D SAY IT'S UP THERE.
THAT WAS ME GROWING UP ON TUCKER'S FARM IN SOUTH AFRICA. HIS FATHER TOOK ME IN WHEN I WAS NINE AFTER MY OLD MAN DIED. WE SPENT OUR DAYS TEARING THROUGH THE BACK FIELDS. HUNTING BOARS, WILD DOGS, OTHER SMALL GAME. GETTING INTO A LITTLE BIT OF TROUBLE - BUT NOTHING TOO RADICAL. AND WE LOVED FILMING STUFF.
ONE DAY WE SNUCK INTO THE WORKERS' HOUSING COMPOUND. TUCKER SPOTTED SOME BLOKE SHAGGING HIS MISSUS. HE WAS ADAMANT WE FILM IT. SO WE SNUCK UP, GOT THIRTY SECONDS AND CREPT AWAY. BUT THE WOMAN SPOTTED US SO HER MAN CHASED US A HALF KILOMETER DOWN THE ROAD.
HIS MACHETE GRAZED TUCKER'S ARM, BOUNCING HIM FROM THE BIKE. I LEAPT OFF GUN IN HAND. TUCKER SCREAMED FOR ME TO KILL HIM. NO WAY, I COULDN'T DO IT. BUT THIS WORKER WOULDN'T BACK DOWN. I WAS SURE HE WAS GOING TO SLICE HIS HEAD OFF.
SO I SHOT A BULLET STRAIGHT THROUGH HIS LEFT EYE.

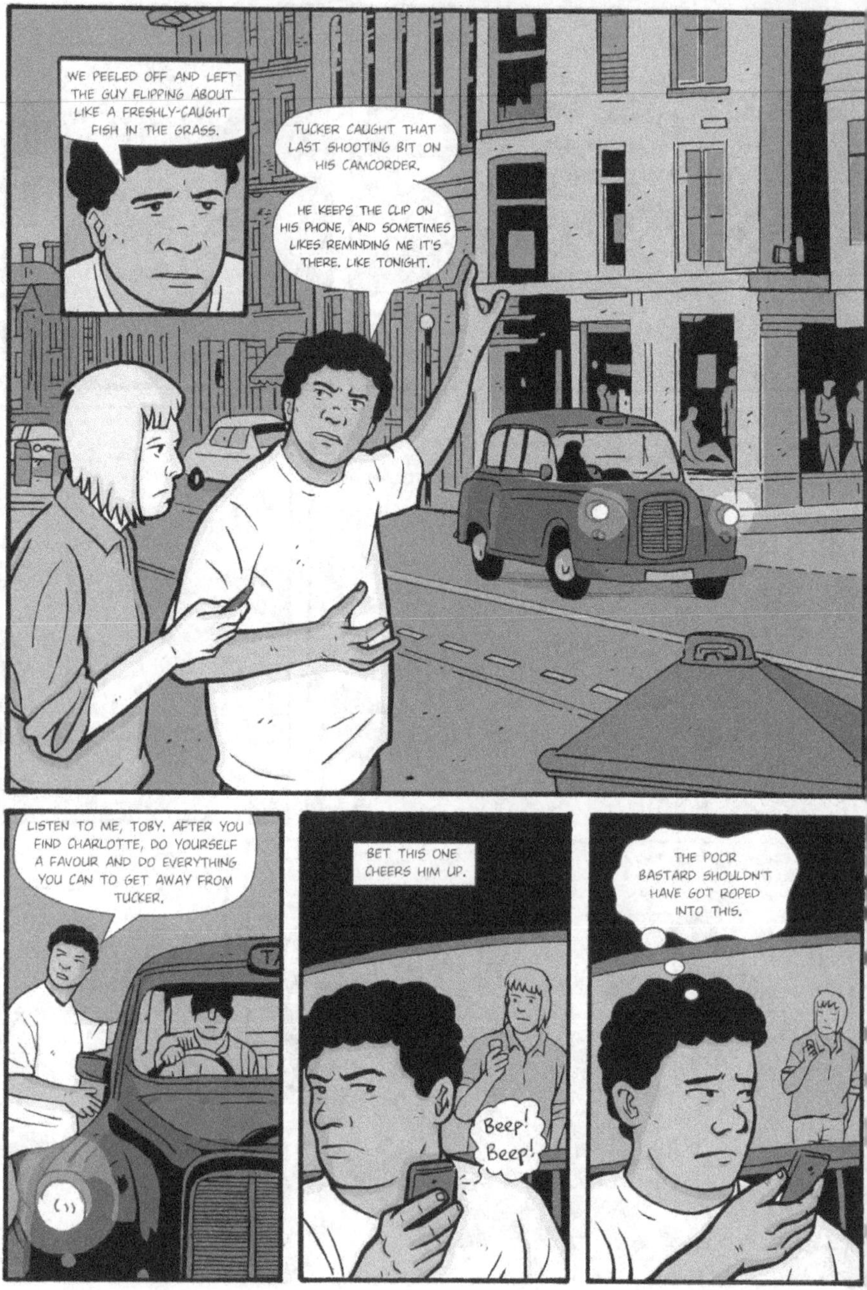
WE PEELED OFF AND LEFT THE GUY FLIPPING ABOUT LIKE A FRESHLY-CAUGHT FISH IN THE GRASS.
TUCKER CAUGHT THAT LAST SHOOTING BIT ON HIS CAMCORDER.
HE KEEPS THE CLIP ON HIS PHONE, AND SOMETIMES LIKES REMINDING ME IT'S THERE. LIKE TONIGHT.
LISTEN TO ME, TOBY. AFTER YOU FIND CHARLOTTE, DO YOURSELF A FAVOUR AND DO EVERYTHING YOU CAN TO GET AWAY FROM TUCKER.
BET THIS ONE CHEERS HIM UP.
Beep! Beep!
THE POOR BASTARD SHOULDN'T HAVE GOT ROPED INTO THIS.

eight

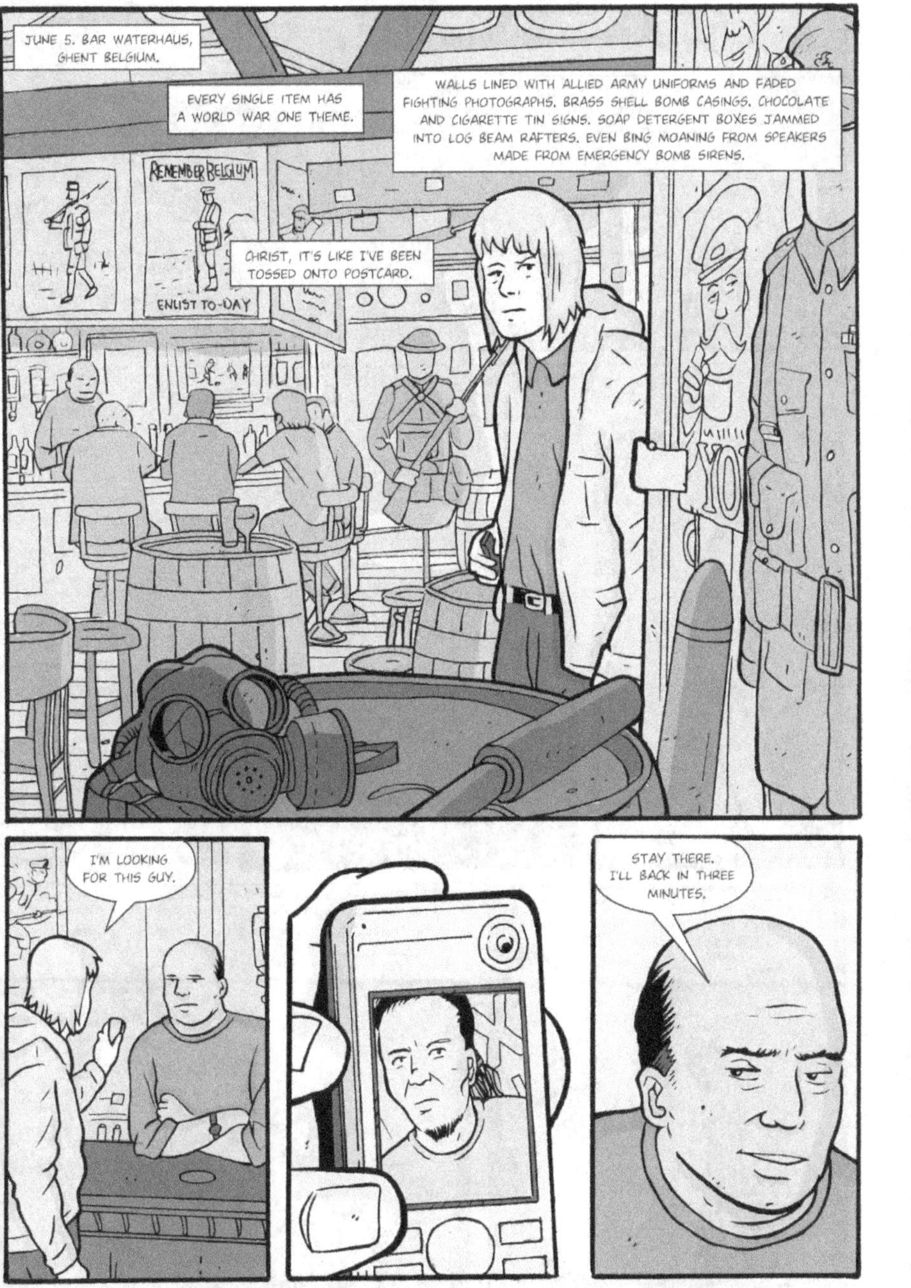

JUNE 5. BAR WATERHAUS, GHENT BELGIUM.
EVERY SINGLE ITEM HAS A WORLD WAR ONE THEME.
WALLS LINED WITH ALLIED ARMY UNIFORMS AND FADED FIGHTING PHOTOGRAPHS. BRASS SHELL BOMB CASINGS. CHOCOLATE AND CIGARETTE TIN SIGNS. SOAP DETERGENT BOXES JAMMED INTO LOG BEAM RAFTERS. EVEN BING MOANING FROM SPEAKERS MADE FROM EMERGENCY BOMB SIRENS.
REMEMBER BELGIUM
ENLIST TO-DAY
CHRIST, IT'S LIKE I'VE BEEN TOSSED ONTO POSTCARD.
I'M LOOKING FOR THIS GUY.
STAY THERE. I'LL BACK IN THREE MINUTES.

Beep! Beep!

SHE'S STILL NUMBER ONE.

1. charlotte's afghan capture 1029k

2. dozen dead albanians dumped from dover trailer 566k

3. killed korean too keen to see southern cousin 439k

4. incarcerated ar*hole's 3rd world hoax-fest 390k

5. vultures pluck, pick n' drop from indian funeral pyre 154k

QUITE A STRONG CONTENDER CRAWLING INTO NUMBER FOUR, DARLING!

SEEMS SOME ANONYMOUS PRISONER SMUGGLED A PHONE INTO HIS CELL. WARDENS ARE SHAKING MUGS AND FLIPPING MATTRESSES IN PENETEN-TARIES ALL OVER EUROPE LOOKING FOR HIM.

USUALLY TRAINED DOGS SNIFF OUT WIRELESSS DEVICES BUT THIS LIFER'S MISSUS SHOVED A TINY MOBILE INSIDE A DEAD PIGEON BEFORE TOSSING IT OVER THE WALL. THEN THE CHUMP SHOVED IT UP HIS A*S, BUT I GUESS THE GUARDS FORGOT TO X-RAY HIM.

THIS GUY LOVES HITTING P*SS POOR FOLKS WITH HOAX TEXT MESSAGES. RENEGADE MELONS INJECTED WITH AIDS IN QATAR, MAD PIG DISEASE SPREADING THROUGH CHINA.

HE'S EVEN CONVINCED A FEW HUNDRED THOUSAND PEASANTS THEY'VE CAUGHT A SICKLY VIRUS WHICH WAS TRANSMITTED VIA THEIR MOBILE.

SUCH MORONS!

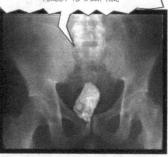

ACTUALLY IDIOT, THE BACTERIA JUMPING FROM THE MOUTH INTO A PHONE RECEIVER MAKES ONE'S MOBILE FILTHIER THAN A PUBLIC LOO.

OH REALLY? WELL YOU BETTER HOPE THIS CHAPS' POPULARITY DOESN'T SPREAD BEFORE JARVIS SENDS THAT MEMORY CHIP. BECAUSE THE SECOND YOUR CLIP SLIPS INTO SECOND, YOU'RE NO LONGER USEFUL.

SO YOU'RE DEAD!

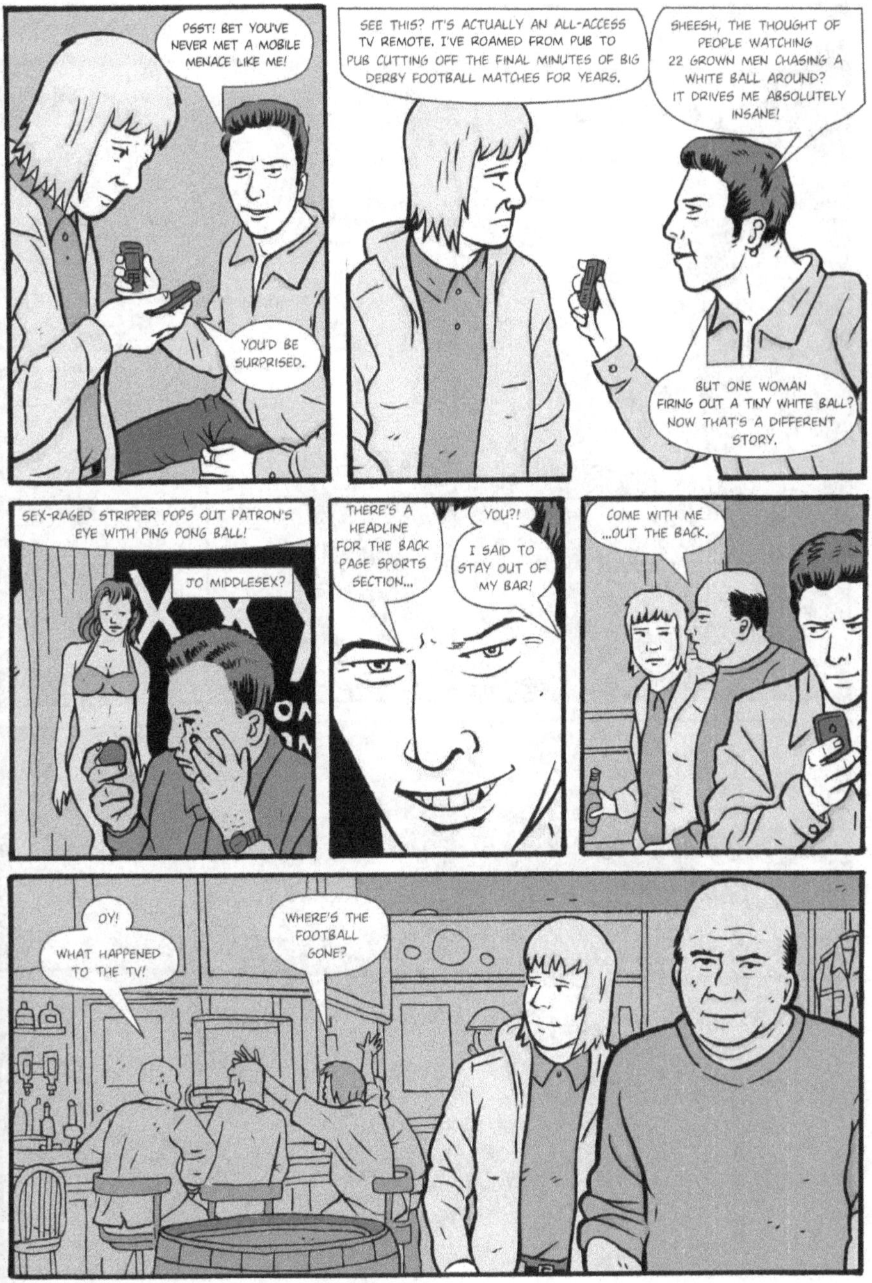
PSST! BET YOU'VE NEVER MET A MOBILE MENACE LIKE ME!
YOU'D BE SURPRISED.
SEE THIS? IT'S ACTUALLY AN ALL-ACCESS TV REMOTE. I'VE ROAMED FROM PUB TO PUB CUTTING OFF THE FINAL MINUTES OF BIG DERBY FOOTBALL MATCHES FOR YEARS.
SHEESH, THE THOUGHT OF PEOPLE WATCHING 22 GROWN MEN CHASING A WHITE BALL AROUND? IT DRIVES ME ABSOLUTELY INSANE!
BUT ONE WOMAN FIRING OUT A TINY WHITE BALL? NOW THAT'S A DIFFERENT STORY.
SEX-RAGED STRIPPER POPS OUT PATRON'S EYE WITH PING PONG BALL!
JO MIDDLESEX?
THERE'S A HEADLINE FOR THE BACK PAGE SPORTS SECTION...
YOU?!
I SAID TO STAY OUT OF MY BAR!
COME WITH ME ...OUT THE BACK.
OY!
WHAT HAPPENED TO THE TV!
WHERE'S THE FOOTBALL GONE?

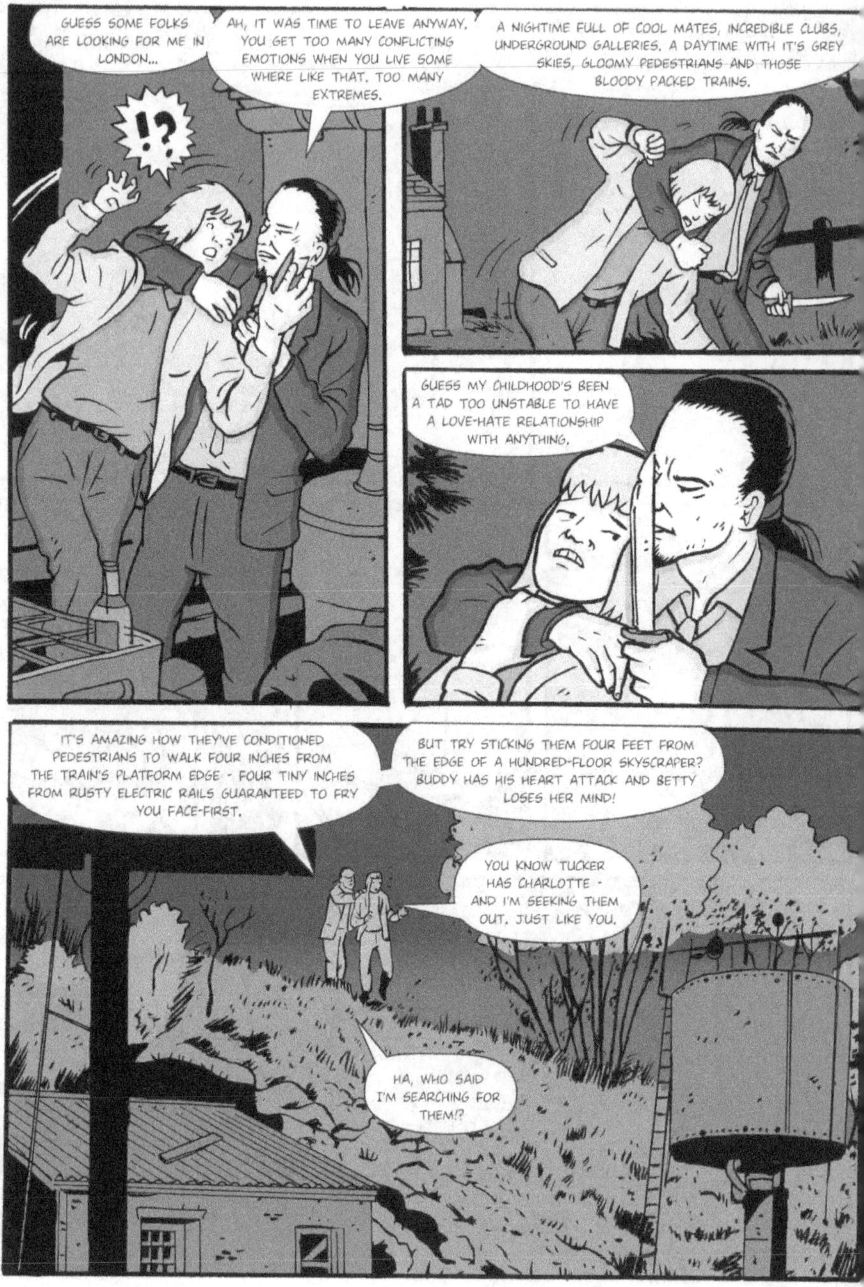

GUESS SOME FOLKS ARE LOOKING FOR ME IN LONDON...
!?
AH, IT WAS TIME TO LEAVE ANYWAY. YOU GET TOO MANY CONFLICTING EMOTIONS WHEN YOU LIVE SOME WHERE LIKE THAT. TOO MANY EXTREMES.
A NIGHTIME FULL OF COOL MATES, INCREDIBLE CLUBS, UNDERGROUND GALLERIES. A DAYTIME WITH IT'S GREY SKIES, GLOOMY PEDESTRIANS AND THOSE BLOODY PACKED TRAINS.
GUESS MY CHILDHOOD'S BEEN A TAD TOO UNSTABLE TO HAVE A LOVE-HATE RELATIONSHIP WITH ANYTHING.
IT'S AMAZING HOW THEY'VE CONDITIONED PEDESTRIANS TO WALK FOUR INCHES FROM THE TRAIN'S PLATFORM EDGE - FOUR TINY INCHES FROM RUSTY ELECTRIC RAILS GUARANTEED TO FRY YOU FACE-FIRST.
BUT TRY STICKING THEM FOUR FEET FROM THE EDGE OF A HUNDRED-FLOOR SKYSCRAPER? BUDDY HAS HIS HEART ATTACK AND BETTY LOSES HER MIND!
YOU KNOW TUCKER HAS CHARLOTTE - AND I'M SEEKING THEM OUT. JUST LIKE YOU.
HA, WHO SAID I'M SEARCHING FOR THEM!?

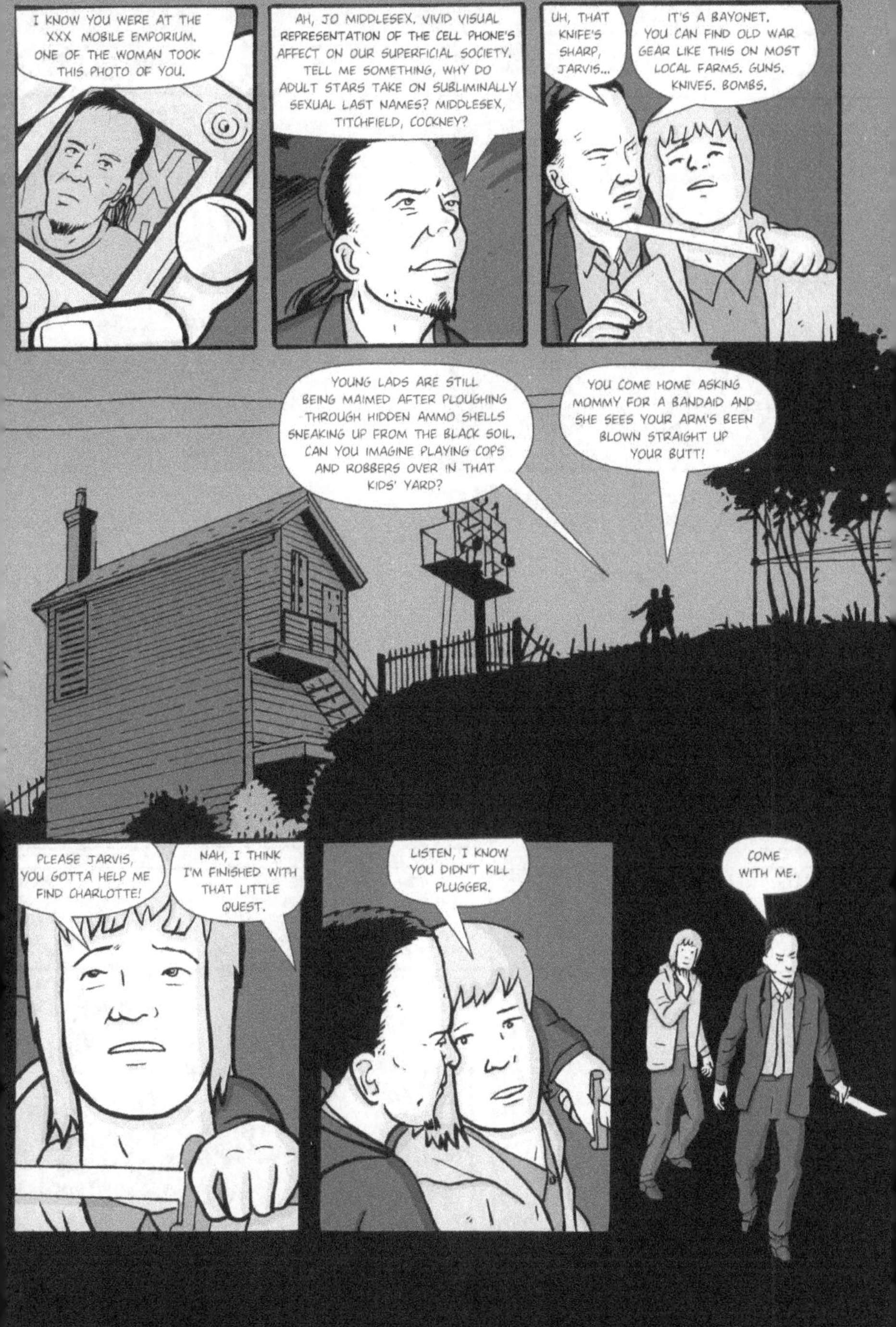
I KNOW YOU WERE AT THE XXX MOBILE EMPORIUM. ONE OF THE WOMAN TOOK THIS PHOTO OF YOU.
AH, JO MIDDLESEX. VIVID VISUAL REPRESENTATION OF THE CELL PHONE'S AFFECT ON OUR SUPERFICIAL SOCIETY. TELL ME SOMETHING, WHY DO ADULT STARS TAKE ON SUBLIMINALLY SEXUAL LAST NAMES? MIDDLESEX, TITCHFIELD, COCKNEY?
UH, THAT KNIFE'S SHARP, JARVIS...
IT'S A BAYONET. YOU CAN FIND OLD WAR GEAR LIKE THIS ON MOST LOCAL FARMS. GUNS. KNIVES. BOMBS.
YOUNG LADS ARE STILL BEING MAIMED AFTER PLOUGHING THROUGH HIDDEN AMMO SHELLS SNEAKING UP FROM THE BLACK SOIL. CAN YOU IMAGINE PLAYING COPS AND ROBBERS OVER IN THAT KIDS' YARD?
YOU COME HOME ASKING MOMMY FOR A BANDAID AND SHE SEES YOUR ARM'S BEEN BLOWN STRAIGHT UP YOUR BUTT!
PLEASE JARVIS, YOU GOTTA HELP ME FIND CHARLOTTE!
NAH, I THINK I'M FINISHED WITH THAT LITTLE QUEST.
LISTEN, I KNOW YOU DIDN'T KILL PLUGGER.
COME WITH ME.

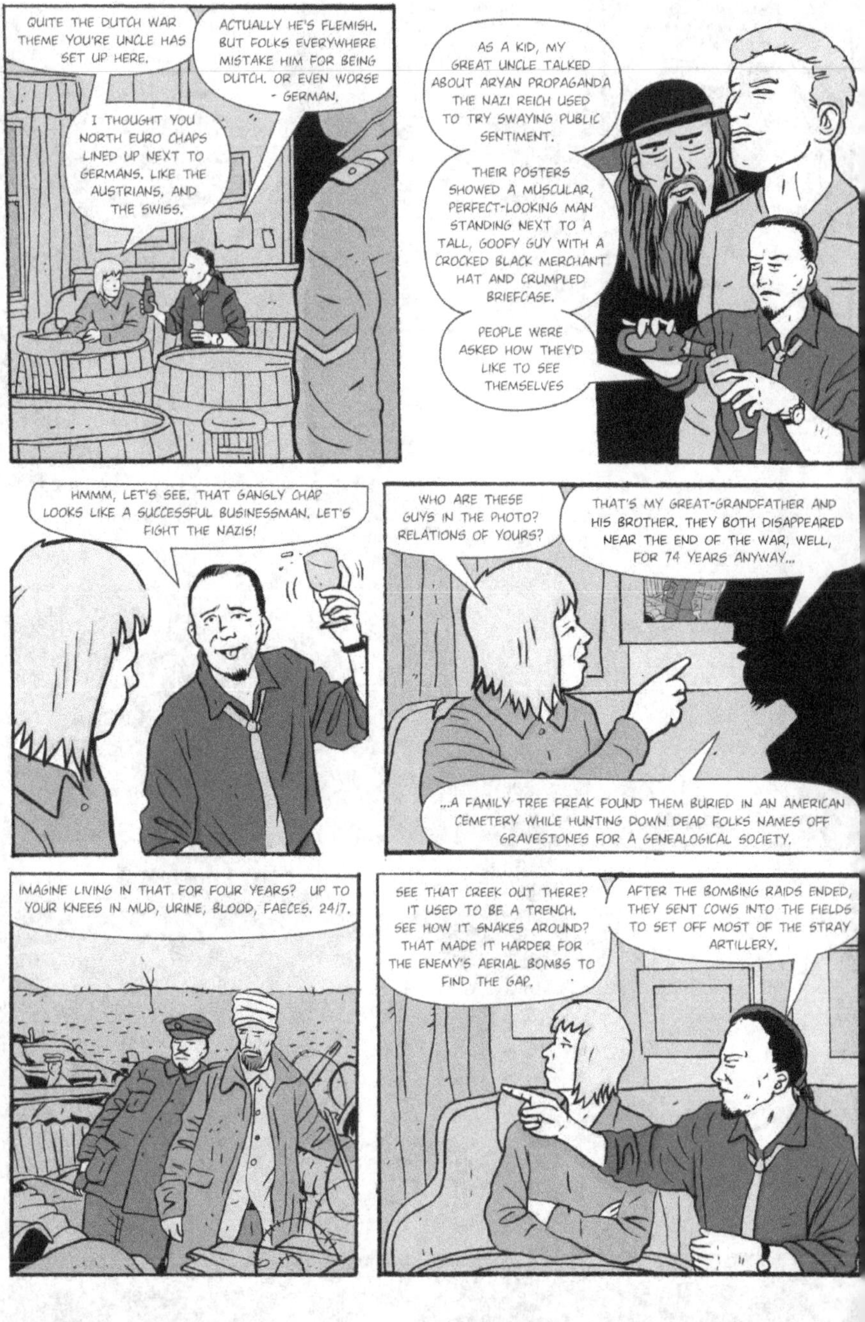
QUITE THE DUTCH WAR THEME YOU'RE UNCLE HAS SET UP HERE.
ACTUALLY HE'S FLEMISH. BUT FOLKS EVERYWHERE MISTAKE HIM FOR BEING DUTCH. OR EVEN WORSE - GERMAN.
I THOUGHT YOU NORTH EURO CHAPS LINED UP NEXT TO GERMANS. LIKE THE AUSTRIANS. AND THE SWISS.
AS A KID, MY GREAT UNCLE TALKED ABOUT ARYAN PROPAGANDA THE NAZI REICH USED TO TRY SWAYING PUBLIC SENTIMENT.
THEIR POSTERS SHOWED A MUSCULAR, PERFECT-LOOKING MAN STANDING NEXT TO A TALL, GOOFY GUY WITH A CROCKED BLACK MERCHANT HAT AND CRUMPLED BRIEFCASE.
PEOPLE WERE ASKED HOW THEY'D LIKE TO SEE THEMSELVES
HMMM, LET'S SEE. THAT GANGLY CHAP LOOKS LIKE A SUCCESSFUL BUSINESSMAN. LET'S FIGHT THE NAZIS!
WHO ARE THESE GUYS IN THE PHOTO? RELATIONS OF YOURS?
THAT'S MY GREAT-GRANDFATHER AND HIS BROTHER. THEY BOTH DISAPPEARED NEAR THE END OF THE WAR, WELL, FOR 74 YEARS ANYWAY...
...A FAMILY TREE FREAK FOUND THEM BURIED IN AN AMERICAN CEMETERY WHILE HUNTING DOWN DEAD FOLKS NAMES OFF GRAVESTONES FOR A GENEALOGICAL SOCIETY.
IMAGINE LIVING IN THAT FOR FOUR YEARS? UP TO YOUR KNEES IN MUD, URINE, BLOOD, FAECES. 24/7.
SEE THAT CREEK OUT THERE? IT USED TO BE A TRENCH. SEE HOW IT SNAKES AROUND? THAT MADE IT HARDER FOR THE ENEMY'S AERIAL BOMBS TO FIND THE GAP.
AFTER THE BOMBING RAIDS ENDED, THEY SENT COWS INTO THE FIELDS TO SET OFF MOST OF THE STRAY ARTILLERY.

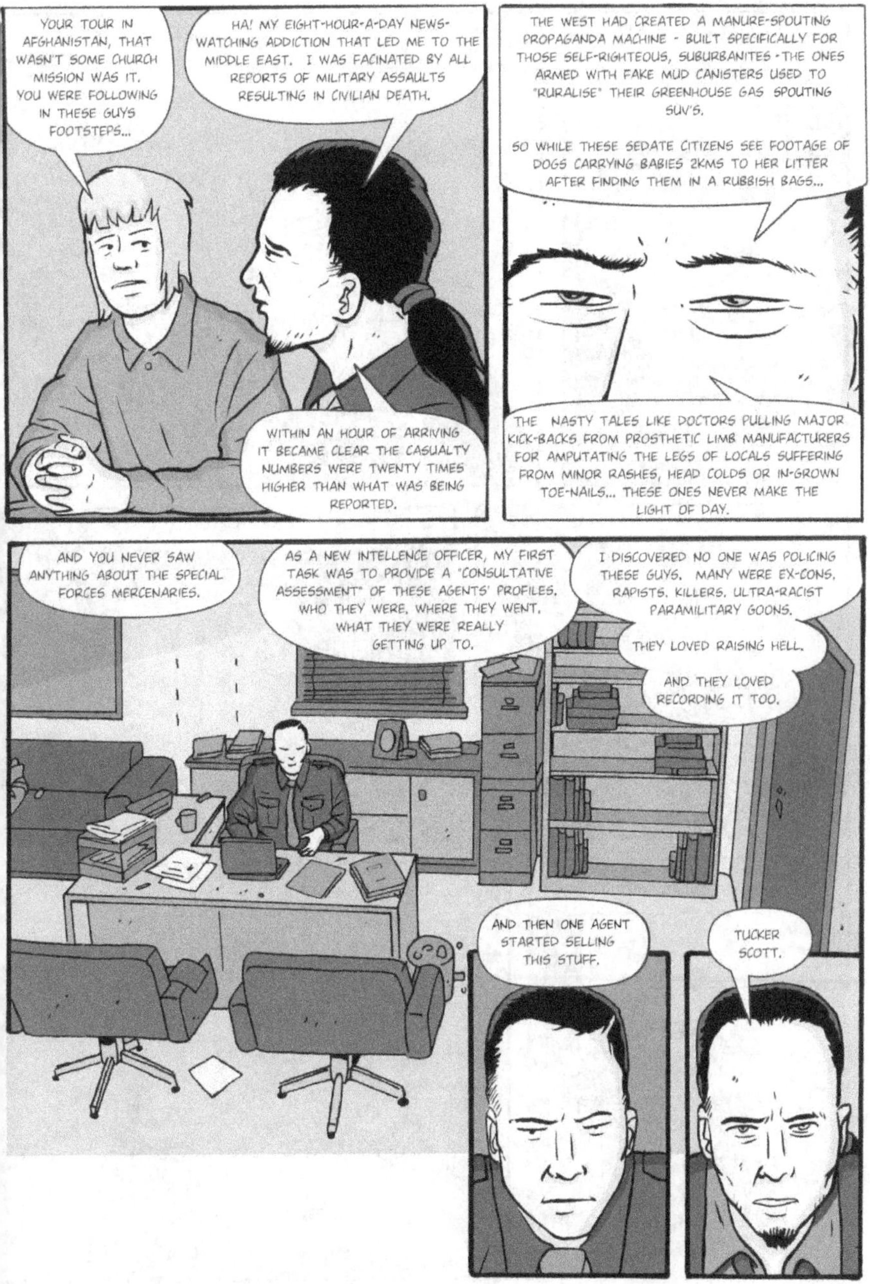
YOUR TOUR IN AFGHANISTAN, THAT WASN'T SOME CHURCH MISSION WAS IT. YOU WERE FOLLOWING IN THESE GUYS FOOTSTEPS...
HA! MY EIGHT-HOUR-A-DAY NEWS-WATCHING ADDICTION THAT LED ME TO THE MIDDLE EAST. I WAS FACINATED BY ALL REPORTS OF MILITARY ASSAULTS RESULTING IN CIVILIAN DEATH.
WITHIN AN HOUR OF ARRIVING IT BECAME CLEAR THE CASUALTY NUMBERS WERE TWENTY TIMES HIGHER THAN WHAT WAS BEING REPORTED.
THE WEST HAD CREATED A MANURE-SPOUTING PROPAGANDA MACHINE - BUILT SPECIFICALLY FOR THOSE SELF-RIGHTEOUS, SUBURBANITES - THE ONES ARMED WITH FAKE MUD CANISTERS USED TO "RURALISE" THEIR GREENHOUSE GAS SPOUTING SUV'S.
SO WHILE THESE SEDATE CITIZENS SEE FOOTAGE OF DOGS CARRYING BABIES 2KMS TO HER LITTER AFTER FINDING THEM IN A RUBBISH BAGS...
THE NASTY TALES LIKE DOCTORS PULLING MAJOR KICK-BACKS FROM PROSTHETIC LIMB MANUFACTURERS FOR AMPUTATING THE LEGS OF LOCALS SUFFERING FROM MINOR RASHES, HEAD COLDS OR IN-GROWN TOE-NAILS... THESE ONES NEVER MAKE THE LIGHT OF DAY.
AND YOU NEVER SAW ANYTHING ABOUT THE SPECIAL FORCES MERCENARIES.
AS A NEW INTELLENCE OFFICER, MY FIRST TASK WAS TO PROVIDE A "CONSULTATIVE ASSESSMENT" OF THESE AGENTS' PROFILES, WHO THEY WERE, WHERE THEY WENT, WHAT THEY WERE REALLY GETTING UP TO.
I DISCOVERED NO ONE WAS POLICING THESE GUYS. MANY WERE EX-CONS, RAPISTS, KILLERS, ULTRA-RACIST PARAMILITARY GOONS.
THEY LOVED RAISING HELL.
AND THEY LOVED RECORDING IT TOO.
AND THEN ONE AGENT STARTED SELLING THIS STUFF.
TUCKER SCOTT.

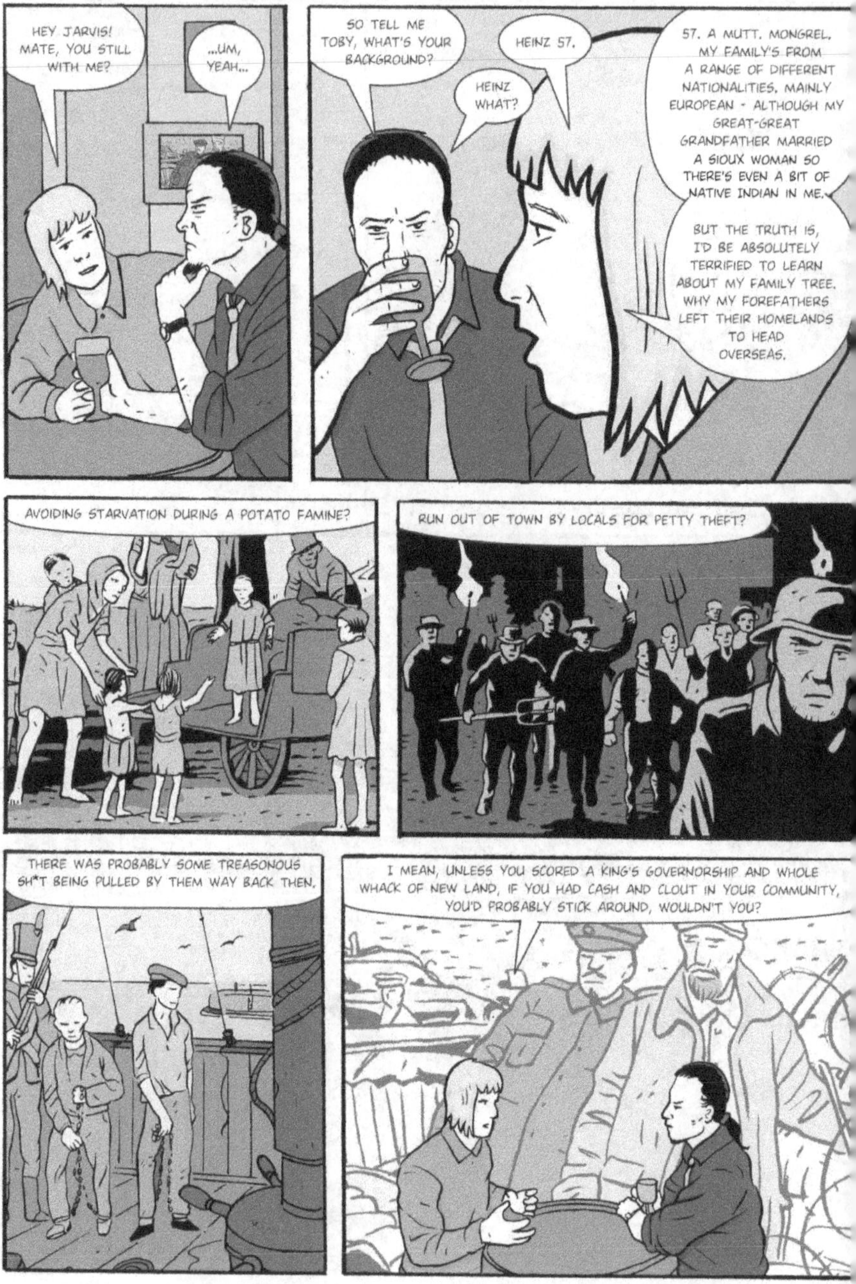
HEY JARVIS! MATE, YOU STILL WITH ME?
...UM, YEAH...
SO TELL ME TOBY, WHAT'S YOUR BACKGROUND?
HEINZ 57.
HEINZ WHAT?
57. A MUTT. MONGREL. MY FAMILY'S FROM A RANGE OF DIFFERENT NATIONALITIES, MAINLY EUROPEAN - ALTHOUGH MY GREAT-GREAT GRANDFATHER MARRIED A SIOUX WOMAN SO THERE'S EVEN A BIT OF NATIVE INDIAN IN ME.
BUT THE TRUTH IS, I'D BE ABSOLUTELY TERRIFIED TO LEARN ABOUT MY FAMILY TREE. WHY MY FOREFATHERS LEFT THEIR HOMELANDS TO HEAD OVERSEAS.
AVOIDING STARVATION DURING A POTATO FAMINE?
RUN OUT OF TOWN BY LOCALS FOR PETTY THEFT?
THERE WAS PROBABLY SOME TREASONOUS SH*T BEING PULLED BY THEM WAY BACK THEN.
I MEAN, UNLESS YOU SCORED A KING'S GOVERNORSHIP AND WHOLE WHACK OF NEW LAND, IF YOU HAD CASH AND CLOUT IN YOUR COMMUNITY, YOU'D PROBABLY STICK AROUND, WOULDN'T YOU?

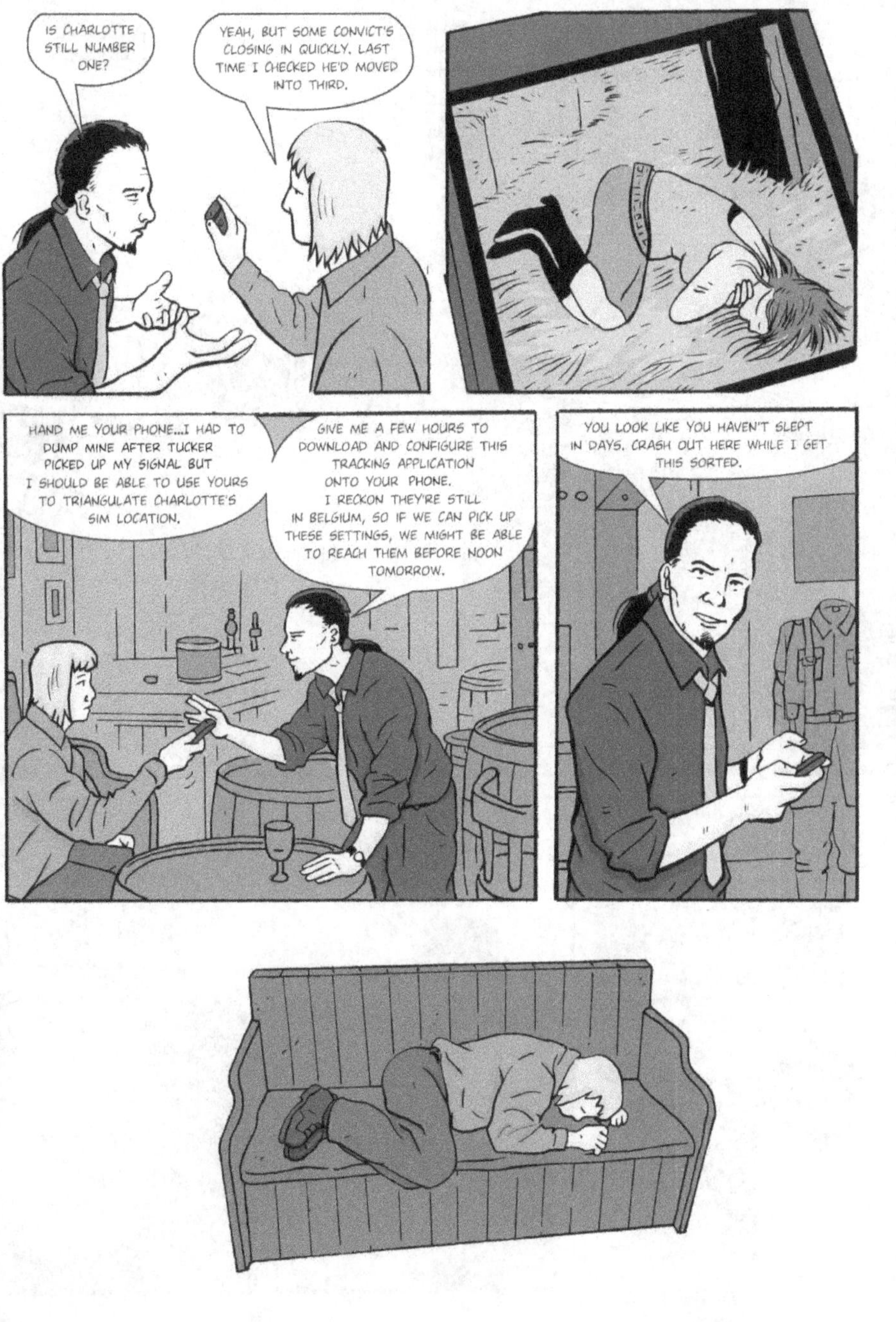
IS CHARLOTTE STILL NUMBER ONE?
YEAH, BUT SOME CONVICT'S CLOSING IN QUICKLY. LAST TIME I CHECKED HE'D MOVED INTO THIRD.
HAND ME YOUR PHONE...I HAD TO DUMP MINE AFTER TUCKER PICKED UP MY SIGNAL BUT I SHOULD BE ABLE TO USE YOURS TO TRIANGULATE CHARLOTTE'S SIM LOCATION.
GIVE ME A FEW HOURS TO DOWNLOAD AND CONFIGURE THIS TRACKING APPLICATION ONTO YOUR PHONE. I RECKON THEY'RE STILL IN BELGIUM, SO IF WE CAN PICK UP THESE SETTINGS, WE MIGHT BE ABLE TO REACH THEM BEFORE NOON TOMORROW.
YOU LOOK LIKE YOU HAVEN'T SLEPT IN DAYS. CRASH OUT HERE WHILE I GET THIS SORTED.

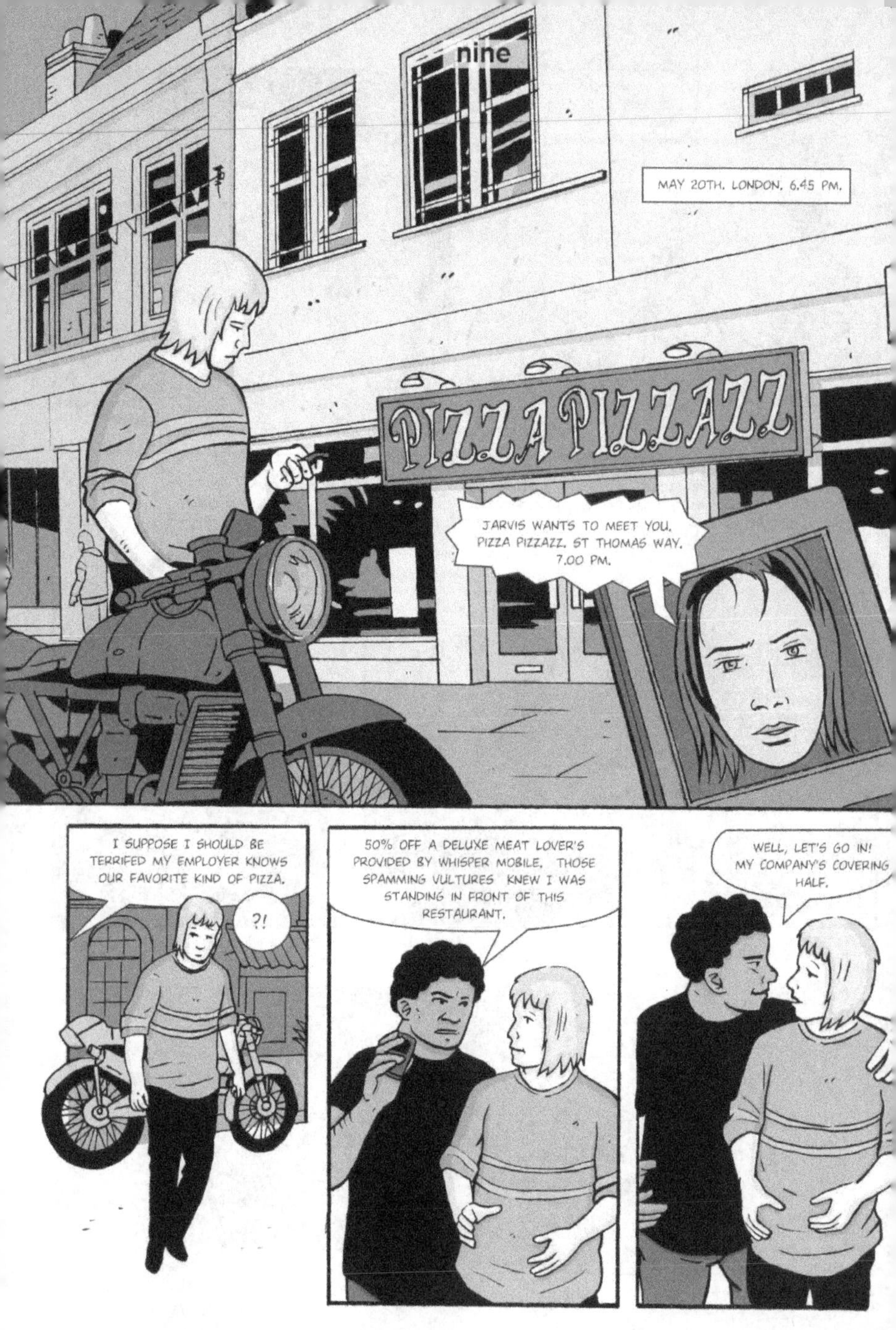
nine
MAY 20TH. LONDON. 6.45 PM.
PIZZA PIZZAZZ
JARVIS WANTS TO MEET YOU. PIZZA PIZZAZZ. ST THOMAS WAY. 7.00 PM.
I SUPPOSE I SHOULD BE TERRIFED MY EMPLOYER KNOWS OUR FAVORITE KIND OF PIZZA.
?!
50% OFF A DELUXE MEAT LOVER'S PROVIDED BY WHISPER MOBILE. THOSE SPAMMING VULTURES KNEW I WAS STANDING IN FRONT OF THIS RESTAURANT.
WELL, LET'S GO IN! MY COMPANY'S COVERING HALF.

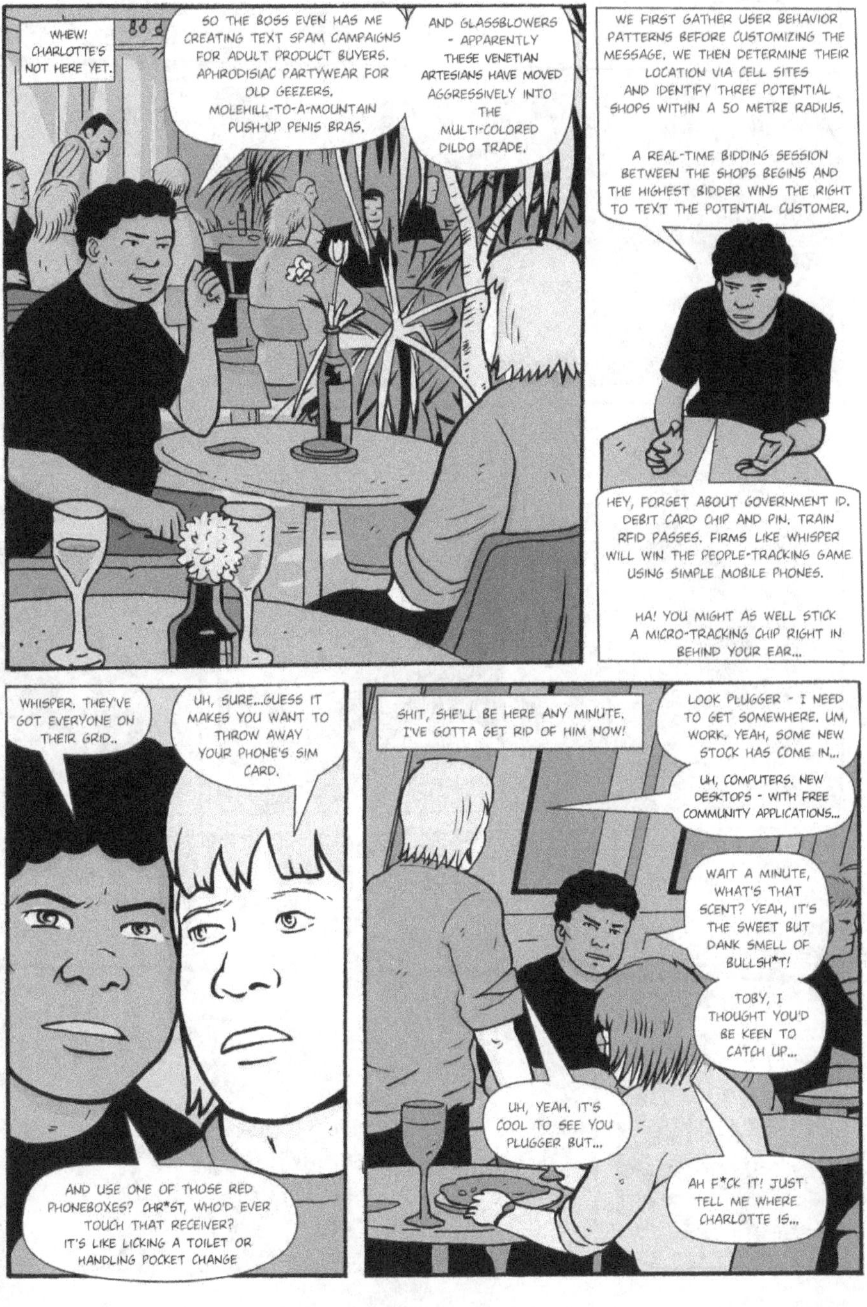
WHEW! CHARLOTTE'S NOT HERE YET.
SO THE BOSS EVEN HAS ME CREATING TEXT SPAM CAMPAIGNS FOR ADULT PRODUCT BUYERS. APHRODISIAC PARTYWEAR FOR OLD GEEZERS. MOLEHILL-TO-A-MOUNTAIN PUSH-UP PENIS BRAS.
AND GLASSBLOWERS - APPARENTLY THESE VENETIAN ARTESIANS HAVE MOVED AGGRESSIVELY INTO THE MULTI-COLORED DILDO TRADE.
WE FIRST GATHER USER BEHAVIOR PATTERNS BEFORE CUSTOMIZING THE MESSAGE. WE THEN DETERMINE THEIR LOCATION VIA CELL SITES AND IDENTIFY THREE POTENTIAL SHOPS WITHIN A 50 METRE RADIUS.
A REAL-TIME BIDDING SESSION BETWEEN THE SHOPS BEGINS AND THE HIGHEST BIDDER WINS THE RIGHT TO TEXT THE POTENTIAL CUSTOMER.
HEY, FORGET ABOUT GOVERNMENT ID. DEBIT CARD CHIP AND PIN. TRAIN RFID PASSES. FIRMS LIKE WHISPER WILL WIN THE PEOPLE-TRACKING GAME USING SIMPLE MOBILE PHONES.
HA! YOU MIGHT AS WELL STICK A MICRO-TRACKING CHIP RIGHT IN BEHIND YOUR EAR...
WHISPER. THEY'VE GOT EVERYONE ON THEIR GRID..
UH, SURE...GUESS IT MAKES YOU WANT TO THROW AWAY YOUR PHONE'S SIM CARD.
AND USE ONE OF THOSE RED PHONEBOXES? CHR*ST, WHO'D EVER TOUCH THAT RECEIVER? IT'S LIKE LICKING A TOILET OR HANDLING POCKET CHANGE
SHIT, SHE'LL BE HERE ANY MINUTE. I'VE GOTTA GET RID OF HIM NOW!
LOOK PLUGGER - I NEED TO GET SOMEWHERE. UM, WORK. YEAH, SOME NEW STOCK HAS COME IN...
UH, COMPUTERS. NEW DESKTOPS - WITH FREE COMMUNITY APPLICATIONS...
WAIT A MINUTE, WHAT'S THAT SCENT? YEAH, IT'S THE SWEET BUT DANK SMELL OF BULLSH*T!
TOBY, I THOUGHT YOU'D BE KEEN TO CATCH UP...
UH, YEAH. IT'S COOL TO SEE YOU PLUGGER BUT...
AH F*CK IT! JUST TELL ME WHERE CHARLOTTE IS...

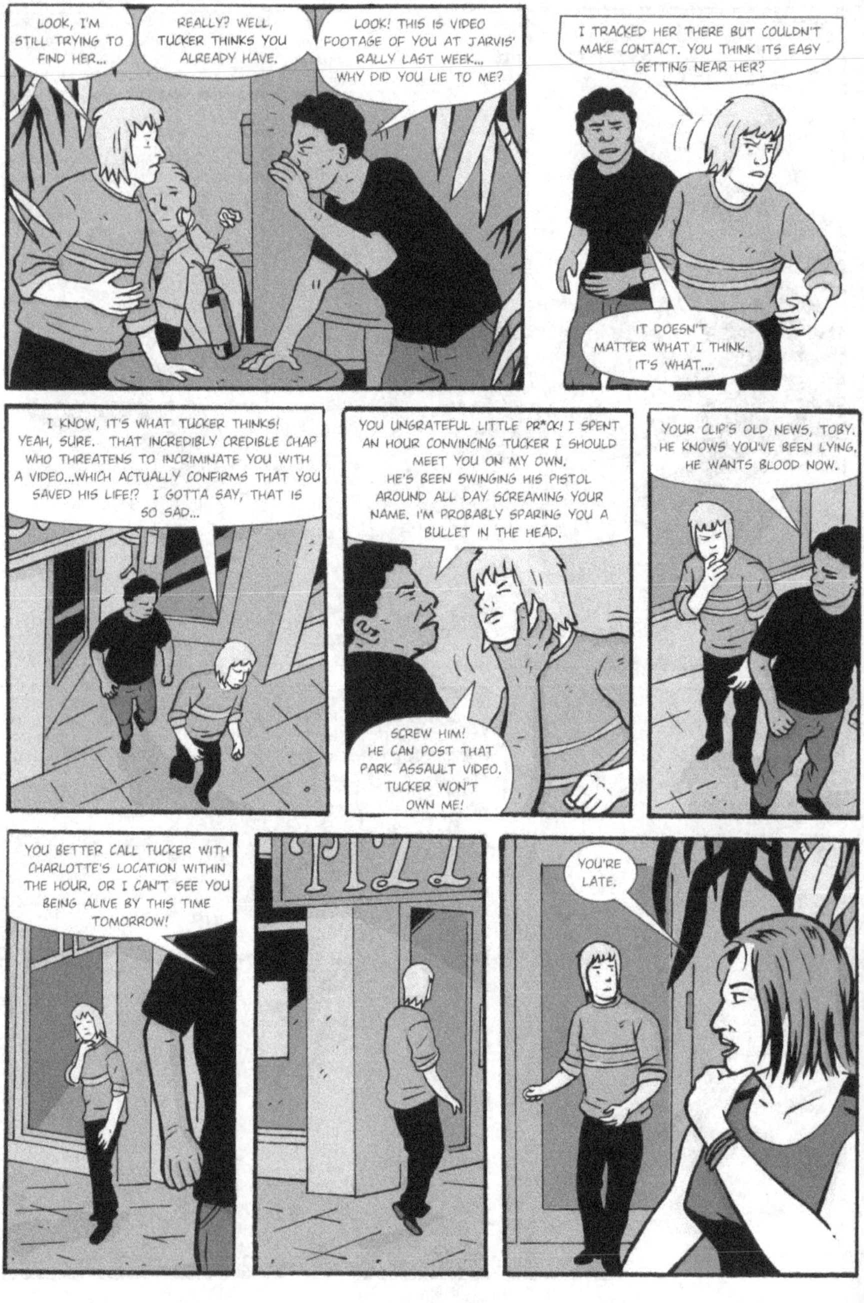
LOOK, I'M STILL TRYING TO FIND HER...
REALLY? WELL, TUCKER THINKS YOU ALREADY HAVE.
LOOK! THIS IS VIDEO FOOTAGE OF YOU AT JARVIS' RALLY LAST WEEK... WHY DID YOU LIE TO ME?
I TRACKED HER THERE BUT COULDN'T MAKE CONTACT. YOU THINK ITS EASY GETTING NEAR HER?
IT DOESN'T MATTER WHAT I THINK. IT'S WHAT....
I KNOW, IT'S WHAT TUCKER THINKS! YEAH, SURE. THAT INCREDIBLY CREDIBLE CHAP WHO THREATENS TO INCRIMINATE YOU WITH A VIDEO...WHICH ACTUALLY CONFIRMS THAT YOU SAVED HIS LIFE!? I GOTTA SAY, THAT IS SO SAD...
YOU UNGRATEFUL LITTLE PR*CK! I SPENT AN HOUR CONVINCING TUCKER I SHOULD MEET YOU ON MY OWN. HE'S BEEN SWINGING HIS PISTOL AROUND ALL DAY SCREAMING YOUR NAME. I'M PROBABLY SPARING YOU A BULLET IN THE HEAD.
SCREW HIM! HE CAN POST THAT PARK ASSAULT VIDEO. TUCKER WON'T OWN ME!
YOUR CLIP'S OLD NEWS, TOBY. HE KNOWS YOU'VE BEEN LYING. HE WANTS BLOOD NOW.
YOU BETTER CALL TUCKER WITH CHARLOTTE'S LOCATION WITHIN THE HOUR. OR I CAN'T SEE YOU BEING ALIVE BY THIS TIME TOMORROW!
YOU'RE LATE.

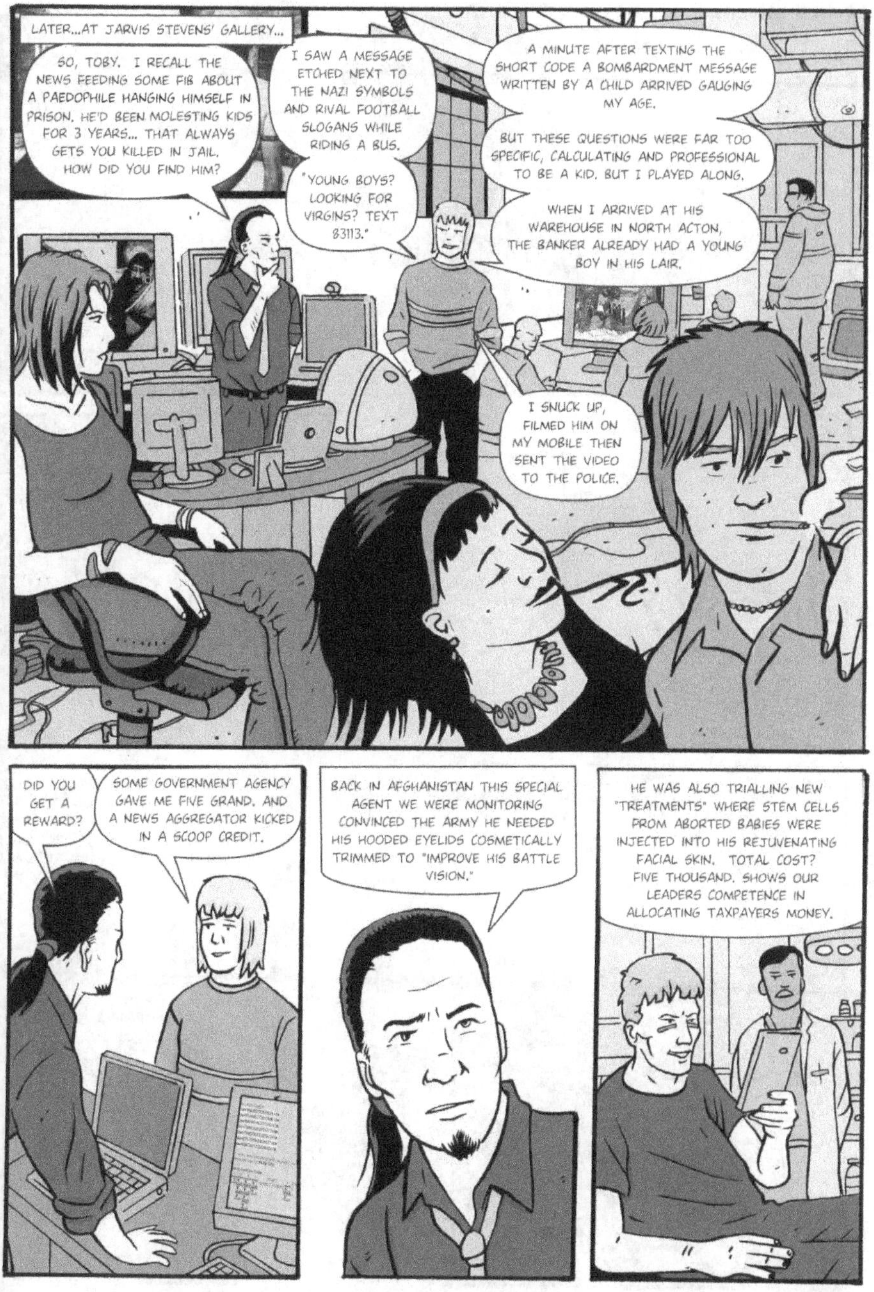
LATER...AT JARVIS STEVENS' GALLERY...
SO, TOBY. I RECALL THE NEWS FEEDING SOME FIB ABOUT A PAEDOPHILE HANGING HIMSELF IN PRISON. HE'D BEEN MOLESTING KIDS FOR 3 YEARS... THAT ALWAYS GETS YOU KILLED IN JAIL. HOW DID YOU FIND HIM?
I SAW A MESSAGE ETCHED NEXT TO THE NAZI SYMBOLS AND RIVAL FOOTBALL SLOGANS WHILE RIDING A BUS.
"YOUNG BOYS? LOOKING FOR VIRGINS? TEXT 83113."
A MINUTE AFTER TEXTING THE SHORT CODE A BOMBARDMENT MESSAGE WRITTEN BY A CHILD ARRIVED GAUGING MY AGE.
BUT THESE QUESTIONS WERE FAR TOO SPECIFIC, CALCULATING AND PROFESSIONAL TO BE A KID. BUT I PLAYED ALONG.
WHEN I ARRIVED AT HIS WAREHOUSE IN NORTH ACTON, THE BANKER ALREADY HAD A YOUNG BOY IN HIS LAIR.
I SNUCK UP, FILMED HIM ON MY MOBILE THEN SENT THE VIDEO TO THE POLICE.
DID YOU GET A REWARD?
SOME GOVERNMENT AGENCY GAVE ME FIVE GRAND. AND A NEWS AGGREGATOR KICKED IN A SCOOP CREDIT.
BACK IN AFGHANISTAN THIS SPECIAL AGENT WE WERE MONITORING CONVINCED THE ARMY HE NEEDED HIS HOODED EYELIDS COSMETICALLY TRIMMED TO "IMPROVE HIS BATTLE VISION."
HE WAS ALSO TRIALLING NEW "TREATMENTS" WHERE STEM CELLS FROM ABORTED BABIES WERE INJECTED INTO HIS REJUVENATING FACIAL SKIN. TOTAL COST? FIVE THOUSAND. SHOWS OUR LEADERS COMPETENCE IN ALLOCATING TAXPAYERS MONEY.

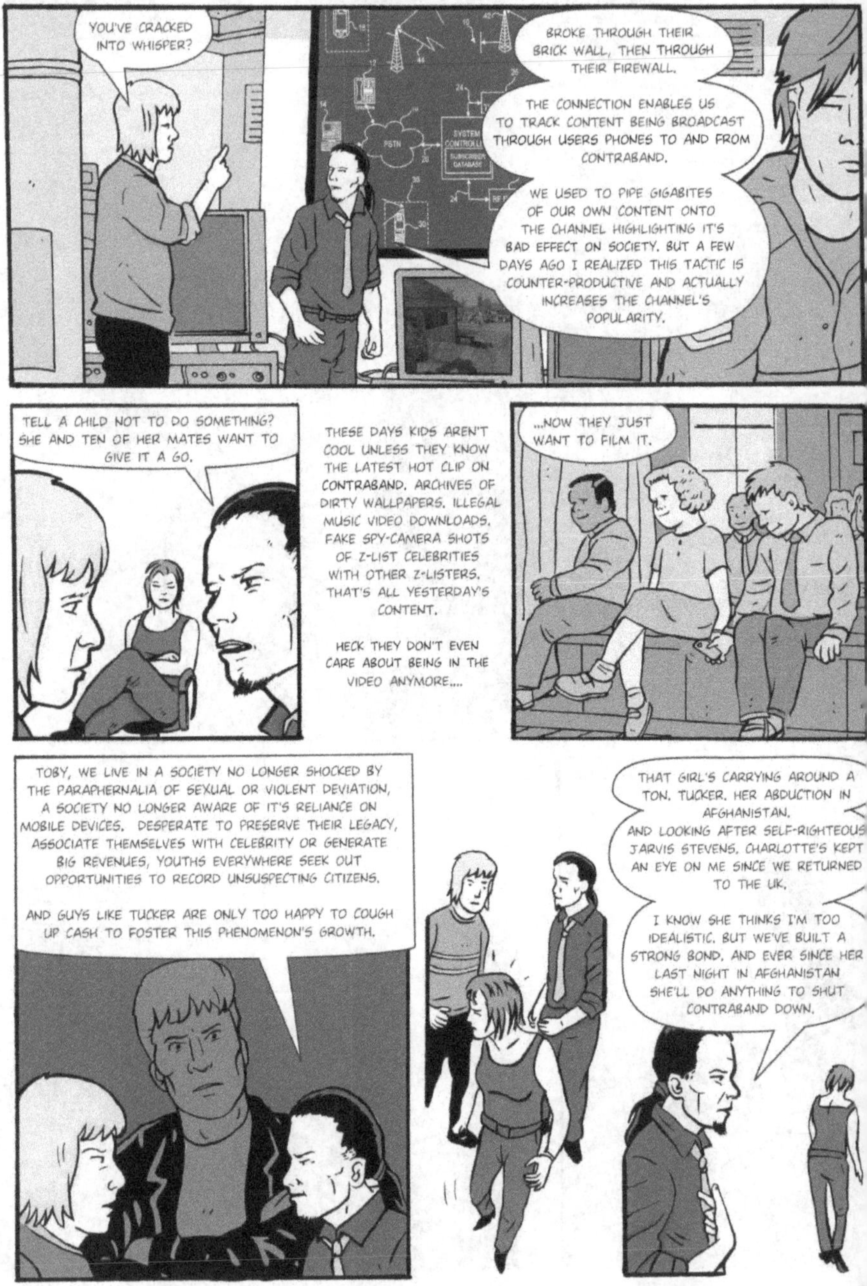
YOU'VE CRACKED INTO WHISPER?
BROKE THROUGH THEIR BRICK WALL, THEN THROUGH THEIR FIREWALL.
THE CONNECTION ENABLES US TO TRACK CONTENT BEING BROADCAST THROUGH USERS PHONES TO AND FROM CONTRABAND.
WE USED TO PIPE GIGABITES OF OUR OWN CONTENT ONTO THE CHANNEL HIGHLIGHTING IT'S BAD EFFECT ON SOCIETY. BUT A FEW DAYS AGO I REALIZED THIS TACTIC IS COUNTER-PRODUCTIVE AND ACTUALLY INCREASES THE CHANNEL'S POPULARITY.
TELL A CHILD NOT TO DO SOMETHING? SHE AND TEN OF HER MATES WANT TO GIVE IT A GO.
THESE DAYS KIDS AREN'T COOL UNLESS THEY KNOW THE LATEST HOT CLIP ON CONTRABAND. ARCHIVES OF DIRTY WALLPAPERS. ILLEGAL MUSIC VIDEO DOWNLOADS. FAKE SPY-CAMERA SHOTS OF Z-LIST CELEBRITIES WITH OTHER Z-LISTERS. THAT'S ALL YESTERDAY'S CONTENT.
HECK THEY DON'T EVEN CARE ABOUT BEING IN THE VIDEO ANYMORE....
...NOW THEY JUST WANT TO FILM IT.
TOBY, WE LIVE IN A SOCIETY NO LONGER SHOCKED BY THE PARAPHERNALIA OF SEXUAL OR VIOLENT DEVIATION, A SOCIETY NO LONGER AWARE OF IT'S RELIANCE ON MOBILE DEVICES. DESPERATE TO PRESERVE THEIR LEGACY, ASSOCIATE THEMSELVES WITH CELEBRITY OR GENERATE BIG REVENUES, YOUTHS EVERYWHERE SEEK OUT OPPORTUNITIES TO RECORD UNSUSPECTING CITIZENS.
AND GUYS LIKE TUCKER ARE ONLY TOO HAPPY TO COUGH UP CASH TO FOSTER THIS PHENOMENON'S GROWTH.
THAT GIRL'S CARRYING AROUND A TON, TUCKER. HER ABDUCTION IN AFGHANISTAN.
AND LOOKING AFTER SELF-RIGHTEOUS JARVIS STEVENS. CHARLOTTE'S KEPT AN EYE ON ME SINCE WE RETURNED TO THE UK.
I KNOW SHE THINKS I'M TOO IDEALISTIC. BUT WE'VE BUILT A STRONG BOND. AND EVER SINCE HER LAST NIGHT IN AFGHANISTAN SHE'LL DO ANYTHING TO SHUT CONTRABAND DOWN.

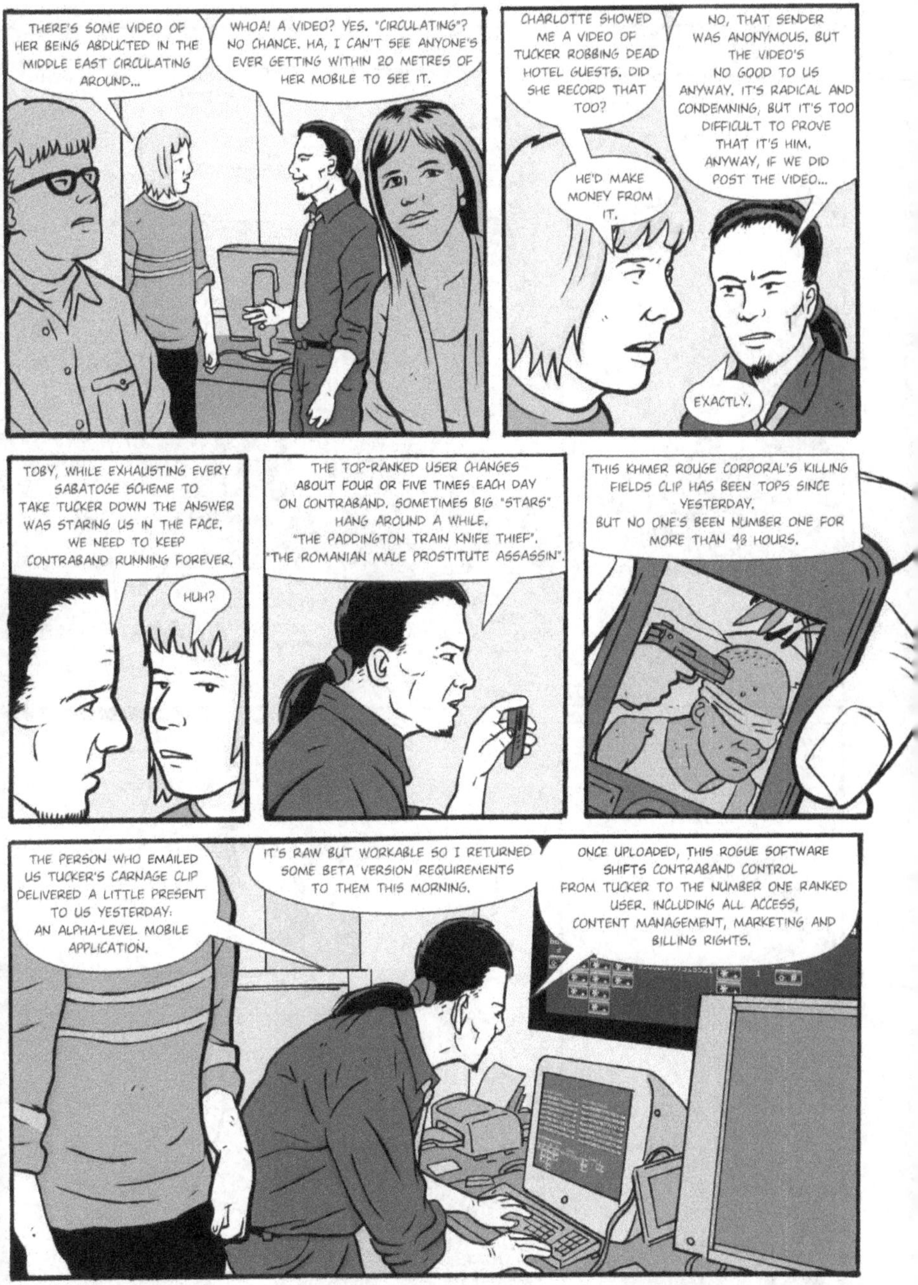
THERE'S SOME VIDEO OF HER BEING ABDUCTED IN THE MIDDLE EAST CIRCULATING AROUND...
WHOA! A VIDEO? YES. "CIRCULATING"? NO CHANCE. HA, I CAN'T SEE ANYONE'S EVER GETTING WITHIN 20 METRES OF HER MOBILE TO SEE IT.
CHARLOTTE SHOWED ME A VIDEO OF TUCKER ROBBING DEAD HOTEL GUESTS. DID SHE RECORD THAT TOO?
NO, THAT SENDER WAS ANONYMOUS. BUT THE VIDEO'S NO GOOD TO US ANYWAY. IT'S RADICAL AND CONDEMNING, BUT IT'S TOO DIFFICULT TO PROVE THAT IT'S HIM. ANYWAY, IF WE DID POST THE VIDEO...
HE'D MAKE MONEY FROM IT.
EXACTLY.
TOBY, WHILE EXHAUSTING EVERY SABATOGE SCHEME TO TAKE TUCKER DOWN THE ANSWER WAS STARING US IN THE FACE. WE NEED TO KEEP CONTRABAND RUNNING FOREVER.
HUH?
THE TOP-RANKED USER CHANGES ABOUT FOUR OR FIVE TIMES EACH DAY ON CONTRABAND. SOMETIMES BIG "STARS" HANG AROUND A WHILE. "THE PADDINGTON TRAIN KNIFE THIEF". "THE ROMANIAN MALE PROSTITUTE ASSASSIN".
THIS KHMER ROUGE CORPORAL'S KILLING FIELDS CLIP HAS BEEN TOPS SINCE YESTERDAY. BUT NO ONE'S BEEN NUMBER ONE FOR MORE THAN 48 HOURS.
THE PERSON WHO EMAILED US TUCKER'S CARNAGE CLIP DELIVERED A LITTLE PRESENT TO US YESTERDAY: AN ALPHA-LEVEL MOBILE APPLICATION.
IT'S RAW BUT WORKABLE SO I RETURNED SOME BETA VERSION REQUIREMENTS TO THEM THIS MORNING.
ONCE UPLOADED, THIS ROGUE SOFTWARE SHIFTS CONTRABAND CONTROL FROM TUCKER TO THE NUMBER ONE RANKED USER. INCLUDING ALL ACCESS, CONTENT MANAGEMENT, MARKETING AND BILLING RIGHTS.

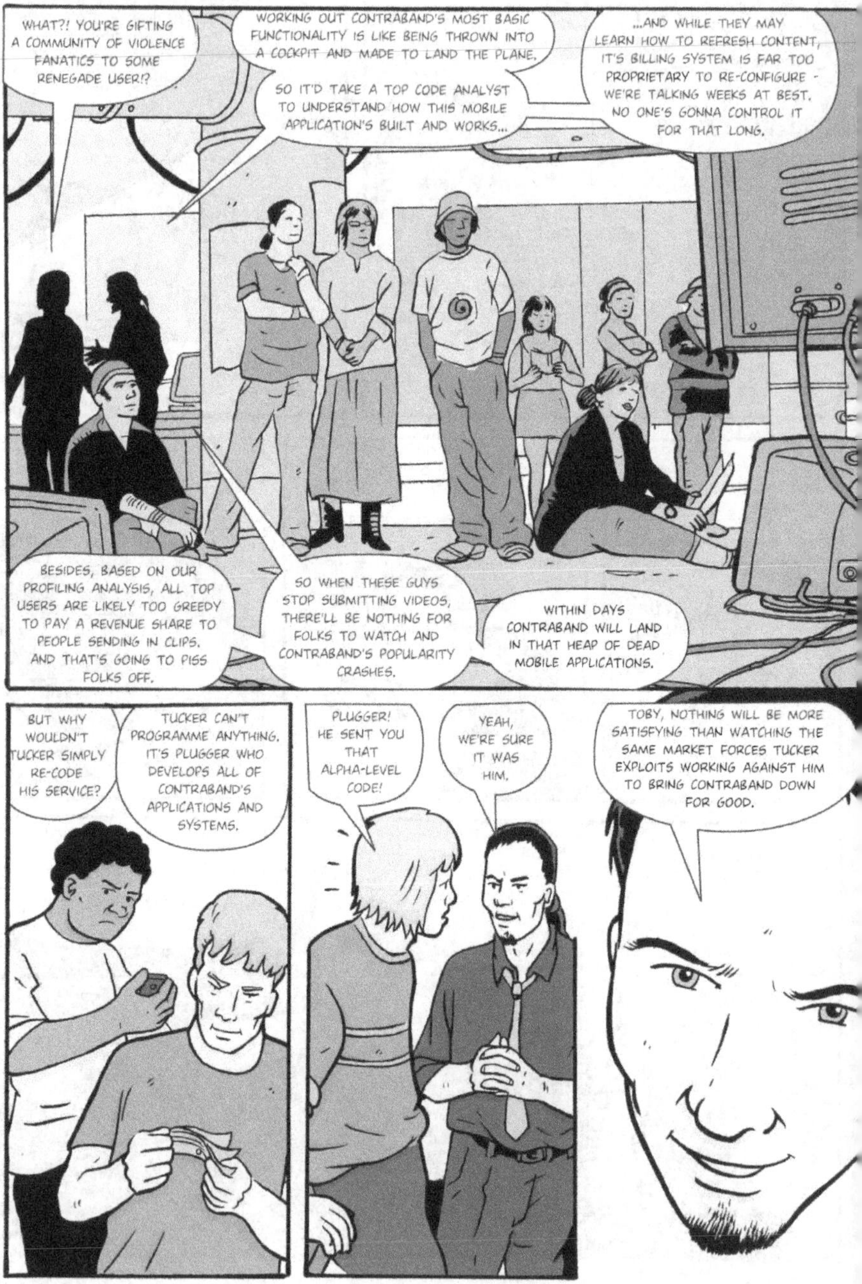
WHAT?! YOU'RE GIFTING A COMMUNITY OF VIOLENCE FANATICS TO SOME RENEGADE USER!?
WORKING OUT CONTRABAND'S MOST BASIC FUNCTIONALITY IS LIKE BEING THROWN INTO A COCKPIT AND MADE TO LAND THE PLANE.
SO IT'D TAKE A TOP CODE ANALYST TO UNDERSTAND HOW THIS MOBILE APPLICATION'S BUILT AND WORKS...
...AND WHILE THEY MAY LEARN HOW TO REFRESH CONTENT, IT'S BILLING SYSTEM IS FAR TOO PROPRIETARY TO RE-CONFIGURE - WE'RE TALKING WEEKS AT BEST. NO ONE'S GONNA CONTROL IT FOR THAT LONG.
BESIDES, BASED ON OUR PROFILING ANALYSIS, ALL TOP USERS ARE LIKELY TOO GREEDY TO PAY A REVENUE SHARE TO PEOPLE SENDING IN CLIPS. AND THAT'S GOING TO PISS FOLKS OFF.
SO WHEN THESE GUYS STOP SUBMITTING VIDEOS, THERE'LL BE NOTHING FOR FOLKS TO WATCH AND CONTRABAND'S POPULARITY CRASHES.
WITHIN DAYS CONTRABAND WILL LAND IN THAT HEAP OF DEAD MOBILE APPLICATIONS.
BUT WHY WOULDN'T TUCKER SIMPLY RE-CODE HIS SERVICE?
TUCKER CAN'T PROGRAMME ANYTHING. IT'S PLUGGER WHO DEVELOPS ALL OF CONTRABAND'S APPLICATIONS AND SYSTEMS.
PLUGGER! HE SENT YOU THAT ALPHA-LEVEL CODE!
YEAH, WE'RE SURE IT WAS HIM.
TOBY, NOTHING WILL BE MORE SATISFYING THAN WATCHING THE SAME MARKET FORCES TUCKER EXPLOITS WORKING AGAINST HIM TO BRING CONTRABAND DOWN FOR GOOD.

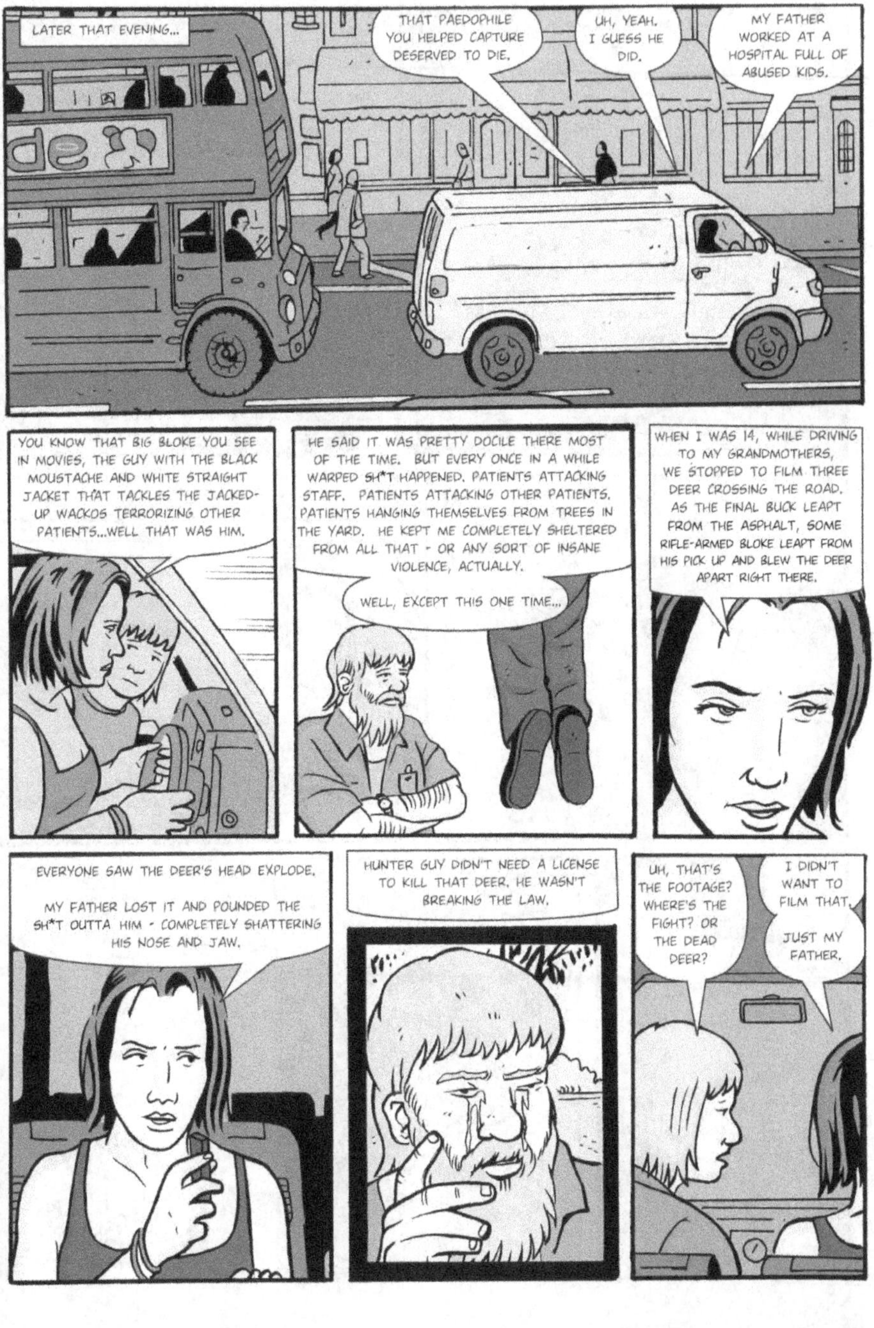
LATER THAT EVENING...
THAT PAEDOPHILE YOU HELPED CAPTURE DESERVED TO DIE.
UH, YEAH. I GUESS HE DID.
MY FATHER WORKED AT A HOSPITAL FULL OF ABUSED KIDS.
YOU KNOW THAT BIG BLOKE YOU SEE IN MOVIES, THE GUY WITH THE BLACK MOUSTACHE AND WHITE STRAIGHT JACKET THAT TACKLES THE JACKED-UP WACKOS TERRORIZING OTHER PATIENTS...WELL THAT WAS HIM.
HE SAID IT WAS PRETTY DOCILE THERE MOST OF THE TIME. BUT EVERY ONCE IN A WHILE WARPED SH*T HAPPENED. PATIENTS ATTACKING STAFF. PATIENTS ATTACKING OTHER PATIENTS. PATIENTS HANGING THEMSELVES FROM TREES IN THE YARD. HE KEPT ME COMPLETELY SHELTERED FROM ALL THAT - OR ANY SORT OF INSANE VIOLENCE, ACTUALLY.
WELL, EXCEPT THIS ONE TIME...
WHEN I WAS 14, WHILE DRIVING TO MY GRANDMOTHERS, WE STOPPED TO FILM THREE DEER CROSSING THE ROAD. AS THE FINAL BUCK LEAPT FROM THE ASPHALT, SOME RIFLE-ARMED BLOKE LEAPT FROM HIS PICK UP AND BLEW THE DEER APART RIGHT THERE.
EVERYONE SAW THE DEER'S HEAD EXPLODE.
MY FATHER LOST IT AND POUNDED THE SH*T OUTTA HIM - COMPLETELY SHATTERING HIS NOSE AND JAW.
HUNTER GUY DIDN'T NEED A LICENSE TO KILL THAT DEER. HE WASN'T BREAKING THE LAW.
UH, THAT'S THE FOOTAGE? WHERE'S THE FIGHT? OR THE DEAD DEER?
I DIDN'T WANT TO FILM THAT.
JUST MY FATHER.

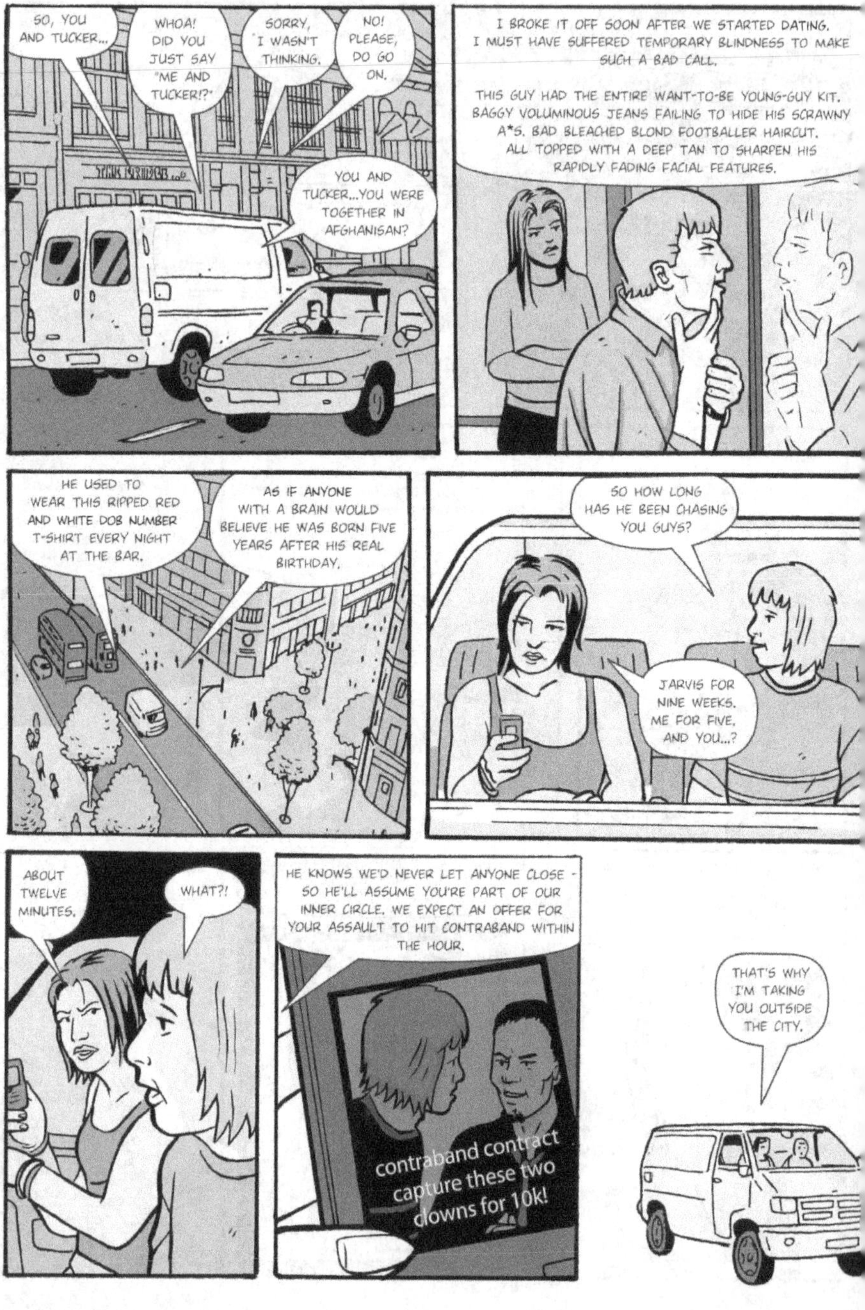
SO, YOU AND TUCKER...
WHOA! DID YOU JUST SAY "ME AND TUCKER!?"
SORRY, I WASN'T THINKING.
NO! PLEASE, DO GO ON.
YOU AND TUCKER...YOU WERE TOGETHER IN AFGHANISAN?
I BROKE IT OFF SOON AFTER WE STARTED DATING. I MUST HAVE SUFFERED TEMPORARY BLINDNESS TO MAKE SUCH A BAD CALL.
THIS GUY HAD THE ENTIRE WANT-TO-BE YOUNG-GUY KIT. BAGGY VOLUMINOUS JEANS FAILING TO HIDE HIS SCRAWNY A*S. BAD BLEACHED BLOND FOOTBALLER HAIRCUT. ALL TOPPED WITH A DEEP TAN TO SHARPEN HIS RAPIDLY FADING FACIAL FEATURES.
HE USED TO WEAR THIS RIPPED RED AND WHITE DOB NUMBER T-SHIRT EVERY NIGHT AT THE BAR.
AS IF ANYONE WITH A BRAIN WOULD BELIEVE HE WAS BORN FIVE YEARS AFTER HIS REAL BIRTHDAY.
SO HOW LONG HAS HE BEEN CHASING YOU GUYS?
JARVIS FOR NINE WEEKS. ME FOR FIVE. AND YOU...?
ABOUT TWELVE MINUTES.
WHAT?!
HE KNOWS WE'D NEVER LET ANYONE CLOSE - SO HE'LL ASSUME YOU'RE PART OF OUR INNER CIRCLE. WE EXPECT AN OFFER FOR YOUR ASSAULT TO HIT CONTRABAND WITHIN THE HOUR.
contraband contract
capture these two
clowns for 10k!
THAT'S WHY I'M TAKING YOU OUTSIDE THE CITY.

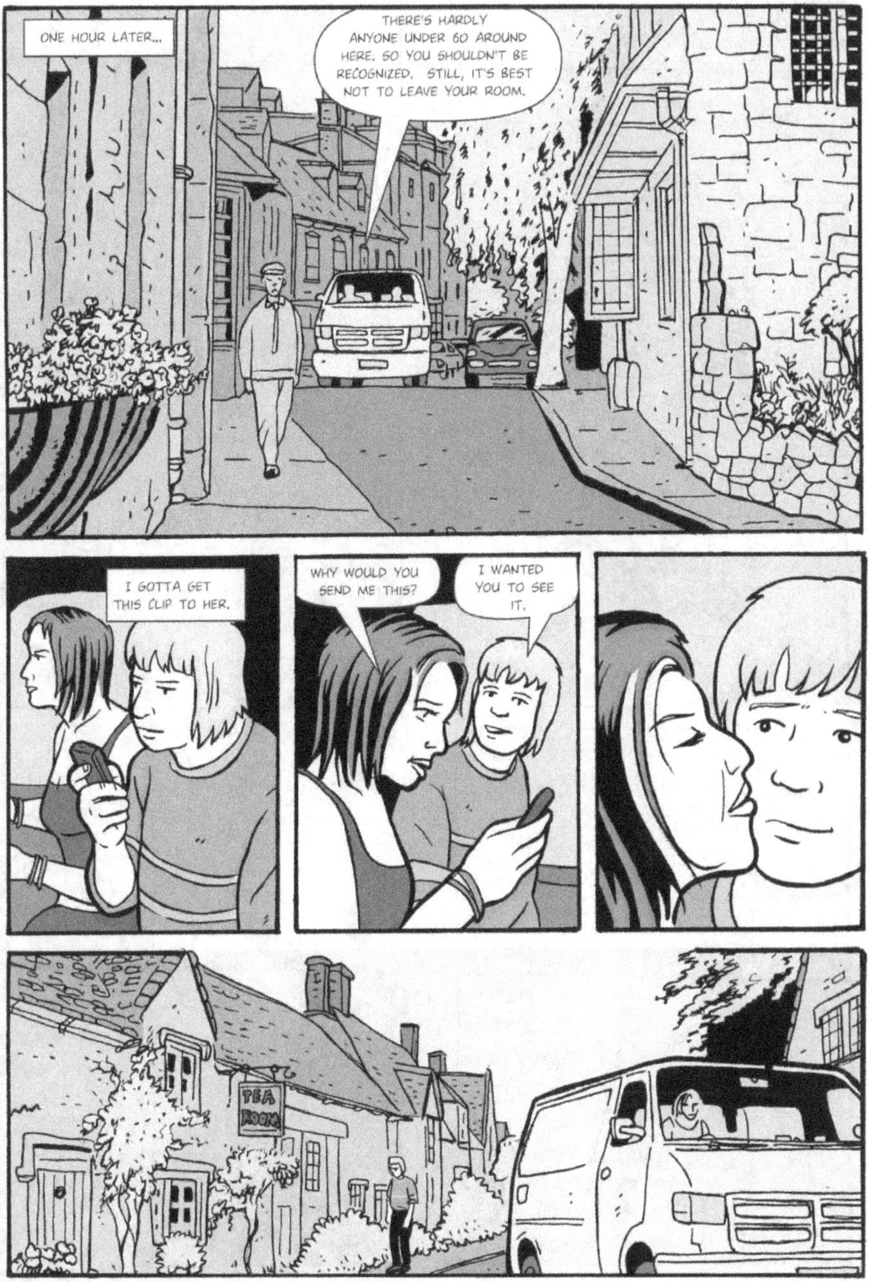
ONE HOUR LATER...
THERE'S HARDLY ANYONE UNDER 60 AROUND HERE. SO YOU SHOULDN'T BE RECOGNIZED. STILL, IT'S BEST NOT TO LEAVE YOUR ROOM.
I GOTTA GET THIS CLIP TO HER.
WHY WOULD YOU SEND ME THIS?
I WANTED YOU TO SEE IT.
TEA ROOM

ten

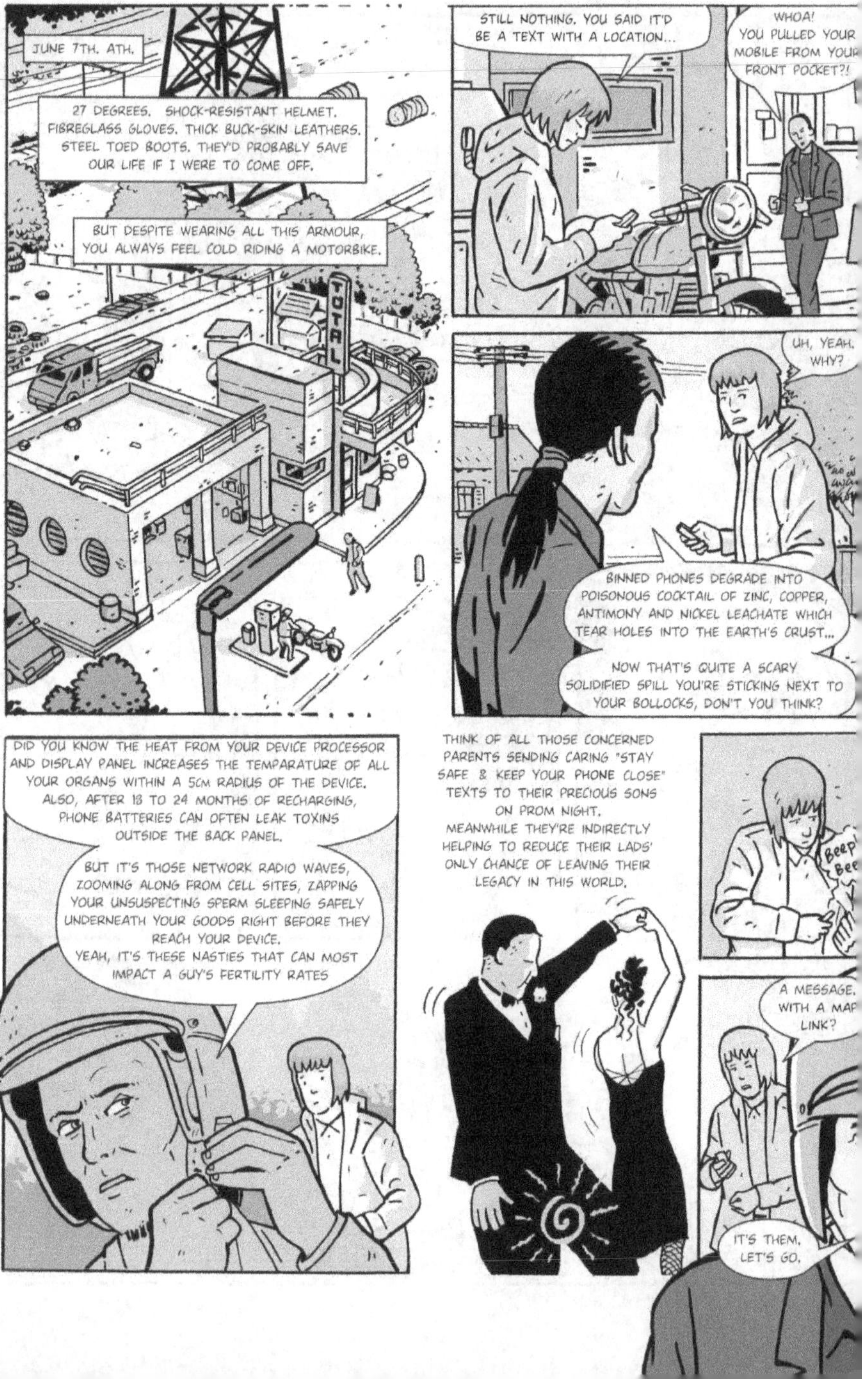

JUNE 7TH. ATH.
27 DEGREES. SHOCK-RESISTANT HELMET. FIBREGLASS GLOVES. THICK BUCK-SKIN LEATHERS. STEEL TOED BOOTS. THEY'D PROBABLY SAVE OUR LIFE IF I WERE TO COME OFF.
BUT DESPITE WEARING ALL THIS ARMOUR, YOU ALWAYS FEEL COLD RIDING A MOTORBIKE.
TOTAL
STILL NOTHING. YOU SAID IT'D BE A TEXT WITH A LOCATION...
WHOA! YOU PULLED YOUR MOBILE FROM YOUR FRONT POCKET?!
UH, YEAH. WHY?
BINNED PHONES DEGRADE INTO POISONOUS COCKTAIL OF ZINC, COPPER, ANTIMONY AND NICKEL LEACHATE WHICH TEAR HOLES INTO THE EARTH'S CRUST...
NOW THAT'S QUITE A SCARY SOLIDIFIED SPILL YOU'RE STICKING NEXT TO YOUR BOLLOCKS, DON'T YOU THINK?
DID YOU KNOW THE HEAT FROM YOUR DEVICE PROCESSOR AND DISPLAY PANEL INCREASES THE TEMPARATURE OF ALL YOUR ORGANS WITHIN A 5CM RADIUS OF THE DEVICE. ALSO, AFTER 18 TO 24 MONTHS OF RECHARGING, PHONE BATTERIES CAN OFTEN LEAK TOXINS OUTSIDE THE BACK PANEL.
BUT IT'S THOSE NETWORK RADIO WAVES, ZOOMING ALONG FROM CELL SITES, ZAPPING YOUR UNSUSPECTING SPERM SLEEPING SAFELY UNDERNEATH YOUR GOODS RIGHT BEFORE THEY REACH YOUR DEVICE. YEAH, IT'S THESE NASTIES THAT CAN MOST IMPACT A GUY'S FERTILITY RATES
THINK OF ALL THOSE CONCERNED PARENTS SENDING CARING "STAY SAFE & KEEP YOUR PHONE CLOSE" TEXTS TO THEIR PRECIOUS SONS ON PROM NIGHT. MEANWHILE THEY'RE INDIRECTLY HELPING TO REDUCE THEIR LADS' ONLY CHANCE OF LEAVING THEIR LEGACY IN THIS WORLD.
Beep! Bee
A MESSAGE. WITH A MAP LINK?
IT'S THEM. LET'S GO.

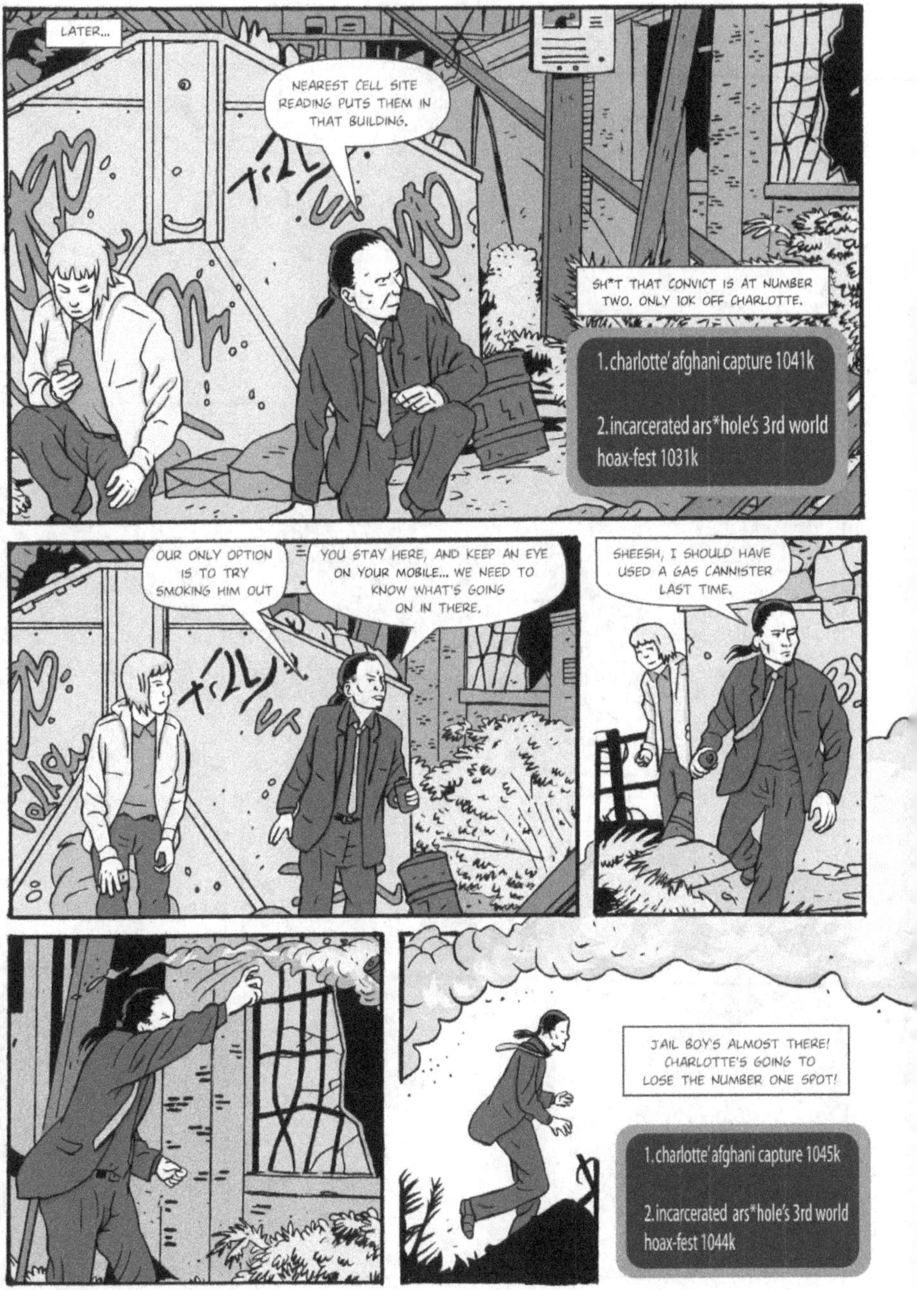

LATER...
NEAREST CELL SITE READING PUTS THEM IN THAT BUILDING.
SH*T THAT CONVICT IS AT NUMBER TWO. ONLY 10K OFF CHARLOTTE.
1. charlotte' afghani capture 1041k
2. incarcerated ars*hole's 3rd world hoax-fest 1031k
OUR ONLY OPTION IS TO TRY SMOKING HIM OUT
YOU STAY HERE, AND KEEP AN EYE ON YOUR MOBILE... WE NEED TO KNOW WHAT'S GOING ON IN THERE.
SHEESH, I SHOULD HAVE USED A GAS CANNISTER LAST TIME.
JAIL BOY'S ALMOST THERE! CHARLOTTE'S GOING TO LOSE THE NUMBER ONE SPOT!
1. charlotte' afghani capture 1045k
2. incarcerated ars*hole's 3rd world hoax-fest 1044k

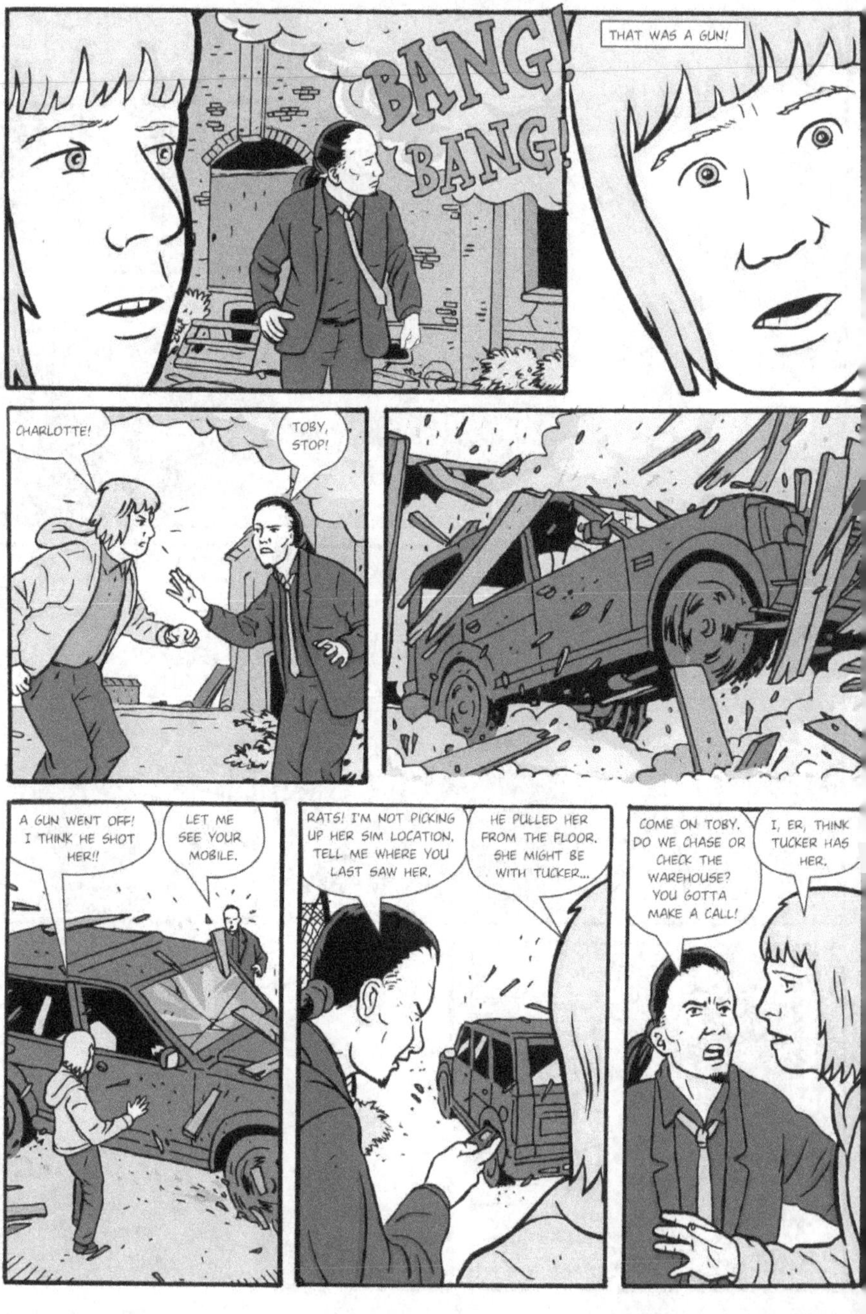
BANG!
BANG!
THAT WAS A GUN!
CHARLOTTE!
TOBY, STOP!
A GUN WENT OFF! I THINK HE SHOT HER!!
LET ME SEE YOUR MOBILE.
RATS! I'M NOT PICKING UP HER SIM LOCATION. TELL ME WHERE YOU LAST SAW HER.
HE PULLED HER FROM THE FLOOR. SHE MIGHT BE WITH TUCKER...
COME ON TOBY. DO WE CHASE OR CHECK THE WAREHOUSE? YOU GOTTA MAKE A CALL!
I, ER, THINK TUCKER HAS HER.

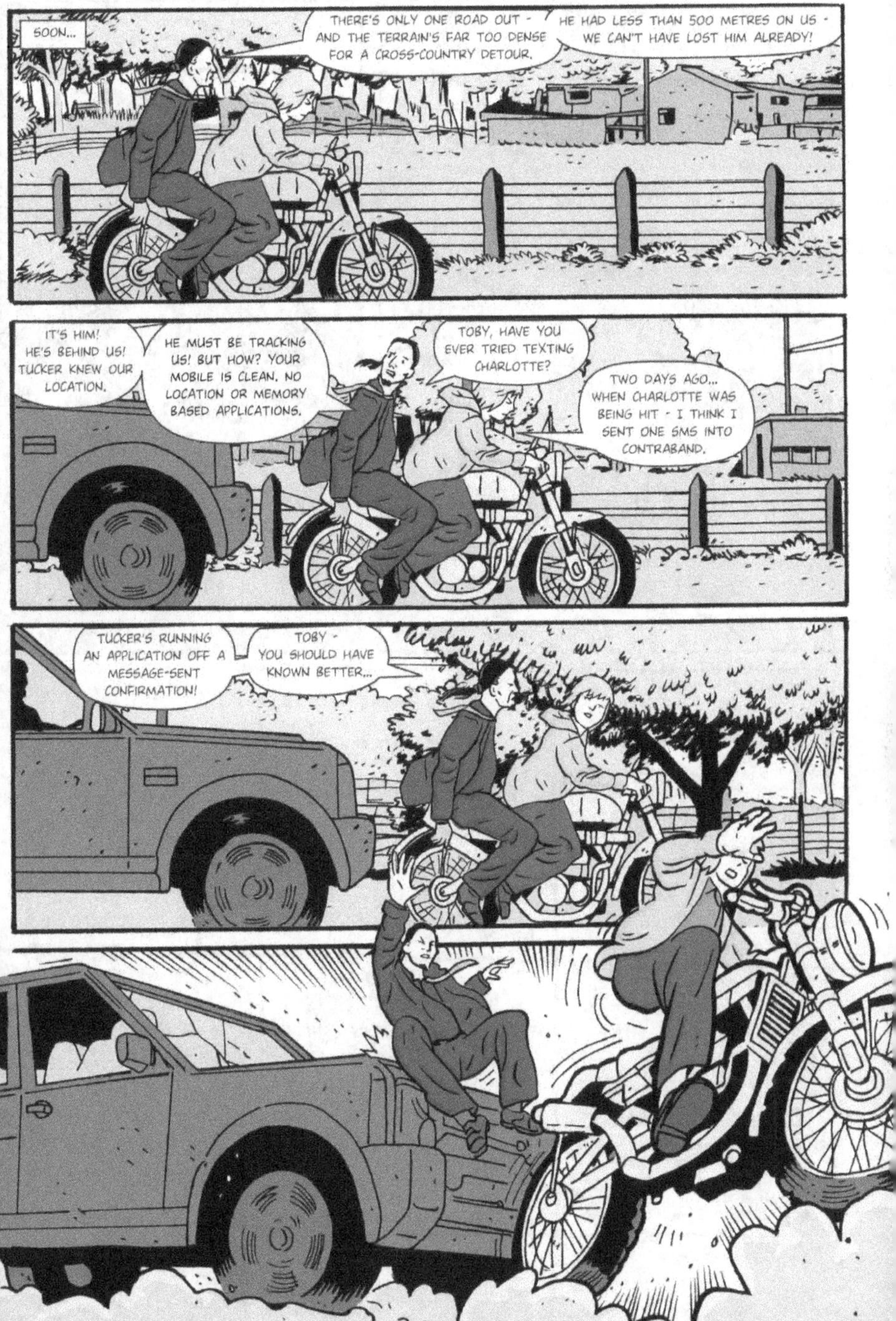
SOON...
THERE'S ONLY ONE ROAD OUT - AND THE TERRAIN'S FAR TOO DENSE FOR A CROSS-COUNTRY DETOUR.
HE HAD LESS THAN 500 METRES ON US - WE CAN'T HAVE LOST HIM ALREADY!
IT'S HIM! HE'S BEHIND US! TUCKER KNEW OUR LOCATION.
HE MUST BE TRACKING US! BUT HOW? YOUR MOBILE IS CLEAN. NO LOCATION OR MEMORY BASED APPLICATIONS.
TOBY, HAVE YOU EVER TRIED TEXTING CHARLOTTE?
TWO DAYS AGO... WHEN CHARLOTTE WAS BEING HIT - I THINK I SENT ONE SMS INTO CONTRABAND.
TUCKER'S RUNNING AN APPLICATION OFF A MESSAGE-SENT CONFIRMATION!
TOBY - YOU SHOULD HAVE KNOWN BETTER...

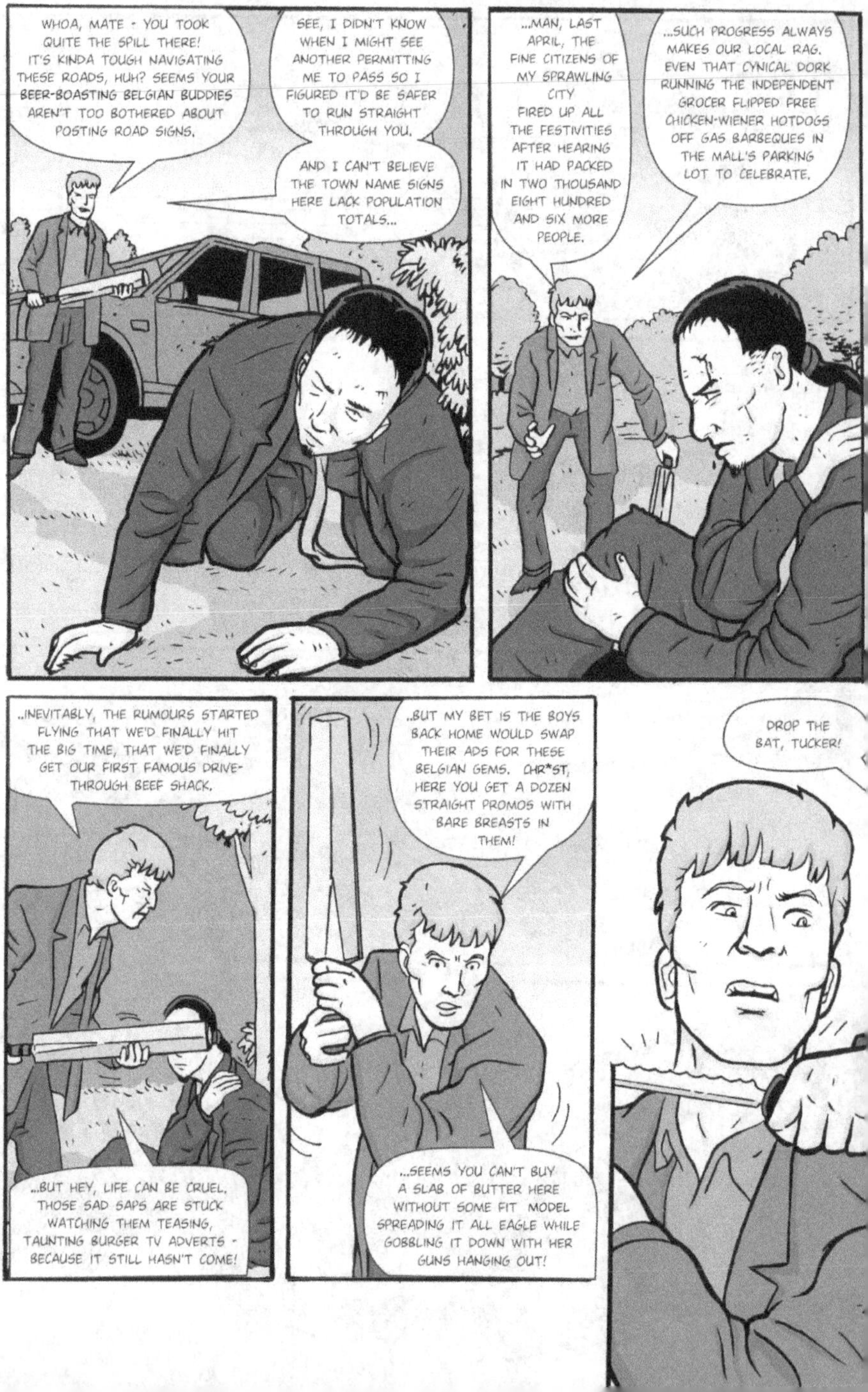
WHOA, MATE - YOU TOOK QUITE THE SPILL THERE! IT'S KINDA TOUGH NAVIGATING THESE ROADS, HUH? SEEMS YOUR BEER-BOASTING BELGIAN BUDDIES AREN'T TOO BOTHERED ABOUT POSTING ROAD SIGNS.
SEE, I DIDN'T KNOW WHEN I MIGHT SEE ANOTHER PERMITTING ME TO PASS SO I FIGURED IT'D BE SAFER TO RUN STRAIGHT THROUGH YOU.
AND I CAN'T BELIEVE THE TOWN NAME SIGNS HERE LACK POPULATION TOTALS...
...MAN, LAST APRIL, THE FINE CITIZENS OF MY SPRAWLING CITY FIRED UP ALL THE FESTIVITIES AFTER HEARING IT HAD PACKED IN TWO THOUSAND EIGHT HUNDRED AND SIX MORE PEOPLE.
...SUCH PROGRESS ALWAYS MAKES OUR LOCAL RAG. EVEN THAT CYNICAL DORK RUNNING THE INDEPENDENT GROCER FLIPPED FREE CHICKEN-WIENER HOTDOGS OFF GAS BARBEQUES IN THE MALL'S PARKING LOT TO CELEBRATE.
..INEVITABLY, THE RUMOURS STARTED FLYING THAT WE'D FINALLY HIT THE BIG TIME, THAT WE'D FINALLY GET OUR FIRST FAMOUS DRIVE-THROUGH BEEF SHACK.
..BUT HEY, LIFE CAN BE CRUEL. THOSE SAD SAPS ARE STUCK WATCHING THEM TEASING, TAUNTING BURGER TV ADVERTS - BECAUSE IT STILL HASN'T COME!
..BUT MY BET IS THE BOYS BACK HOME WOULD SWAP THEIR ADS FOR THESE BELGIAN GEMS. CHR*ST, HERE YOU GET A DOZEN STRAIGHT PROMOS WITH BARE BREASTS IN THEM!
...SEEMS YOU CAN'T BUY A SLAB OF BUTTER HERE WITHOUT SOME FIT MODEL SPREADING IT ALL EAGLE WHILE GOBBLING IT DOWN WITH HER GUNS HANGING OUT!
DROP THE BAT, TUCKER!

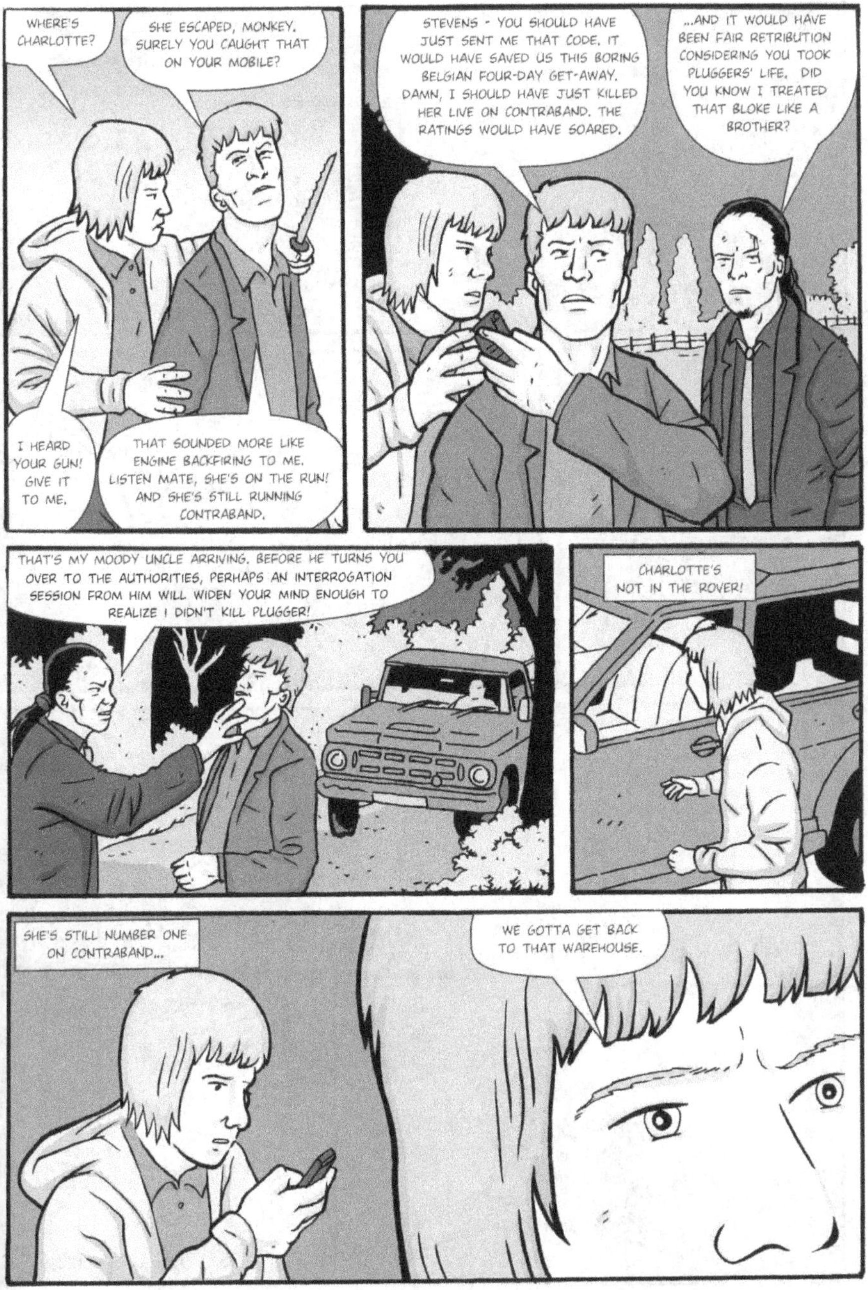
WHERE'S CHARLOTTE?
SHE ESCAPED, MONKEY. SURELY YOU CAUGHT THAT ON YOUR MOBILE?
I HEARD YOUR GUN! GIVE IT TO ME.
THAT SOUNDED MORE LIKE ENGINE BACKFIRING TO ME. LISTEN MATE, SHE'S ON THE RUN! AND SHE'S STILL RUNNING CONTRABAND.
STEVENS - YOU SHOULD HAVE JUST SENT ME THAT CODE. IT WOULD HAVE SAVED US THIS BORING BELGIAN FOUR-DAY GET-AWAY. DAMN, I SHOULD HAVE JUST KILLED HER LIVE ON CONTRABAND. THE RATINGS WOULD HAVE SOARED.
...AND IT WOULD HAVE BEEN FAIR RETRIBUTION CONSIDERING YOU TOOK PLUGGERS' LIFE. DID YOU KNOW I TREATED THAT BLOKE LIKE A BROTHER?
THAT'S MY MOODY UNCLE ARRIVING. BEFORE HE TURNS YOU OVER TO THE AUTHORITIES, PERHAPS AN INTERROGATION SESSION FROM HIM WILL WIDEN YOUR MIND ENOUGH TO REALIZE I DIDN'T KILL PLUGGER!
CHARLOTTE'S NOT IN THE ROVER!
SHE'S STILL NUMBER ONE ON CONTRABAND...
WE GOTTA GET BACK TO THAT WAREHOUSE.

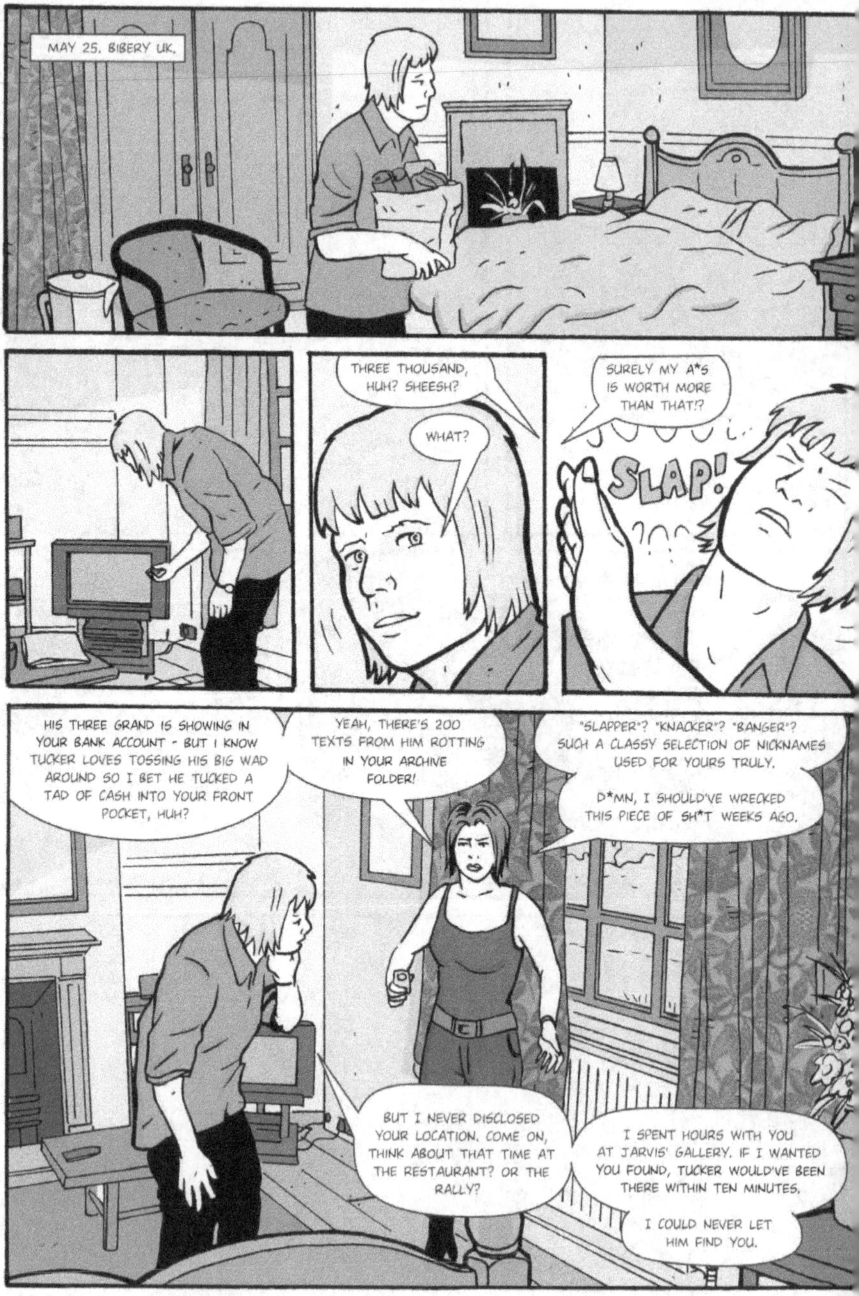
MAY 25. BIBERY UK.
THREE THOUSAND, HUH? SHEESH?
WHAT?
SURELY MY A*S IS WORTH MORE THAN THAT!?
SLAP!
HIS THREE GRAND IS SHOWING IN YOUR BANK ACCOUNT - BUT I KNOW TUCKER LOVES TOSSING HIS BIG WAD AROUND SO I BET HE TUCKED A TAD OF CASH INTO YOUR FRONT POCKET, HUH?
YEAH, THERE'S 200 TEXTS FROM HIM ROTTING IN YOUR ARCHIVE FOLDER!
"SLAPPER"? "KNACKER"? "BANGER"? SUCH A CLASSY SELECTION OF NICKNAMES USED FOR YOURS TRULY.
D*MN, I SHOULD'VE WRECKED THIS PIECE OF SH*T WEEKS AGO.
BUT I NEVER DISCLOSED YOUR LOCATION. COME ON, THINK ABOUT THAT TIME AT THE RESTAURANT? OR THE RALLY?
I SPENT HOURS WITH YOU AT JARVIS' GALLERY. IF I WANTED YOU FOUND, TUCKER WOULD'VE BEEN THERE WITHIN TEN MINUTES.
I COULD NEVER LET HIM FIND YOU.

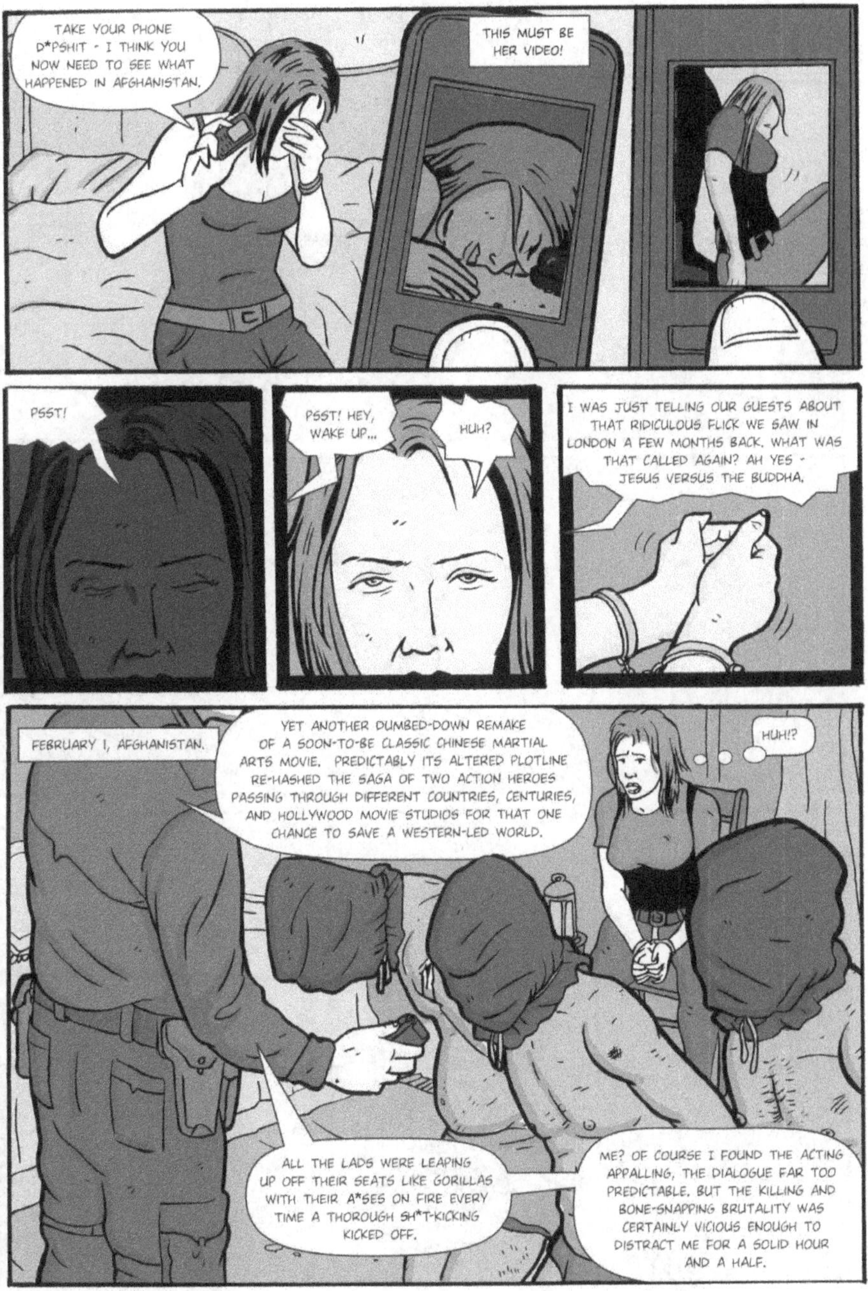
TAKE YOUR PHONE D*PSHIT - I THINK YOU NOW NEED TO SEE WHAT HAPPENED IN AFGHANISTAN.
THIS MUST BE HER VIDEO!
PSST!
PSST! HEY, WAKE UP...
HUH?
I WAS JUST TELLING OUR GUESTS ABOUT THAT RIDICULOUS FLICK WE SAW IN LONDON A FEW MONTHS BACK. WHAT WAS THAT CALLED AGAIN? AH YES - JESUS VERSUS THE BUDDHA.
FEBRUARY 1, AFGHANISTAN.
YET ANOTHER DUMBED-DOWN REMAKE OF A SOON-TO-BE CLASSIC CHINESE MARTIAL ARTS MOVIE. PREDICTABLY ITS ALTERED PLOTLINE RE-HASHED THE SAGA OF TWO ACTION HEROES PASSING THROUGH DIFFERENT COUNTRIES, CENTURIES, AND HOLLYWOOD MOVIE STUDIOS FOR THAT ONE CHANCE TO SAVE A WESTERN-LED WORLD.
HUH!?
ALL THE LADS WERE LEAPING UP OFF THEIR SEATS LIKE GORILLAS WITH THEIR A*SES ON FIRE EVERY TIME A THOROUGH SH*T-KICKING KICKED OFF.
ME? OF COURSE I FOUND THE ACTING APPALLING, THE DIALOGUE FAR TOO PREDICTABLE. BUT THE KILLING AND BONE-SNAPPING BRUTALITY WAS CERTAINLY VICIOUS ENOUGH TO DISTRACT ME FOR A SOLID HOUR AND A HALF.

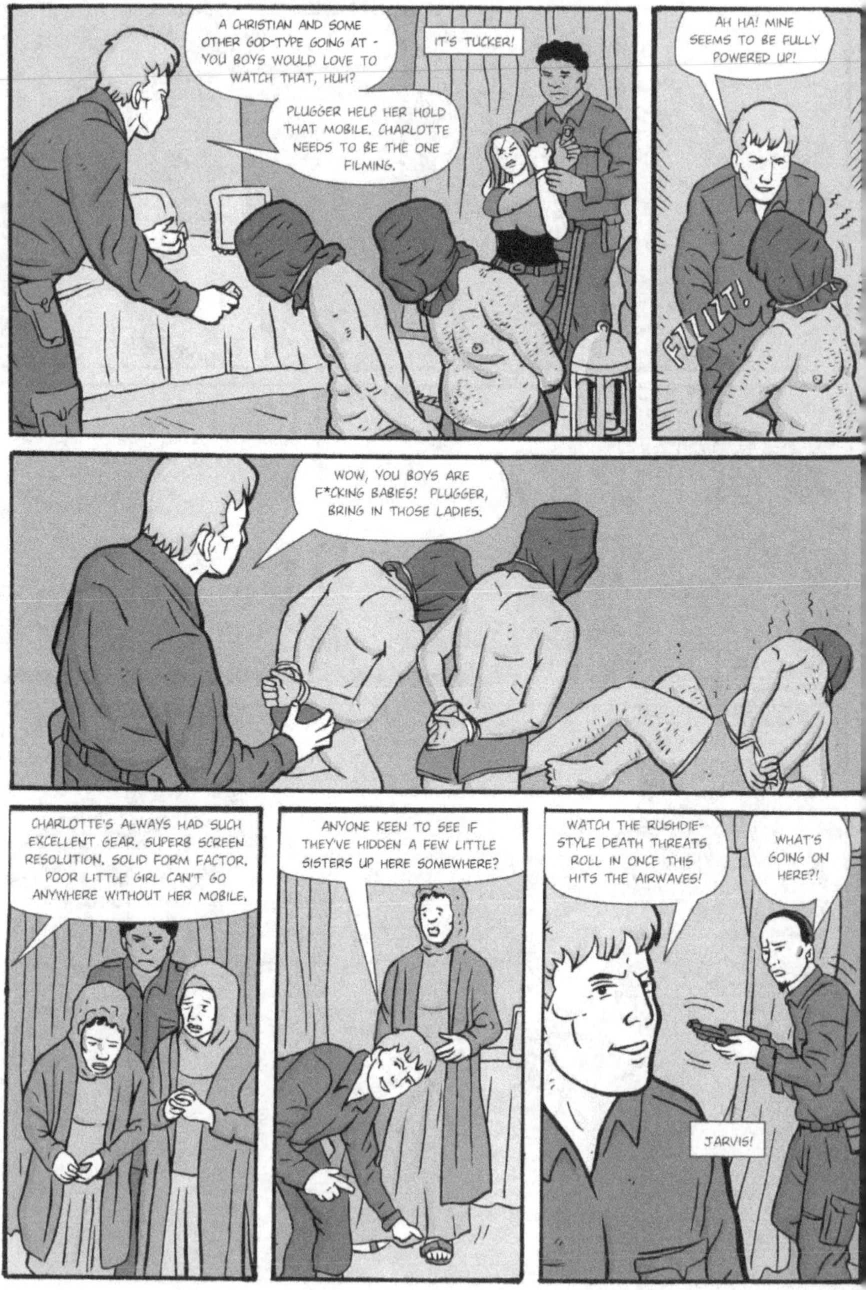
A CHRISTIAN AND SOME OTHER GOD-TYPE GOING AT - YOU BOYS WOULD LOVE TO WATCH THAT, HUH?
PLUGGER HELP HER HOLD THAT MOBILE. CHARLOTTE NEEDS TO BE THE ONE FILMING.
IT'S TUCKER!
AH HA! MINE SEEMS TO BE FULLY POWERED UP!
FZZIZT!
WOW, YOU BOYS ARE F*CKING BABIES! PLUGGER, BRING IN THOSE LADIES.
CHARLOTTE'S ALWAYS HAD SUCH EXCELLENT GEAR. SUPERB SCREEN RESOLUTION. SOLID FORM FACTOR. POOR LITTLE GIRL CAN'T GO ANYWHERE WITHOUT HER MOBILE.
ANYONE KEEN TO SEE IF THEY'VE HIDDEN A FEW LITTLE SISTERS UP HERE SOMEWHERE?
WATCH THE RUSHDIE-STYLE DEATH THREATS ROLL IN ONCE THIS HITS THE AIRWAVES!
WHAT'S GOING ON HERE?!
JARVIS!

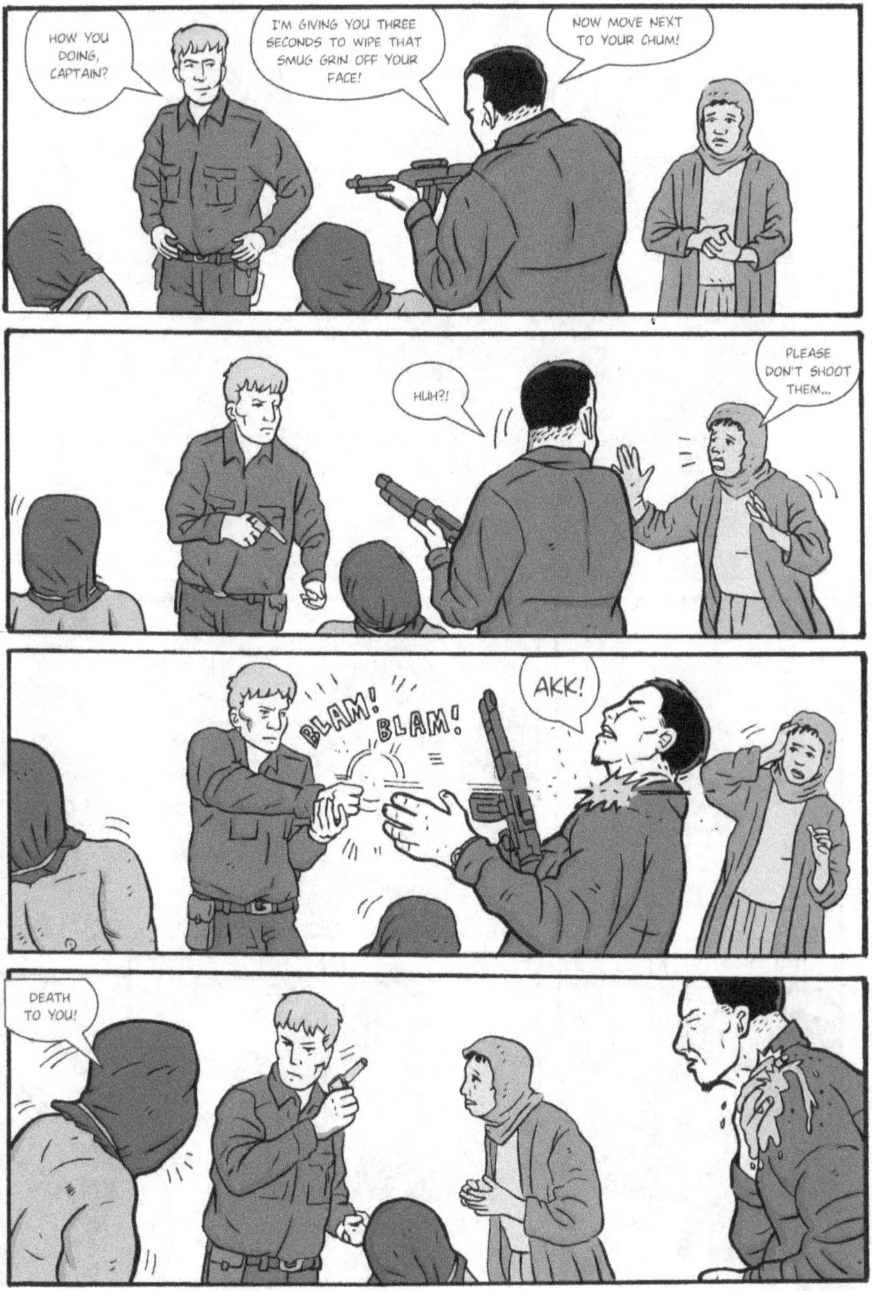
HOW YOU DOING, CAPTAIN?
I'M GIVING YOU THREE SECONDS TO WIPE THAT SMUG GRIN OFF YOUR FACE!
NOW MOVE NEXT TO YOUR CHUM!
HUH?!
PLEASE DON'T SHOOT THEM...
BLAM! BLAM!
AKK!
DEATH TO YOU!

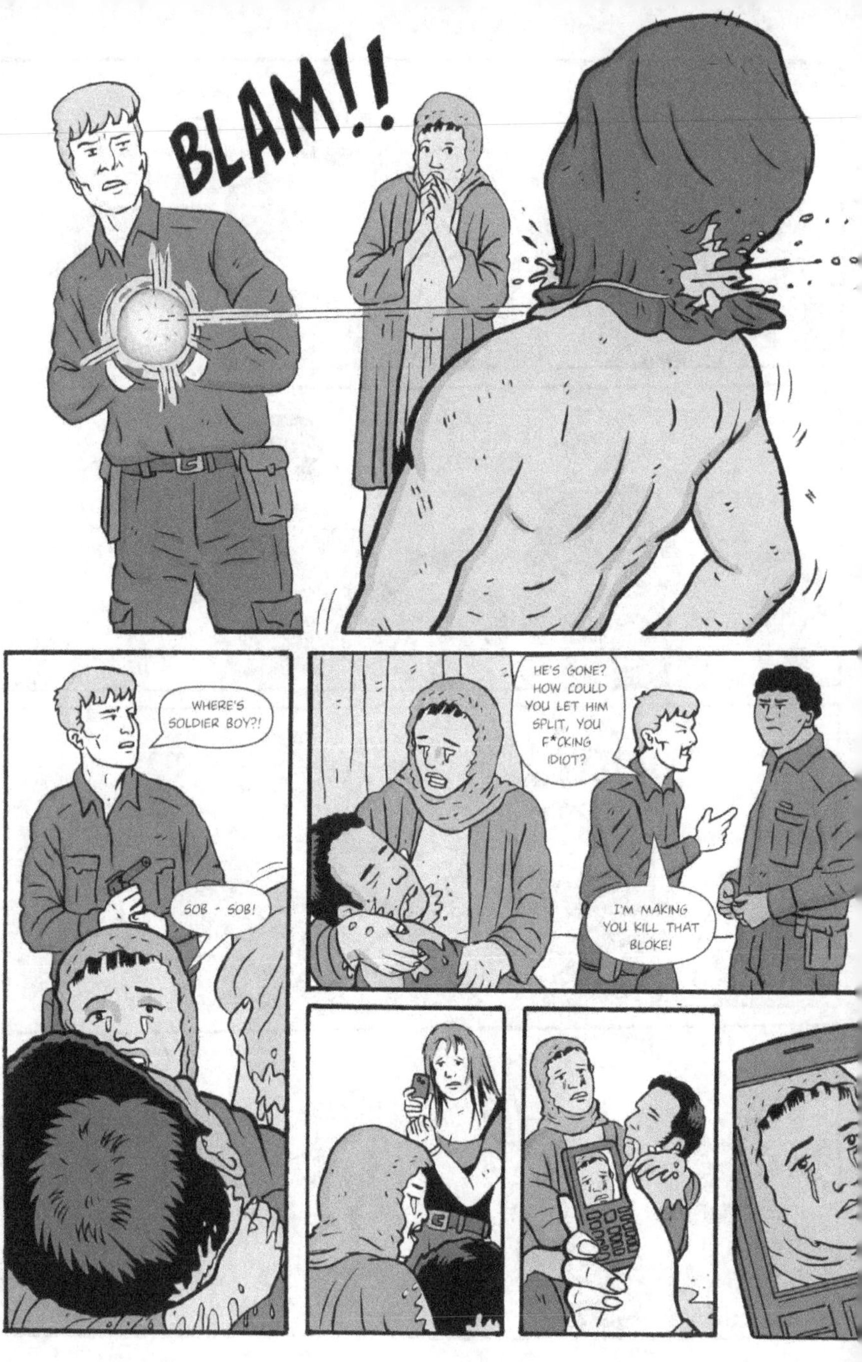
BLAM!!
WHERE'S SOLDIER BOY?!
SOB - SOB!
HE'S GONE? HOW COULD YOU LET HIM SPLIT, YOU F*CKING IDIOT?
I'M MAKING YOU KILL THAT BLOKE!

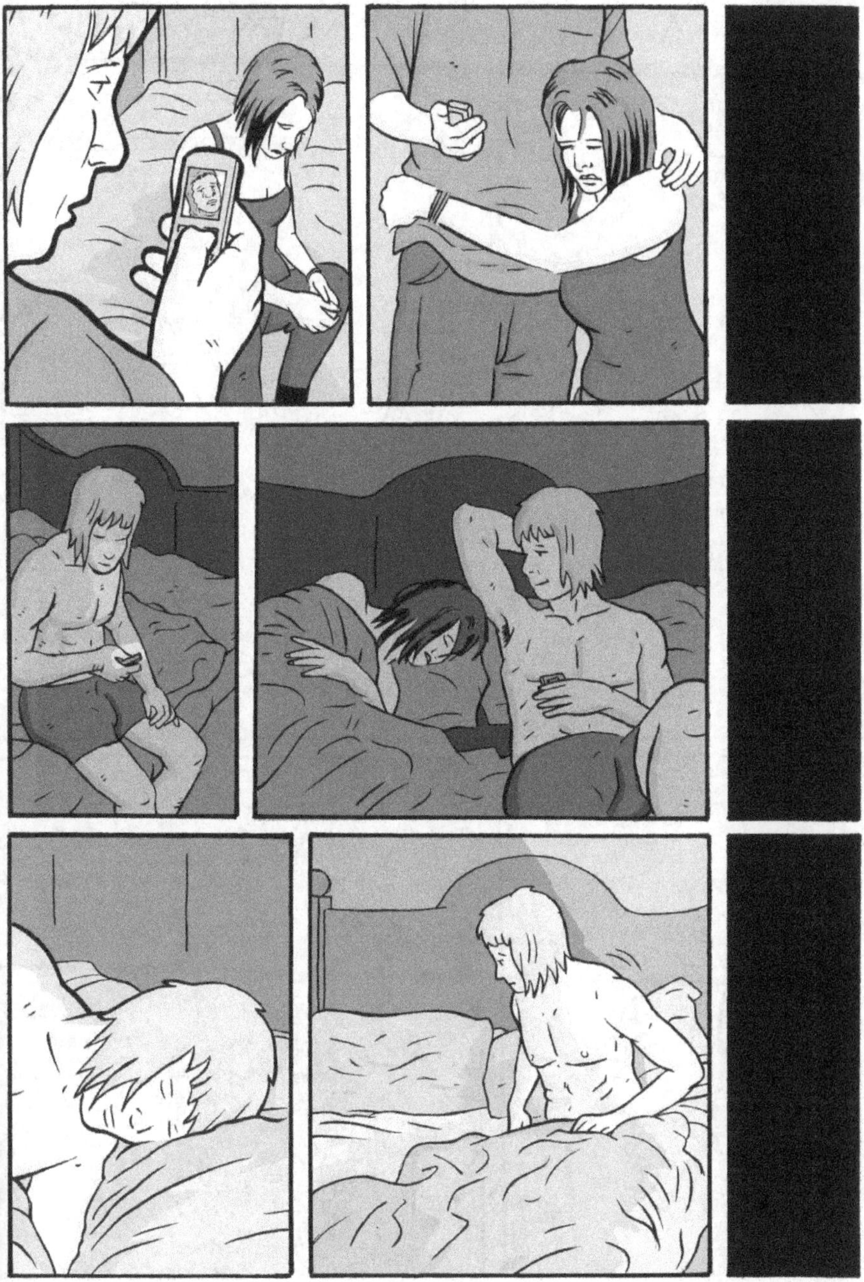

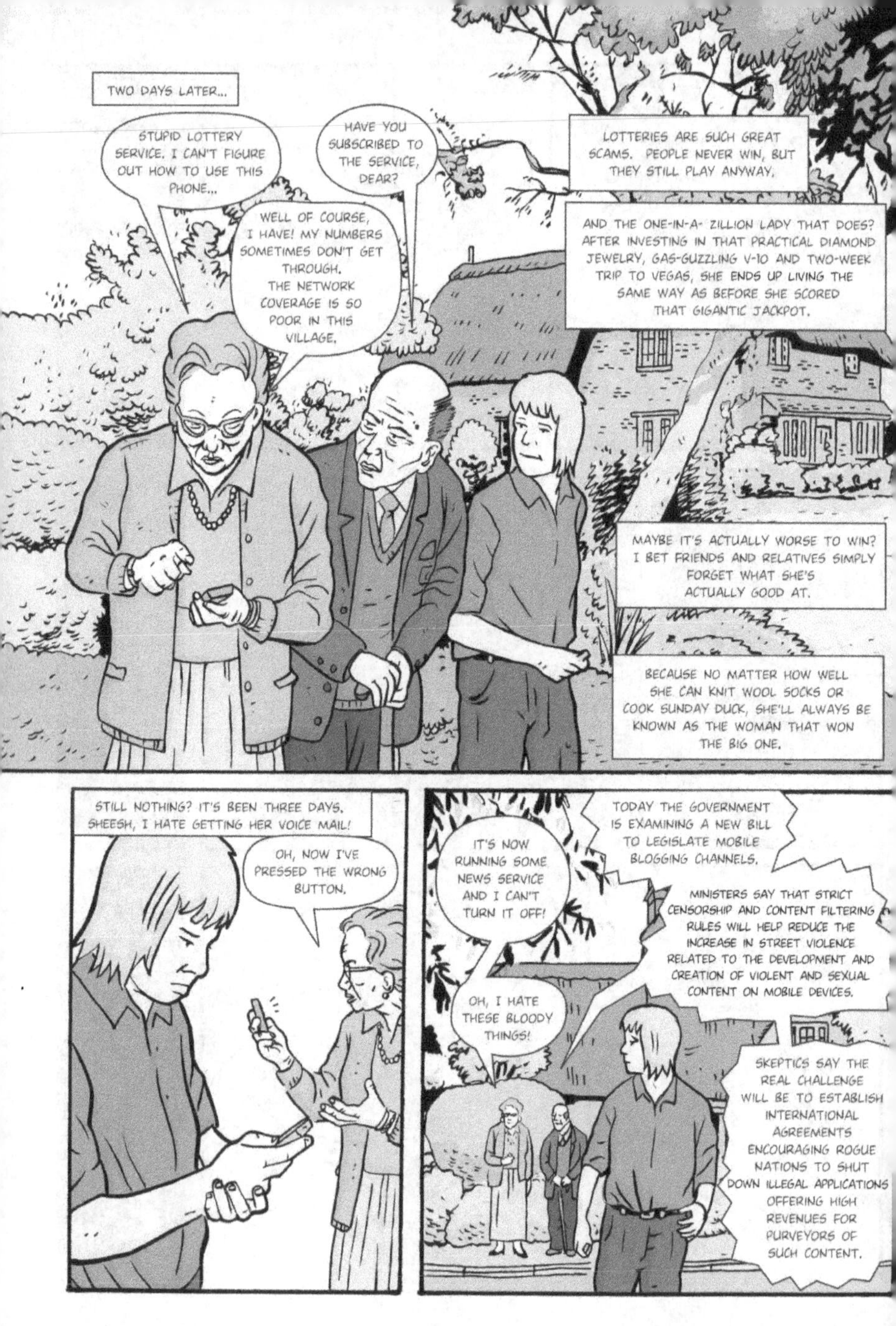

TWO DAYS LATER...
STUPID LOTTERY SERVICE. I CAN'T FIGURE OUT HOW TO USE THIS PHONE...
HAVE YOU SUBSCRIBED TO THE SERVICE, DEAR?
WELL OF COURSE, I HAVE! MY NUMBERS SOMETIMES DON'T GET THROUGH. THE NETWORK COVERAGE IS SO POOR IN THIS VILLAGE.
LOTTERIES ARE SUCH GREAT SCAMS. PEOPLE NEVER WIN, BUT THEY STILL PLAY ANYWAY.
AND THE ONE-IN-A- ZILLION LADY THAT DOES? AFTER INVESTING IN THAT PRACTICAL DIAMOND JEWELRY, GAS-GUZZLING V-10 AND TWO-WEEK TRIP TO VEGAS, SHE ENDS UP LIVING THE SAME WAY AS BEFORE SHE SCORED THAT GIGANTIC JACKPOT.
MAYBE IT'S ACTUALLY WORSE TO WIN? I BET FRIENDS AND RELATIVES SIMPLY FORGET WHAT SHE'S ACTUALLY GOOD AT.
BECAUSE NO MATTER HOW WELL SHE CAN KNIT WOOL SOCKS OR COOK SUNDAY DUCK, SHE'LL ALWAYS BE KNOWN AS THE WOMAN THAT WON THE BIG ONE.
STILL NOTHING? IT'S BEEN THREE DAYS. SHEESH, I HATE GETTING HER VOICE MAIL!
OH, NOW I'VE PRESSED THE WRONG BUTTON.
IT'S NOW RUNNING SOME NEWS SERVICE AND I CAN'T TURN IT OFF!
TODAY THE GOVERNMENT IS EXAMINING A NEW BILL TO LEGISLATE MOBILE BLOGGING CHANNELS.
MINISTERS SAY THAT STRICT CENSORSHIP AND CONTENT FILTERING RULES WILL HELP REDUCE THE INCREASE IN STREET VIOLENCE RELATED TO THE DEVELOPMENT AND CREATION OF VIOLENT AND SEXUAL CONTENT ON MOBILE DEVICES.
OH, I HATE THESE BLOODY THINGS!
SKEPTICS SAY THE REAL CHALLENGE WILL BE TO ESTABLISH INTERNATIONAL AGREEMENTS ENCOURAGING ROGUE NATIONS TO SHUT DOWN ILLEGAL APPLICATIONS OFFERING HIGH REVENUES FOR PURVEYORS OF SUCH CONTENT.

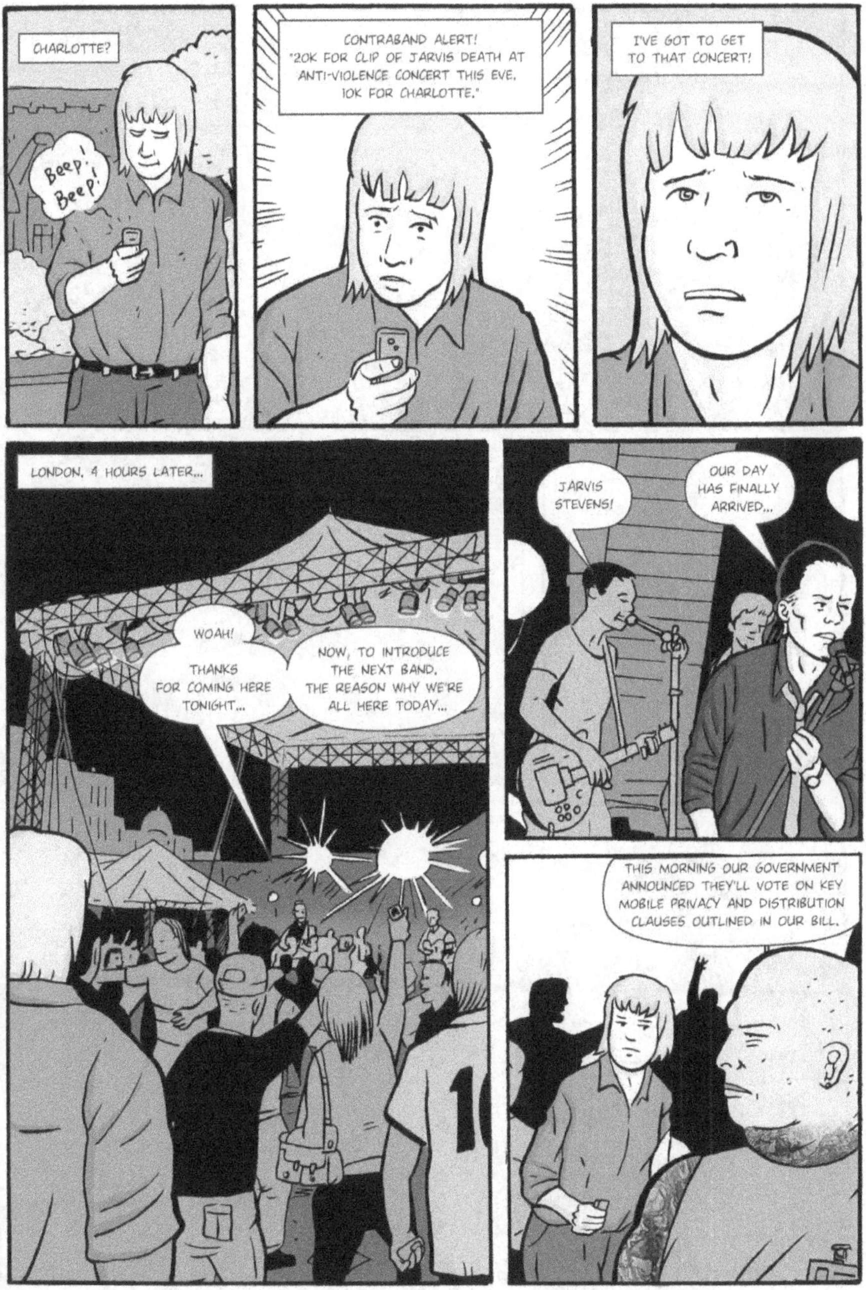
CHARLOTTE?
Beep! Beep!
CONTRABAND ALERT! "20K FOR CLIP OF JARVIS DEATH AT ANTI-VIOLENCE CONCERT THIS EVE. 10K FOR CHARLOTTE."
I'VE GOT TO GET TO THAT CONCERT!
LONDON, 4 HOURS LATER...
WOAH! THANKS FOR COMING HERE TONIGHT...
NOW, TO INTRODUCE THE NEXT BAND, THE REASON WHY WE'RE ALL HERE TODAY...
JARVIS STEVENS!
OUR DAY HAS FINALLY ARRIVED...
THIS MORNING OUR GOVERNMENT ANNOUNCED THEY'LL VOTE ON KEY MOBILE PRIVACY AND DISTRIBUTION CLAUSES OUTLINED IN OUR BILL.

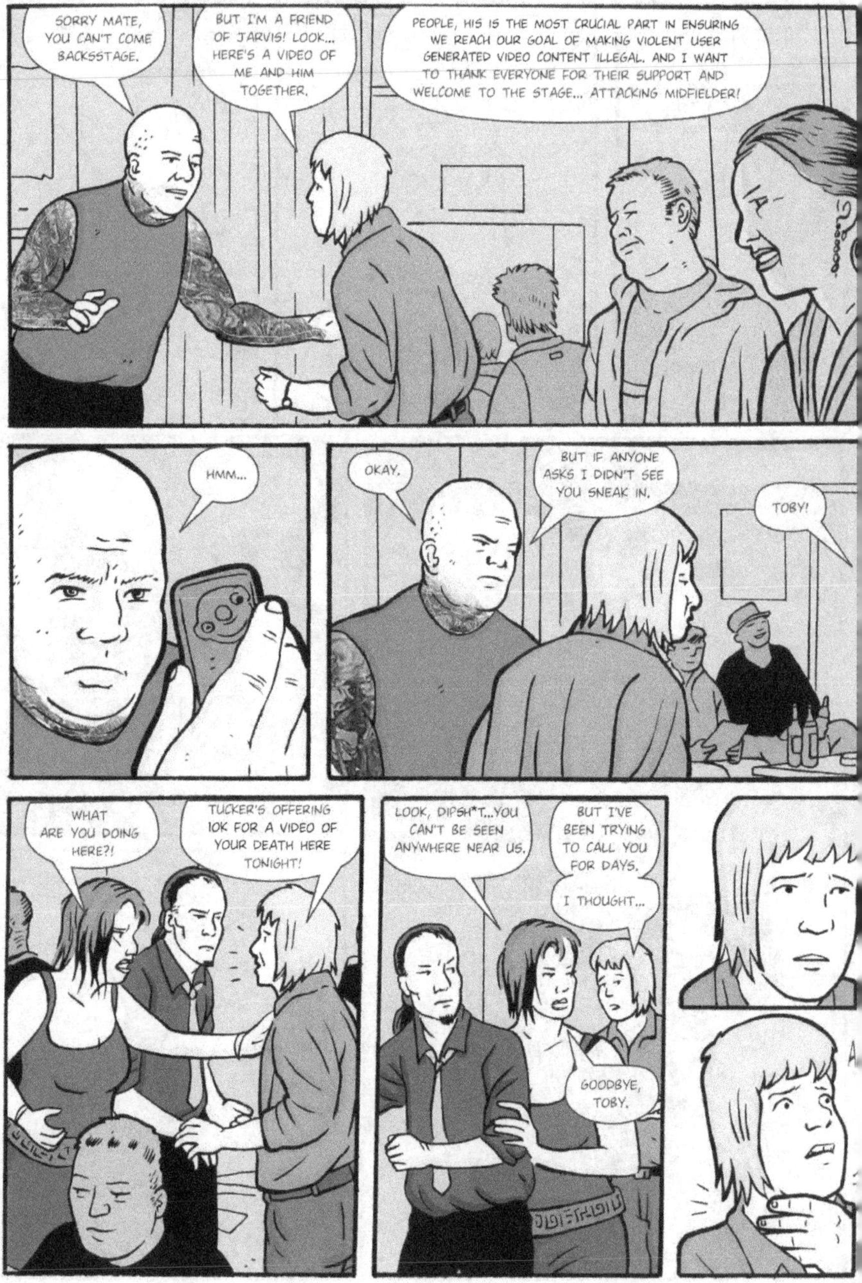
SORRY MATE, YOU CAN'T COME BACKSSTAGE.
BUT I'M A FRIEND OF JARVIS! LOOK... HERE'S A VIDEO OF ME AND HIM TOGETHER.
PEOPLE, HIS IS THE MOST CRUCIAL PART IN ENSURING WE REACH OUR GOAL OF MAKING VIOLENT USER GENERATED VIDEO CONTENT ILLEGAL. AND I WANT TO THANK EVERYONE FOR THEIR SUPPORT AND WELCOME TO THE STAGE... ATTACKING MIDFIELDER!
HMM...
OKAY.
BUT IF ANYONE ASKS I DIDN'T SEE YOU SNEAK IN.
TOBY!
WHAT ARE YOU DOING HERE?!
TUCKER'S OFFERING 10K FOR A VIDEO OF YOUR DEATH HERE TONIGHT!
LOOK, DIPSH*T...YOU CAN'T BE SEEN ANYWHERE NEAR US.
BUT I'VE BEEN TRYING TO CALL YOU FOR DAYS.
I THOUGHT...
GOODBYE, TOBY.

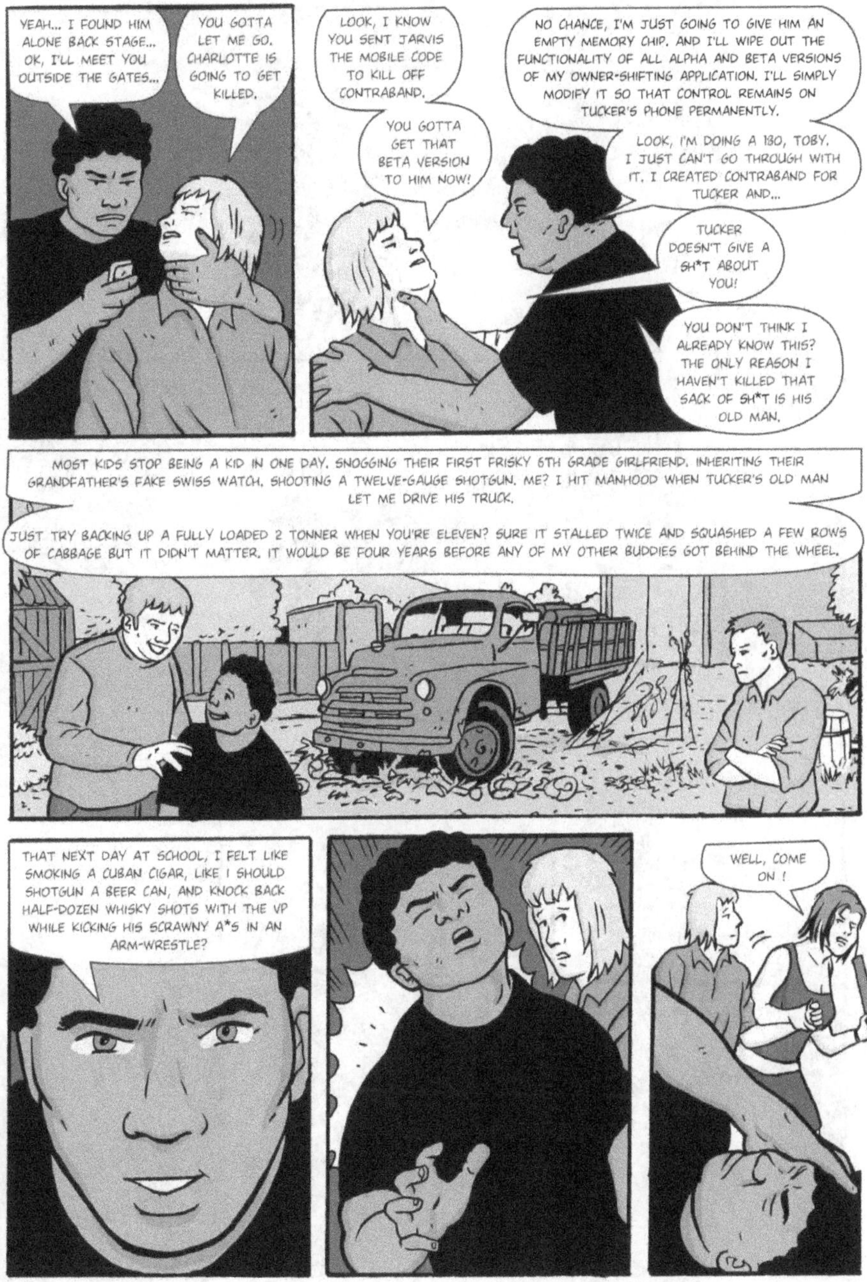
YEAH... I FOUND HIM ALONE BACK STAGE... OK, I'LL MEET YOU OUTSIDE THE GATES...
YOU GOTTA LET ME GO. CHARLOTTE IS GOING TO GET KILLED.
LOOK, I KNOW YOU SENT JARVIS THE MOBILE CODE TO KILL OFF CONTRABAND.
YOU GOTTA GET THAT BETA VERSION TO HIM NOW!
NO CHANCE, I'M JUST GOING TO GIVE HIM AN EMPTY MEMORY CHIP. AND I'LL WIPE OUT THE FUNCTIONALITY OF ALL ALPHA AND BETA VERSIONS OF MY OWNER-SHIFTING APPLICATION. I'LL SIMPLY MODIFY IT SO THAT CONTROL REMAINS ON TUCKER'S PHONE PERMANENTLY.
LOOK, I'M DOING A 180, TOBY. I JUST CAN'T GO THROUGH WITH IT. I CREATED CONTRABAND FOR TUCKER AND...
TUCKER DOESN'T GIVE A SH*T ABOUT YOU!
YOU DON'T THINK I ALREADY KNOW THIS? THE ONLY REASON I HAVEN'T KILLED THAT SACK OF SH*T IS HIS OLD MAN.
MOST KIDS STOP BEING A KID IN ONE DAY. SNOGGING THEIR FIRST FRISKY 6TH GRADE GIRLFRIEND. INHERITING THEIR GRANDFATHER'S FAKE SWISS WATCH. SHOOTING A TWELVE-GAUGE SHOTGUN. ME? I HIT MANHOOD WHEN TUCKER'S OLD MAN LET ME DRIVE HIS TRUCK.
JUST TRY BACKING UP A FULLY LOADED 2 TONNER WHEN YOU'RE ELEVEN? SURE IT STALLED TWICE AND SQUASHED A FEW ROWS OF CABBAGE BUT IT DIDN'T MATTER. IT WOULD BE FOUR YEARS BEFORE ANY OF MY OTHER BUDDIES GOT BEHIND THE WHEEL.
THAT NEXT DAY AT SCHOOL, I FELT LIKE SMOKING A CUBAN CIGAR, LIKE I SHOULD SHOTGUN A BEER CAN, AND KNOCK BACK HALF-DOZEN WHISKY SHOTS WITH THE VP WHILE KICKING HIS SCRAWNY A*S IN AN ARM-WRESTLE?
WELL, COME ON !

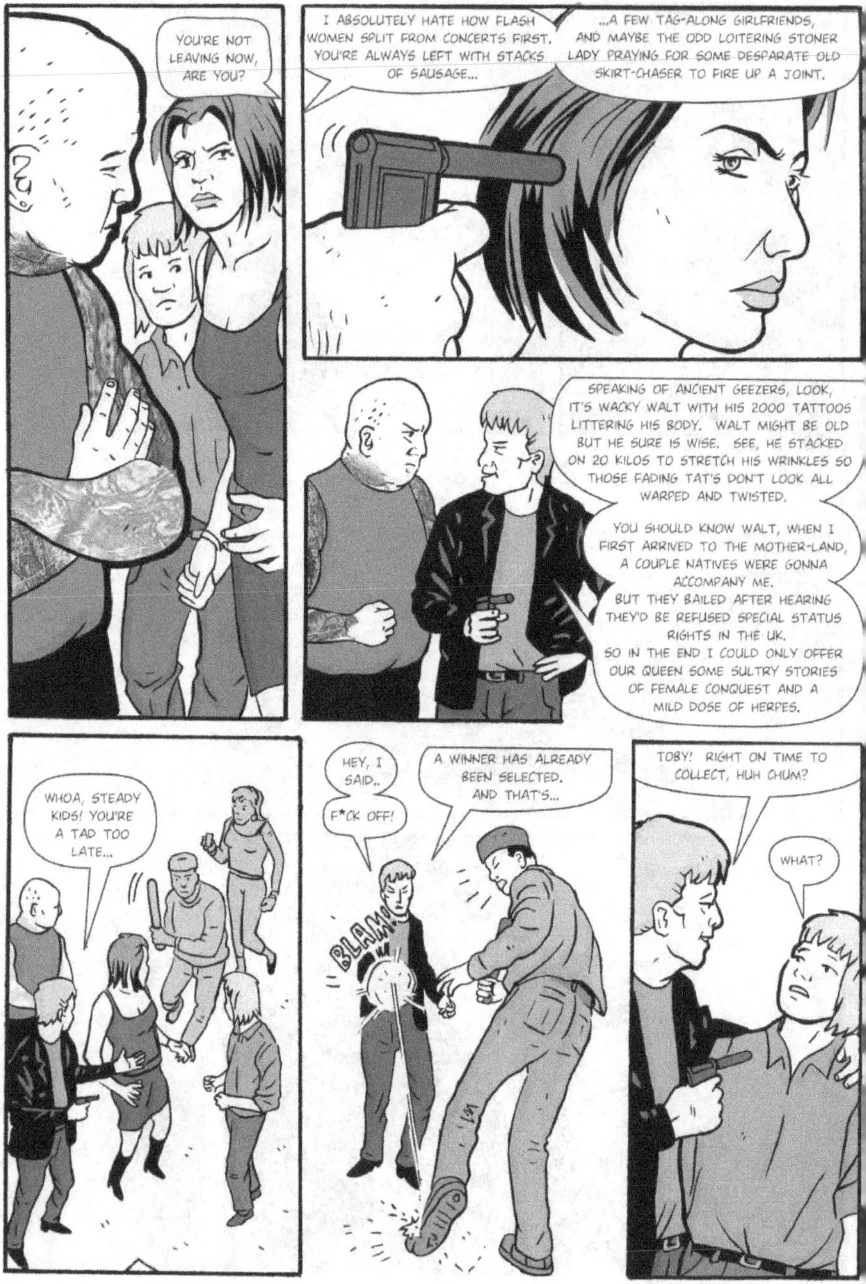
YOU'RE NOT LEAVING NOW, ARE YOU?
I ABSOLUTELY HATE HOW FLASH WOMEN SPLIT FROM CONCERTS FIRST. YOU'RE ALWAYS LEFT WITH STACKS OF SAUSAGE...
...A FEW TAG-ALONG GIRLFRIENDS, AND MAYBE THE ODD LOITERING STONER LADY PRAYING FOR SOME DESPARATE OLD SKIRT-CHASER TO FIRE UP A JOINT.
SPEAKING OF ANCIENT GEEZERS, LOOK, IT'S WACKY WALT WITH HIS 2000 TATTOOS LITTERING HIS BODY. WALT MIGHT BE OLD BUT HE SURE IS WISE. SEE, HE STACKED ON 20 KILOS TO STRETCH HIS WRINKLES SO THOSE FADING TAT'S DON'T LOOK ALL WARPED AND TWISTED.
YOU SHOULD KNOW WALT, WHEN I FIRST ARRIVED TO THE MOTHER-LAND, A COUPLE NATIVES WERE GONNA ACCOMPANY ME. BUT THEY BAILED AFTER HEARING THEY'D BE REFUSED SPECIAL STATUS RIGHTS IN THE UK. SO IN THE END I COULD ONLY OFFER OUR QUEEN SOME SULTRY STORIES OF FEMALE CONQUEST AND A MILD DOSE OF HERPES.
WHOA, STEADY KIDS! YOU'RE A TAD TOO LATE...
HEY, I SAID..
F*CK OFF!
A WINNER HAS ALREADY BEEN SELECTED. AND THAT'S...
BLAM!
TOBY! RIGHT ON TIME TO COLLECT, HUH CHUM?
WHAT?

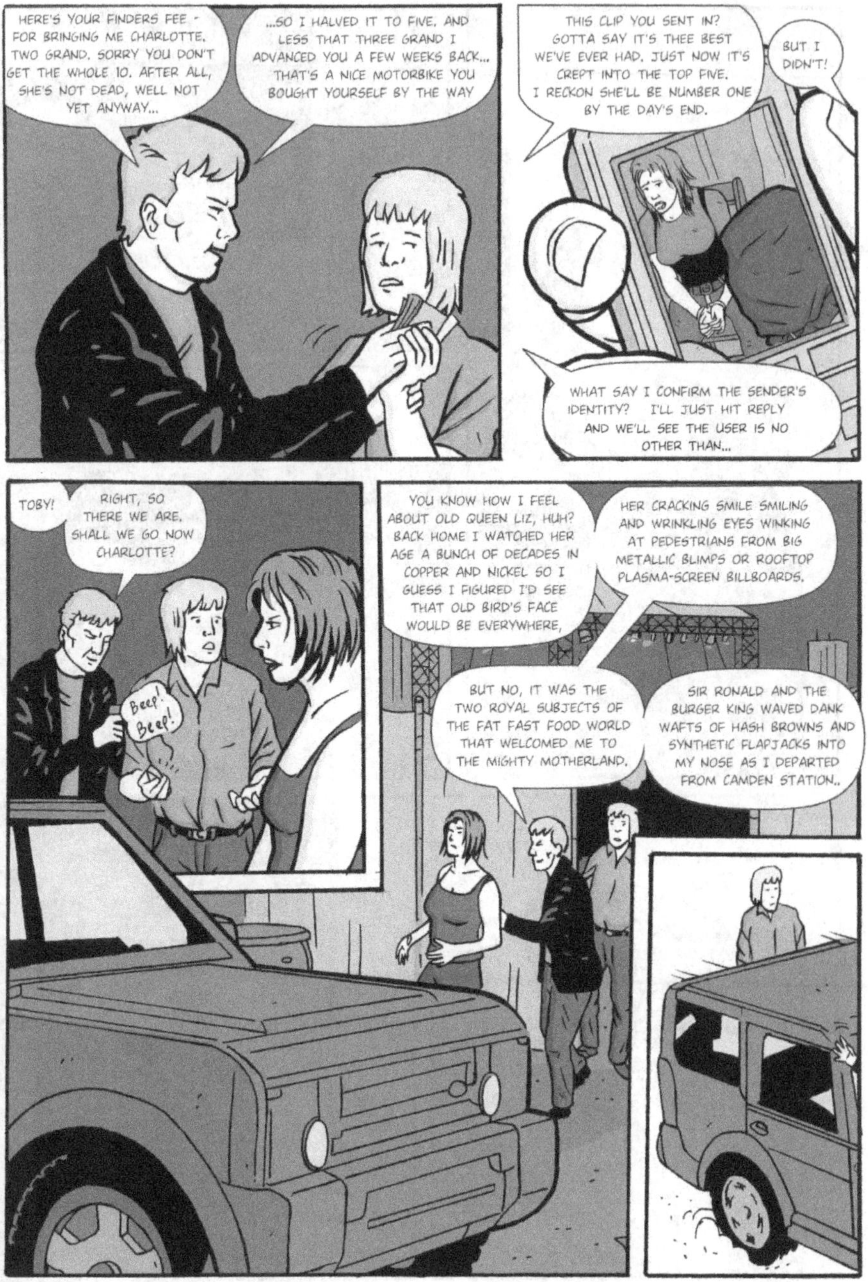
HERE'S YOUR FINDERS FEE - FOR BRINGING ME CHARLOTTE. TWO GRAND. SORRY YOU DON'T GET THE WHOLE 10. AFTER ALL, SHE'S NOT DEAD, WELL NOT YET ANYWAY...
...SO I HALVED IT TO FIVE, AND LESS THAT THREE GRAND I ADVANCED YOU A FEW WEEKS BACK... THAT'S A NICE MOTORBIKE YOU BOUGHT YOURSELF BY THE WAY
THIS CLIP YOU SENT IN? GOTTA SAY IT'S THEE BEST WE'VE EVER HAD. JUST NOW IT'S CREPT INTO THE TOP FIVE. I RECKON SHE'LL BE NUMBER ONE BY THE DAY'S END.
BUT I DIDN'T!
WHAT SAY I CONFIRM THE SENDER'S IDENTITY? I'LL JUST HIT REPLY AND WE'LL SEE THE USER IS NO OTHER THAN...
TOBY!
RIGHT, SO THERE WE ARE. SHALL WE GO NOW CHARLOTTE?
Beep! Beep!
YOU KNOW HOW I FEEL ABOUT OLD QUEEN LIZ, HUH? BACK HOME I WATCHED HER AGE A BUNCH OF DECADES IN COPPER AND NICKEL SO I GUESS I FIGURED I'D SEE THAT OLD BIRD'S FACE WOULD BE EVERYWHERE,
HER CRACKING SMILE SMILING AND WRINKLING EYES WINKING AT PEDESTRIANS FROM BIG METALLIC BLIMPS OR ROOFTOP PLASMA-SCREEN BILLBOARDS.
BUT NO, IT WAS THE TWO ROYAL SUBJECTS OF THE FAT FAST FOOD WORLD THAT WELCOMED ME TO THE MIGHTY MOTHERLAND.
SIR RONALD AND THE BURGER KING WAVED DANK WAFTS OF HASH BROWNS AND SYNTHETIC FLAPJACKS INTO MY NOSE AS I DEPARTED FROM CAMDEN STATION..

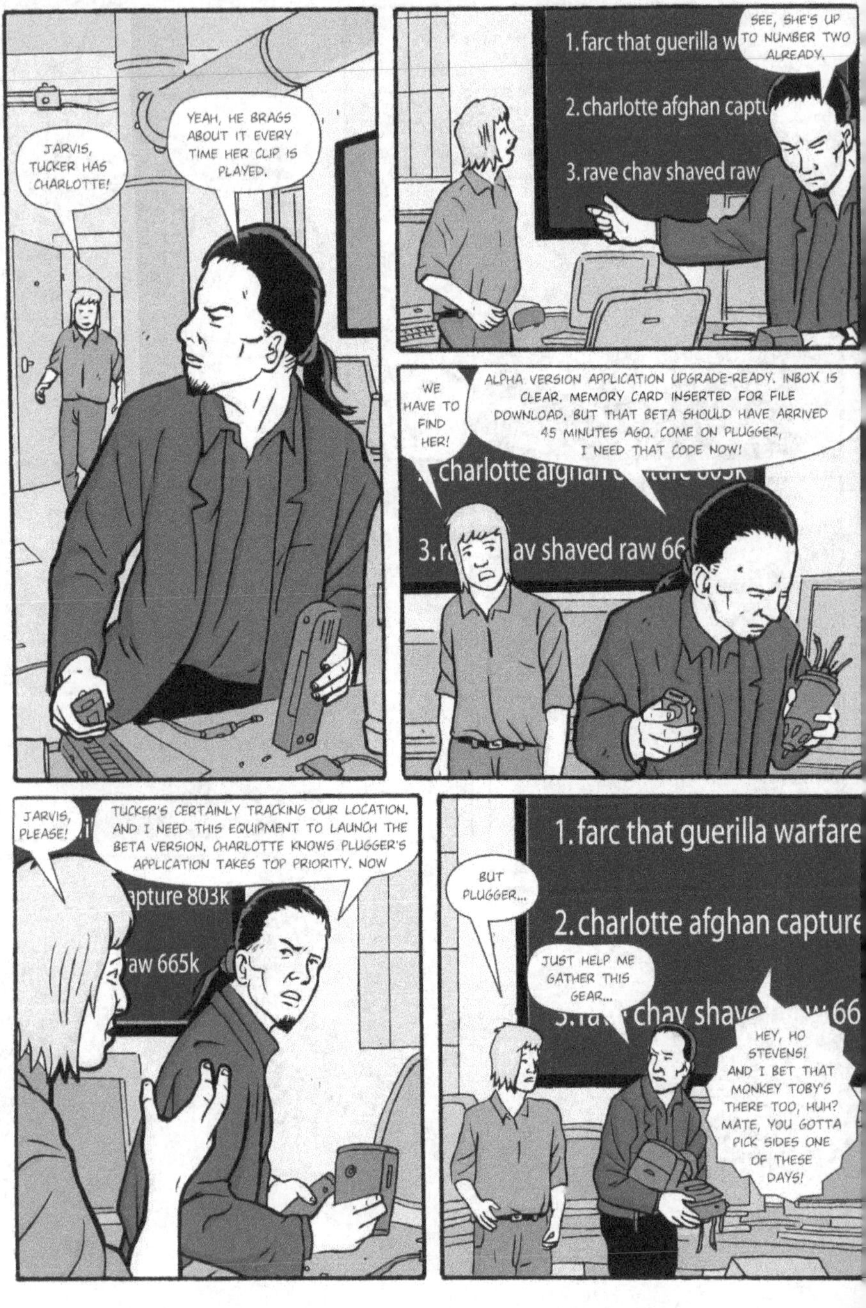
JARVIS, TUCKER HAS CHARLOTTE!
YEAH, HE BRAGS ABOUT IT EVERY TIME HER CLIP IS PLAYED.
1. farc that guerilla w
2. charlotte afghan captu
3. rave chav shaved raw
SEE, SHE'S UP TO NUMBER TWO ALREADY.
WE HAVE TO FIND HER!
ALPHA VERSION APPLICATION UPGRADE-READY. INBOX IS CLEAR. MEMORY CARD INSERTED FOR FILE DOWNLOAD. BUT THAT BETA SHOULD HAVE ARRIVED 45 MINUTES AGO. COME ON PLUGGER, I NEED THAT CODE NOW!
JARVIS, PLEASE!
TUCKER'S CERTAINLY TRACKING OUR LOCATION. AND I NEED THIS EQUIPMENT TO LAUNCH THE BETA VERSION. CHARLOTTE KNOWS PLUGGER'S APPLICATION TAKES TOP PRIORITY. NOW
1. farc that guerilla warfare
2. charlotte afghan capture
BUT PLUGGER...
JUST HELP ME GATHER THIS GEAR...
HEY, HO STEVENS! AND I BET THAT MONKEY TOBY'S THERE TOO, HUH? MATE, YOU GOTTA PICK SIDES ONE OF THESE DAYS!

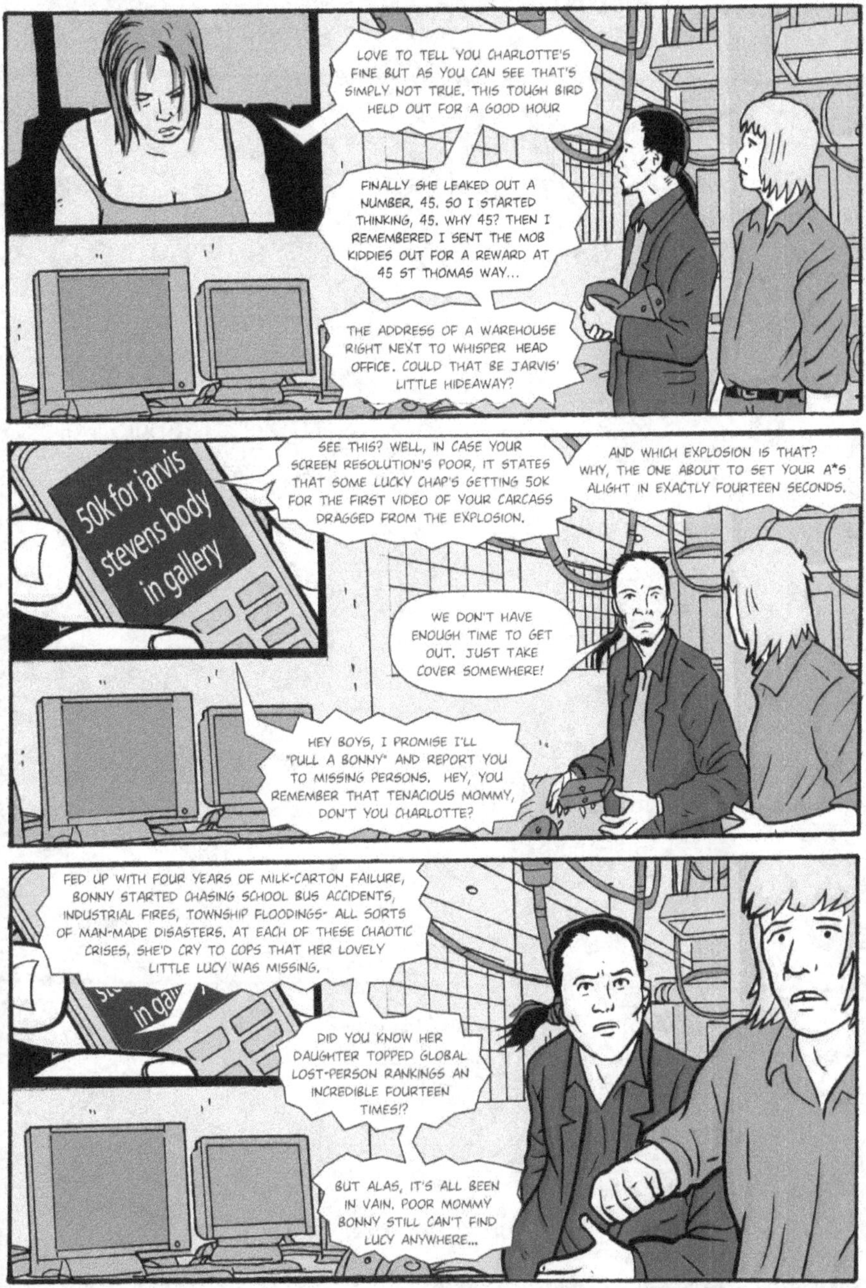

LOVE TO TELL YOU CHARLOTTE'S FINE BUT AS YOU CAN SEE THAT'S SIMPLY NOT TRUE. THIS TOUGH BIRD HELD OUT FOR A GOOD HOUR
FINALLY SHE LEAKED OUT A NUMBER. 45. SO I STARTED THINKING, 45. WHY 45? THEN I REMEMBERED I SENT THE MOB KIDDIES OUT FOR A REWARD AT 45 ST THOMAS WAY...
THE ADDRESS OF A WAREHOUSE RIGHT NEXT TO WHISPER HEAD OFFICE. COULD THAT BE JARVIS' LITTLE HIDEAWAY?
50k for jarvis stevens body in gallery
SEE THIS? WELL, IN CASE YOUR SCREEN RESOLUTION'S POOR, IT STATES THAT SOME LUCKY CHAP'S GETTING 50K FOR THE FIRST VIDEO OF YOUR CARCASS DRAGGED FROM THE EXPLOSION.
AND WHICH EXPLOSION IS THAT? WHY, THE ONE ABOUT TO SET YOUR A*S ALIGHT IN EXACTLY FOURTEEN SECONDS.
WE DON'T HAVE ENOUGH TIME TO GET OUT. JUST TAKE COVER SOMEWHERE!
HEY BOYS, I PROMISE I'LL "PULL A BONNY" AND REPORT YOU TO MISSING PERSONS. HEY, YOU REMEMBER THAT TENACIOUS MOMMY, DON'T YOU CHARLOTTE?
FED UP WITH FOUR YEARS OF MILK-CARTON FAILURE, BONNY STARTED CHASING SCHOOL BUS ACCIDENTS, INDUSTRIAL FIRES, TOWNSHIP FLOODINGS- ALL SORTS OF MAN-MADE DISASTERS. AT EACH OF THESE CHAOTIC CRISES, SHE'D CRY TO COPS THAT HER LOVELY LITTLE LUCY WAS MISSING.
DID YOU KNOW HER DAUGHTER TOPPED GLOBAL LOST-PERSON RANKINGS AN INCREDIBLE FOURTEEN TIMES!?
BUT ALAS, IT'S ALL BEEN IN VAIN. POOR MOMMY BONNY STILL CAN'T FIND LUCY ANYWHERE...

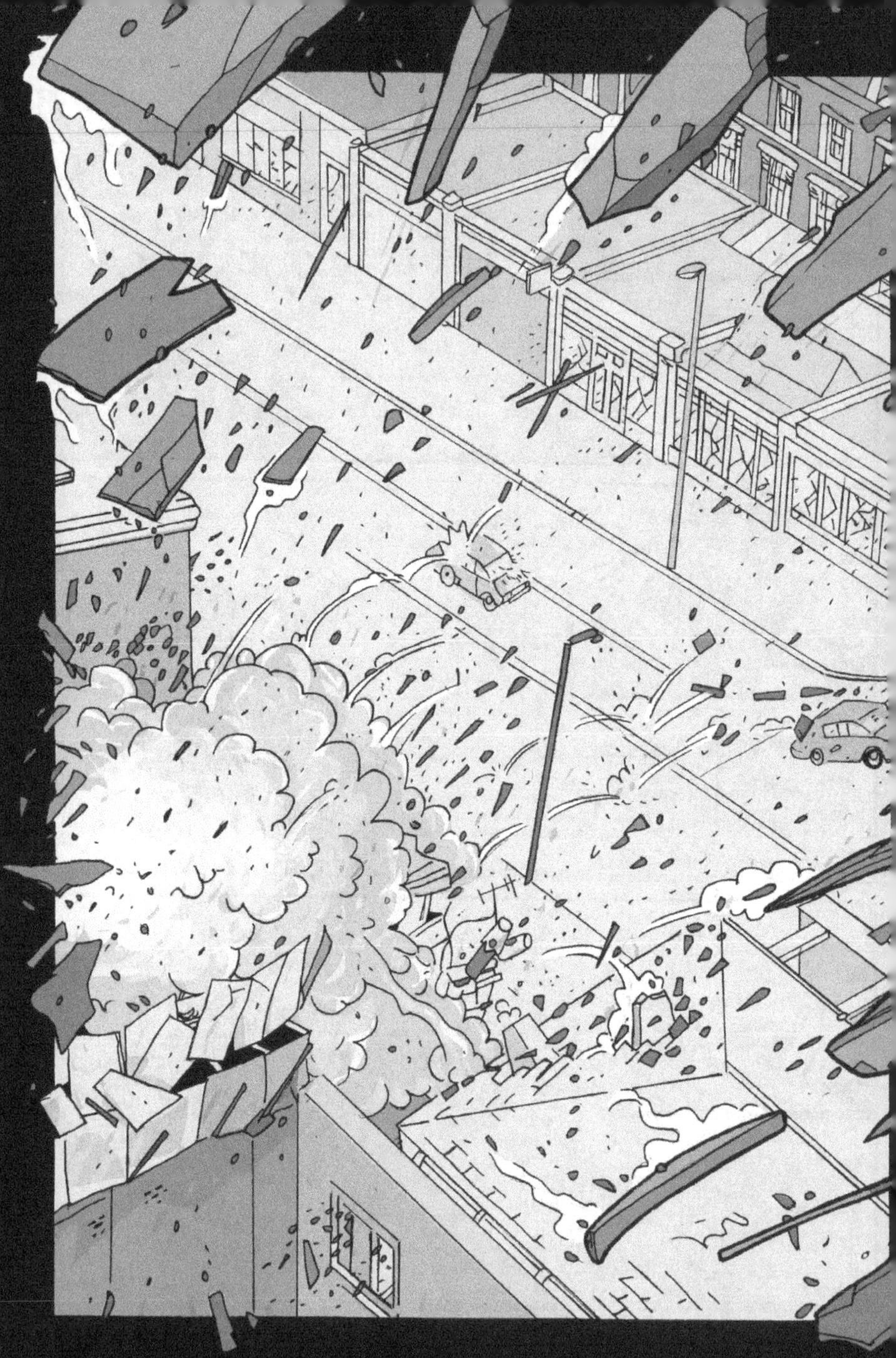

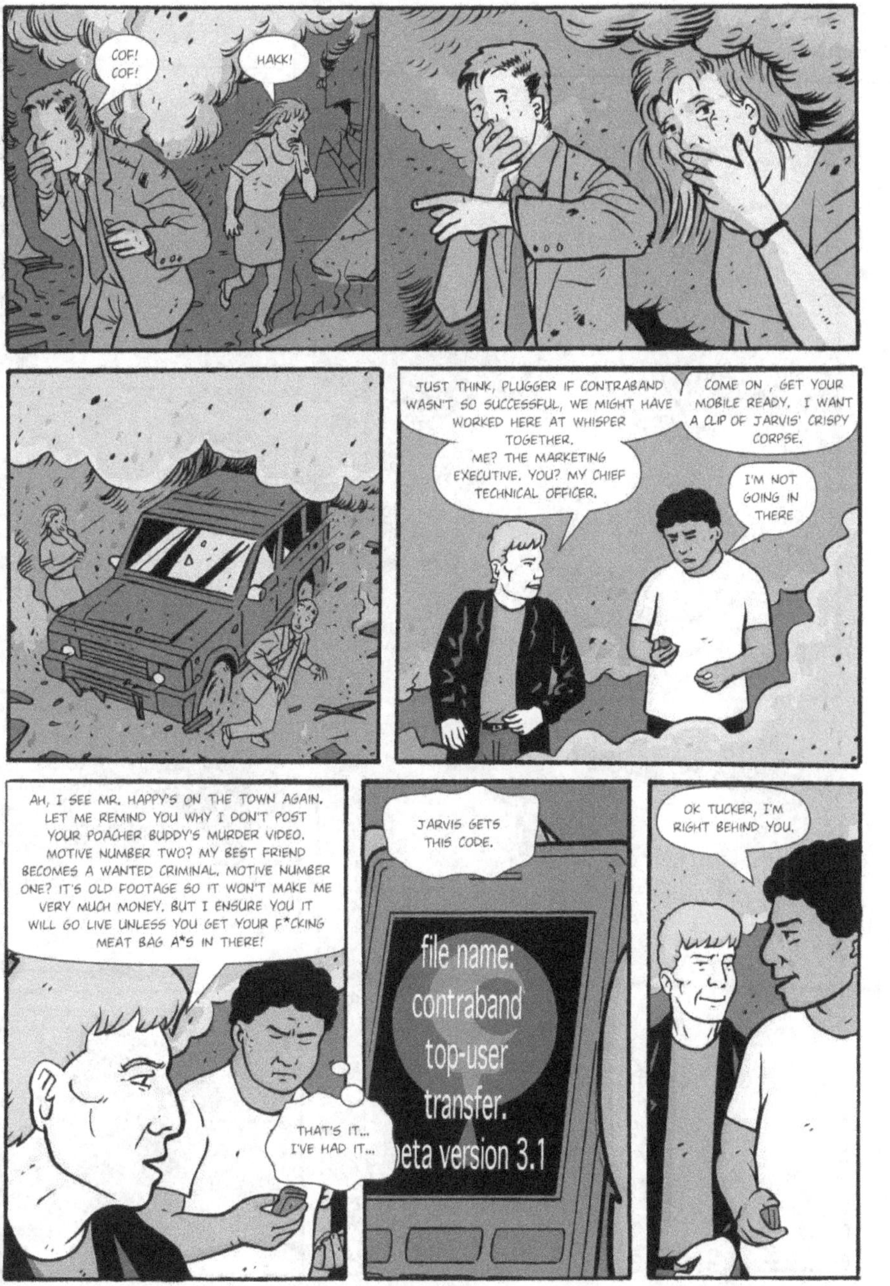
COF! COF!
HAKK!
JUST THINK, PLUGGER IF CONTRABAND WASN'T SO SUCCESSFUL, WE MIGHT HAVE WORKED HERE AT WHISPER TOGETHER. ME? THE MARKETING EXECUTIVE. YOU? MY CHIEF TECHNICAL OFFICER.
COME ON , GET YOUR MOBILE READY. I WANT A CLIP OF JARVIS' CRISPY CORPSE.
I'M NOT GOING IN THERE
AH, I SEE MR. HAPPY'S ON THE TOWN AGAIN. LET ME REMIND YOU WHY I DON'T POST YOUR POACHER BUDDY'S MURDER VIDEO. MOTIVE NUMBER TWO? MY BEST FRIEND BECOMES A WANTED CRIMINAL. MOTIVE NUMBER ONE? IT'S OLD FOOTAGE SO IT WON'T MAKE ME VERY MUCH MONEY. BUT I ENSURE YOU IT WILL GO LIVE UNLESS YOU GET YOUR F*CKING MEAT BAG A*S IN THERE!
THAT'S IT... I'VE HAD IT...
JARVIS GETS THIS CODE.
file name: contraband top-user transfer. beta version 3.1
OK TUCKER, I'M RIGHT BEHIND YOU.

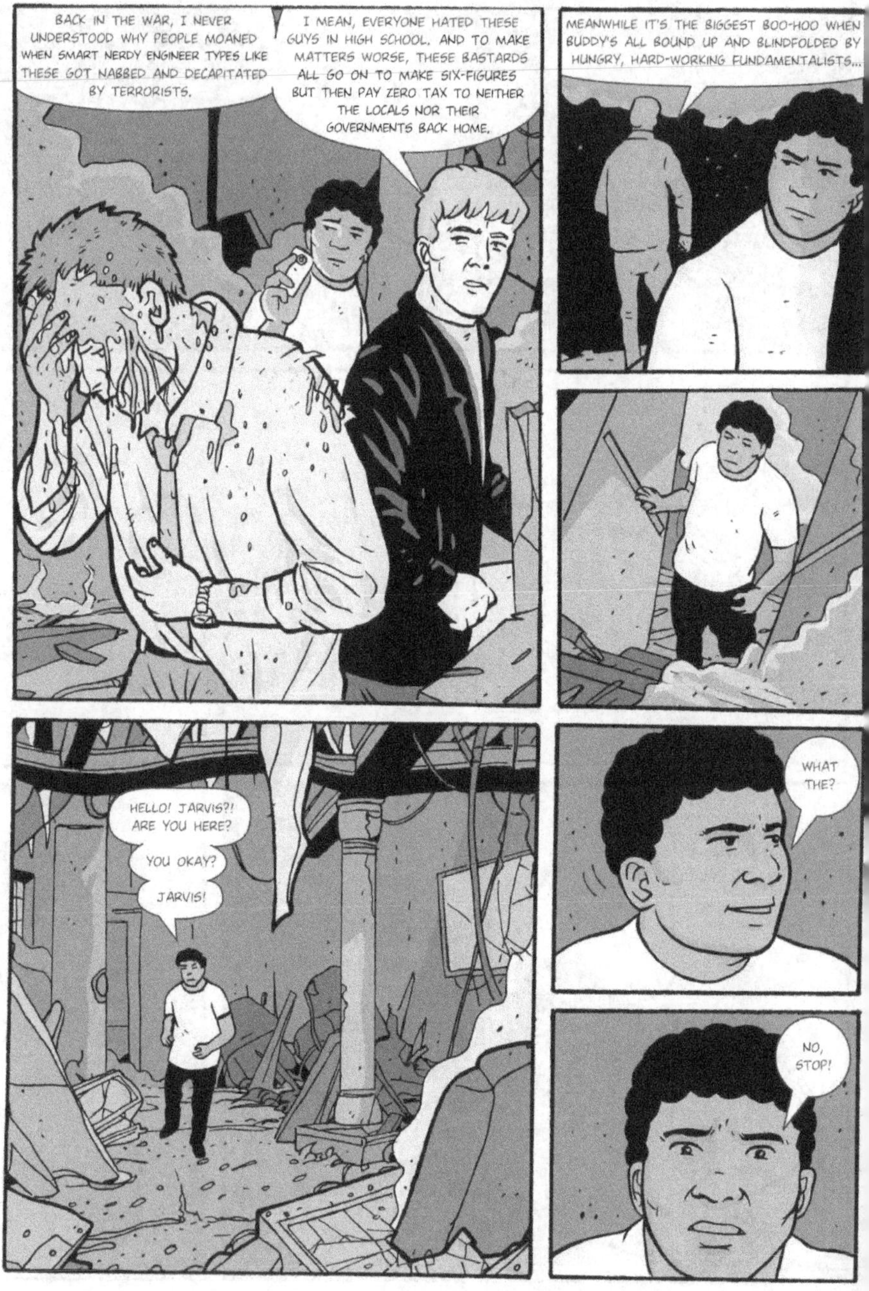
BACK IN THE WAR, I NEVER UNDERSTOOD WHY PEOPLE MOANED WHEN SMART NERDY ENGINEER TYPES LIKE THESE GOT NABBED AND DECAPITATED BY TERRORISTS.
I MEAN, EVERYONE HATED THESE GUYS IN HIGH SCHOOL. AND TO MAKE MATTERS WORSE, THESE BASTARDS ALL GO ON TO MAKE SIX-FIGURES BUT THEN PAY ZERO TAX TO NEITHER THE LOCALS NOR THEIR GOVERNMENTS BACK HOME.
MEANWHILE IT'S THE BIGGEST BOO-HOO WHEN BUDDY'S ALL BOUND UP AND BLINDFOLDED BY HUNGRY, HARD-WORKING FUNDAMENTALISTS...
HELLO! JARVIS?! ARE YOU HERE?
YOU OKAY?
JARVIS!
WHAT THE?
NO, STOP!

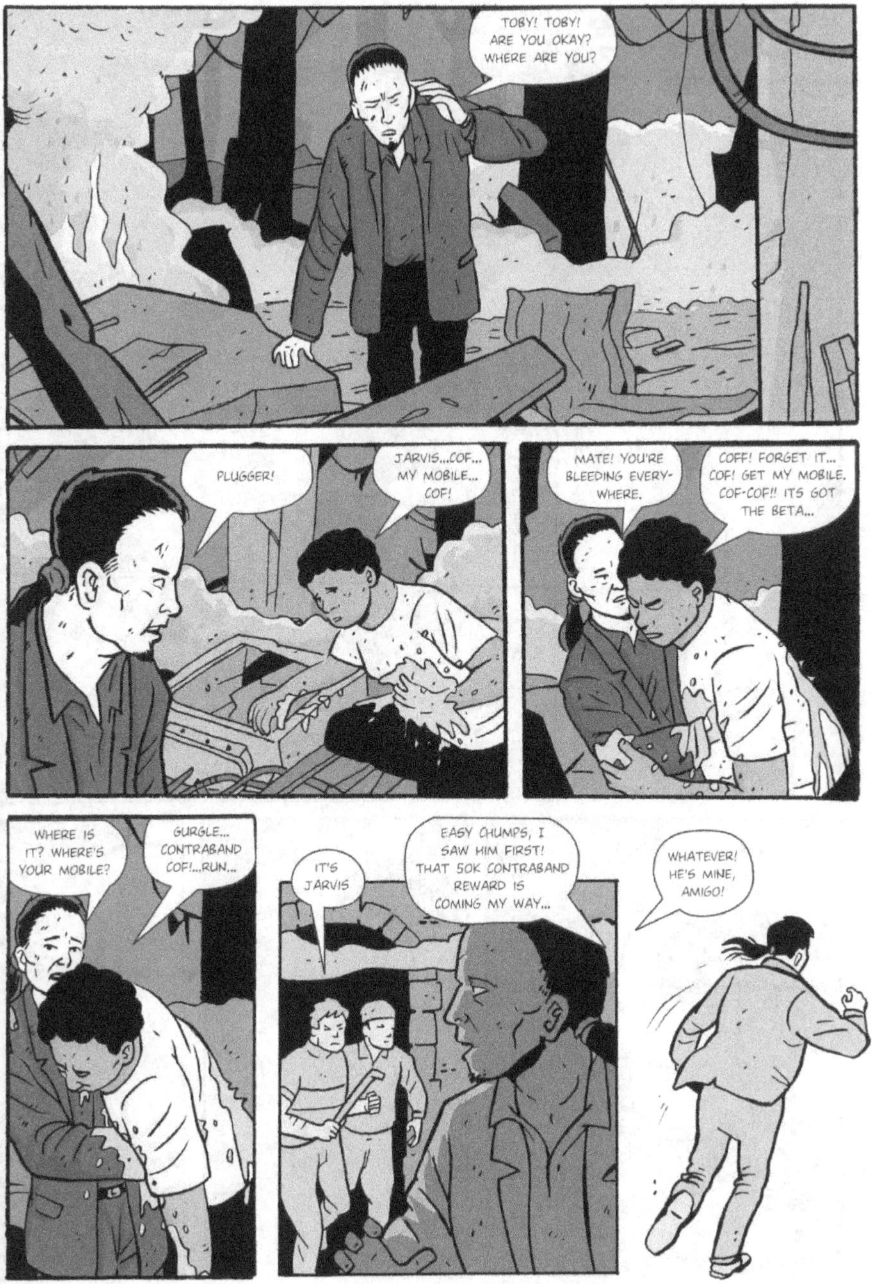
TOBY! TOBY! ARE YOU OKAY? WHERE ARE YOU?
PLUGGER!
JARVIS...COF... MY MOBILE... COF!
MATE! YOU'RE BLEEDING EVERY-WHERE.
COFF! FORGET IT... COF! GET MY MOBILE. COF-COF!! ITS GOT THE BETA...
WHERE IS IT? WHERE'S YOUR MOBILE?
GURGLE... CONTRABAND COF!...RUN...
IT'S JARVIS
EASY CHUMPS, I SAW HIM FIRST! THAT 50K CONTRABAND REWARD IS COMING MY WAY...
WHATEVER! HE'S MINE, AMIGO!

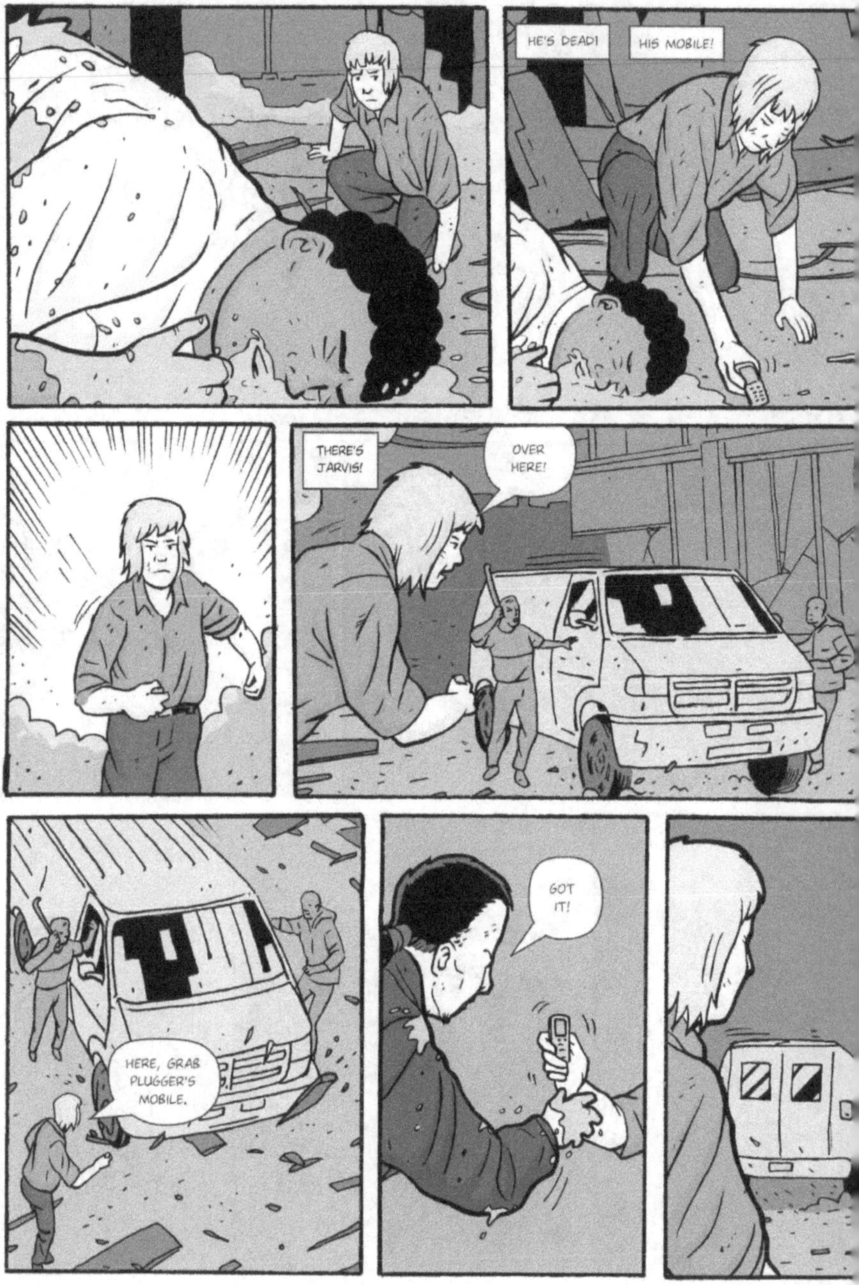
HE'S DEAD!
HIS MOBILE!
THERE'S JARVIS!
OVER HERE!
HERE, GRAB PLUGGER'S MOBILE.
GOT IT!

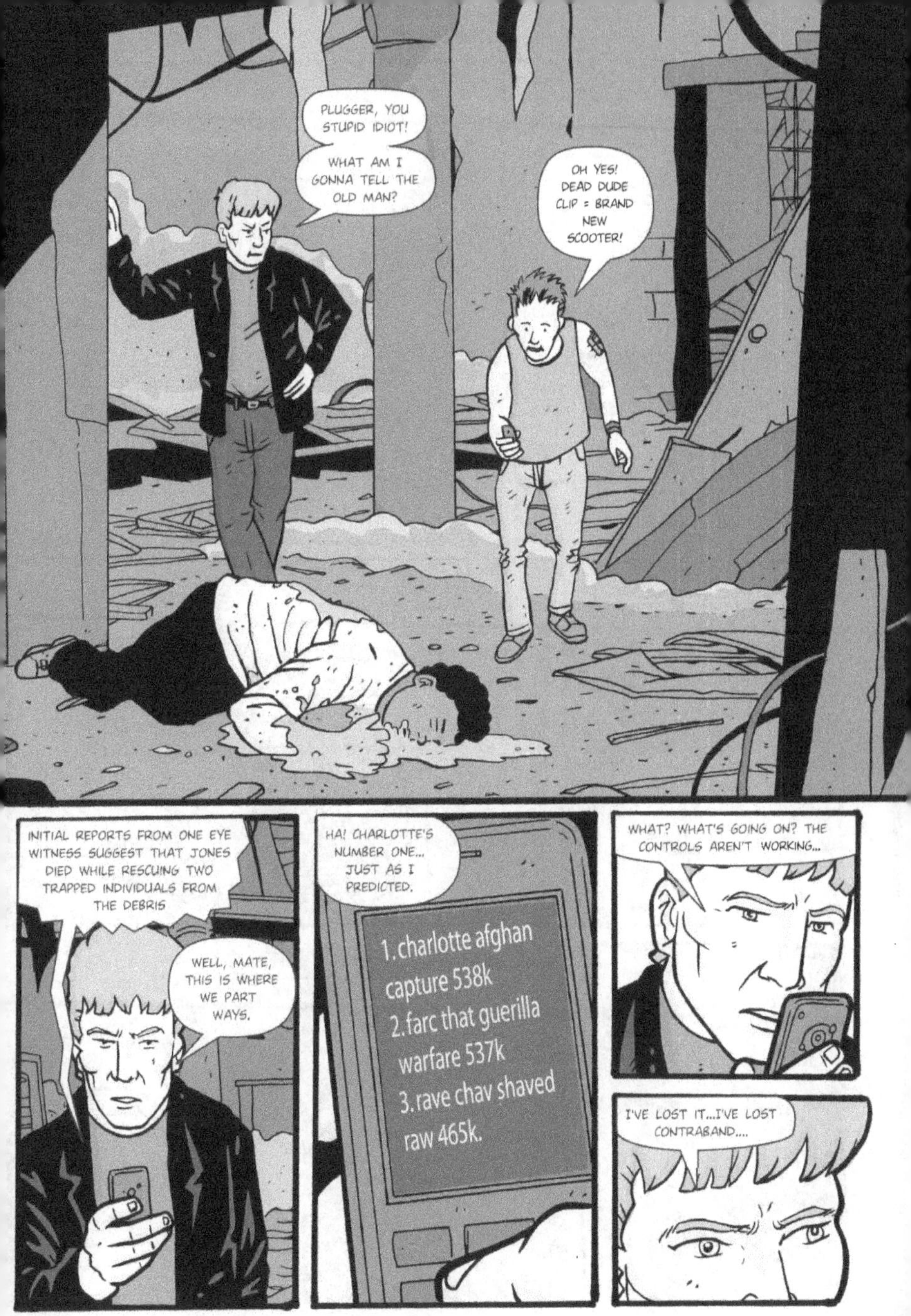
PLUGGER, YOU STUPID IDIOT!
WHAT AM I GONNA TELL THE OLD MAN?
OH YES! DEAD DUDE CLIP = BRAND NEW SCOOTER!
INITIAL REPORTS FROM ONE EYE WITNESS SUGGEST THAT JONES DIED WHILE RESCUING TWO TRAPPED INDIVIDUALS FROM THE DEBRIS
WELL, MATE, THIS IS WHERE WE PART WAYS.
HA! CHARLOTTE'S NUMBER ONE... JUST AS I PREDICTED.
1. charlotte afghan capture 538k
2. farc that guerilla warfare 537k
3. rave chav shaved raw 465k.
WHAT? WHAT'S GOING ON? THE CONTROLS AREN'T WORKING...
I'VE LOST IT...I'VE LOST CONTRABAND....

twelve

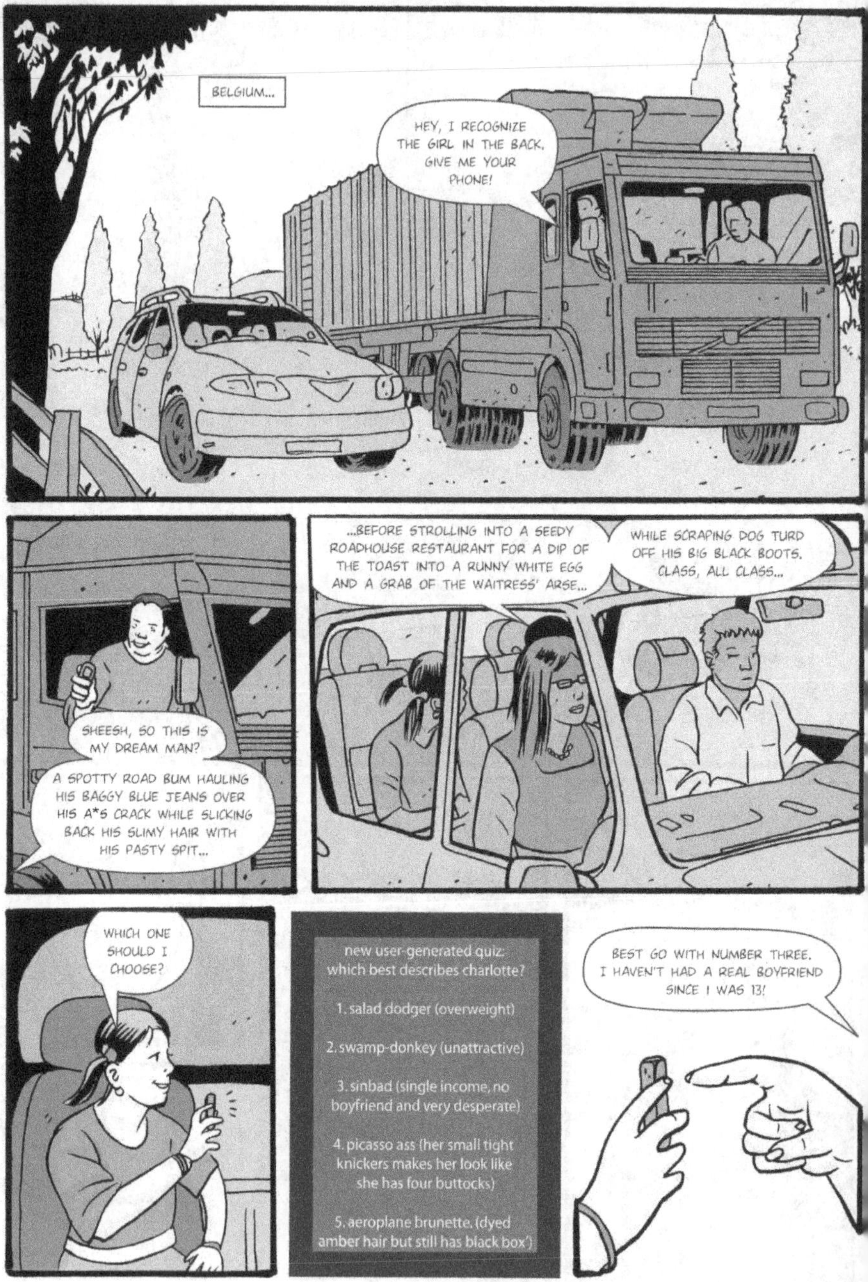
BELGIUM...
HEY, I RECOGNIZE THE GIRL IN THE BACK. GIVE ME YOUR PHONE!
SHEESH, SO THIS IS MY DREAM MAN?
A SPOTTY ROAD BUM HAULING HIS BAGGY BLUE JEANS OVER HIS A*S CRACK WHILE SLICKING BACK HIS SLIMY HAIR WITH HIS PASTY SPIT...
...BEFORE STROLLING INTO A SEEDY ROADHOUSE RESTAURANT FOR A DIP OF THE TOAST INTO A RUNNY WHITE EGG AND A GRAB OF THE WAITRESS' ARSE...
WHILE SCRAPING DOG TURD OFF HIS BIG BLACK BOOTS. CLASS, ALL CLASS...
WHICH ONE SHOULD I CHOOSE?
new user-generated quiz: which best describes charlotte?
1. salad dodger (overweight)
2. swamp-donkey (unattractive)
3. sinbad (single income, no boyfriend and very desperate)
4. picasso ass (her small tight knickers makes her look like she has four buttocks)
5. aeroplane brunette. (dyed amber hair but still has black box')
BEST GO WITH NUMBER THREE. I HAVEN'T HAD A REAL BOYFRIEND SINCE I WAS 13!

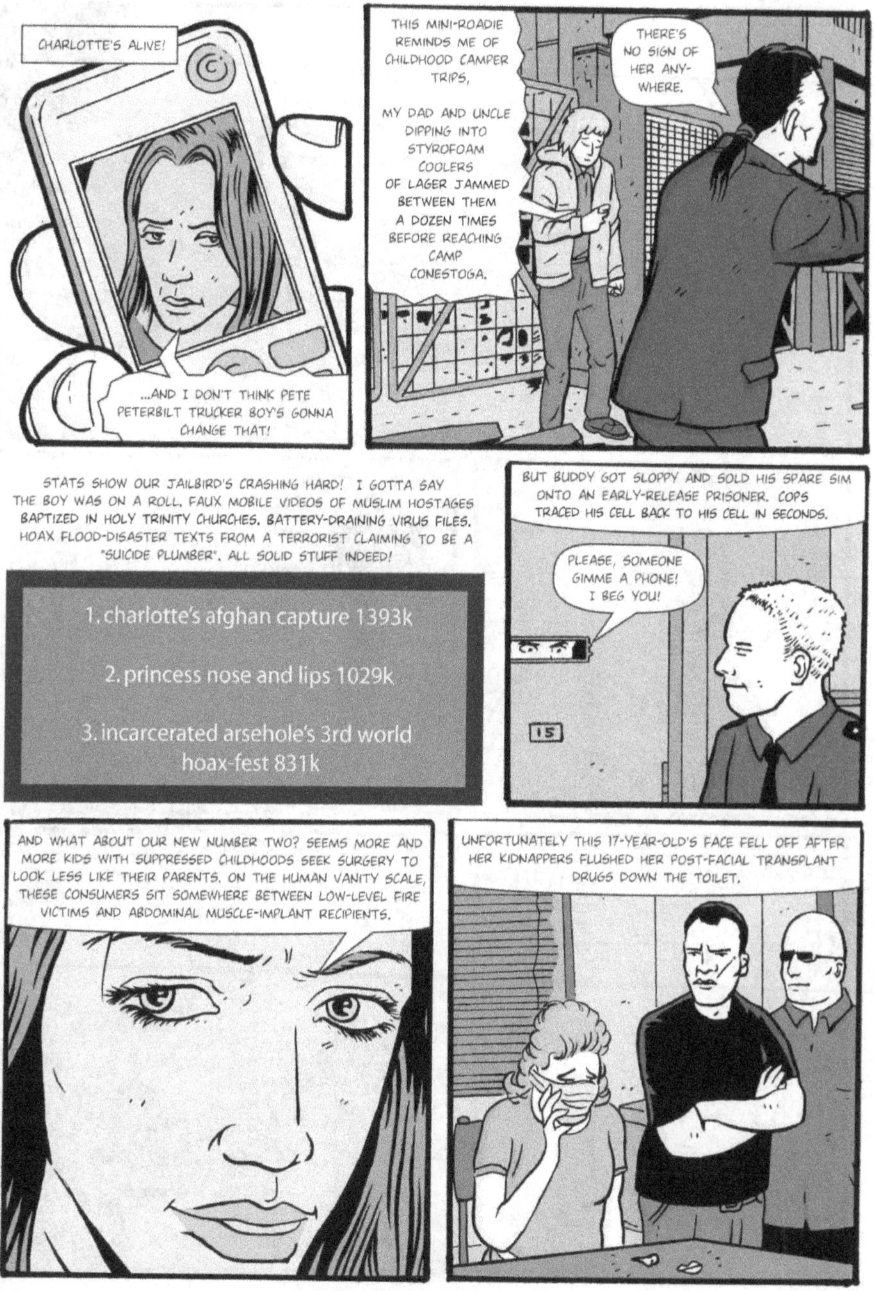

CHARLOTTE'S ALIVE!
...AND I DON'T THINK PETE PETERBILT TRUCKER BOY'S GONNA CHANGE THAT!
THIS MINI-ROADIE REMINDS ME OF CHILDHOOD CAMPER TRIPS,
MY DAD AND UNCLE DIPPING INTO STYROFOAM COOLERS OF LAGER JAMMED BETWEEN THEM A DOZEN TIMES BEFORE REACHING CAMP CONESTOGA.
THERE'S NO SIGN OF HER ANY-WHERE.
STATS SHOW OUR JAILBIRD'S CRASHING HARD! I GOTTA SAY THE BOY WAS ON A ROLL. FAUX MOBILE VIDEOS OF MUSLIM HOSTAGES BAPTIZED IN HOLY TRINITY CHURCHES. BATTERY-DRAINING VIRUS FILES. HOAX FLOOD-DISASTER TEXTS FROM A TERRORIST CLAIMING TO BE A "SUICIDE PLUMBER". ALL SOLID STUFF INDEED!
1. charlotte's afghan capture 1393k
2. princess nose and lips 1029k
3. incarcerated arsehole's 3rd world hoax-fest 831k
BUT BUDDY GOT SLOPPY AND SOLD HIS SPARE SIM ONTO AN EARLY-RELEASE PRISONER. COPS TRACED HIS CELL BACK TO HIS CELL IN SECONDS.
PLEASE, SOMEONE GIMME A PHONE! I BEG YOU!
15
AND WHAT ABOUT OUR NEW NUMBER TWO? SEEMS MORE AND MORE KIDS WITH SUPPRESSED CHILDHOODS SEEK SURGERY TO LOOK LESS LIKE THEIR PARENTS. ON THE HUMAN VANITY SCALE, THESE CONSUMERS SIT SOMEWHERE BETWEEN LOW-LEVEL FIRE VICTIMS AND ABDOMINAL MUSCLE-IMPLANT RECIPIENTS.
UNFORTUNATELY THIS 17-YEAR-OLD'S FACE FELL OFF AFTER HER KIDNAPPERS FLUSHED HER POST-FACIAL TRANSPLANT DRUGS DOWN THE TOILET.

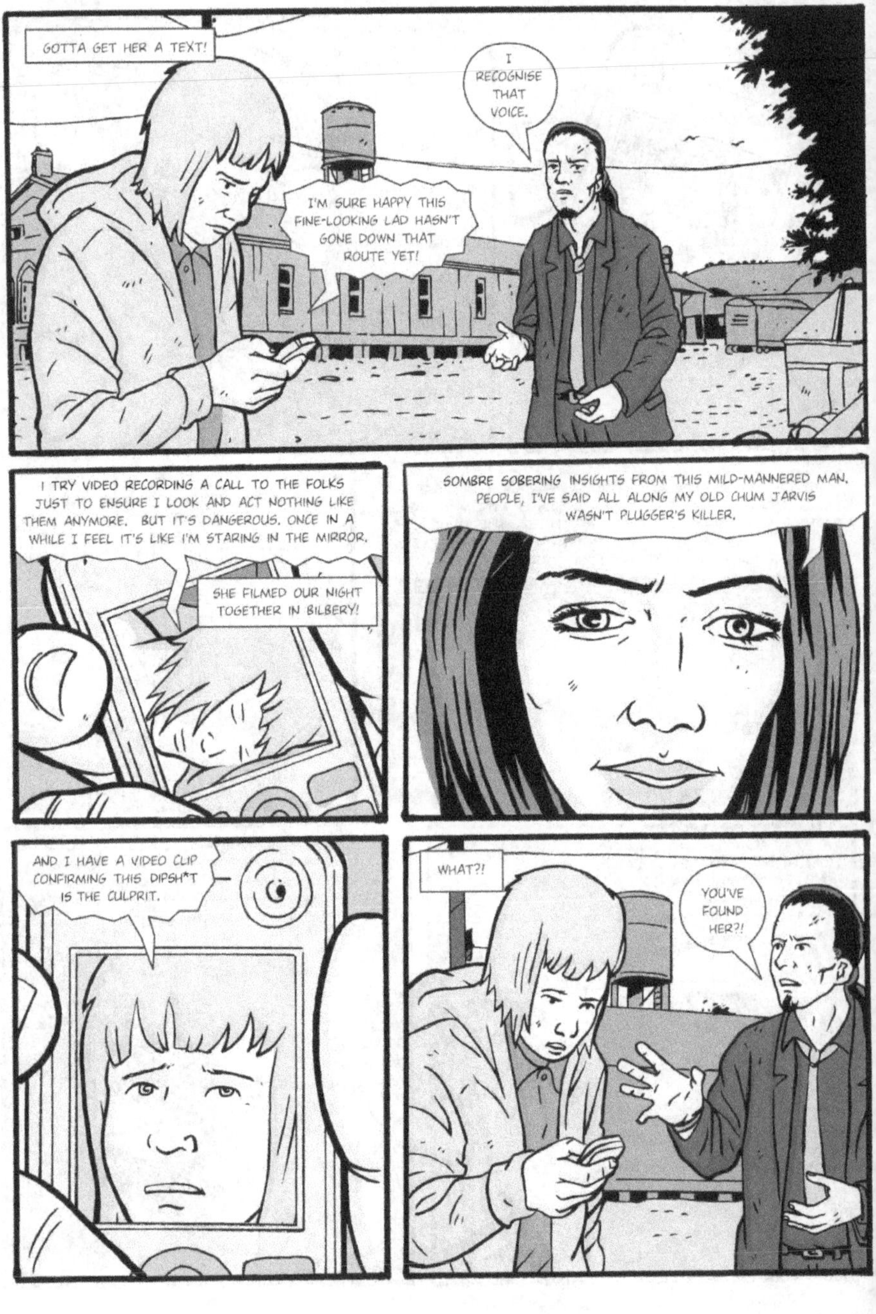
GOTTA GET HER A TEXT!
I RECOGNISE THAT VOICE.
I'M SURE HAPPY THIS FINE-LOOKING LAD HASN'T GONE DOWN THAT ROUTE YET!
I TRY VIDEO RECORDING A CALL TO THE FOLKS JUST TO ENSURE I LOOK AND ACT NOTHING LIKE THEM ANYMORE. BUT IT'S DANGEROUS. ONCE IN A WHILE I FEEL IT'S LIKE I'M STARING IN THE MIRROR.
SHE FILMED OUR NIGHT TOGETHER IN BILBERY!
SOMBRE SOBERING INSIGHTS FROM THIS MILD-MANNERED MAN. PEOPLE, I'VE SAID ALL ALONG MY OLD CHUM JARVIS WASN'T PLUGGER'S KILLER.
AND I HAVE A VIDEO CLIP CONFIRMING THIS DIPSH*T IS THE CULPRIT.
WHAT?!
YOU'VE FOUND HER?!

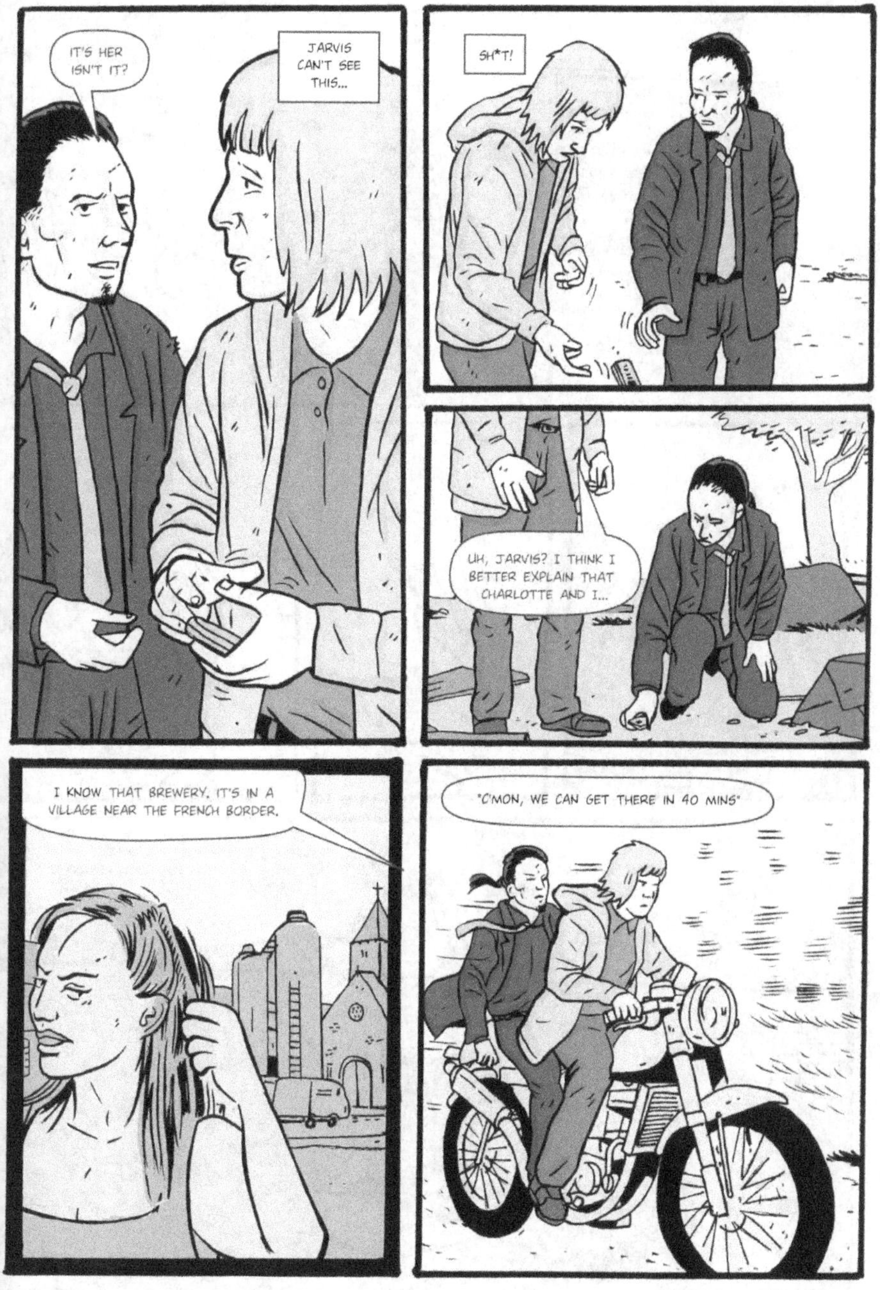

IT'S HER ISN'T IT?
JARVIS CAN'T SEE THIS...
SH*T!
UH, JARVIS? I THINK I BETTER EXPLAIN THAT CHARLOTTE AND I...
I KNOW THAT BREWERY. IT'S IN A VILLAGE NEAR THE FRENCH BORDER.
"C'MON, WE CAN GET THERE IN 40 MINS"

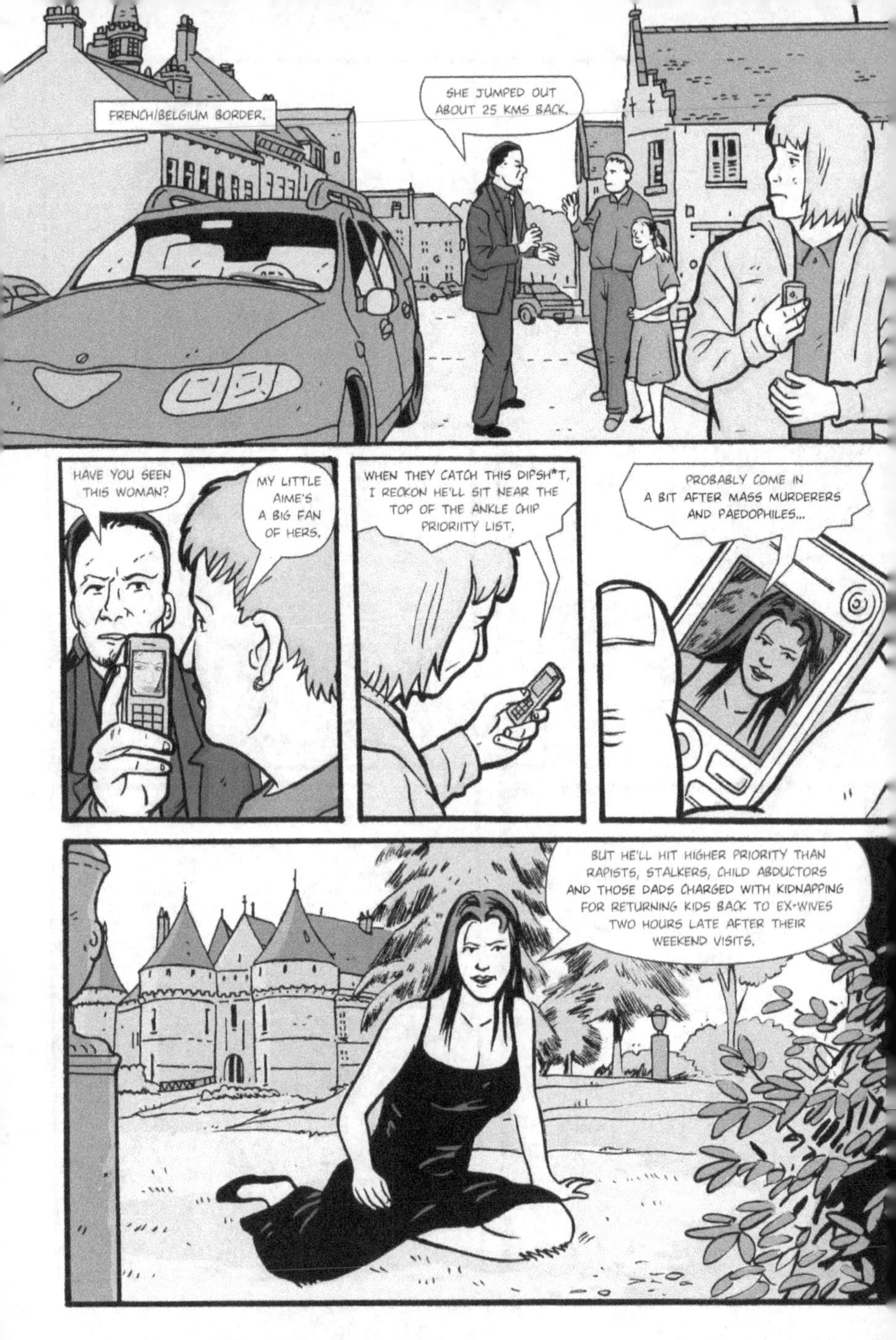
FRENCH/BELGIUM BORDER.
SHE JUMPED OUT ABOUT 25 KMS BACK.
HAVE YOU SEEN THIS WOMAN?
MY LITTLE AIME'S A BIG FAN OF HERS.
WHEN THEY CATCH THIS DIPSH*T, I RECKON HE'LL SIT NEAR THE TOP OF THE ANKLE CHIP PRIORIITY LIST.
PROBABLY COME IN A BIT AFTER MASS MURDERERS AND PAEDOPHILES...
BUT HE'LL HIT HIGHER PRIORITY THAN RAPISTS, STALKERS, CHILD ABDUCTORS AND THOSE DADS CHARGED WITH KIDNAPPING FOR RETURNING KIDS BACK TO EX-WIVES TWO HOURS LATE AFTER THEIR WEEKEND VISITS.

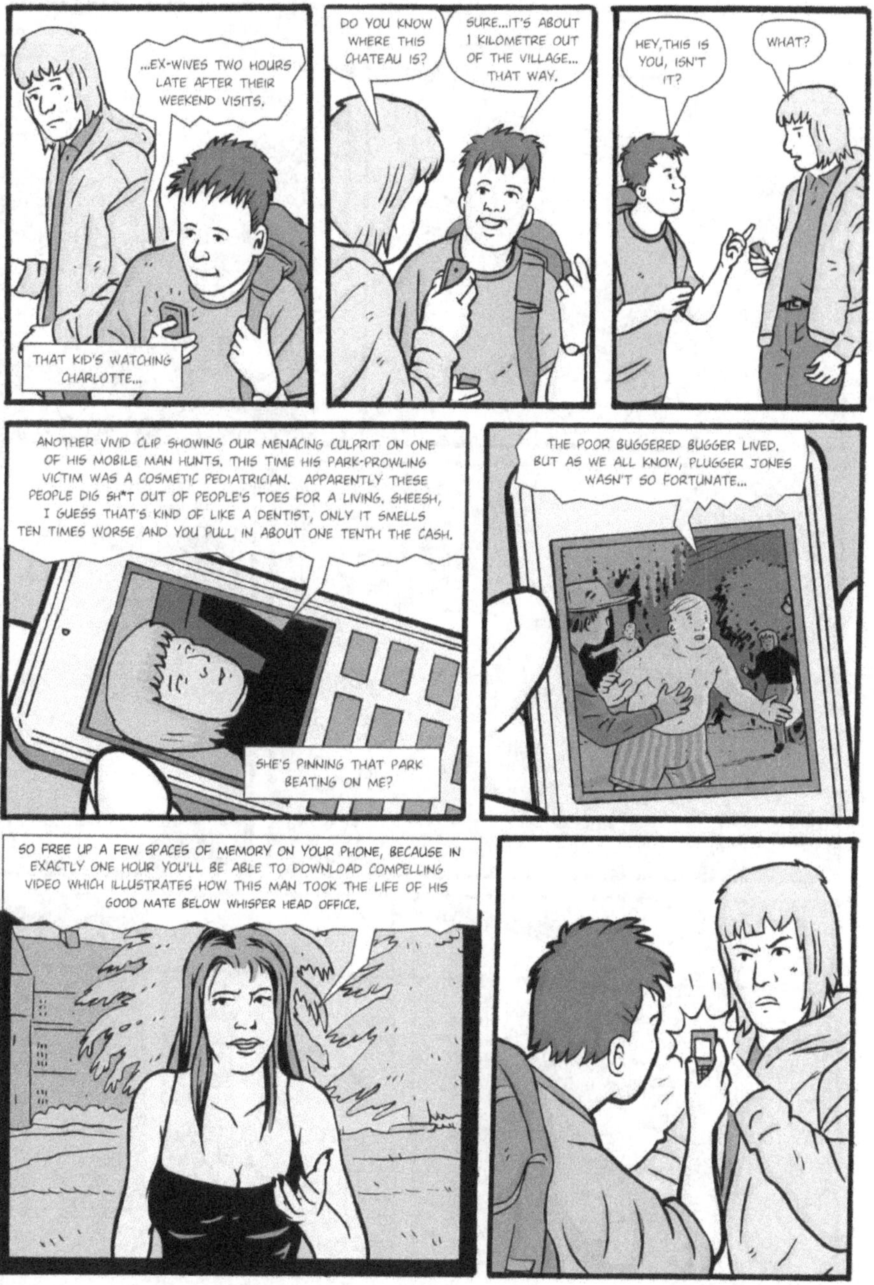
...EX-WIVES TWO HOURS LATE AFTER THEIR WEEKEND VISITS.
THAT KID'S WATCHING CHARLOTTE...
DO YOU KNOW WHERE THIS CHATEAU IS?
SURE...IT'S ABOUT 1 KILOMETRE OUT OF THE VILLAGE... THAT WAY.
HEY, THIS IS YOU, ISN'T IT?
WHAT?
ANOTHER VIVID CLIP SHOWING OUR MENACING CULPRIT ON ONE OF HIS MOBILE MAN HUNTS. THIS TIME HIS PARK-PROWLING VICTIM WAS A COSMETIC PEDIATRICIAN. APPARENTLY THESE PEOPLE DIG SH*T OUT OF PEOPLE'S TOES FOR A LIVING. SHEESH, I GUESS THAT'S KIND OF LIKE A DENTIST, ONLY IT SMELLS TEN TIMES WORSE AND YOU PULL IN ABOUT ONE TENTH THE CASH.
SHE'S PINNING THAT PARK BEATING ON ME?
THE POOR BUGGERED BUGGER LIVED. BUT AS WE ALL KNOW, PLUGGER JONES WASN'T SO FORTUNATE...
SO FREE UP A FEW SPACES OF MEMORY ON YOUR PHONE, BECAUSE IN EXACTLY ONE HOUR YOU'LL BE ABLE TO DOWNLOAD COMPELLING VIDEO WHICH ILLUSTRATES HOW THIS MAN TOOK THE LIFE OF HIS GOOD MATE BELOW WHISPER HEAD OFFICE.

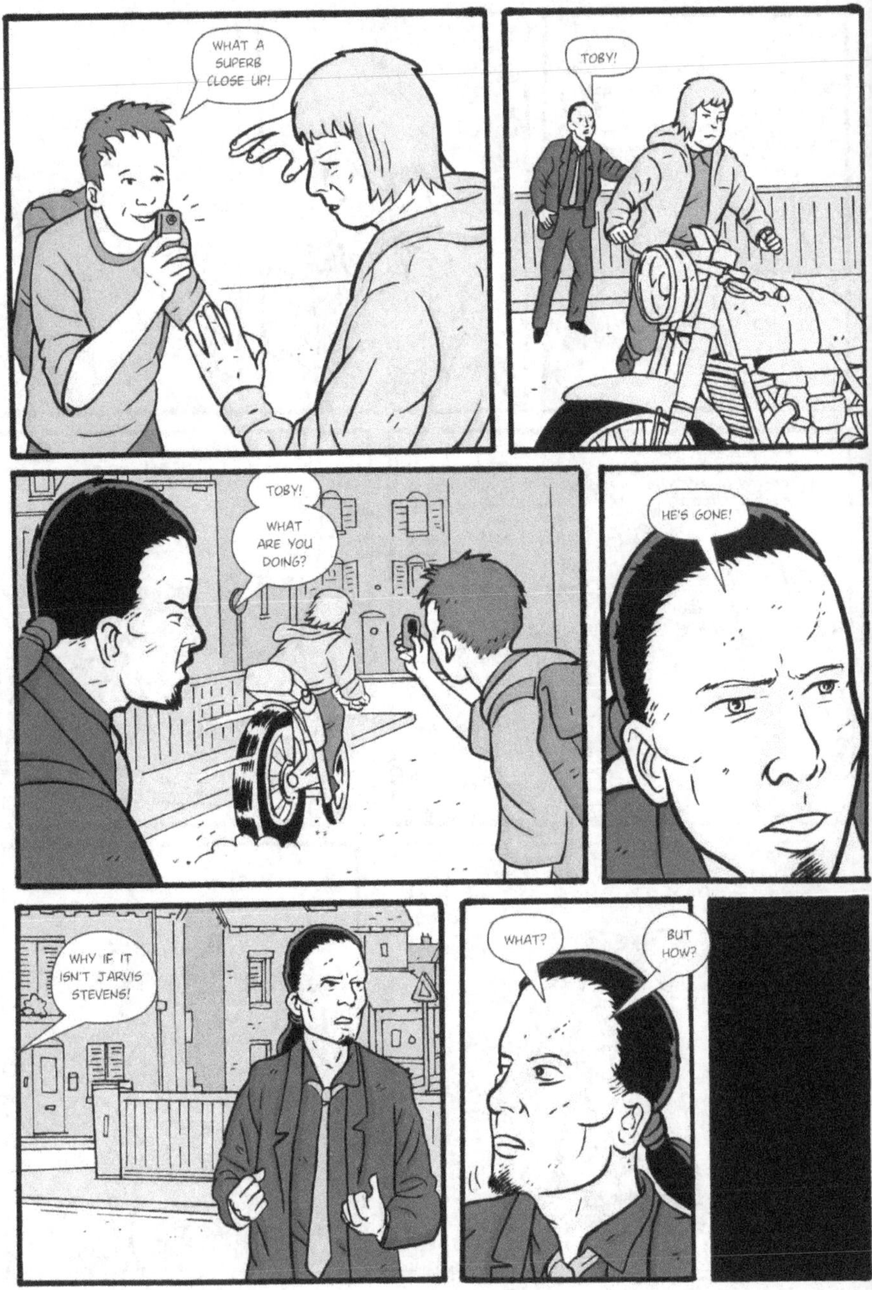
WHAT A SUPERB CLOSE UP!
TOBY!
TOBY!
WHAT ARE YOU DOING?
HE'S GONE!
WHY IF IT ISN'T JARVIS STEVENS!
WHAT?
BUT HOW?

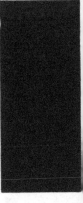

thirteen

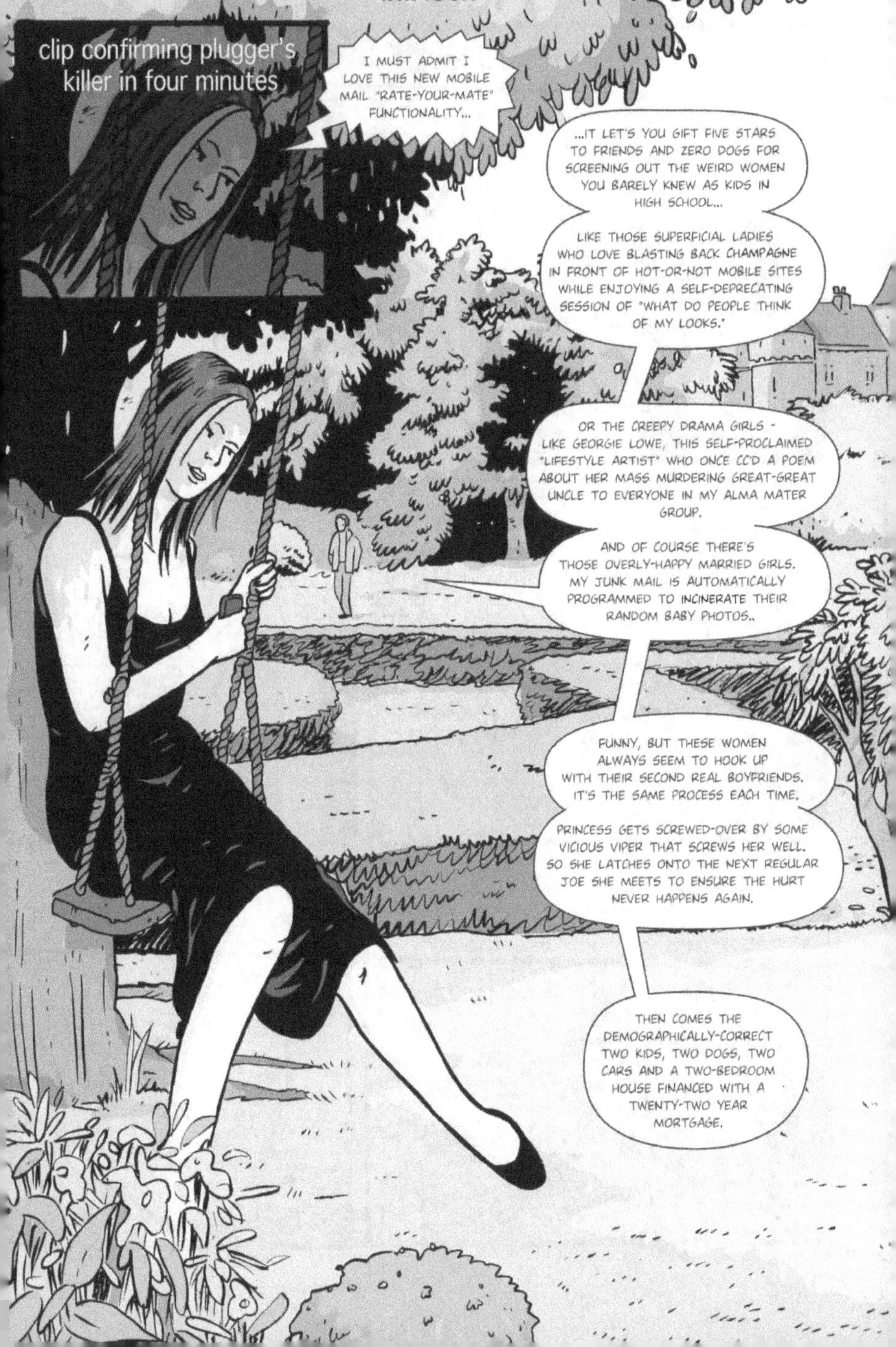

clip confirming plugger's killer in four minutes
I MUST ADMIT I LOVE THIS NEW MOBILE MAIL "RATE-YOUR-MATE" FUNCTIONALITY...
...IT LET'S YOU GIFT FIVE STARS TO FRIENDS AND ZERO DOGS FOR SCREENING OUT THE WEIRD WOMEN YOU BARELY KNEW AS KIDS IN HIGH SCHOOL...
LIKE THOSE SUPERFICIAL LADIES WHO LOVE BLASTING BACK CHAMPAGNE IN FRONT OF HOT-OR-NOT MOBILE SITES WHILE ENJOYING A SELF-DEPRECATING SESSION OF "WHAT DO PEOPLE THINK OF MY LOOKS."
OR THE CREEPY DRAMA GIRLS - LIKE GEORGIE LOWE, THIS SELF-PROCLAIMED "LIFESTYLE ARTIST" WHO ONCE CC'D A POEM ABOUT HER MASS MURDERING GREAT-GREAT UNCLE TO EVERYONE IN MY ALMA MATER GROUP.
AND OF COURSE THERE'S THOSE OVERLY-HAPPY MARRIED GIRLS. MY JUNK MAIL IS AUTOMATICALLY PROGRAMMED TO INCINERATE THEIR RANDOM BABY PHOTOS..
FUNNY, BUT THESE WOMEN ALWAYS SEEM TO HOOK UP WITH THEIR SECOND REAL BOYFRIENDS. IT'S THE SAME PROCESS EACH TIME.
PRINCESS GETS SCREWED-OVER BY SOME VICIOUS VIPER THAT SCREWS HER WELL. SO SHE LATCHES ONTO THE NEXT REGULAR JOE SHE MEETS TO ENSURE THE HURT NEVER HAPPENS AGAIN.
THEN COMES THE DEMOGRAPHICALLY-CORRECT TWO KIDS, TWO DOGS, TWO CARS AND A TWO-BEDROOM HOUSE FINANCED WITH A TWENTY-TWO YEAR MORTGAGE.

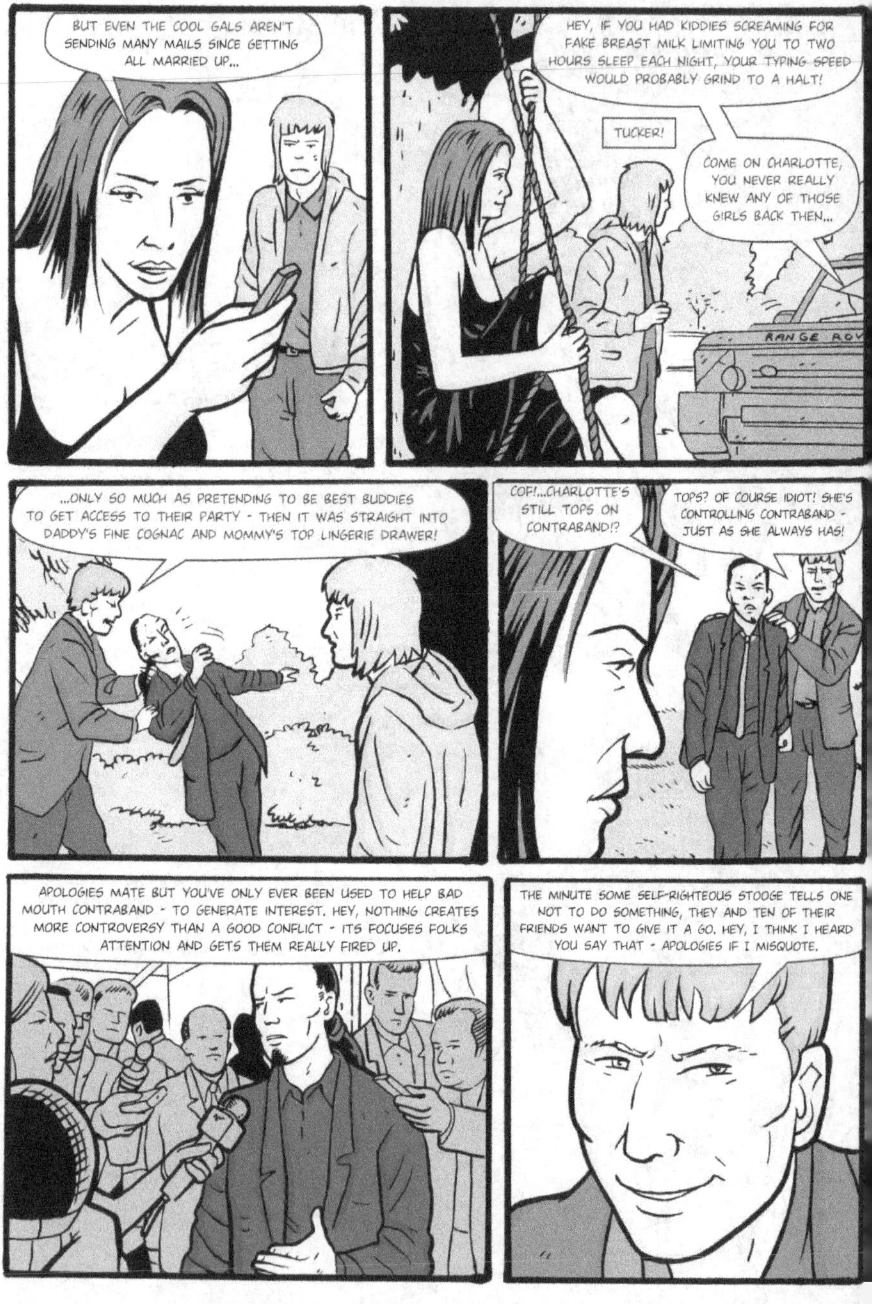
BUT EVEN THE COOL GALS AREN'T SENDING MANY MAILS SINCE GETTING ALL MARRIED UP...
HEY, IF YOU HAD KIDDIES SCREAMING FOR FAKE BREAST MILK LIMITING YOU TO TWO HOURS SLEEP EACH NIGHT, YOUR TYPING SPEED WOULD PROBABLY GRIND TO A HALT!
TUCKER!
COME ON CHARLOTTE, YOU NEVER REALLY KNEW ANY OF THOSE GIRLS BACK THEN...
RANGE ROV
...ONLY SO MUCH AS PRETENDING TO BE BEST BUDDIES TO GET ACCESS TO THEIR PARTY - THEN IT WAS STRAIGHT INTO DADDY'S FINE COGNAC AND MOMMY'S TOP LINGERIE DRAWER!
COF!...CHARLOTTE'S STILL TOPS ON CONTRABAND!?
TOPS? OF COURSE IDIOT! SHE'S CONTROLLING CONTRABAND - JUST AS SHE ALWAYS HAS!
APOLOGIES MATE BUT YOU'VE ONLY EVER BEEN USED TO HELP BAD MOUTH CONTRABAND - TO GENERATE INTEREST. HEY, NOTHING CREATES MORE CONTROVERSY THAN A GOOD CONFLICT - ITS FOCUSES FOLKS ATTENTION AND GETS THEM REALLY FIRED UP.
THE MINUTE SOME SELF-RIGHTEOUS STOOGE TELLS ONE NOT TO DO SOMETHING, THEY AND TEN OF THEIR FRIENDS WANT TO GIVE IT A GO. HEY, I THINK I HEARD YOU SAY THAT - APOLOGIES IF I MISQUOTE.

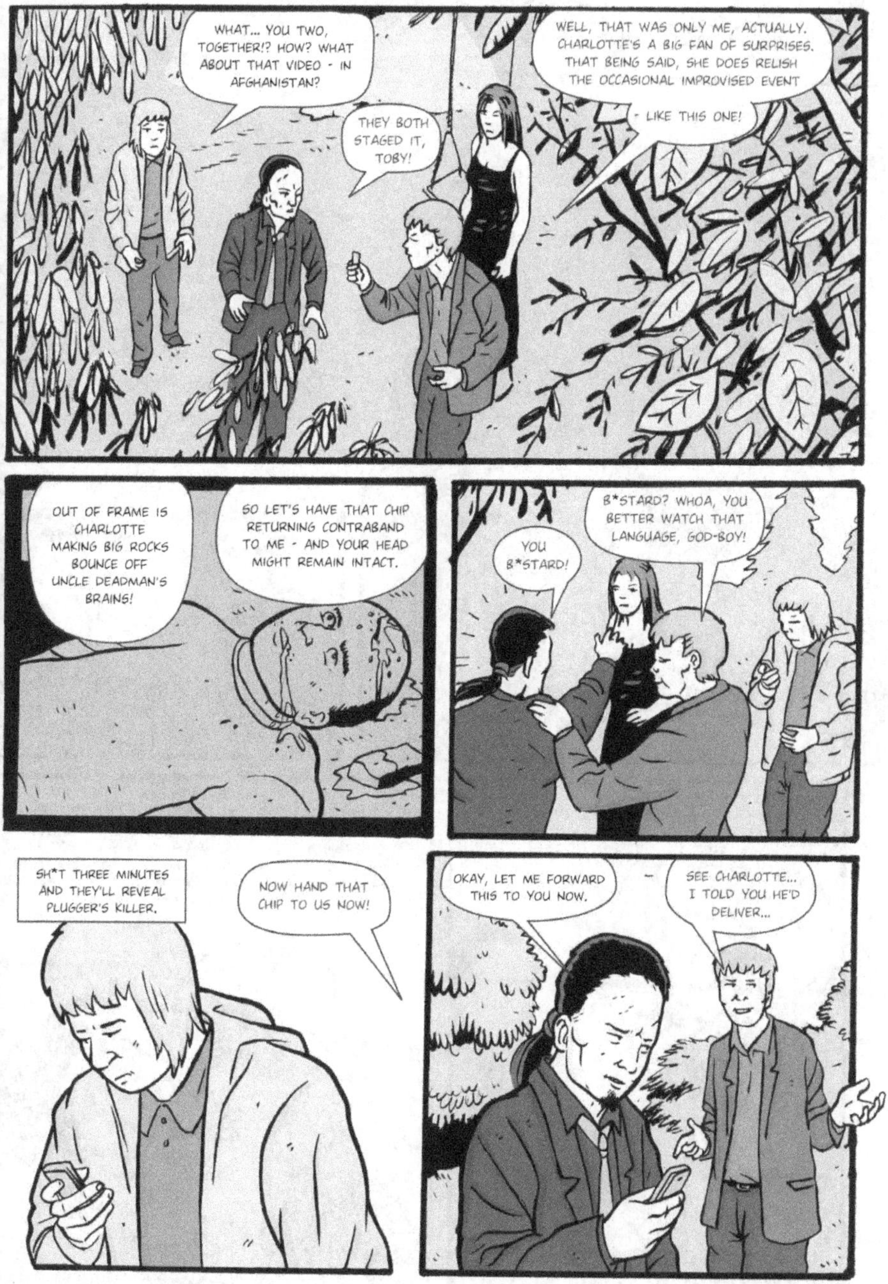
WHAT... YOU TWO, TOGETHER!? HOW? WHAT ABOUT THAT VIDEO - IN AFGHANISTAN?
THEY BOTH STAGED IT, TOBY!
WELL, THAT WAS ONLY ME, ACTUALLY. CHARLOTTE'S A BIG FAN OF SURPRISES. THAT BEING SAID, SHE DOES RELISH THE OCCASIONAL IMPROVISED EVENT
- LIKE THIS ONE!
OUT OF FRAME IS CHARLOTTE MAKING BIG ROCKS BOUNCE OFF UNCLE DEADMAN'S BRAINS!
SO LET'S HAVE THAT CHIP RETURNING CONTRABAND TO ME - AND YOUR HEAD MIGHT REMAIN INTACT.
YOU B*STARD!
B*STARD? WHOA, YOU BETTER WATCH THAT LANGUAGE, GOD-BOY!
SH*T THREE MINUTES AND THEY'LL REVEAL PLUGGER'S KILLER.
NOW HAND THAT CHIP TO US NOW!
OKAY, LET ME FORWARD THIS TO YOU NOW.
SEE CHARLOTTE... I TOLD YOU HE'D DELIVER...

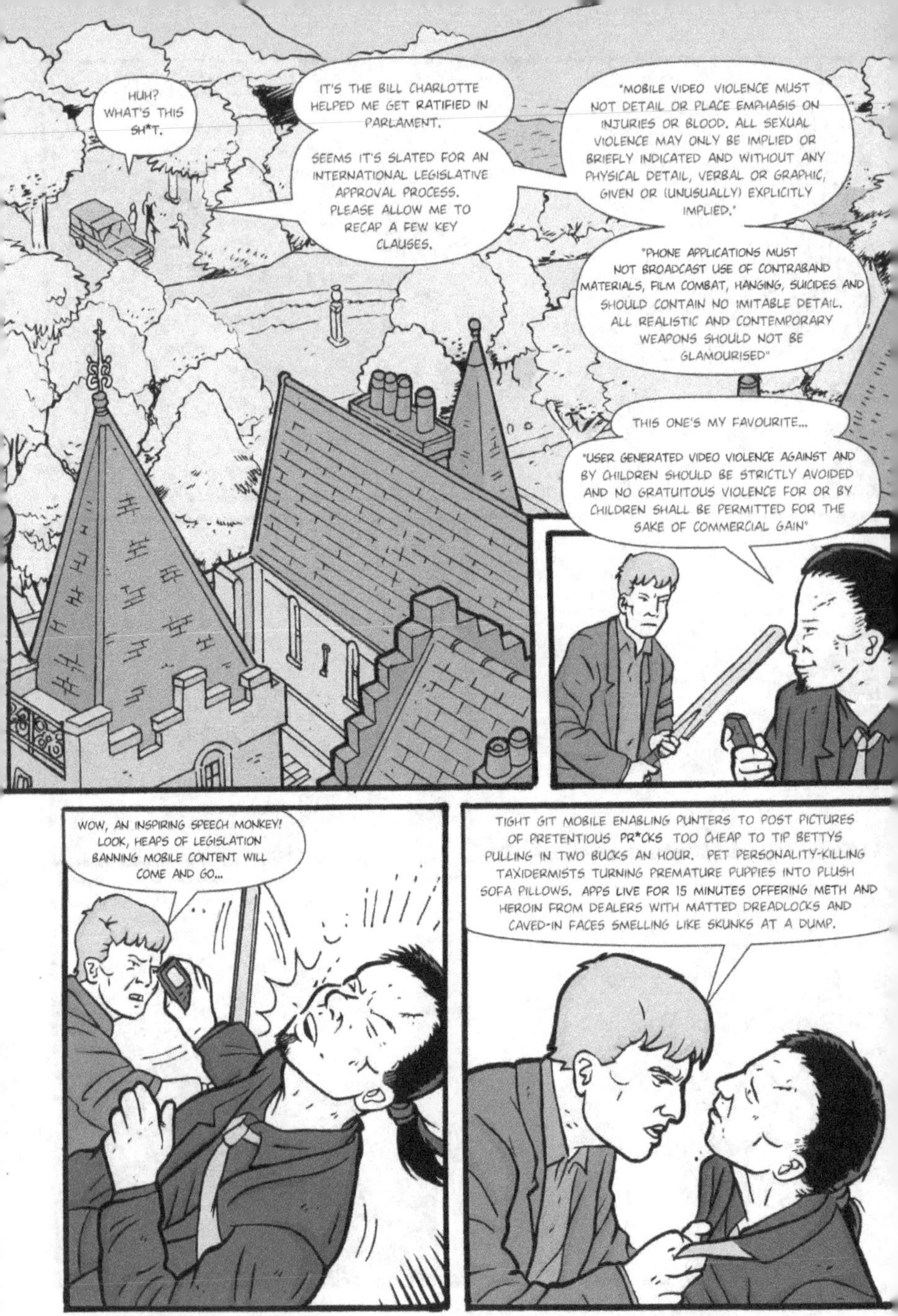
HUH? WHAT'S THIS SH*T.
IT'S THE BILL CHARLOTTE HELPED ME GET RATIFIED IN PARLAMENT.
SEEMS IT'S SLATED FOR AN INTERNATIONAL LEGISLATIVE APPROVAL PROCESS. PLEASE ALLOW ME TO RECAP A FEW KEY CLAUSES.
"MOBILE VIDEO VIOLENCE MUST NOT DETAIL OR PLACE EMPHASIS ON INJURIES OR BLOOD. ALL SEXUAL VIOLENCE MAY ONLY BE IMPLIED OR BRIEFLY INDICATED AND WITHOUT ANY PHYSICAL DETAIL, VERBAL OR GRAPHIC, GIVEN OR (UNUSUALLY) EXPLICITLY IMPLIED."
"PHONE APPLICATIONS MUST NOT BROADCAST USE OF CONTRABAND MATERIALS, FILM COMBAT, HANGING, SUICIDES AND SHOULD CONTAIN NO IMITABLE DETAIL. ALL REALISTIC AND CONTEMPORARY WEAPONS SHOULD NOT BE GLAMOURISED"
THIS ONE'S MY FAVOURITE...
"USER GENERATED VIDEO VIOLENCE AGAINST AND BY CHILDREN SHOULD BE STRICTLY AVOIDED AND NO GRATUITOUS VIOLENCE FOR OR BY CHILDREN SHALL BE PERMITTED FOR THE SAKE OF COMMERCIAL GAIN"
WOW, AN INSPIRING SPEECH MONKEY! LOOK, HEAPS OF LEGISLATION BANNING MOBILE CONTENT WILL COME AND GO...
TIGHT GIT MOBILE ENABLING PUNTERS TO POST PICTURES OF PRETENTIOUS PR*CKS TOO CHEAP TO TIP BETTYS PULLING IN TWO BUCKS AN HOUR. PET PERSONALITY-KILLING TAXIDERMISTS TURNING PREMATURE PUPPIES INTO PLUSH SOFA PILLOWS. APPS LIVE FOR 15 MINUTES OFFERING METH AND HEROIN FROM DEALERS WITH MATTED DREADLOCKS AND CAVED-IN FACES SMELLING LIKE SKUNKS AT A DUMP.

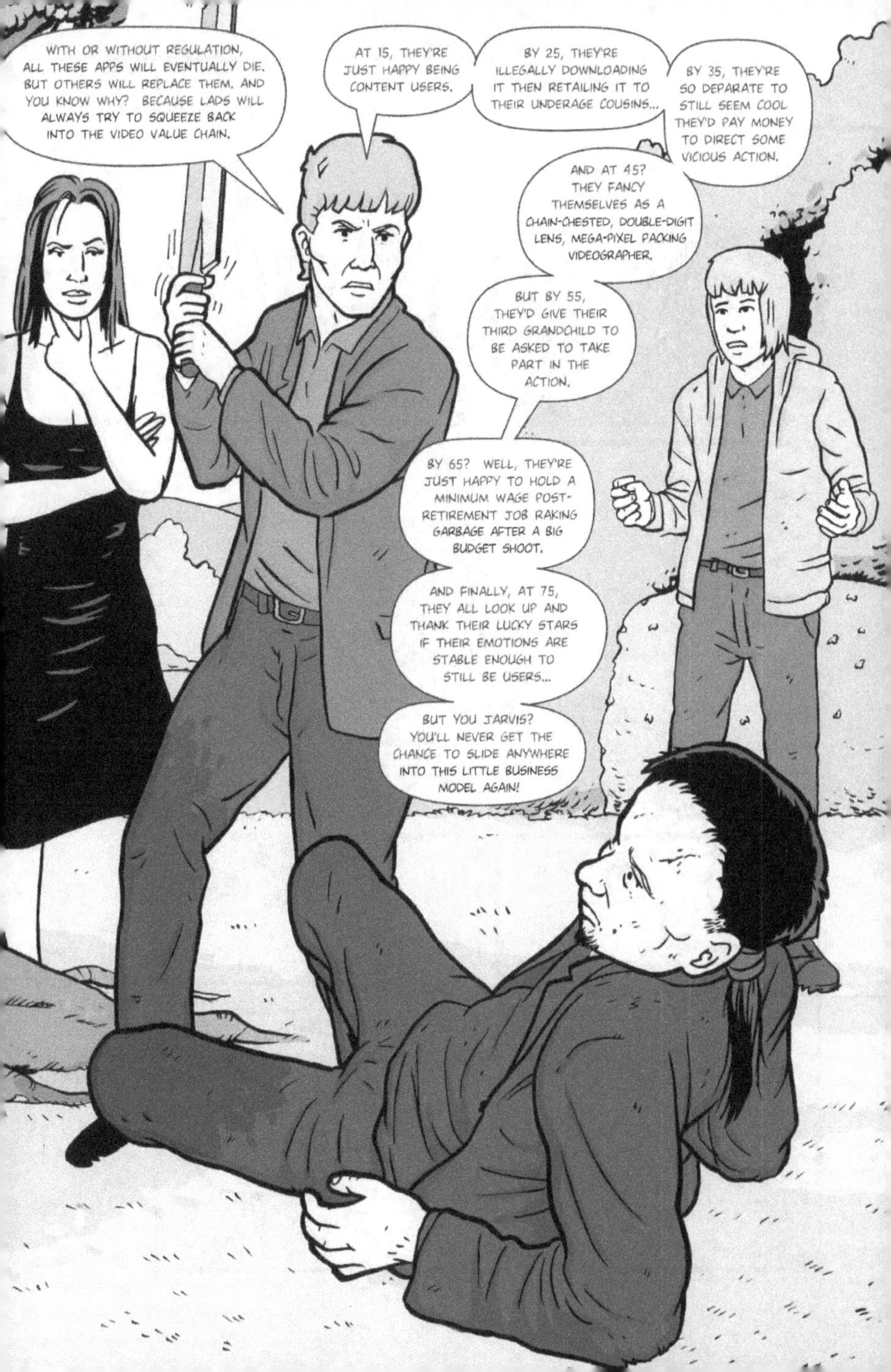
WITH OR WITHOUT REGULATION, ALL THESE APPS WILL EVENTUALLY DIE. BUT OTHERS WILL REPLACE THEM. AND YOU KNOW WHY? BECAUSE LADS WILL ALWAYS TRY TO SQUEEZE BACK INTO THE VIDEO VALUE CHAIN.
AT 15, THEY'RE JUST HAPPY BEING CONTENT USERS.
BY 25, THEY'RE ILLEGALLY DOWNLOADING IT THEN RETAILING IT TO THEIR UNDERAGE COUSINS...
BY 35, THEY'RE SO DEPARATE TO STILL SEEM COOL THEY'D PAY MONEY TO DIRECT SOME VICIOUS ACTION.
AND AT 45? THEY FANCY THEMSELVES AS A CHAIN-CHESTED, DOUBLE-DIGIT LENS, MEGA-PIXEL PACKING VIDEOGRAPHER.
BUT BY 55, THEY'D GIVE THEIR THIRD GRANDCHILD TO BE ASKED TO TAKE PART IN THE ACTION.
BY 65? WELL, THEY'RE JUST HAPPY TO HOLD A MINIMUM WAGE POST-RETIREMENT JOB RAKING GARBAGE AFTER A BIG BUDGET SHOOT.
AND FINALLY, AT 75, THEY ALL LOOK UP AND THANK THEIR LUCKY STARS IF THEIR EMOTIONS ARE STABLE ENOUGH TO STILL BE USERS...
BUT YOU JARVIS? YOU'LL NEVER GET THE CHANCE TO SLIDE ANYWHERE INTO THIS LITTLE BUSINESS MODEL AGAIN!

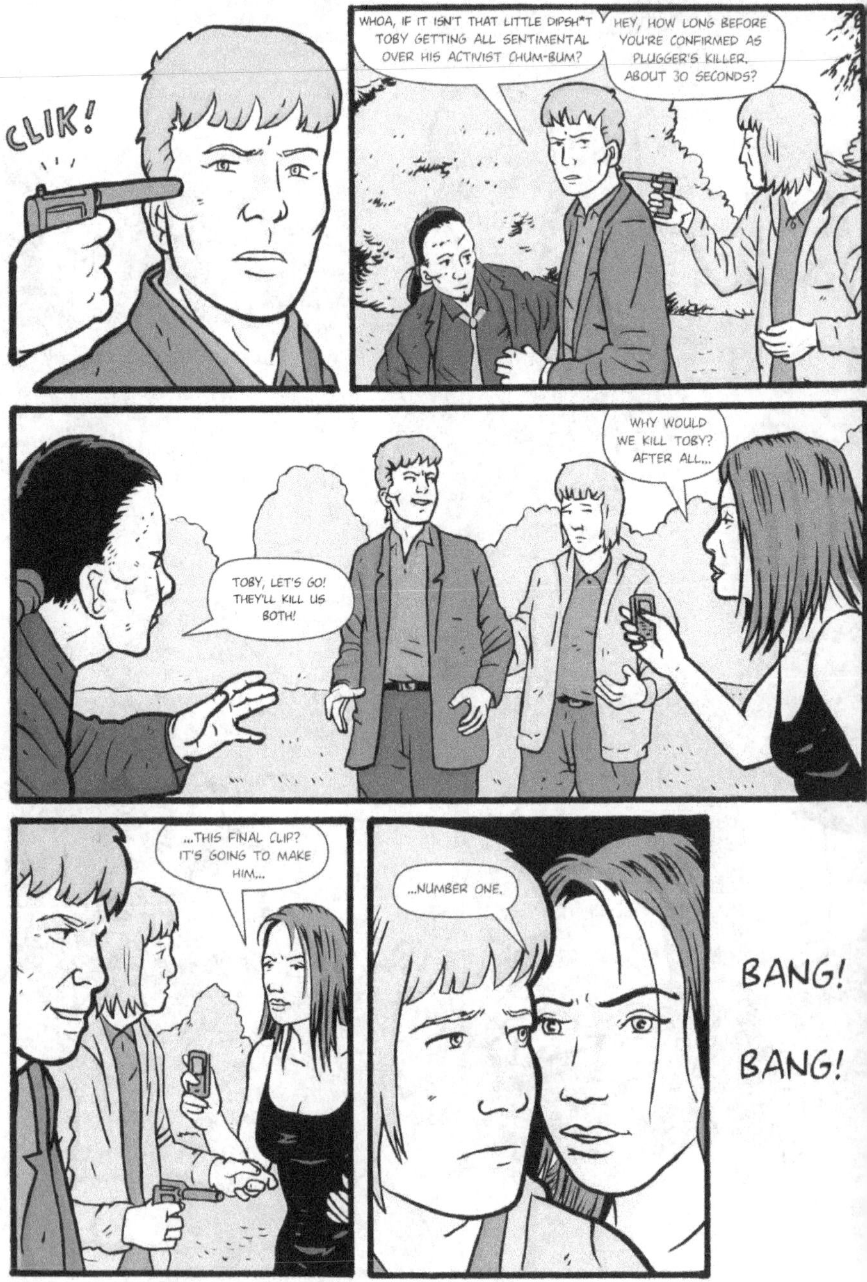
CLIK!
WHOA, IF IT ISN'T THAT LITTLE DIPSH*T TOBY GETTING ALL SENTIMENTAL OVER HIS ACTIVIST CHUM-BUM?
HEY, HOW LONG BEFORE YOU'RE CONFIRMED AS PLUGGER'S KILLER. ABOUT 30 SECONDS?
TOBY, LET'S GO! THEY'LL KILL US BOTH!
WHY WOULD WE KILL TOBY? AFTER ALL...
...THIS FINAL CLIP? IT'S GOING TO MAKE HIM...
...NUMBER ONE.
BANG!
BANG!

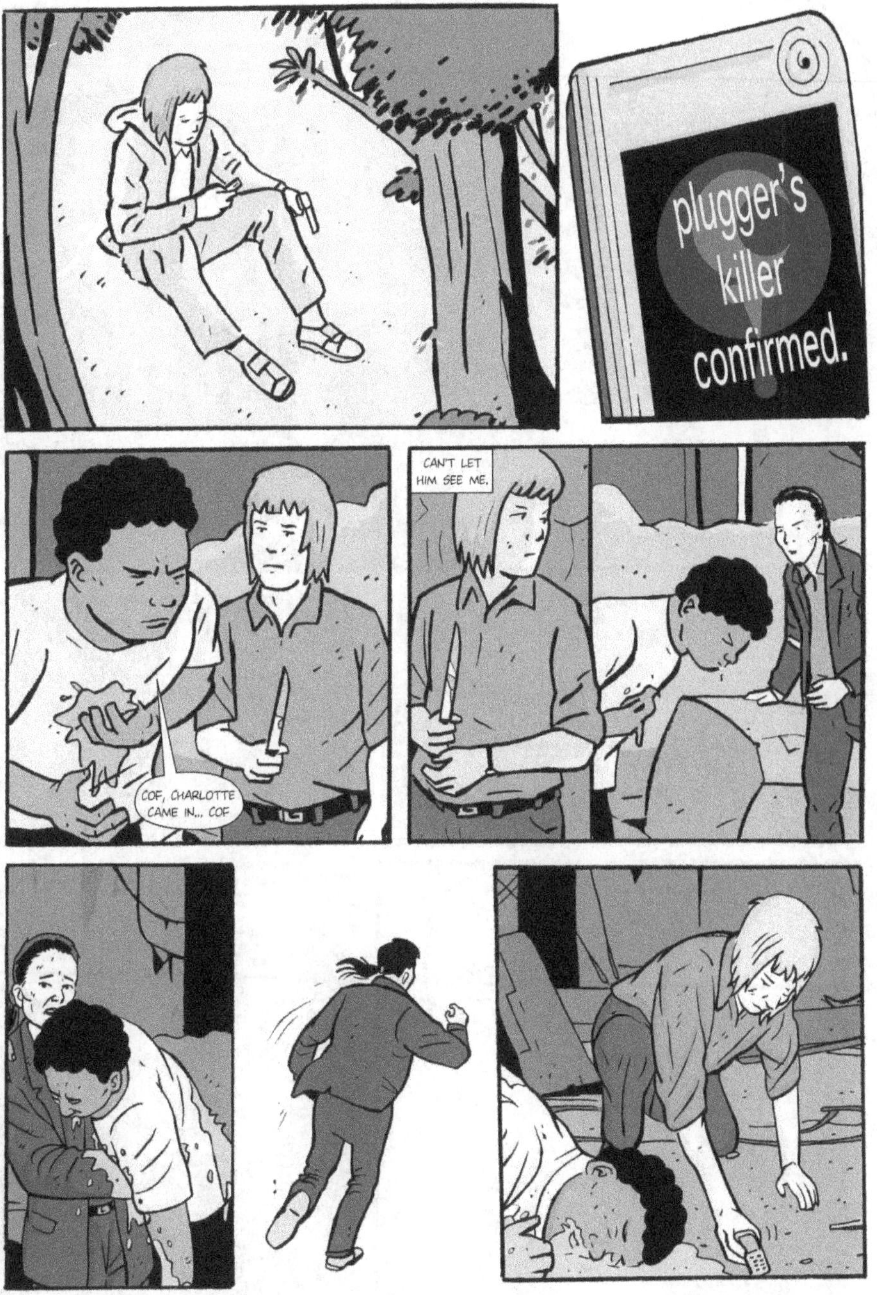
plugger's killer confirmed.
CAN'T LET HIM SEE ME.
COF, CHARLOTTE CAME IN... COF

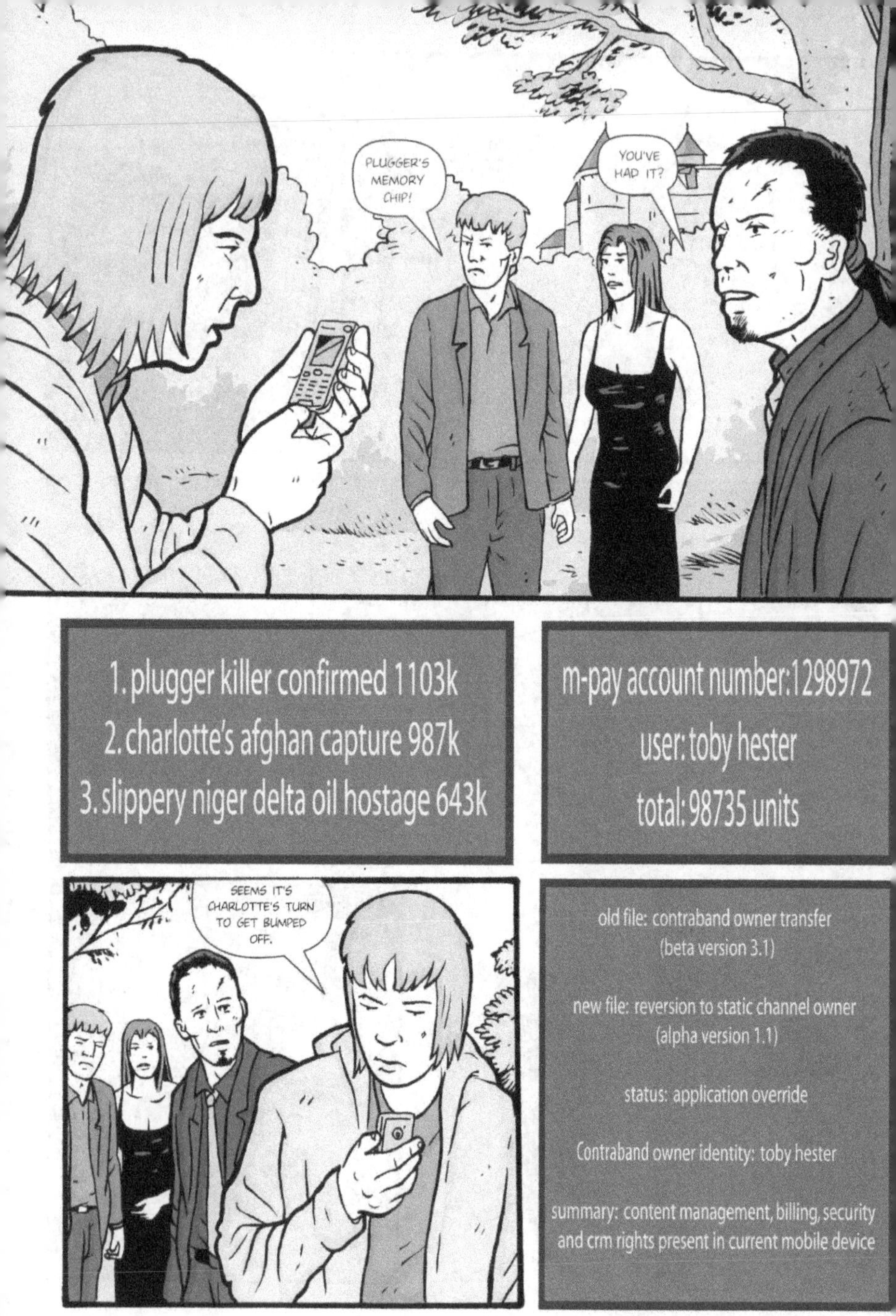
PLUGGER'S MEMORY CHIP!
YOU'VE HAD IT?
1. plugger killer confirmed 1103k
2. charlotte's afghan capture 987k
3. slippery niger delta oil hostage 643k
m-pay account number:1298972
user: toby hester
total: 98735 units
SEEMS IT'S CHARLOTTE'S TURN TO GET BUMPED OFF.
old file: contraband owner transfer (beta version 3.1)
new file: reversion to static channel owner (alpha version 1.1)
status: application override
Contraband owner identity: toby hester
summary: content management, billing, security and crm rights present in current mobile device

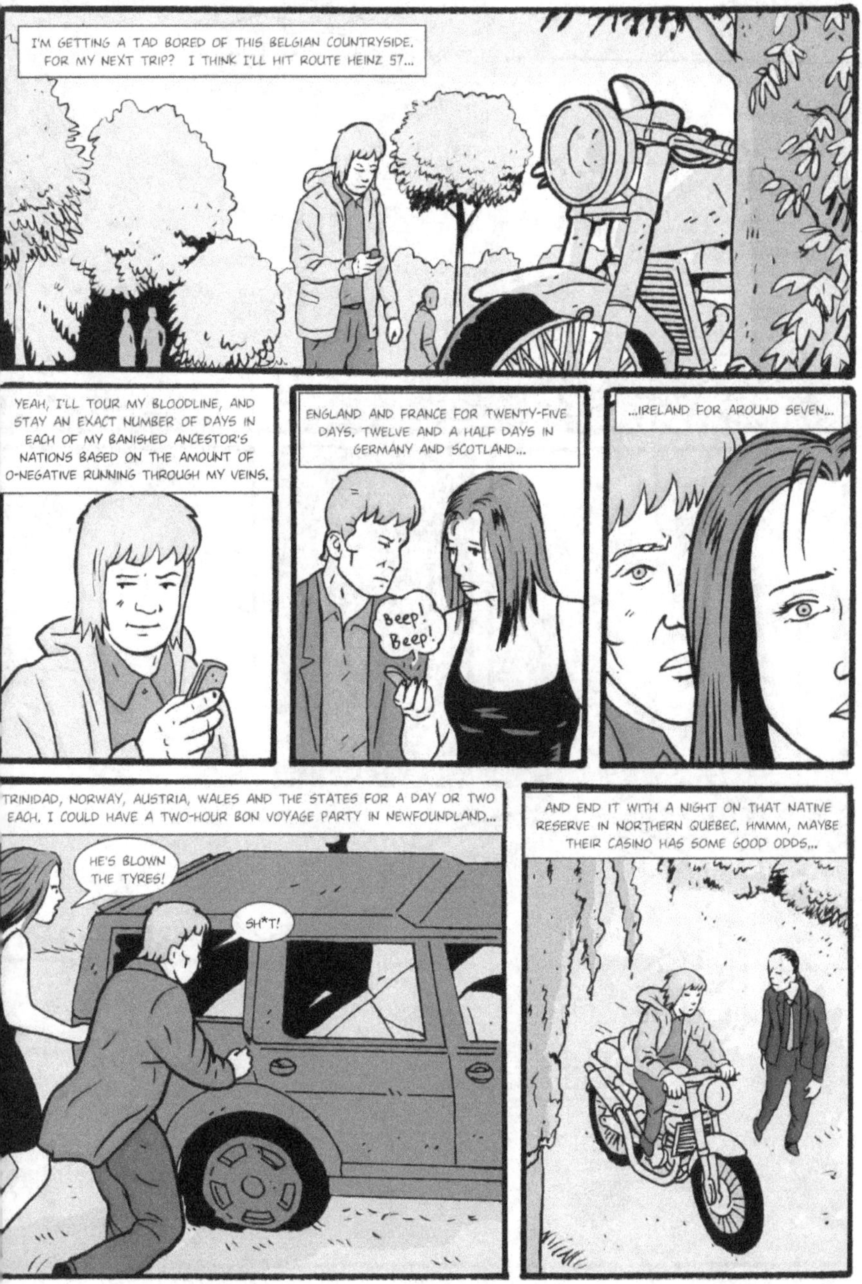
I'M GETTING A TAD BORED OF THIS BELGIAN COUNTRYSIDE. FOR MY NEXT TRIP? I THINK I'LL HIT ROUTE HEINZ 57...
YEAH, I'LL TOUR MY BLOODLINE, AND STAY AN EXACT NUMBER OF DAYS IN EACH OF MY BANISHED ANCESTOR'S NATIONS BASED ON THE AMOUNT OF O-NEGATIVE RUNNING THROUGH MY VEINS.
ENGLAND AND FRANCE FOR TWENTY-FIVE DAYS. TWELVE AND A HALF DAYS IN GERMANY AND SCOTLAND...
Beep! Beep!
...IRELAND FOR AROUND SEVEN...
TRINIDAD, NORWAY, AUSTRIA, WALES AND THE STATES FOR A DAY OR TWO EACH. I COULD HAVE A TWO-HOUR BON VOYAGE PARTY IN NEWFOUNDLAND...
HE'S BLOWN THE TYRES!
SH*T!
AND END IT WITH A NIGHT ON THAT NATIVE RESERVE IN NORTHERN QUEBEC. HMMM, MAYBE THEIR CASINO HAS SOME GOOD ODDS...

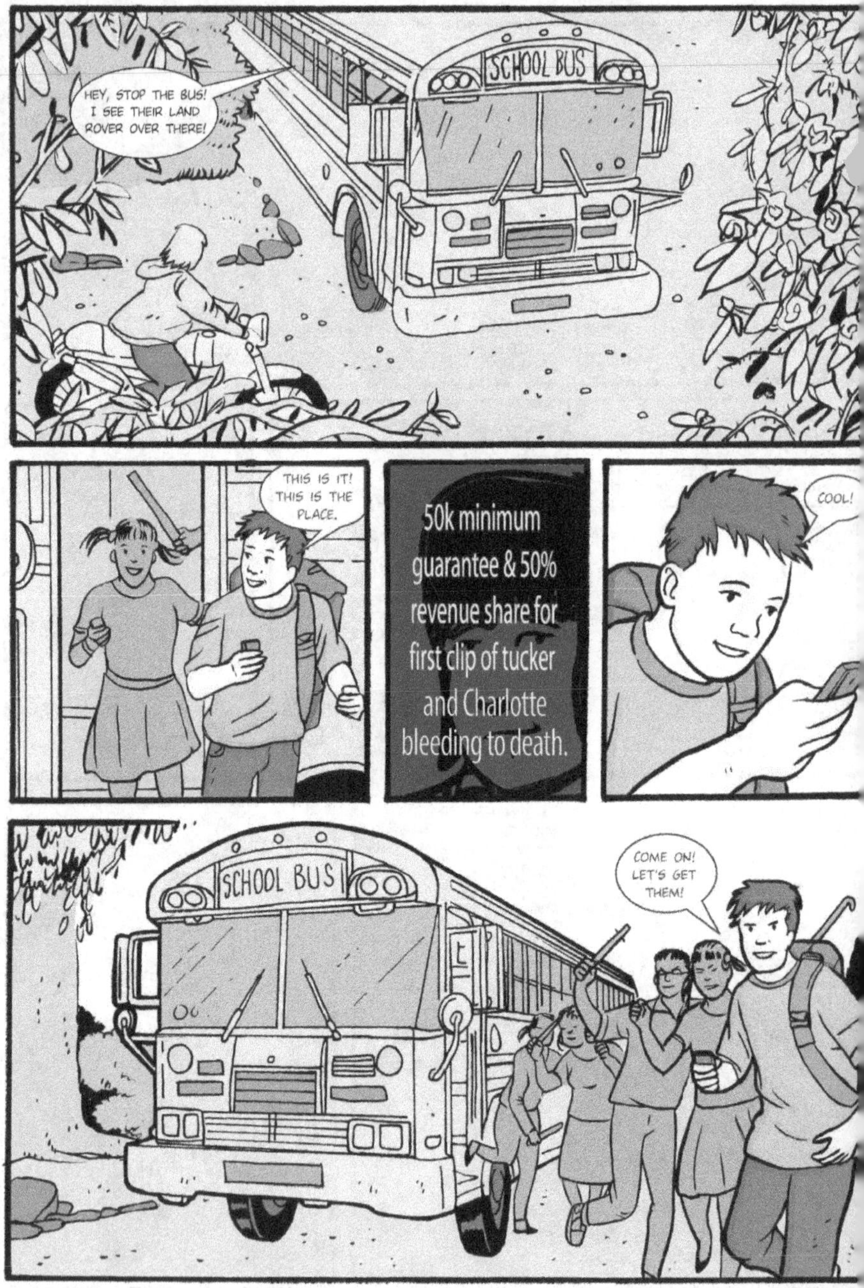
HEY, STOP THE BUS! I SEE THEIR LAND ROVER OVER THERE!
SCHOOL BUS
THIS IS IT! THIS IS THE PLACE.
50k minimum guarantee & 50% revenue share for first clip of tucker and Charlotte bleeding to death.
COOL!
SCHOOL BUS
COME ON! LET'S GET THEM!

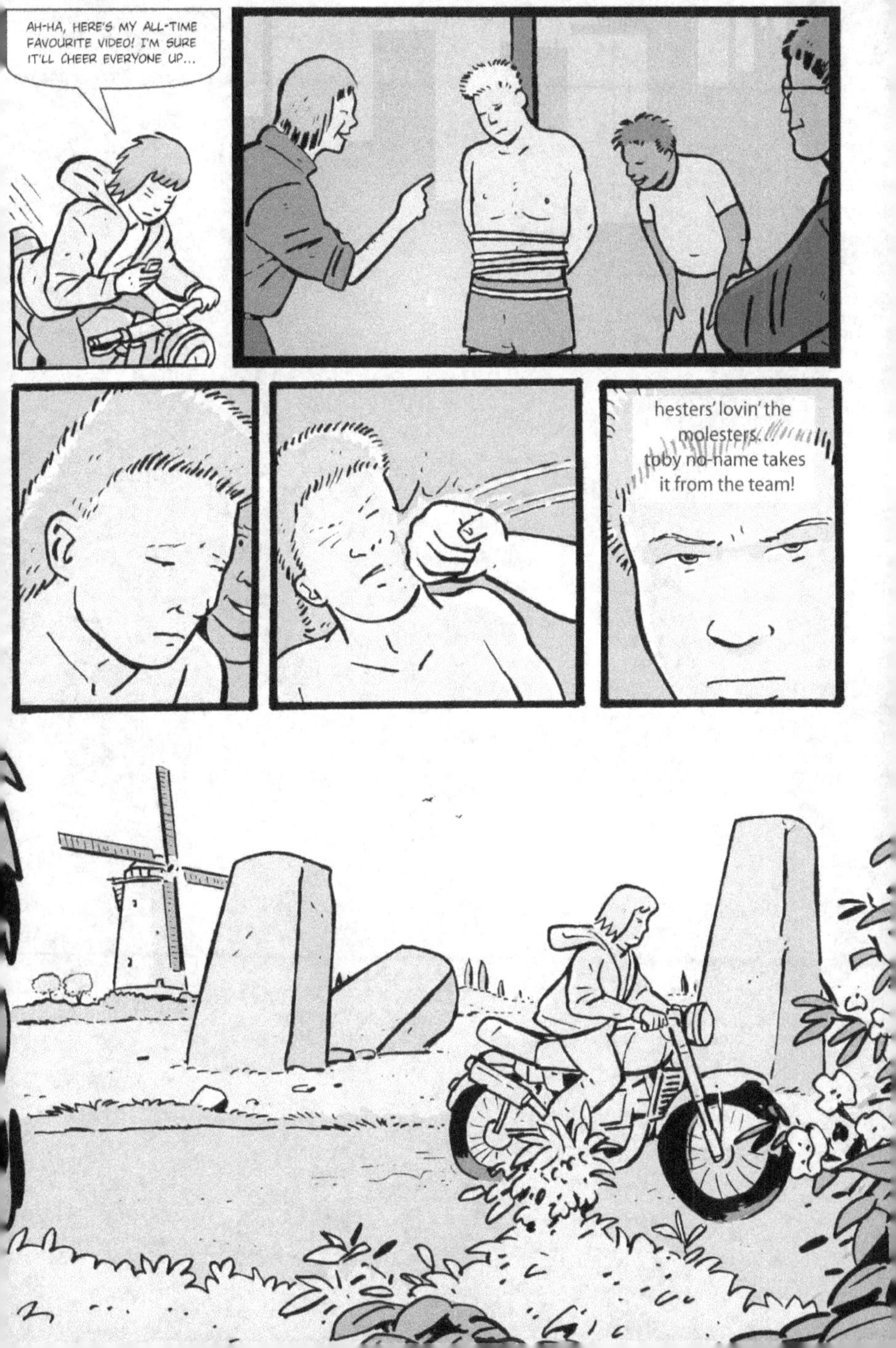
AH-HA, HERE'S MY ALL-TIME FAVOURITE VIDEO! I'M SURE IT'LL CHEER EVERYONE UP...
hesters' lovin' the molesters.
toby no-name takes it from the team!

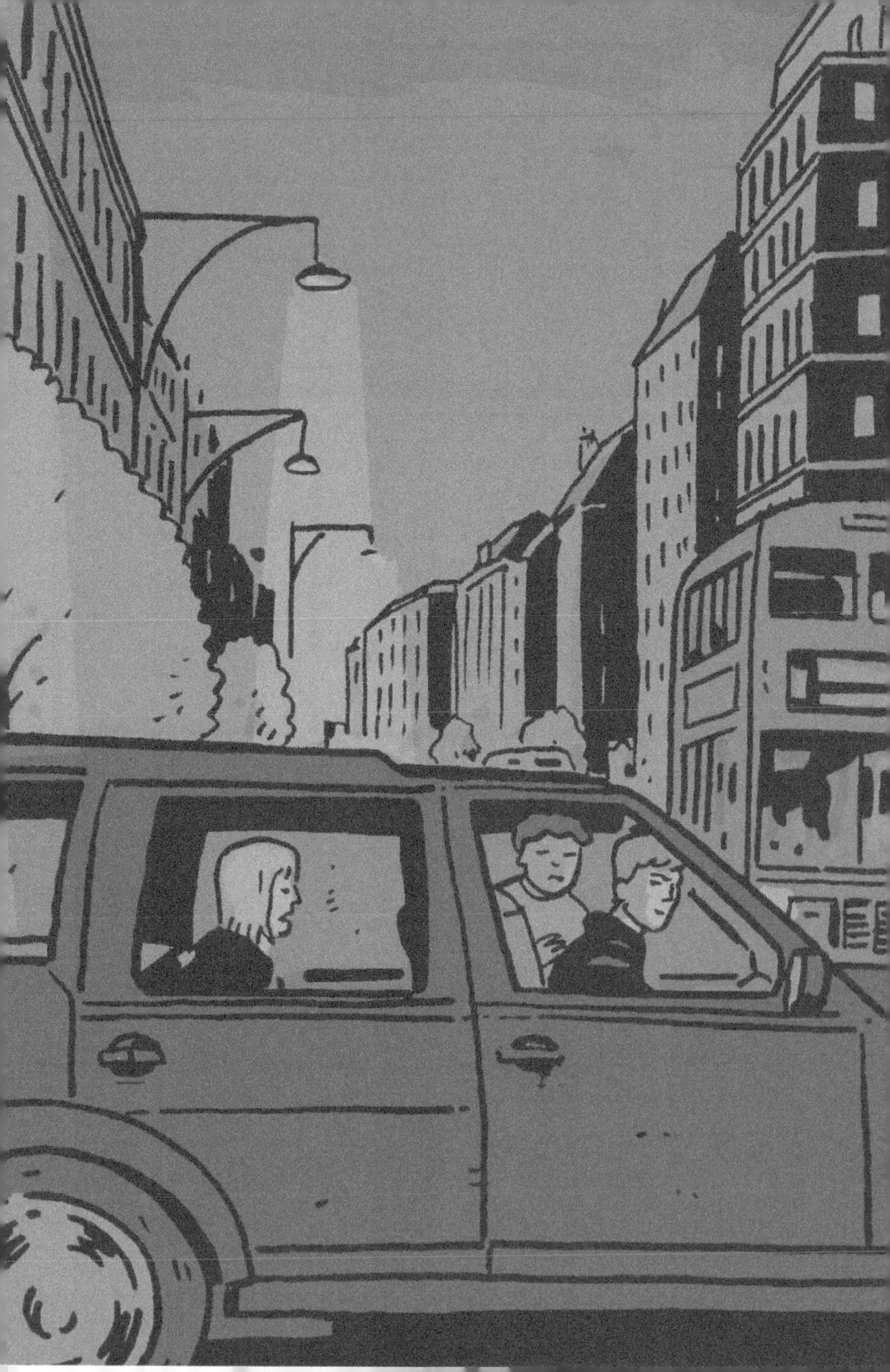

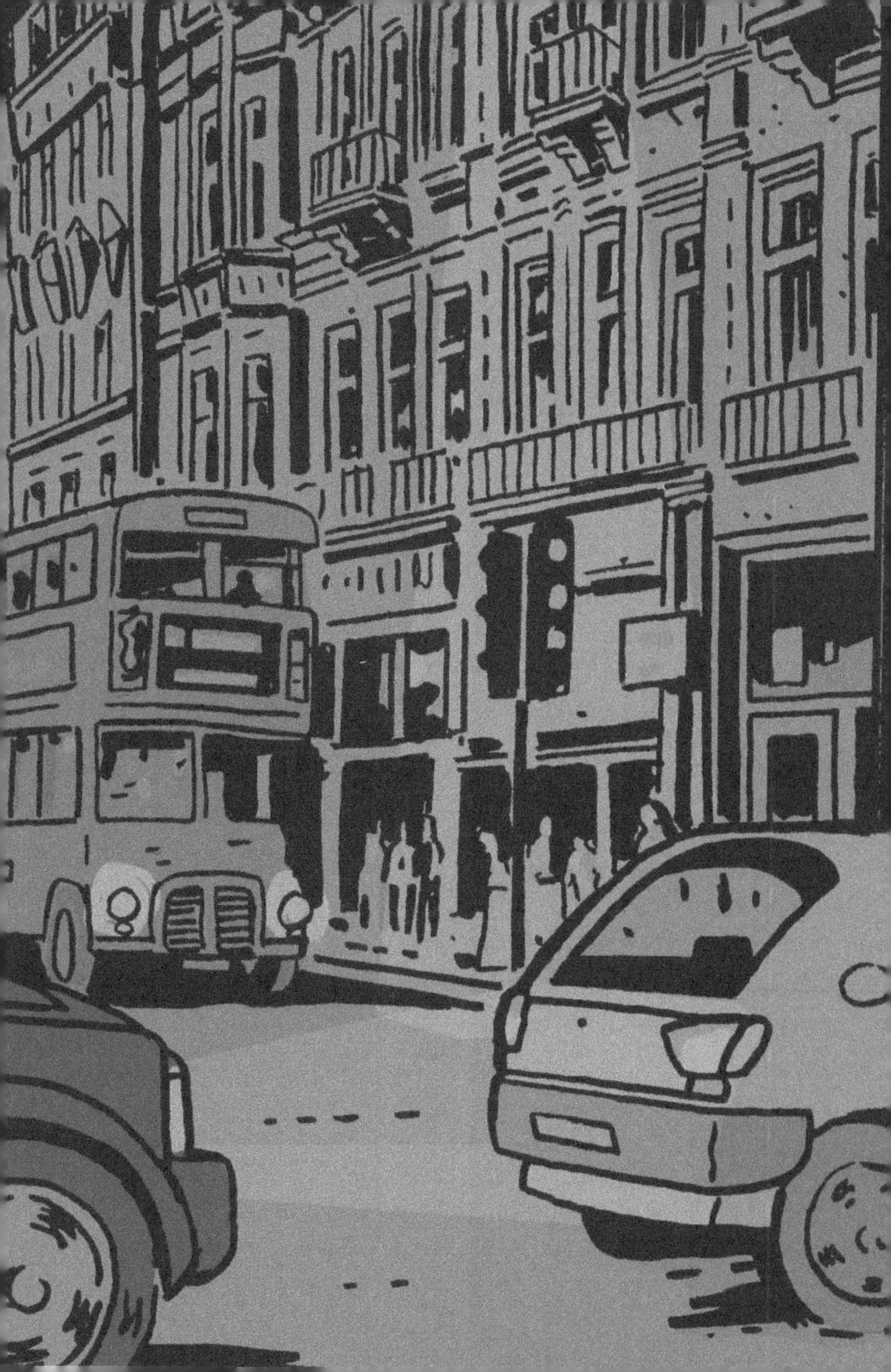

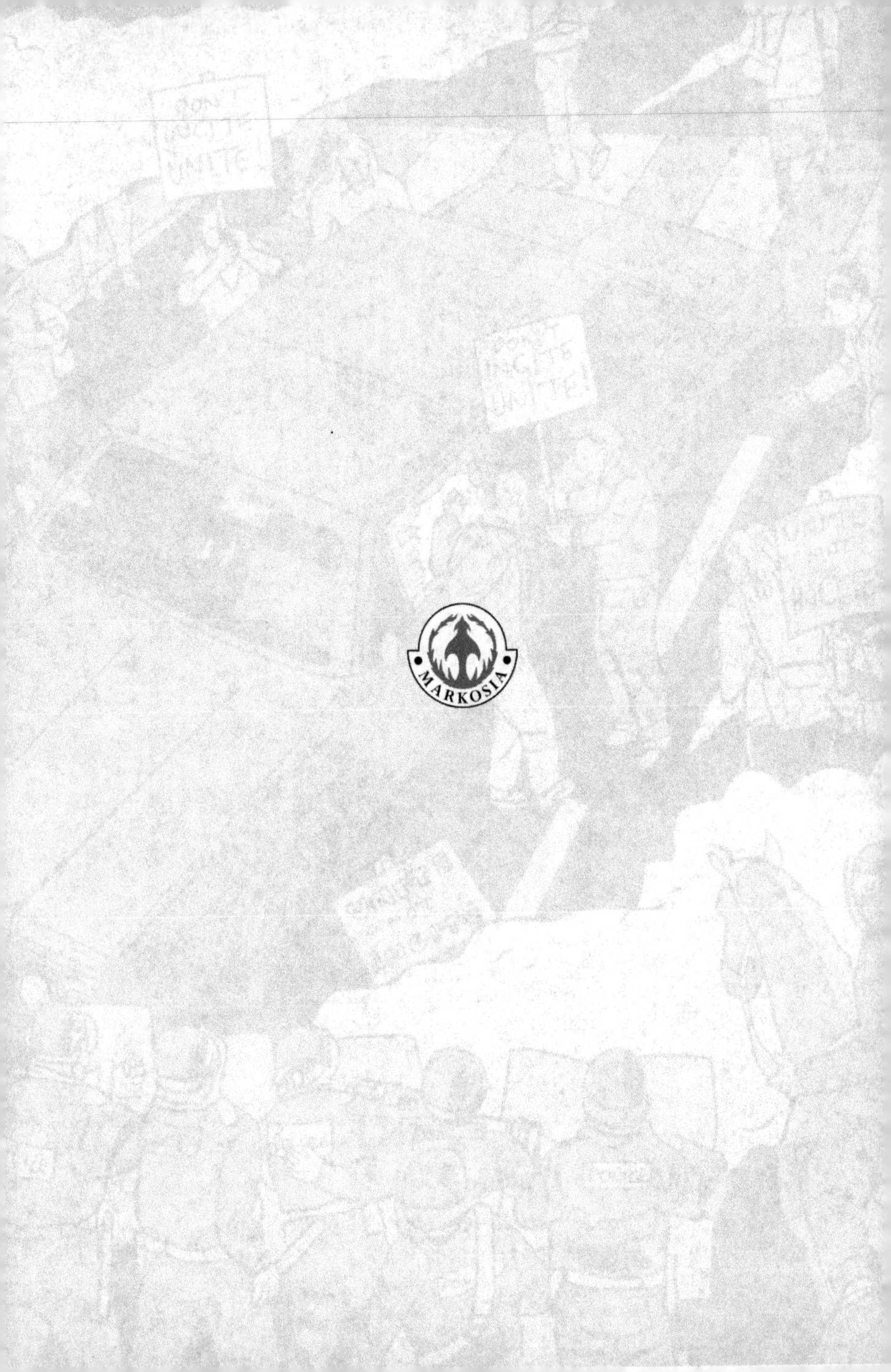
DON'T INCITE UNITE
DON'T INCITE UNITE!

MARKOSIA

CPSIA information can be obtained
at www.ICGtesting.com
Printed in the USA
BVHW041256140521
607364BV00014B/229

9 781913 802608